D1736996

During the late eighteenth century the Bible underwent a shift in interpretation so radical as to make it virtually a different book from what it had been a hundred years earlier. Even as historical criticism suggested that, far from being divinely inspired or even a rock of certainty in a world of flux, its text was neither stable nor original, the new notion of the Bible as a cultural artifact became a paradigm of all literature. While formal religion declined, the prestige of the Bible as a literary and aesthetic model rose to new heights. Not merely was English, German, and even French Romanticism steeped in biblical references of a new kind, but hermeneutics and, increasingly, theories of literature and criticism were biblically derived. The Romantic Bible became simultaneously a single novel-like narrative work, an on-going tradition of interpretation and a 'metatype': an all-embracing literary form giving meaning to all other writing.

By the same author

Coleridge and Wordsworth: the Poetry of Growth (1970)

Romanticism and Religion: the Tradition of Coleridge and Wordsworth in the Victorian Church (1976)

Victorian Fantasy (1979)

The Romantics (ed.) (1982)

Words and the 'Word': Language, Poetics and Biblical Interpretation (1986)

Reading the Text: Biblical Criticism and Literary Theory (ed.) (1991)

The Bible (Landmarks of World Literature Series, 1991)

ORIGINS OF NARRATIVE

William Blake, 'Jacob's Ladder' (1808).
Reproduced by permission of the British Museum.

ORIGINS OF NARRATIVE

The Romantic appropriation of the Bible

STEPHEN PRICKETT

Regius Professor of English, University of Glasgow

CAMBRIDGE
UNIVERSITY PRESS

Published by the Press Syndicate of the University of Cambridge
The Pitt Building, Trumpington Street, Cambridge CB2 IRP
40 West 20th Street, New York, NY 10011–4211, USA
10 Stamford Road, Oakleigh, Melbourne 3166, Australia

First published 1996

Printed in Great Britain at the University Press, Cambridge

A catalogue record for this book is available from the British Library

Library of Congress cataloguing in publication data
Prickett, Stephen.
Origins of narrative: the romantic appropriation of the Bible /
Stephen Prickett.
p.   cm.
Includes bibliographical references.
ISBN 0 521 44543 4 (hardback)
1. Bible and literature.   2. Bible – Hermeneutics.   3. Romanticism.
1. Title.
BS535.P75   1996
220'.09'033 – dc20   95–21587   CIP

ISBN 0 521 44543 4 hardback

CE

For Maria

All the classical poems of the ancients are coherent, inseparable; they form an organic whole, they constitute, properly viewed, only a single poem, the only one in which poetry itself appears in perfection. In a similar way, in a perfect literature all books should be only a single book, and in such an eternally developing book, the gospel of humanity and culture will be revealed.

(Friedrich Schlegel, *Ideas*, 95)

the deeper we sound, the further down into the lower world of the past we probe and press, the more do we find that the earliest foundations of humanity, its history and culture, reveal themselves unfathomable.

(Thomas Mann, *Joseph and his Brothers*)

Contents

Preface

To start with what this book is *not*: it is not about the use of biblical plots or themes in Romantic literature, nor is it about the naturalising of supernaturalism associated with M.H. Abrams. Neither is it a literary analysis of the Bible of the kinds pioneered by Hans Frei or Northrop Frye. All are interesting topics, and much yet remains to be written on them. My theme, however, concerns the way in which the Romantics read the Bible itself: how it was responsible not merely for much Romantic literary theory, but had, in the process, been so irrevocably altered by the new hermeneutic assumptions it had engendered that it became for the nineteenth century virtually a different book from that of a century before. Beyond this lie other, more elusive, snarks: why, for instance, was the Romantic fascination with the evolution of self-consciousness so linked with notions of the origins of the Bible? And, perhaps even more important, how far is the creativeness and vitality of our literary tradition related to its biblical origins?

Moreover, as I began to trace this almost unnoticed Romantic transformation of the Bible, I quickly realised that it was far from being a unique event. Behind that particular and unusually well-documented story of hermeneutic re-interpretation lies another, of successive earlier appropriations resting upon one another, layer upon layer, until the question of an original biblical 'ur-text' becomes lost in the archaeology of time. Indeed, as any study of its textual history will show, the Bible is better described in terms of an on-going tradition of interpretation than as a specific individual work. It was then that the word 'appropriation' forced its way into my mind as being, if not a trap to catch a snark, at least a trace of a trace, as it were a footprint, of where it might have passed.

The Bible's own original myth of appropriation, that of Jacob and Esau, brought a second word to my attention: the word 'blessing'. As a gift, an inheritance, a tradition to be transmitted from generation to generation the Hebrew carried a much greater charge than the vague supernaturally sanctioned good wishes the modern English often seems to imply. But that original blessing of Jacob by his father, Isaac, highlights a profound ambiguity, latent in even the *Oxford English Dictionary* (*OED*) definition of 'an authoritative declaration of divine favour'. On the one hand, it was experienced as an inalienable patriarchal tradition, passed from father to son, with full divine endorsement. On the other, it is perhaps more typical of patriarchy than many would like to admit that, in practice, it was not merely up for grabs, but its chronic vulnerability to such appropriative seizure was actually one of its central attributes, and was to become one of the strangest yet most persistent characteristics both of the Hebrew scriptures and of the Christian Bible. Not surprisingly, for the Romantics, Jacob's blessing was to provide an almost irresistible nexus of imagery. Among its concomitant attributes were the idea of inspiration and a kind of consciousness of self and of personal identity that has been more often investigated by writers and literary critics than by theologians – who, if they have recognised it at all, have often been more prone to view it as a cause of sin than as a mark of divine favour. Those nineteenth-century critics as the brothers Julius and Augustus Hare, who attempted to discuss these developments holistically, were correspondingly marginalised.

Such marginalisation was only one symptom of the way in which the main European cultural tradition of textual interpretation had been deeply damaged at the end of the eighteenth century by the progressive separation of biblical from literary studies. In *Words and the 'Word'* I epitomised this arbitrary amputation in Wilhelm von Humboldt's decision in 1809 to separate the study of theology from that of the other humanities in the new University of Berlin. One (no doubt jaundiced) academic reviewer commented that this was possibly the only example in human history of the decision of a university administrator turning out to be of importance. Though it is unlikely that either Humboldt or anyone else foresaw the long-term consequences, the effect of his reorganisation was to isolate one form of literary study from all the rest. As a result, not merely was secular literary criticism impoverished, but theology also – though it has taken more than a hundred years for it to become aware of the ache in its missing limb. Only while theologians believed that their discipline was possessed of sources and ways of knowing that were, in some sense, immune from the processes normal in other, secular, literary traditions could it afford to stand aloof from developments in literary criticism. Ironically, it was precisely during this period in the nineteenth century that it fell prey to the most hard-headed and pseudo-scientific forms of materialist historicism. More effort was frequently devoted by liberal theologians to showing how and why particular miracles could not have happened than to investigating the nature and origins of the narratives and traditions in which particular miracles were embedded. When, for instance, in 1862, the liberal-minded Bishop of Natal, John Colenso, published the first volume of his *Critical Examination of the Pentateuch* (1862–79), arguing (what is now a critical commonplace) that the first five books of the Bible were not by Moses at all but dated from post-Exilic times, and were therefore 'forgeries', the Bishop of Cape Town excommunicated him (he was later re-instated). Even where, as in the case of the so-called 'mythological school', there was some awareness of how these narratives might have arisen, the idea of myth still carried with it suggestions of primitiveness and non-historical origins. Conversely, secular literary criticism rapidly lost any sense it might have had of the biblical origins of its craft.

As we shall see, though the twentieth century has done something to redress the historical imbalance, much remains to be done. I believe our most urgent critical task is now to try and reverse that surgery and see how the two separated disciplines might again be reunited – not in a return to the eighteenth century, but as a prelude to the twenty-first. This book is one step, at least, in that direction – though no doubt it is also about many other things that, with the help of others, I shall only slowly become conscious of.

Acknowledgements

Anyone seeking to tackle an interdisciplinary and comparative topic spanning some four thousand years may plausibly be accused of asking for trouble. In so far as I have avoided it, it is due to the help and advice of many friends and colleagues. Without the constant stream of notes, reflections and ideas from Ward Allen, this book would probably never have been started, let alone completed. We have as yet never met: but he is one of the world's great correspondents. Others, too, have been unstinting in time and advice. Paul and Rosanne Weaver have opened my eyes to new and ancient intellectual horizons – and spotted numerous typos; Tim Clark has probed and reinforced my knowledge of contemporary critical theory; Donald Mackenzie's knowledge of the finer points of theology has been matched only by his generosity in expounding them to me; Colin Smethurst has kindly shared with me a fraction of his knowledge of Chateaubriand. Working with Iain McCalman, the finest of Romantic historians, has been a privilege and an education in itself. Christopher Burdon, Françoise Deconnick-Brossard, Elizabeth Jay, Robert Maslen, Roger Stephenson and Peter Walsh, have all kindly allowed me to make use of their research or shared ideas with me. Yet others, Jonathan Bordo, David Jasper and Werner Jeanrond, may even be unaware of chance remarks or observations that have set me off on new lines of thought. Finally, I should like to thank my wife, whose reading of the manuscript has saved me not only from errors of typography and grammar, but from needless ambiguity, unconscious solecism and occasional unnecessary obscurity.

The Introduction draws on material summarised in chapter 1 of *The Bible* in the Landmarks of World Literative series. Part of chapter 2 has appeared in *Translating Religious Texts*, edited by David Jasper (Macmillan 1993) and part of chapter 4 in *Sense and Transcendence: Essays in Honour of Hermann Servotte*, edited by Ortwin de Graef (Louvain

University Press, 1995). I am grateful to the editors concerned for their permission to reproduce the material.

My thanks are also due to the Australian Research Council, whose 1989 grant enabled me to start work on this project, and to the director and staff of the Humanities Research Centre, at the Australian National University, who gave me a year-long visiting scholarship in 1994 to complete it. To Graham Clark, Iain McCalman, Jodi, Leena and Stephanie, and a panorama of like-minded visiting scholars I owe an unpayable debt. To the Department of English Literature and Faculty of Arts at Glasgow University I owe corresponding thanks for allowing me to take the leave when I did.

Introduction

'The history of appropriation', writes Jonathan Bate in *Shakespearean Constitutions*, 'may suggest that "Shakespeare" is not a man who lived from 1564 to 1616 but a body of work that is refashioned by each subsequent age in the image of itself'.[1] If that is true of the Romantic use of Shakespeare, it is doubly so of the Bible, which during the eighteenth century underwent a similar but altogether more profound 'refashioning'. Though, for obvious reasons, this did not involve the same liberties with the text, an increasing use of the Bible (as against the classics) in almost every form of public and private discourse was accompanied by a largely unnoticed shift in reading and interpretation so radical as to make of it virtually a new book from a hundred years earlier. Even as formal religious observance was by the end of the century declining towards a nadir unequalled at any time since,[2] the prestige of the Bible as a literary and aesthetic model had risen to new heights. Not merely was Romantic thought in England, Germany and even France, steeped through and through in biblical references but, less obviously, Romantic criticism, its accompanying concept of 'literature' and even the theory of hermeneutics was no less biblically derived. The Romantic Bible was at once a single narrative work, an on-going tradition of interpretation, and what I have called in these pages a 'metatype': a kind of all-embracing literary form that was invoked to encompass and give meaning to all other books.

But though this construction was unique – and in some ways uniquely potent – it was, as many critics were aware, by no means the first time such a reconstruction had occurred. Historical criticism, much of it dating from the second half of the eighteenth century, was

---

[1] Jonathan Bate, *Shakespearean Constitutions: Politics, Theatre, Criticism 1730–1830*, Oxford: Clarendon Press, 1989, p. 3.

[2] See the statistics in Robert Currie, Alan Gilbert and Lee Horsely (eds.), *Churches and Churchgoers: Patterns of Growth in the British Isles Since 1700*, Oxford: Clarendon Press, 1977.

already beginning to suggest that the text of the Bible, so far from being, as contemporary pietistic and Evangelical rhetoric was wont to claim, a rock of certainty in a world of flux, was itself a midrashic composition of endless revisions and appropriations of earlier writings. In that, it could be, and was seen by some as, a paradigm of our entire literary culture – and ultimately of the collective hermeneutical process by which any culture develops and inculcates its distinctive way of understanding the world. For the young Friedrich Schlegel, as for Coleridge, the Bible was the central literary form and thus the ideal of every book, a new supreme genre, which provided a goal for representatives of all other genres.[3]

Reading has never been a simple or straightforward activity. It has always been accompanied by a theory of how a piece of writing should be read and interpreted. Each change in the practice of textual interpretation has required corresponding changes in theory. Such theories, taking a wide variety of social, political and religious forms, have always been used to justify the long sequence of shifting hermeneutics that forms the invisible sub-structure to any particular cultural milieu. Coming to consciousness within our apparently secular world, it is not always easy for us to see the ways in which it has been shaped by that longwinded and somewhat quirky product of an ancient Semitic people we call by our generic word for 'book', yet the fact remains that the Bible, simply in cultural terms, has been the most important single book in the history of Western civilisation, if not of the world. As the Romantics were well aware, we owe to it even our idea of a book itself. The Bible was traditionally 'the Book of Books': an ambiguous phrase implying both that it was a collection of works somehow contributing to a mysterious unity greater than the sum of its parts, and, at the same time, *the* pre-eminent and superlative book – as it were the class-definer, the book by which all other books were to be known *as books*. The importance of this for the development of European literature and thought can scarcely be over-estimated. To begin with, it suggests a curious ambiguity between implied pluralism and effective singularity. Thus the English word 'Bible' is derived, via the French *bible*, from the late Latin *biblia*, a feminine singular noun that meant simply 'the book'. In its older Latin form, however, *biblia* was not understood as the feminine singular, but as the (identical) neuter plural form, which was, in turn, derived from the Greek *ta biblia*,

---

[3] See Jack Forstman, *A Romantic Triangle: Schleiermacher and Early German Romanticism*, Misoula, Mont.: Scolars Press, 1977, p. 22.

which meant 'the books' – essentially no more than a collection of individual works. This shift in meaning reflects the changing physical conditions of the book (or books) themselves. Before the invention of the codex, or bound manuscript volume, the biblical texts were held as individual scrolls often stored together in a wooden chest or cupboard. Under such conditions the question of what works did, or did not constitute the scriptures, or their exact order, though it might have been a matter of doctrinal debate, was not an immediately practical one. Individual scrolls could be read in whatever order one chose. The invention of the codex, however, with its immediate practical advantages of compactness, ease of handling and storage, meant that potential flexibility was lost. From then on the books had to come in a specific order – and it is significant that the process of creating a canon for both for the Hebrew Bible and for the New Testament coincides historically with the widespread introduction of the codex. Even so, in a world of laboriously transcribed manuscripts, content and order of books remained relatively unstable until as late as the thirteenth century[4] and only the introduction of printing in the fifteenth completed this transition from utterance to artifact.[5] What began as 'the books' had, literally and physically, become 'the book' – and in the process a new dimension had been added to the notion of narrative.

As a result the idea of what constitutes a book came to include within itself that notion of unity with diversity, of openness and plain meaning with secrets and polysemous layers of meaning.[6] The concept of narrative that was to evolve with the novel assumed the possibility of many parallel stories – sometimes apparently unrelated; it took for granted sub-plot and main plot; stories within stories; parallel, complementary and even contradictory stories that may link thematically rather than by direct influence. It is no accident, for instance, that many of the foundational works of English literature: Malory's *Morte Darthur*, Chaucer's *Canterbury Tales* or Spenser's *Faerie Queene* are also, in effect, collections of stories relating in various ways to a single common theme. The same kind of structures were used by Boccaccio in Italy and Rabelais in France. Similarly, the frequency of two or more

---

[4] See Teresa Webber's review of *The Early Mediaeval Bible* (Cambridge, 1994), *Times Literary Supplement*, 27 January 1995, p. 26.

[5] See Walter J. Ong, *Orality and Literacy: the Technologising of the Word*, Routledge, 1982, p. 125. (Apart from publications of university presses, the place of publication, if not given in the reference, is London.)

[6] A point made by Erich Auerbach in his comparison between biblical and Homeric modes of narration. See *Mimesis*, Princeton University Press, 1953, p. 19.

thematically related plots in Elizabethan drama – and most notably in Shakespeare – emphasises the origins of English drama in the biblical models provided by the mediaeval Miracle Plays. Again, popular drama had similar origins on the continent – in Italy, France and Germany; it was only later that the French Court imposed on a francophile Europe a taste for the more austere and concentrated classical unities.

Though, as we shall see, there has always been a powerful classical influence, even on the reading and interpretation of the Bible, it is primarily to this biblical idea of a book that we owe our peculiar set of expectations about the world. Because the biblical writers took it for granted that there was a meaning to the whole cycle of human existence, and later interpreters developed this to assume that every event described in the Bible, however trivial it might seem, had a figurative, typological or, as we would now say, symbolic relation to the whole, it became habitual in other areas of existence also to look for narrative, with a pattern of hidden meaning, rather than expect a mere chronicle of events. This expectation runs very deep in Western society, affecting not merely fiction, but biography, history, law and, of course, science – that distinctive product of a belief in a rational and stable universe where every part has its meaning in relation to the greater 'story' of the whole. Ironically such a belief in the grand narrative of science was common to both Newton and his most trenchant critic of the Romantic period, Goethe.[7] It is still rarely appreciated (especially by those puzzled by Newton's obsessive interest in biblical history and prophecy[8]) that the scientific revolution of the seventeenth century owed as much to Hebrew mysticism as to Greek rationality.[9] Similarly alongside the open, rational, tradition there have always co-existed others, arcane and hidden, whose essence is secret meanings and the capacity to interpret signs totally invisible to the uninitiated.

But whether open or secret, we find the idea that a book was, by its very nature, interpretative. This was a quality already present in the Hebrew Bible, but the Christian project of appropriating the Hebrew scriptures and presenting itself as the legitimised heir to Judaism gave the process a new urgency. After the first generation, the Church

[7] See Roger Stephenson, *Goethe's Conception of Knowledge and Science*, Edinburgh University Press, 1995, p. 68.
[8] Among other works by Isaac Newton, see, for instance, *The Chronology of the Ancient Kingdoms Amended* (1728) or *Observations on the Prophecies of Daniel and St. John* (1733).
[9] See E.A. Burtt, *The Metaphysical Foundations of Modern Science*, Routledge, 1933.

Fathers – Ambrose, Augustine, Cyprian, Jerome, Tertullian and the rest – were not Jews but classically trained scholars coming to the Bible with a quite different set of aesthetic and philosophical assumptions from the Apostles. In its literal sense, much of what now became the 'Old Testament' bore little or no relation to the superstructure constructed upon it. In many cases, indeed, its narratives and even ethical teachings actually seemed to contradict those of the New Testament. The need to interpret texts was thus not an incidental phenomenon of the new religion, but a response to a problem that was essential to its foundation and subsequent development. In this sense at least, critical theory was what Christianity was all about.

Moreover, because Christianity began with a sense that it differed radically from the world that preceded it, and that even its own sacred texts had to be effectively defamiliarised, the interpretative function of narrative was uniquely central right from the start. When the Greek historian Herodotus visited Thebes in Egypt, he gazed with awe at 300 generations of high priests of the Theban temple listed in its inscriptions, as he realised that they went back for thousands of years before the dawn of Greek history. J.H. Plumb has contrasted this disturbing experience, which began to give meaning and shape to the idea of history for the Greeks, with the untroubled serenity of the Chinese chroniclers, for whom the succession of one emperor after another for upwards of 5,000 years was simply a sequence of time.[10] In contrast with the Chinese, the compilers of the New Testament, like Herodotus, saw in the past not merely a sequence of events, but a problem with a meaning that had to be explained.

This sense of the past as a problem was compounded by the events of the first few centuries of the Christian era. The biblical world was never a monoculture existing in isolation from surrounding societies. On the contrary, it clung to a marginal existence at the intersection of great powers, and Jewish political and cultural life flowered only in the brief intervals between the waning and waxing of foreign imperial ambitions – Egyptians, Assyrians, Babylonians, Persians, Greeks and Romans. One reason, perhaps, why Christianity, rather than its many rivals, was able to ride out the destruction of the Roman Empire was that it already contained within its own literature models not merely for the destruction of empires, but for something much more important: a *meaningful* pattern to their rise and fall.

---

[10] *The Death of the Past*, Macmillan, 1969, p. 111.

It is therefore hardly surprising if, in our biblically based culture, the inherent expectations of a book include not merely narrative but *revelation*: a sense that some hidden mystery is to be unfolded and even explained. Even the sense of antiquity, the realisation of the age and alienness of the biblical texts served to reinforce this sense of a tradition of wisdom handed down from generation to generation. The concept of intertextuality is, in effect, as old as Western civilisation itself, for Europe's past is rooted in a translated book – not merely a translation for modern Europeans, but essentially and in its very origins. As the Romantics were quick to recognise, this is as characteristic of the internal structure of the Bible as it is of its later history. Though the Bible is presented as arising from the peculiar experience of one particular people, it is in fact itself a palimpsest of languages and contexts. If the Old Testament, for instance, is written almost entirely in Hebrew, substantial parts of it incorporate translation or paraphrase of other Near Eastern texts – Mesopotamian, Egyptian, Canaanite and others. Because it has taken its very existence from the intersection of other languages and cultures, the Bible has always been at once marginal and assimilative: culturally meek, perhaps, but fully prepared to inherit the earth.

In short, so far from being simply instrumental, our idea of a book has always been one of our most powerfully and ideologically charged cultural constructs, affecting the whole basis, and even the metaphysical legitimacy of our civilisation. European literary criticism was born from the problematic relationship between the Hebrew and Christian Bibles and the biblical writings and the classical literature of Greece and Rome. But if this duality of Europe's past, its conflicting ideologies and their different interpretations of human destiny[11] had worried such classical scholars as, for instance, Augustine and Jerome, from that problem was to stem, not merely our hermeneutics, but our peculiar sense of history, many of the great questions of Western philosophy, and, not least, the peculiar dynamics of our literary tradition.

That sense of a dynamic literary tradition stemming from many sources, but above all from the Bible, lies at the heart of Romantic literary theory. If, on the one hand, it was to transform cultural awareness of the Bible itself from a God-given monolith to a living and changing interpretative tradition, it was, on the other, to involve a similar rereading of all subsequent literature. In the following pages we

[11] *Ibid.*, p. 136.

shall be tracing first of all the romantic inheritance: a book whose earliest myths rested not merely upon appropriation, but on Jacob's blessing – that peculiar and paradoxical myth of mis-appropriation. It was a dynamic that was to be repeated with the Christian appropriation of the Hebrew scriptures, and arguably yet again with the Reformation. In the second part we shall be looking at how the contingencies of the aesthetic, political, intellectual and religious context of late eighteenth- and early nineteenth-century Europe led towards a quite new way of reading the scriptures that was to reach its most explicit form in Schleiermacher's hermeneutics. But it would be a mistake to see this sea-change as being solely or even primarily theological – at least in any institutional sense. One of the most significant facts about the Romantic appropriation of the Bible was its freedom from any ecclesiastical or doctrinal control, Protestant or Catholic. Though we shall be looking at some sermons, they will range from those of that most anarchic and undoctrinal clergyman, Laurence Sterne, to the equally unorthodox 'speeches' of Schleiermacher to his anti-clerical friends. As befits the holistic strivings of the fragmented Romantic sensibility, we shall also be looking at many other fields affected by the shift in biblical theory: landscape gardening, novels, painting, psychology, revolutionary and counter-revolutionary polemic – not to mention Swedenborg's impressively detailed reports on the prevailing class distinctions among angels. If the particular examples seem on occasions arbitrary, selective and historically disparate, they represent the tradition at least in terms of that archetypal Romantic metaphor of a prism whose fragmentary incompleteness reflects an essentially unachievable totality. In the words of Julius Hare: 'Is not every Gothic minster unfinished? and for the best of reasons, because it is infinite.' There is always more.

PART I

Jacob's blessing

CHAPTER I

The stolen birthright

GENESIS

We begin, fittingly enough, with the story of a blessing and an imposture: that of Jacob and Esau.

And Rebekah took goodly raiment of her eldest son Esau, which were with her in the house, and put them upon Jacob, her younger son: and she put the skins of the kids of the goats upon his hands, and upon the smooth of his neck: and she gave the savoury meat and the bread, which she had prepared, into the hand of her son Jacob.

And he came unto his father, and said, My father: and he said, Here am I; who art thou, my son?

And Jacob said unto his father, I am Esau thy firstborn; I have done according as thou badest me: arise, I pray thee, sit and eat of my venison, that thy soul may bless me ...

And Isaac said unto Jacob, Come near, I pray thee, that I may feel thee my son, whether thou be my very son Esau or not. And Jacob went near unto Isaac his father; and he felt him, and said, The voice is Jacob's voice, but the hands are the hands of Esau. And he discerned him not, because his hands were hairy, as his brother Esau's hands: so he blessed him. And he said Art thou my very son Esau? And he said, I am. And he said, Bring it near to me, and I will eat of my son's venison, that my soul may bless thee. And he brought it near to him, and he did eat: and he brought him wine, and he drank.

And his father Isaac said unto him, Come near now, and kiss me my son. And he came near, and kissed him: and he smelled the smell of his raiment, and blessed him, and said, See the smell of my son is as the smell of a field which the Lord hath blessed: Therefore God give thee the dew of heaven, and the fatness of the earth, and plenty of corn and wine: Let people serve thee, and nations bow down to thee: be lord over thy brethren, and let thy mother's sons bow down to thee: cursed be every one that curseth thee, and blessed be he that blesseth thee.

And it came to pass, as soon as Isaac had made an end of blessing Jacob, and Jacob was yet scarce gone out from the presence of Isaac his father, that

Esau his brother came in from his hunting. And he also had made savoury
meat, and brought it unto his father, and said unto his father, Let my father
arise, and eat of his son's venison, that thy soul may bless me.

And Isaac his father said unto him, Who art thou? And he said, I am thy
son, thy firstborn Esau. And Isaac trembled very exceedingly, and said, Who?
where is he that hath taken venison, and brought it me, and I have eaten of all
before thou camest, and have blessed him? yea, and he shall be blessed.

And when Esau heard the words of his father, he cried with a great and
exceeding bitter cry, and said unto his father, Bless me, even me also, O my
father.

And he said, Thy brother came with subtilty, and hath taken away thy
blessing. (Genesis 27: 15–35, AV)

Some 3,550 years later (according to the most accurate count then
available),[1] in September 1791, the Revolutionary French National
Assembly was formally presented by its Secretary, the former aristocrat
Constantin-François Chassebœuf de Volney, with a short monograph
entitled *Les Ruines, ou méditation sur les révolutions des empires*. The enigmatic
title gave little clue to its real thesis, which, in the form of a
mythological vision, concerned the origins of religion, and in particular
of Christianity. According to Volney, not merely all Indo-European
and Semitic religion but even astrology as well could be traced back to
a common origin in ancient Egypt at least 17,000 years ago.[2] All
modern forms of supernatural and revealed religion were, he claimed,
in reality nothing more than the misplaced products of primitive
nature-worship, time and the accidents of historical diffusion. Thus the
gods of Egypt had been appropriated by the Aryans into their own
pantheon before being eventually reduced to a single deity in Persia in
the sixth century BCE. This new syncretistic monotheism had in turn
been adopted by the Israelites when released from the Babylonian
captivity by the Persians, transmitted to the Christians and thence
eventually to the Bedouin tribesmen of the Arabian desert: 'Jews,
Christians, Mahometans, howsoever lofty may be your pretensions,
you are in your spiritual and immaterial system, only the blundering
followers of Zoroaster.'[3] In keeping with the uniformitarian assumptions of the Enlightenment, miracles were attributed to the power of

---

[1] *The History of the Old and New Testaments Extracted from the Sacred Scriptures, the Holy Fathers, and
Other Ecclesiastical Writers ...*, 4th impression, 1712, p. 31. Though it does not say so, I assume
that the particular calculation is made on the basis of Archbishop Ussher's dating – which
was still in use in such conservative quarters as the Cambridge Theological Tripos as late as
the 1840s.

[2] *The Ruins: or a Survey of the Revolutions of Empires*, T. Allman, 1851, pp. 135–6.

[3] *Ibid.* p. 113.

imagination, the gods to their origins in the forces of nature and the regulation of human society to the operation of natural law and self-love.[4] Volney supported this argument by a dazzling and curious display of erudition ranging from Hindu cosmology to the esoteric doctrines of the Essenes.[5] That, together with its strongly revolutionary and anti-clerical context, was sufficient to account for the book's immediate popularity both inside and outside France. The first English translation was published in 1792 by Joseph Johnson, the radical publisher and friend of, among others, Blake, Godwin and Paine – though Volney himself is known to have expressed some doubts about its mildness of tone. At least two other translations had appeared by the end of the 1790s, and it was still being reprinted (in its mildest version) by free-thinking and radical groups in Britain as late as the 1880s.

What connects these two very different accounts, one from and the other about the origins of the Bible, is that the second is in a curious sense only a repetition of the first. Both concern the appropriation of a tradition. If the Genesis narrative is part of one of the great foundation myths of the Old Testament about the inheritance of Israel itself, Volney's myth of biblical origins summarises, and in many ways epitomises the way in which the Romantics historicised the Bible and transformed it from divine revelation into a cultural and aesthetic artifact.

The story of Jacob and Esau is so well known that it is easy for the reader brought up on it to miss how disturbing and deeply paradoxical it really is. Even for someone who had never encountered it before, two things are at once clear. The first is that whatever is being transmitted by means of the 'blessing' is of unique and unrepeatable importance. The second is that it was here acquired by means that were at once illegitimate and somehow irreversible.

Though blessings are a common feature of the Old Testament, a little investigation brings to light two interesting facts about this particular case. The first is that though this is assumed to be the earliest and one of the most important examples of a biblical blessing, it is unique in that, though God is assumed to be in some sense a guarantor, it nowhere expicitly invokes any kind of divine assistance or sanction.[6] Isaac's actual words refer first of all to the land and its fertility, then to

---

[4] *Ibid.* pp. 21–5; 132–3.
[5] *Ibid.* pp. 115–7; 120.
[6] Claus Westermann, *Blessing in the Bible and in the Life of the Church*, trs. Keith Crim, Philadelphia: Fortress Press, 1978, pp. 53–9.

the son who is here viewed as a nation, to wish him a place of first rank.[7] Claus Westermann comments:

Characteristic of the blessing is that its setting in life is leave-taking or farewell (Gen. 24: 60); this is the situation out of which it is to be understood; it is vitality that is passed on by the one who is departing from life to the one who is continuing in life; in this process no distinction is made between the corporeal and the spiritual and so both action and word are required. Because the blessing is concerned with vitality as a whole, the blessing cannot return or be subsequently altered.[8]

Nevertheless, though God is nowhere invoked in the blessing, what is being transmitted has everything to do with a consciousness of Him. The line of descent from Abraham to Jacob/Israel and thence to Joseph and his twelve brothers is crucial to any understanding of the Hebrew scriptures. Isaac is the God-given son of Abraham, doubly precious both on account of his miraculous birth, which, we are told, occurred when his mother, Sarah, was well past child-bearing; and also because his father had received him again from God after Abraham had shown himself willing to sacrifice his only son. Now Isaac is passing on the blessing to his heir: not just as the eldest son of his father, but also as the chosen one to carry the worship of the new god, Yahweh, whose repeated promise had been that Abraham's descendants should be 'as the stars of the heaven, and as the sand which is upon the sea shore' and in whom 'all the nations of the earth' should 'be blessed' (Genesis 22: 17–18; 26: 4). The patriarchal blessing is, therefore, not just a family matter, but one on which the future of a nation and – as Volney correctly asserted – no fewer than three great world religions were to depend. Right at the outset of this tremendous destiny, however, the line of true descent is hijacked by a scheming mother and her ambitious son. And neither Isaac, nor, it seems, even God himself, is willing or able to do anything about it. Instead of Eliphaz, Reuel, Jeush, Jaalam and Korah, the sons of Esau (Genesis 36), from now on the story of God's people is to be that of Jacob's twelve sons – the boastful dreamer, Joseph, and his resentful brothers – founders of the twelve tribes of Israel. Not for the last time in the Bible, the main tradition of the descent of the people of God and their seemingly unique revelation is channelled through a blatantly usurped line of succession – with little or no attempt to conceal the fact.

[7] See Gerhard von Rad, *Genesis: a Commentary*, trs. John H. Marks, 3rd revised edn, SCM Press, 1972, p. 278.

[8] Claus Westermann, *Genesis 12–36: a Commentary*, trs. John J. Scullion SJ, SPCK, 1986, p. 436.

The second point is a historical one, and that is simply how rare it is for commentators to question the meaning of this blessing.[9] Yet without some idea of its meaning it is not easy for the modern reader to see exactly *what* it is that has been stolen by Jacob. Moreover the fuzziness of such historical and theoretical answers that we have do little to address the question of the story's subsequent history and the part it has played in the imagery and discourse of later, and apparently unrelated civilisations. It is perhaps worth looking for a moment therefore at this 'blessing' not primarily in anthropological, archaeological, cultic or thelogical terms, but, as it were *phenomenologically* – to ask, in effect, what, in the light of later events, did Jacob actually take from Esau that was of such irreversible significance? What, if any, was the *advantage* gained for Jacob and his descendants by deceiving his blind and dying father?

The immediate answer, when we stop to think about it, is both very obvious and at the same time very curious: what they gained was the story itself. What has come down to us across almost three and a half thousand years or more is simply the narrative of this primaeval appropriation, with its consequences for the family tradition and all its mythic reverberations. In the end, what was achieved by Jacob/Israel was that writers through succeeding ages to the very end of the twentieth century – and doubtless beyond – should be writing about the incident and debating its significance. In short, the story has come across the millennia to serve as a *metaphor* of appropriation, encapsulating at once both the essential vitality and the inherent illegitimacy of the process.

That we should come to the story from the outset encrusted as it were with legend and commentary is for us part of its cultural presence. Thus the shocking enormity of this incident – almost as shocking as Cain's earlier elimination of his brother Abel – has tended to be played down or simply justified, not least because, unlike the earlier example, God himself seemed so ready to accept it. Regardless of the fact that Esau appears to have forgotten all about the deal with his brother when he comes to claim his blessing, the story of him selling his birthright for a mess of pottage (Genesis 25: 29–34) has often been used to justify the switch of inheritance by biblical exegetes, who have, almost without exception, been quick to side with the winner and to declare that all was for the best. Readers of Donne's Holy Sonnet XI,

[9] See *ibid.*

'Spit in my face you Jewes ...', have sometimes been puzzled by the parallel between Jacob and Christ in the lines:

> And Jacob came cloth'd in vile harsh attire
> But to suplant, and with gainfull intent:
> God cloth'd himself in vile mans flesh, that so
> He might be weake enough to suffer woe.

But in fact, so far from being one of Donne's more outrageous conceits, the figure was a standard one – even to the overt anti-semitism of the opening lines. A later seventeenth-century commentary, for instance, is quite clear about the dire warnings contained in the typology of the story. Esau is

in this respect (as the Fathers observe) a Figure of those, who, desirous to unite GOD *and the* World *together, cast about how they may enjoy the Comforts of* Heaven *and the Pleasures of the* Earth *both at once ...*

> *This Mysterious History throughout, represents to us in all parts of it* Jesus Christ, *cloathed in the outward appearance of a* Sinner, *as* Jacob *here was in that of* Esau. *It is also an admirable Figure of the Reprobation of the* Jews, *who desired nothing but the good things of the* World; *and of the Election of the* Church, *which* (like *David*) *desires but one thing of* GOD, *and requests but one* Blessing.

> *We must have a care* (as S. *Paul* saith) *not to imitate* Esau, *who having sold his Birthright to* Jacob, *and desiring afterwards, as being the Eldest, to receive the* Blessing *of his Father, was rejected, without being able to persuade his Father to revoke what he had pronounced in Favour of* Jacob, *notwithstanding his entreating it with many Tears. For as he had despised* GOD, GOD *also despised his Cries and Tears, as not proceeding from a sincere Repentance, nor from a true Change of Heart.*[10]

By the early nineteenth century, however, such comforting typologies had given way to distinct unease. Mrs Trimmer, in a popular Evangelical commentary, is clearly more than a little worried about the moral aspects of the story, does her best to clear Jacob, and concludes by speculating openly about God's motives in the whole exercise:

Jacob, in obedience to his mother, acts against his own conscience. Our Reason will show us that these are not things we should imitate in Isaac, Rebekah, and Jacob; therefore no remarks are made upon them by the sacred writer of their history. What we are particularly to observe here, is, that GOD made the faults of these three persons contribute to bring about his own good purposes. GOD knew beforehand what they would do; he also knew that Jacob, though he would do many wrong things, would keep from idol worship, and reverence his Creator, and bring up his family in the true religion; and that Esau on the contrary would marry among idolators, and depart from the right

---

[10] *History of the Old and New Testaments*, p. 31.

way; and GOD, possibly for this reason, ordained that Jacob rather than Esau should be the head of the great nation through which all the families of the earth should be blessed.[11]

Nevertheless, it is clear that whatever the original rights and wrongs of the case, Jacob's triumph has been complete. Esau had the misfortune never to write a book – and history, as we are constantly reminded, is told from the point of view of the victors. After all, Moses – by tradition at least, the author of the first five books of the Bible, the Pentateuch – was of the tribe of Levi, and a descendant of Jacob, and not of Esau, who has accordingly been relegated to the also-rans of history. But, as the examples above illustrate, there is something more to Jacob's victory than control of the media. What is really significant about this story is not that Esau was supplanted, but that this account, the official narrative of the descendants of Jacob/Israel, *tells* us that he was. In other words, the story of this appropriated blessing is somehow so important an element in the much larger national saga of who the children of Israel felt themselves to be that the need to repeat it has over-ridden the obvious moral difficulties in justifying the legitimacy of the succession. The result was to give those thus legitimised, from thenceforth distinctively the 'children' of Israel, a peculiar kind of consciousness of who they were and how they had become so – a consciousness that in turn finds expression in the biblical text through a new interpretative theory.

Hence another incident embedded in the larger narrative: the story of Jacob's ladder (Genesis 29: 10–22). Fleeing from the wrath of his cheated brother, Jacob goes to sleep in the open and dreams of a ladder reaching to heaven, with angels of God ascending and descending upon it. It is here, at the place ever afterwards to be known as Bethel, that God makes three promises that are to be fundamental to the story of Israel: possession of the land; innumerable descendants; and finally, through those descendants, a blessing to 'all the families of the earth'. Once again, this is, of course, Jacob's own version of events – dreams are unverifiable – but though it repeats and conveniently confirms possession of the blessing, there is a special rider that transforms it from a family squabble into an ideology. A new interpretative theory has been enunciated, replete with universal significance. Thus not merely is the story both a reminder of the great saga of Israel, and

[11] Mrs (Sarah) Trimmer, *Help to the Unlearned in the Study of the Holy Scriptures*, 2nd edn, 1806, pp. 32–3.

a key text for Christian inclusiveness, it has also long been interpreted, both typologically and symbolically, as a metaphor of divine inspiration. As generations of writers and artists have since observed, it has served as a constant reminder of the unexpected, even arbitrary, nature of the transcendent – here in the form of a theophany occurring literally in the middle of nowhere, to a guilty man on the run.

The success of that theory is attested by the fact that the two commentaries cited above, totally different as they may appear to be at first glance, both rest their defences on it. The clue comes at the beginning of Genesis 28:

> And Isaac called Jacob, and blessed him, and charged him, and said unto him, Thou shalt not take a wife of the daughters of Canaan. Arise, go to Padan-aram, to the house of Bethuel thy mother's father; and take thee a wife from thence of the daughters of Laban thy mother's brother.

This is a repetition of Abraham's instruction to his servant concerning the marriage of Isaac in Genesis 24: 3: 'I will make thee swear by the Lord, the God of heaven, and the God of the earth, that thou shalt not take a wife unto my son of the daughters of the Canaanites, among whom I dwell ...' At the heart of the biblical story of the Patriarchs is the absolute prohibition of polytheism; to preserve the new religion revealed to Abraham there is to be *no* intermarriage with the Canaanites. That way lay a return to the old religion of the land: Baal-worship, polytheism and infidelity. For the Hebrew Bible it is the ultimate sin.[12] This is a constant refrain that will echo throughout the Pentateuch and the entire history of Israel in the books of Judges, Samuel, Kings and Chronicles. If one wishes to extend the dichotomy, it can be found in the New Testament enmity between the Jews, the descendants of those who had endured the Captivity and kept the old faith in Babylon, and the Samaritans, the descendants of those who had stayed and mingled with new settlers planted by the conquerors. The Samaritans (however much they too might claim to have kept their distinctive faith) had, in the eyes of the returned exiles, committed the unforgivable sin of setting up a rival temple to Jerusalem in Samaria – a move which was seen as threatening a return to the polytheism of the local Canaanite culture. The dangers of any weakening of the doctrine of one temple, one god, were well illustrated,

---

[12] A case of 'do as I say, not as I do' since Abraham himself takes a Canaanite wife, Keturah (Genesis 25: 1). 'Not too nice a choice' comments Thomas Mann (*Joseph and his Brothers*, trs. H.T. Lowe-Porter, Penguin, 1988, p. 83).

to orthodox eyes, by the syncretism of the new settlers, who were very willing to add what was, to them, the local cult of Yahweh to their existing pantheon.[13] To take it a stage further, that continuing hostility to the native Canaanites can even arguably be seen to underlie the enmity between the Palestinian Arabs and the Jews in twentieth-century Israel.

The biblical consequences of that patriarchal prohibition were far-reaching enough. From it stems Jacob's flight to Bethel, his famous dream, the fourteen years' service under Laban, his uncle, the consequent marriages with his cousins Leah and Rachel, and his fathering of the twelve tribes of Israel. And there we have it: by a marriage of cousins the purity of the descent – and therefore of the monotheism, the religion of Yahweh – was guaranteed. What is significant is that it is only *after* Jacob has appropriated the blessing intended for his elder twin that we find Isaac insisting that he may not marry a Canaanite. Esau, we are told in the previous chapter, had already married two Hittite wives (Genesis 26: 34–5) – and so, it is implied, had already endangered the monotheistic line of succession. Both this and the story of his selling his birthright (which again, interestingly, places Jacob in a bad light) prepare the way for his loss of the blessing.

The effectiveness of this reading as a hermeneutic principle can be judged by the two extracts from critical commentaries quoted above. The first is, as one would expect from a seventeenth-century interpretation, primarily typological: Esau, rather startlingly in view of what has just been said, is taken as the 'type' of the Jews; Jacob of the Christian Church. What is important, however, is not so much the roles assigned as their *relationship* to one another. Just as Isaac's blessing, apparently destined for Esau, had been appropriated by Jacob, so, with the coming of the New Dispensation, the blessing intended for the Jews is appropriated by the Christians. The earlier appropriation foreshadows and justifies the later; the line of religious descent has passed to the Christians, who must now, in their turn, take care not to backslide or intermarry with the Jews. As we shall see, there is in this typological linking of Jacob with the Church a theme of central significance to the later history of appropriation.

---

[13] See II Kings 17: 24–41. This account of Samaritan syncretism and the fragility of monotheism is given more plausibility by recent archaeological discoveries of the existence of such apparently syncretistic Jewish communities as far afield as upper Egypt (see John Romer, *Testament: the Bible and History*, Michael O'Mara, 1988, pp. 115–16).

By the end of the eighteenth century, however, there has been a radical shift of mood. It is true that the central plank of Mrs Trimmer's account remains the assertion that it is Jacob, rather than Esau, who will 'keep from idol worship ... and bring up his family in the true religion'. To that extent the traditional critical principle has triumphed: for the proto-Victorian what was important was still the *family* line as the only guarantee of the true faith. Small wonder that figures and tropes of the family remained as central to New Testament Christianity in a metaphorical sense as they were literally to Old Testament Judaism. Yet though, at first sight, such sentiments could have been those of Ezra or any of the prophets, there is a sense in which Mrs Trimmer is closer to the iconoclastic Volney than to her pietistic seventeenth-century predecessors.

The distancing of typology is no longer available to her. Forced by the bare narrative to reach after a new mode of reading the scriptures, she instinctively takes the story of Jacob as she might a novel, and is clearly embarrassed by the doubtful morality she finds there. Behind her acknowledgement of the family principle is a wholly modern unease at the means taken to ensure its success. Though for her the historical accuracy is still not to be questioned, once the narrative is stripped of its typological accretions we have to be assured that these figures are not role-models. Her solution is the familiar critical assumption of dramatic space between author and character. As befits the universal novel written by the Supreme Author, the deadpan narratives of the Old Testament have been replaced by a saga of irony and guilt.

If Mrs Trimmer reads biblical narrative in terms of fictional history and contemporary morality, Volney, like the German Higher Critics, discovers in its moral contradictions and intolerance an appropriation of earlier Near-Eastern cults. The two writers' assumptions mirror a cultural and national divide that we shall explore in later chapters. Though we are more likely to associate the impact of Volney's methodology in Victorian Britain with later names like those of Hennell, Feuerbach or Strauss,[14] this is more because his association with the French Revolution effectively served to discredit his scholarship among the clergy and the world of the Anglican establishment

---

[14] Charles Hennell, *Enquiry Concerning the Origins of Christianity*, 1838; David Freidrich Strauss, *The Life of Jesus*, (1835) trs. George Eliot, 1846; Ludwig Feuerbach, *The Essence of Christianity*, (1841) trs. George Eliot, New York: Harper, 1854. See Stephen Prickett, 'Romantics to Victorians: from Typology to Symbolism', in S. Prickett (ed.), *Reading the Text: Biblical Criticism and Literary Theory*, Oxford: Blackwell, 1991.

than because his arguments were themselves ineffective. Volney remains a key figure in the history of interpretation theory, and, as the number of translations suggests, he had a considerable direct impact on English radicals at the end of the eighteenth and beginning of the nineteenth centuries.[15] Tom Paine drew heavily on him both in the *Rights of Man* and *The Age of Reason*, and remarks such as 'the Christian theory is little else than the idolatry of the ancient Mythologists accommodated to the purposes of power and revenue'[16] read like direct quotations. Thomas Spence published lengthy extracts from *The Ruins* in his journal *Pig's Meat or Universal School of Man's Rights*.[17] It was also extensively summarised in the Freethinking *Christian's Magazine*[18] and the strongly anti-Christian *Theological Enquirer*, as well as in other pamphlets by its editor, George Cannon, an ex-Spencean turned (among other things) pornographer, who published a number of eruditely ironic pseudo-theological works under the pen-name of the Reverend Erasmus Perkins.[19] One of the contributors to Cannon's *Enquirer* was the young poet Percy Bysshe Shelley, who allowed him to publish extracts from both his 'Refutation of Deism' and 'Queen Mab' in the first issue of March 1815.[20] If 'Queen Mab', which was to become one of the classic texts of early nineteenth-century radicalism, shows unmistakable evidence of Volney's influence,[21] the same is equally true of Shelley's now better-known poem of 1817, 'Ozymandias'. After all, Ramases II (Ozymandias is the Greek form of the name) was, of course, not merely an earthly tyrant, but also a god. Like Blake – who also knew Volney's book – Shelley was quick to see the connections between earthly and spiritual tyranny. That same year, 1817, Mary Shelley, the poet's wife, was to give the *Ruins of Empire* further mythopoeic status by putting it on the Monster's educational reading-list in *Frankenstein*.

To use a word which, though it was just coming into fashion, would probably not have occurred to contemporaries in this context, the *Ruins*

---

[15] See, for instance, E.P. Thompson, *The Making of the English Working Class*, Gollancz, 1965, pp. 107–8.
[16] *Complete Writings of Thomas Paine*, ed. P.S. Foner, 2 vols, New York: Citadel Press, 1945, vol. I, p. 464.
[17] See Iain McCalman, *Radical Underworld: Prophets, Revolutionaries and Pornographers in London, 1745–1840*, Cambridge University Press, 1988, p. 24.
[18] *Ibid.*, p. 74.
[19] *Ibid.*, pp. 78–9.
[20] *Ibid.*, pp. 80–1.
[21] For a discussion of the relationship between the two see Gerald McNeice, *Shelley and the Revolutionary Idea*, Cambridge, Mass., 1969, pp. 123–4; also Richard Holmes, *Shelley: the Pursuit*, Quartet Books, 1976, p. 202.

is a highly 'Romantic' piece of writing – which is not least among the reasons for its appeal to iconoclastic members of the next generation of writers and poets like Shelley. As we shall see, it is also true that the idea of appropriation, in the sense in which it is used by modern criticism and hermeneutic theory, is itself a highly Romantic one. Though there was little in the general thesis of Volney's syncretistic and diffusionist argument that was specifically new, and that had not appeared earlier in the writings of, say, Vico, Holbach, Sir William Jones' studies of classical Indian languages and religion,[22] or in such eighteenth-century German historical critics of the Bible as Eichhorn, Reimarus and Lessing, it was perhaps the first time that a polemical work of this kind had caught the popular imagination to this degree. Most earlier syncretistic and diffusionist accounts of religion had been essentially conservative in that they had taken the supremacy of the Bible as their starting-point. William Stukeley, the antiquarian, for instance, in his *Stonehenge* (1740) and *Avebury* (1743), had accepted the tacit implication of the deist John Toland's book, *A Critical History of the Druids* (1723), that the Church of England had appropriated the pagan priestcraft of the Celts. For Stukeley, however, there was nothing sinister or corrupt in this because the druids had inherited *their* religion (via Phoenician traders) directly from the Old Testament Patriarchs themselves. The Anglican Church was, therefore, custodian of the pure biblical revelation untainted by the far more dangerous corruptions of Rome. More universal in its syncretism, Jacob Bryant's *A New System* (1744) had claimed that all ancient pagan mythologies were based on degraded and fragmentary memories of biblical history – preserved by societies that had been scattered and cut off from their common root by the catastrophe of the Flood. Sun worship was thus not the pagan origin of monotheism, but, on the contrary, a dim recollection of an original spiritual monotheism now lost and overlaid by animism and superstition.[23]

---

[22] 'The *Sanscrit* language, whatever may be its antiquity, is of a wonderful structure; more perfect than the *Greek*, more copious than the *Latin*, and more exquisitely refined than either, yet bearing to both of them a stronger affinity, both in the roots of the verbs and in the forms of the grammar, than could possibly have been produced by accident; so strong indeed, that no philologer could examine them all three, without believing them to have sprung from some common source, which, perhaps, no longer exists: there is a similar reason, though not quite so forcible, for supposing that both the Gothick and the Celtic, though blended with a very different idiom, had the same origin with the Sanscrit; and the old Persian might be added to the same family.' Sir William Jones, 'Third Anniversary Discourse on the Hindus, Feb. 2, 1786', in *Works*, ed. Lord Teignmouth, vol. III, London, 1807, p. 34.

[23] See Jon Mee, *Dangerous Enthusiasm: William Blake and the Culture of Radicalism in the 1790s*, Oxford: Clarendon Press, 1992, pp. 92–6; 132.

But Volney's refusal to allow Christianity a clear supremacy over other Near-Eastern religions was by no means the most shocking of his conclusions. Worse, perhaps, was his claim that the Bible had antecedents that might extend back over a period of up to 17,000 years. As we have just seen, standard biblical commentaries of the eighteenth century were often in the habit of including not merely the dates BC of particular events, but also the dates of those events after the Creation of the world – which, as everyone knew, following the famous calculations of Archbishop Ussher, had occurred in 4004 BC.[24] Even this date, of course, itself represented a form of historicism: the mere attempt to make such a calculation was a gesture away from mythology towards the new idea of a verifiable dating. Moreover, the odd 4 on this date was because Ussher also believed that Jesus had been born in the year AD 4 and not in the year 1, as the conventional Christian calendar (dating from the eighth century) had assumed. But Volney's implied attack on conventional biblical dating was probably less disturbing for many orthodox Christians than another implicit suggestion of his: that the Old Testament – and in particular the book of Genesis – was not the earliest known written text.

For many contemporary scholars it was still an article of faith that Hebrew was the oldest known language – containing at least elements of the original unfallen Adamic language where words stood in an essential rather than a contingent and arbitrary relationship to the things they described.[25] Thus Johann Gottfried Herder, in his great literary study of the Old Testament, *The Spirit of Hebrew Poetry*, published only ten years before, had done no more than sum up conventional wisdom when he took it for granted that Hebrew poetry 'expresses the earliest perceptions, the simplest forms, by which the human soul expressed its thoughts, the most uncorrupted affections that bound and guided it'.[26] But Herder had still been a clergyman – however unorthodox a one. The idea that there might be behind Genesis a nexus of yet older literary texts, and that the first book of the Bible, so far from being in every sense the beginning of written human

---

[24] See, for instance, *History of the Old and New Testaments*, p. 38.

[25] See Hans Aarsleff, *From Locke to Saussure: Essays on the Study of Intellectual History*, Minneapolis: University of Minnesota Press, 1982, pp. 58–60. Working from similar biblical premises, James Parsons argued in *The Remains of Japhet* (1767; repr. Meriston: Scholar Press, 1968) that Irish and Welsh were in fact older than Hebrew, being the remains of 'Japhetan', the original antediluvian language. (pp. x–xii).

[26] J.G. Herder, *The Spirit of Hebrew Poetry* (Dessau 1782–3) 3rd edn, Marburg, 1822; trs. James Marsh, Burlington, Vermont: Edward Smith, 1833, pp. 45–6.

experience, the fount and origin of all history, was in some sense a rewriting or a commentary on those texts, constituted for many as great a challenge to contemporary thought as the sixteenth-century substitution of the Copernican for the Ptolemaic astronomical system, or Darwin's nineteenth-century placement of man within the chain of evolutionary biology. Far from being the foundation document of Christian civilisation, laid down by divine fiat, it now seemed possible, to those prepared to consider Volney's iconoclastic arguments, that the Bible in some sense had begun as an appropriation of the mythological and historical writings of other earlier civilisations. It was, perhaps understandably, less commented upon that this might in turn only parallel the appropriation of Esau's blessing by Jacob, not to mention the much better documented appropriation of the Hebrew scriptures by the early Church for the creation of the Christian Bible.

Later biblical scholarship has built a huge and, it must be said, still largely speculative, edifice that in effect augments and substantiates Volney's diffusionist thesis. The so-called 'documentary hypothesis', that Genesis in particular is a redaction or compilation of a number of earlier source documents, has been persuasively and powerfully restated in the middle of this century by Gerhard von Rad, who saw Hebrew history writing as a product of imperial court circles in the period of David and Solomon.[27] According to this view, court historians of the golden age 'enlightenment' adapted earlier sources (now lost) to produce in Genesis a Creation narrative that would lead naturally forward to the achievements of their own age. Others, such as W.F. Albright, drawing on the discovery of a number of religious texts during excavations at the Canaanite city of Ugarit, have seen the kind of epic history represented by Genesis as inspired by earlier Canaanite or Ugaritic works (of which, it must be added, few satisfactory examples have yet been found).[28]

If the details of this putative appropriation of older material remained shadowy and controversial, for others the principles on which the redactors worked appeared easier to perceive. In von Rad's words: 'The Israelites came to a historical way of thinking, and then to historical writing, by way of their belief in the sovereignty of God in

---

[27] John Van Seters, *In Search of History: Historiography in the Ancient World and the Origins of Biblical History*, Yale University Press, 1983, pp. 213–16.

[28] W.F. Albright, *Yahweh and the Gods of Canaan*, Athlone Press, 1968, pp. 1–52; F.M. Cross, *Canaanite Myth and Hebrew Epic*, Cambridge, Mass.: Harvard University Press, 1973. For examples of Canaanite influence on the Bible see ch. 2, below.

history.'[29] The historical monotheism that we have seen as the critical principle at work in the Jacob and Esau story became for many twentieth-century critics a key to all mythologies: by appropriating and incorporating the legends of Canaan, Babylon and Egypt it alone was seen as making sense of, and a meaningful narrative from, the mass of conflicting stories of the heroes and deities of the region. Thus the Flood narrative of Genesis is remarkably similar to that written in Hurrian, the language of a tribe which seems to have entered the ancient Near East from north India around 1600 BCE. The name of its hero, Nahmizuli, contains the (vowel-less) Hebrew word for Noah, *Nhm*, and his ark also comes to rest on Mount Ararat – which, though it is some way from Canaan, happens to have been right in the heart of the ancient Hurrian Empire. But whereas that story ends with the goddess Ishtar pledging a marvellous necklace, 'the Jewels of Heaven', that she will save humanity from the god Enlil's wrath in future, the biblical account ends with the covenant between man and God, with the rainbow as its sign.[30]

Nor, of course, has this process of reworking and appropriation ceased with any of the 'final' arrangements of the biblical canon – of which there have been several. Though such arguments may be presented in a scholarly fashion, with whatever evidence as can be adduced, we should not lose sight of the fact that what they are presenting us with is, in effect, yet another re-interpretation of the Bible – a new theory of reading. Similarly Volney's suggestion that the Christian scriptures, and, indeed, the Hebrew Bible on which they in turn were founded, are nothing but an appropriation of yet earlier religious texts, is, of course, itself part of a further attempt at appropriation – in effect, an effort to replace one myth by another. As the official presentation to the National Assembly indicated, his book was part of a concerted strategy to make it impossible to read the Christian Bible, and therefore by implication, the doctrines of the Catholic Church, except through the lens of his particular brand of historicism. If in the end Volney's attempted appropriation was to prove only partially successful, the strategy itself embodied a prophetic insight. As we have seen, despite, or, rather, *because* of its innocent guise of neutral scholarship, historicism was to prove one of the nineteenth century's most

[29] Gerhard von Rad, 'The Beginnings of Historical Writing in Ancient Israel', in *The Problem of the Hexateuch and Other Essays*, trs. E.W. Dicken, Edinburgh and London, Oliver and Boyd, 1966, p. 170.

[30] John Romer, *Testament: the Bible and History*, Michael O'Mara, 1988, pp. 30–2.

effective new methodological mythologies. Whereas in classical and mediaeval thought 'earliest' implied 'best' (an idea mirrored in the meaning of the Latin verb *praecedere*, which translates into English not merely as 'to appear first' but also 'to surpass'[31]) Romantic and nineteenth-century historicism was tacitly evolutionist in its assumptions. By concentrating less on the final form of a religion than on where it had supposedly originated, and through what variations it was held to have developed, it provided a seemingly 'scientific' and scholarly means of destabilising *all* forms of religious belief. To explain a belief in terms of its origins was tacitly also to identify its essence with its crudest and most primitive manifestations. Moreover the effect of suggesting that an idea might have evolved through many obviously incompatible forms was ultimately to cast doubt on all of them. If the monotheism of Moses could be shown to be part of a seamless web stretching back to the most simple forms of polytheism or even animism in pre-Dynastic Egypt then it presumably owed so much the less to Revelation. If miraculous or quasi-miraculous biblical events, such as the Deluge, which had hitherto been treated as unique, could be shown to have parallels in the mythology of the neighbouring cultures of Mesopotamia, then the likelihood of such events having actually occurred in the way described seemed correspondingly remote. In this context, the accusation of appropriation was itself a highly effective appropriative manoeuvre – nor is it accidental that Volney's suggestion that historical appropriation lay at the root of Christian mythology should be part of a further covertly appropriative act, itself to be justified by a new diffusionist theory of history.

HISTORICISM AND HERMENEUTICS

It is, perhaps, time to look further at the history of this highly romantic concept of 'appropriation', and how it is used in contemporary critical and philosophical thought – not to mention how it has come to denote the process by which readers make sense of what they read. The Latin root verb *appropriare* was formed by the prefix *ad* (or 'to') plus *proprius* ('own') meaning 'rendering or making one's own' (a derivation that was even clearer in one late legal variant *adpropriare*). As the *OED* reminds us, in pre-Reformation ecclesiastical law it was the legal word used to describe the transfer of tithes or endowed benefices from a parish to a

---

[31] See David Norton, *A History of the Bible as Literature*, vol. I: *From Antiquity to 1700*, Cambridge University Press, 1993, pp. 51–2.

monastic house; by an obvious connection of ideas, it became at the English Reformation the euphemism commonly used to describe the looting of those same monastic houses with well-rewarded zeal by a member of Henry's newly Protestant merchant-aristocracy. Lacking a Reformation in the sixteenth century, France had to wait until the 1790s for the revolution that was to bring about a parallel dissolution and appropriation of many of her monasteries, but the identically spelt French word *appropriation* has behind it, nevertheless, a network of similar connotations. In the Larousse *Universel* dictionary, among the given synonyms of the reflexive form of the verb *s'approprier* is *usurper*: 'to usurp'. Perhaps because of the inevitable suggestion that such transfers, whatever the pretext, were often morally dubious, even in metaphorical usage, the French word, like the English, always carried with it implications that fell something short of respectability. The taking over of someone else's property, however it may be justified legally, has never been generally seen as a morally glamorous activity; indeed, such has been the usual English opinion of the law, that any suggestion that the word might carry some quasi-legal force merely served to reinforce its already faintly disreputable aura.

There is an ironic twist to this linguistic history in that the negative form of the word, 'misappropriation', a fairly late development, which one would logically have expected to have had the effect of legitimising the idea of appropriation itself, signally failed to do so in practice. This may result from the ambiguous context in which it made its appearance. In view of the legal history of the original word it seems no accident that the first recorded use in the *OED* of this negative form is from a speech of Edmund Burke at the trial of Warren Hastings in 1794. The resonances of the word become still more murky if one notes that Hastings was, against all apparent justice, finally acquitted of charges of corruption after a seven-year trial. The deadpan account of Hastings' life in the *Dictionary of National Biography* records, among the many events of his Indian rule, that in 1781 he had 'deposed Chait Singh and appropriated his treasure'. Consciously or unconsciously this echoes Burke's charge of 'the violent misappropriation of the revenues of the Nabob'. We might say that what was at stake in that trial was not just Hastings' dubious conduct of affairs, but the whole legal legitimacy of the idea of appropriation – specifically, as it had previously been understood in the colonial context, but also more generally throughout British legal history. Burke may have lost the case, but there is a sense in which he won the linguistic argument.

Never again was India to be governed in such a buccaneering style[32] –
and within a very few years 'misappropriation' had passed into legal
terminology. Its connotations, however, continued to suggest that it
was not so much the opposite of appropriation (as in the parallel
formations of 'mistreat', 'mistake' or 'mis-adventure') as a peculiarly
extreme form, in which the latent injustices of appropriation have
become so blatant as to be clearly against the law, rather than merely
exploiting its loopholes.

Other resonances to the word echo around Hastings. He was
godfather to Jane Austen's cousin, and later sister-in-law, Eliza
Hancock (that he was very possibly her real father suggests a different
kind of appropriation). The Austen family followed the trial of their
wealthy patron and friend with intense partisan interest. Mrs Austen's
great-uncle had in his time been an even more successful 'appropriator'
than Hastings himself – between 1705 and 1711, as Paymaster-General
to the Forces Abroad, he had, as it was tactfully put, 'skimmed off' the
sum of £15,374,689 from the funds under his control.[33]

Nor, perhaps, is it accidental that the idea of appropriation should
have acquired such Oriental associations. For Edward Said, contemplating the European creation, construction and subsequent control of
'the Orient', such a process is reprehensible and inevitably destructive
to both sides; yet, as he also tacitly concedes, it is only one example
from many of the normal process by which one culture comes to
understand another by modelling it in its own terms.[34] In contrast, the
corresponding German word *aneignen*, meaning 'to make one's own'
what was initially 'alien', conveys no such pejorative undertones. It
comes to prominence in the late eighteenth century from linguistic
roots that are biological and organic rather than legal – to be
associated more with that untranslatable romantic word *Bildung* (the
Goethean idea of 'growth' or 'self-development') than it is with 'theft'.
Thus in the twentieth century Walter Benjamin, who was not in other
contexts notably free of what Ricoeur calls the 'hermeneutics of
suspicion', describes the sensual appreciation of architecture as a form
of 'appropriation' with the suggestion that it not merely contributes to
individual growth, but that this process, taken collectively, creates a

[32] For an account of the context of these changes, see John Clive, *Thomas Babington Macaulay*,
Secker and Warburg, 1973, pp. 304–8.
[33] See Park Honan, *Jane Austen*, Weidenfield and Nicholson, 1987, Part 1, ch. 4; and 167; Alistair
Duckworth, *The Improvement of the Estate: a Study of Jane Austen's Novels*, Baltimore, Md.: Johns
Hopkins University Press, 1971, p. 45.
[34] Edward W. Said, *Orientalism: Western Constructions of the Orient*, new edn, Penguin, 1995.

cultural tradition and thus becomes the source of canonical values.[35] In the same (marxist) tradition Robert Weimann has stressed the two-way process whereby 'the socializing of the individual and the personalizing of the social' both involve 'the process of *Aneignung*, the imaginative appropriation of the world and the nature of one's own existence in it'.[36]

Behind these two very different traditions of meaning lies a theoretical conflict that goes back to the classical world: between what might be called the Ciceronian and the Aristotelian concepts of society. Whereas the Romans saw their society in essentially formal and legal terms, the Greeks always saw themselves primarily in terms of the possession of a common ideology[37] – and it is this strand that is also uppermost in the German word. Perhaps to avoid the implicit Latin legalism of the Anglo-French tradition Paul Ricoeur explicitly draws on Gadamer and, behind him, Heidegger, when he wishes to deploy the concept himself.[38] For Ricoeur, whose philosophy was formed in deliberate reaction to the process of distancing and even scepticism almost inevitably created by historicism, there is a fundamental distinction to be made between hermeneutics and historicism. In seeking to explain the ideas and beliefs of the past by viewing them comparatively, historicism (as in the case of Volney) is also a powerful distancing agent. In what might be called its 'strong' form, exemplified best perhaps in Hegel and Marx, historicism could involve a claim to the status of a natural science, and to explain the nature, processes and above all the outcome of human history. The hidden agenda behind the claims of so-called 'scientific' predictive historicism has been rightly pilloried by such anti-marxist historiographers as Karl Popper,[39] but even in its more prevalent, 'weak' version, simply as a comparative analysis of the past, historicism has almost inevitably been the vehicle for a destructive relativism. (The great exception to this, of course, would be Hegel himself, who uses historicism as a route to absolutism:

[35] Walter Benjamin, 'The Work of Art in the Age of Mechanical Reproduction', in *Illuminations*, ed. Hannah Arendt, trs. Harry Zohn, Fontana/Collins, 1973, p. 242.

[36] Robert Weimann, *Structure and Society in Literary History*, Charlottesville: University Press of Virginia, 1976, p. 9.

[37] The fullest account of this is probably in Eric Voegelin's massive study, *Order and History*, Baton Rouge: Louisiana State University Press, 1956–87, vol. 3, but such accounts as that in Charles Cochrane's, *Christianity and Classical Culture*, Oxford University Press, 1944, are more accessible.

[38] Hans Georg Gadamer, *Wahrheit und Methode*, Tübingen: J.C.B. Mohr, 1960; English translation: *Truth and Method*, Sheed and Ward, 1975.

[39] *The Poverty of Historicism*, Routledge, 1957.

but, in a classic appropriative manoeuvre, he insists that since, in his own interpretation, history merges with the Absolute, it is not itself susceptible to historicisation.) In contrast hermeneutics, as Ricoeur uses the word, seeks not to explain, from a detached standpoint, but to *understand* the writings of the past and to allow us to comprehend the meanings they held for both their writers and their audiences. 'The aim of all hermeneutics', he writes, 'is to struggle against cultural distance and historical alienation.'[40] 'Appropriation' or *Aneignen* is his word for that complex process by which a reader takes an alien concept from another cultural context and so assimilates it as to render it a part of his or her own personal world.

There is in this nothing shady, underhand or disreputable: on the contrary, it is essentially only a description of how the human mind operates. Ricoeur is thus at some pains to dissociate this use of the word from the crude notion of simply 'taking possession' implied by the Latin legal root of the Anglo-French word. For him, the process of making an initially alien idea one's own does not involve so much seizure and control, as a kind of surrender to what *it* has to say. Appropriation is primarily a 'letting-go'[41] distinguished from any form of 'taking possession' by a corresponding 'relinquishment'. At this point we have clearly passed from what purports to be merely descriptive to some kind of normative or even ethical statement. For Ricoeur this gesture of self-abnegation or surrender to what is alien and new in the 'other' creates the possibility of revelation – in both its secular sense and in the more precise theological sense that is never far behind his hermeneutics. 'The letters of St Paul', he writes, 'are no less addressed to me than to the Romans, the Galatians, the Corinthians.'[42] Revelation is not merely revelation of *something*, it is at the same time also *self*-revelation. Appropriation 'is the process by which the revelation of new modes of being ... gives the subject new capacities for knowing himself'.[43]

The link between appropriation and revelation is, in my view, the cornerstone of a hermeneutics which seeks to overcome the failures of historicism and to remain faithful to the original intention of Schleiermacher's hermeneutics. To understand an author better than he understood himself is to unfold the

[40] Paul Ricoeur, 'Appropriation', in *Hermeneutics and the Human Sciences*, ed., trs. and introduced by John B. Thompson, Cambridge University Press, 1981, p. 185.
[41] *Ibid.*, p. 191.
[42] *Ibid.*, p. 191.
[43] *Ibid.*, p. 192.

revelatory power implicit in his discourse, beyond the limited horizon of his own existential situation.[44]

But attractive as such confidence in self-discovery through the processes of appropriation is, it has also has dangers. Jürgen Habermas, from the explicitly historicist Frankfurt School, has criticised the facile optimism of Gadamer (and by implication, therefore, also of Ricoeur), pointing out that there are in practice severe restrictions to all claims of hermeneutical understanding. For him 'Hermeneutical consciousness is incomplete so long as it has not incorporated into itself reflection on the limit of hermeneutical understanding.'[45] Habermas raises, as an example, the case where 'systematically distorted patterns of communication' occur in normal speech – such as when two people talking fail to notice, as an observer might, that they are at cross-purposes.[46] If such things happen in trivial everyday conversations, it is no less likely that they can also happen in ways much more difficult to detect when we are dealing with the documents of the past. We should therefore, perhaps, retain some degree of scepticism about the more ambitious claims made for hermeneutics.

Even while we may applaud the ideal of moving beyond the limitations inherent in any individual's perspective, and sympathise with Ricoeur's desire to break with the 'failures of historicism', for many of his critics there is a dangerous hubris implicit in the idea that the hermeneut can be privileged to remain faithful to 'the original intention of Schleiermacher's hermeneutics'. Intentionality is a difficult and dangerous concept at the best of times, and, as we shall see, it is doubly difficult in the case of Schleiermacher, the exact meaning of whose ideas on hermeneutics have been the battleground for one of the most famous recent debates over appropriation. Even more problematic is the confidence that we might be capable of understanding an author better than he understood himself. Though this was a keystone in Schleiermacher's own hermeneutics, as we shall see, his focus on the conditions bringing author and reader together arose from the specific and highly unusual context of 'Jena' Romanticism – and, in particular, from his friendship with Friedrich Schlegel.[47] It was left to Wilhelm Dilthey, Schleiermacher's most influential disciple, to make the more

---

[44] *Ibid.*
[45] Jürgen Habermas, 'On Hermeneutics' Claim to Universality', in Kurt Mueuer-Vollmer (ed.), *The Hermeneutics Reader*, Oxford: Basil Blackwell, 1986, p. 302.
[46] *Ibid.*, p. 192.
[47] See below, ch. 4, pp. 180–203.

general claim that this was 'the necessary conclusion of the doctrine of unconscious creation'.[48] As such, it was a claim about the possibility of historical understanding, not, of course, a claim to knowledge of absolute meaning. There was, for Schleiermacher, no formula that would uncover a final meaning: 'understanding is an unending task'.[49]

It seems then that there is a dilemma right at the heart of this debate that crucially affects the way in which we understand what we mean by appropriation. Hermeneutics' apparent promise of a way of over-coming the inevitable distancing and scepticism engendered by histori-cism is only at the price of claiming an insight that seems in the last resort to be dangerously subjective and self-constructed. We cannot altogether dispense with the implication of the Latin tradition that appropriation is a disguised form of 'theft': a wrenching of an idea, a story (or even a 'blessing') from its original context and placing it in a new setting where it may come to mean something very different. Yet by itself that interpretation of the word is obviously inadequate and too negative; appropriation in the positive sense is also clearly a necessary and essential quality of the process described by Benjamin, what Newman called 'real' as distinct from 'notional assent'[50] or what Michael Polanyi called 'personal knowledge'[51] – that process of taking a new and alien idea and so incorporating it into the structure of one's thought and feeling that it becomes a personal (and personalised) possession. It might, perhaps, be a better working hypothesis to suggest that there is in the very idea of 'appropriation' *both* a quality of thinly disguised theft *and* a recognition that such a take-over is a necessary part of the way in which any person, or even society, makes an idea its own – that appropriation is, in other words, a normal condition of intellectual and cultural vitality. Such a hypothesis would also involve the recognition that there is, intrinsic to the phenomenon we are attempting to describe, a quality of 'living dangerously' – as Jacob was to discover when he had to flee from Esau. Just as there will have been occasions when the appropriation of an idea, a text, or some other form of knowledge, has transformed and enriched the life of an individual or the cultural landscape of a society, so there will have been others when a similar appropriative act will have effectively inhibited,

[48] Wilhelm Dilthey, 'The Development of Hermeneutics' (1900), reprinted in David E. Klemm (ed.), *Hermeneutical Inquiry*, vol. 1: *The Interpretation of Texts*, Atlanta: Scolars Press, 1986, p. 104.

[49] *Hermeneutics, the Handwritten Manuscripts*, ed. H. Kimmerle, trs. J. Duke and J. Forstmann, Missoula, Mont.: Scolars Press, 1977, p. 41 (sect. A, Bibl.).

[50] John Henry Newman, *A Grammar of Assent* (1870), ed. C.F. Harrold, Longman, 1957.

[51] Michael Polanyi, *Personal Knowledge: Towards a Post-Critical Philosophy*, Routledge, 1958.

distorted or even destroyed that idea, and prevented what we, from another perspective, might well see as its true development. Which is also to say, as Kuhn has suggested of scientific paradigms,[52] that any particular hermeneutic perspective will inevitably *exclude* other alternative ways of thinking, feeling and perceiving.

We have one such example of an exclusion immediately to hand in the history of hermeneutics. In considering the slow development of linguistic theories Gadamer notes that 'it was precisely the religious tradition of the Christian West that hindered serious thought about language, so that the question of the origin of language could be posed in a new way only at the time of the Enlightenment'.[53] The identification of the whole Bible with the *logos*, the divine Word of God of John's Gospel, rapidly became central to early Christianity, and was the main principle behind its tradition of biblical interpretation until well after the Reformation. Christianity's new critical theory was nothing less than the claim that Jesus was the promised Messiah of the Hebrew scriptures, and that *only* by reading them in this light could they be properly understood. The 'New Testament' was thus the culmination and fulfilment of those scriptures, now suitably re-arranged and transformed into an incomplete but forward-looking collection of books now collectively to be known as the 'Old Testament'.[54] Since this involved an extensive process of re-interpretation, often of an elaborately figurative nature, the traditional Hebrew belief that every word was of vital and God-given significance (a conviction itself, of course, open to a wide variety of interpretations) was obviously as important to the new appropriators of the scriptures as it was to their original possessors – and could, once again, be appropriated into the Greek notion of the *logos* as a source of divine inspiration. That this might also prevent any discussion of the human origins of language was clearly not something that could easily be perceived until an extensive body of secular writings, from both the modern and the ancient worlds, had become easily available through printing. As is clear from the first serious modern attempts by Vico, Herder, von Humboldt and others,[55]

---

[52] Thomas Kuhn, *The Structure of Scientific Revolutions*, University of Chicago Press, 1962.

[53] Hans Georg Gadamer, 'Man and Language' (1966), in *Philosophical Hermeneutics*, trs. and ed. David E. Linge, University of California Press, 1976. p. 60.

[54] See Prickett (ed.), *Reading the Text*, pp. 1–5.

[55] See Giambattista Vico, *The New Science* (1744), trs. Thomas Goddard Bergin and Max Harrold Frisch, Ithaca, N.Y.: Cornell University Press, 1968; Johann Gottfried Herder, 'Essay on the Origin of Language' (1772), in *Herder on Social and Political Culture*, trs. and ed. by F.M. Barnard, Cambridge University Press, 1969; Wilhelm von Humboldt, *On Language* (1836), trs. Peter

even eighteenth-century attempts to think about the origins of language
still felt, in various ways, the massive pull of these traditional religious
assumptions.

Such an example, like that of Jacob and Esau, also serves to remind
us that to seek the ambiguities of appropriation only in the thickets of
twentieth-century theory is to ignore the way in which it has lain at the
roots of our cultural consciousness ever since the dawn of literacy.
Indeed, it will be our argument that the primeval tension between theft
and creative acquisition is not an accident of the written word, but in
some way endemic to it. Genesis begins with the Fall and ends with the
story of Jacob. At some very deep level that tension may actually be
essential to our idea of what constitutes a book, as if the original sin of
Eden were not merely part of the foundation myth of Western
civilisation, but was also somehow encapsulated, even mirrored, within
the form by which that myth has been transmitted. If so, it has also
been our *felix culpa*, the means whereby the written word has become
not just a means for the transmission of legal codes – the oldest known
piece of writing is claimed to be the Code of Hamurabi – but for myth-
making, story-telling and invention. Similarly metafiction, the way in
which one story draws upon another, is not the product of modern
critical theory, but is a constant and inescapable presence in the written
word, constituting at once a revision of the past and a legitimation of
the present. At its most formal, this classical instinct towards appropriation obeyed what Ernst Curtius has called 'the fundamental law of life
that applied throughout Antiquity': 'according to which the sanction
for all new creations was in the traditional works from which they
derived and to which they had to refer: as the colony to the mother
city; the statue to the founder, the song to the Muses, the copy to the
original, and the work of art to the model'.[56]

But, whatever the theory, the practice was not always so ordered
and hierarchical as this might suggest. According to Manus O'Don-
nell's *Life of St Columba*, the original Battle of the Books concerned the
ownership of a Psalter which Bishop Finnian of Druin-Finn had loaned
to the Irish saint. When Columba secretly had a copy made, Finnian,
hearing of it, demanded that it, too, should be returned with the
original. The matter was referred to the king, Diarmait mac Cer-béil,

Heath, introduction by Hans Aarsleff, Cambridge University Press, 1988; and Aarsleff, *From Locke to Saussure.*

[56] Ernst Curtius, 'Virgil', in *Essays on European Literature*, trs. Michael Kowal, Princeton University Press, 1973, p. 7.

who ruled that 'If I had loaned you my cow, and it had calved while in your byre, would you not have returned both to me?' In the ensuing battle of Cúl-Dremne, we are told, thousands perished, and Columba, also under threat of excommunication from the Synod of Tailtiu, was forced to flee (apparently still with Psalter) to Iona.[57] What was claimed to be the disputed book was later adopted as the 'battler' of the O'Donnells, and carried into war by them.

Such are the perils of unclear copyright laws. But whatever the historical truth behind the story of Columba's Psalter, it captures something of that tension over appropriation that no doubt the classical rules of legitimation were designed to ease. This is as true of individual words and ideas as of moments whose outcomes portended major cultural transformations.

TROY, GREECE AND ROME

If we have so far made the Bible central to our argument it is because the history of that book, though unique, is peculiarly important to our understanding of the phenomenon of appropriation. Indeed, it seems to epitomise the process. As we have come to suspect more and more over the past 200 years since Volney, much of its narrative is grounded in mythologies, beliefs and texts that have been acquired from else-where; moreover, the moments of greatest influence in that transmission have been both irreversible and, not infrequently, seemingly illegitimate as well. Yet that, essentially romantic, interpretation of the Christian Bible needs to be seen in the context of other non-biblical processes of appropriation that were already centuries old at the beginning of the Christian era.

The two great homeric epics, *The Iliad* and *The Odyssey*, had told the story and the subsequent consequences of the overthrow and destruction of another earlier society, that of the Trojans. The story of the defeat and appropriation of Trojan civilisation was as fundamental to the Greeks' sense of cultural identity as the story of Jacob and Esau was to the Hebrews'. Not least because of its power to articulate that peculiar European sense of the 'otherness' and difference of a lost past, the story of Troy was to provide an alternative mythological under-pinning of later cultures almost as powerful as the Bible itself. But it would be a mistake to assume that the opposition between Europe's

[57] See J.F. Kenny, *The Sources for the Early History of Ireland* (1929), reprinted, Dublin: Irish University Press, 1968, pp. 391, 435 and 630.

pasts, pagan and Christian, classical and biblical, was as absolute as Plumb's reference to the problem of Europe's 'dual past' might suggest. To Tertullian's question 'What has Athens to do with Jerusalem?'[58] the historical answer, at any rate, seems to be, 'Quite a lot'. At least from the Jewish side there are repeated attempts from the third century BCE onwards to suggest a shared cultural lineage with Hellenism. There is, for instance, the tradition attributed by both Josephus and Eusebius to the otherwise unknown second-century writer, Cleodemus Malchus, that among Abraham's many children were three sons who joined with Heracles in his war against the Libyan giant Antaeus. After his victory, the Greek hero marries the daughter of one of these sons of Abraham, whose name, Africa, is then given to the whole continent.[59]

Perhaps in reference to this same legend, 1 Maccabees 12: 20–3 has a correspondence between the Jews and Arius 1, King of the Spartans, in which the latter acknowledge their kinship with the Jews, both being 'of Abraham's blood'. The story is again taken up by Josephus.[60] Commenting on these stories, Erich Gruen dismisses the idea that these Jewish stories should be interpreted as an attempt at 'a ticket of admission to the Hellenic club'.[61] On the contrary, he argues, the naming of Abraham as the common forefather makes it plain that the Jews were trying to bring the Greeks within their own traditions rather than subordinating themselves to Hellenism.[62] The logical corollary of Hebrew monotheism was that, just as in the Exodus stories, where Yahweh's power over the Egyptians had to be demonstrated, the new dominant Mediterranean force of Hellenism had to be seen also to acknowledge the only true God. So far from being a gesture towards the Greek world, it should rather be seen as the ultimate affirmation of the uncompromising nature of Judaism.

But before we dismiss these slightly absurd Jewish attempts to appropriate the Hellenic tradition as mere curiosities of history we should pause to consider their outcome. Perhaps no less remarkable than the spread of Christianity across the ancient world in the first few centuries of our era was the new fusion of the biblical and classical worlds that resulted. Often referred to as the 'Hellenising of

---

[58] *De praescriptione haereticorum*, 7.
[59] Jos. *A.J.* 1.239–41; Eus. *P.E.* 9.20. 2–4.
[60] *Ibid.*, p. 10. (I Macc. 12: 20–3; Jos. *A.J.* 12.225–7).
[61] As claimed by E.J. Bickerman, *The Jews in the Greek Age*, Cambridge, Mass.: Harvard University Press, 1988, p. 184.
[62] Erich S. Gruen, 'Cultural Fictions and Cultural Identity', *University of California, Berkeley Transactions of the American Philological Association*, 123 (1993), pp. 11–12.

Christianity' it might in many ways be better described as the 'Judaising of Hellenism'. At the centre of the new and all-conquering religio-philosophic synthesis was not the pantheon of Greece, but the God of the Hebrew scriptures. As Richard Jenkyns, among others, has noted, one of the most extraordinary (and least remarked) features of Indo-European societies was the extinction of all their major European religious systems within a very few years of encountering Christianity.

Once any new system of belief has commended itself to a considerable body of people it is seldom altogether eradicated; Zoroastrianism, founded more than two and a half thousand years ago, has survived for the past millennium or so with less than 150,000 adherents ... Religions do not die; they become cataleptic ... To this general rule there is one enormous exception. The growth of Christianity completely destroyed the great Indo-European pantheons, Norse, German, and Greco-Roman. Some time in the sixth century A.D. the last man died who believed in the existence of Juno, Venus and Apollo, and in the succeeding centuries Asgard and Niflheim went the way of Olympus.[63]

Given the relative numbers involved, however, one wonders if Zoroastrianism might not be the exception rather than the rule. Certainly in Asia Hinduism and Buddism, also both Indo-European in origin, are alive and well – but of the dramatic collapse of the European pagan religions in the face of Christianity there can be no doubt.

And here, and in the light of its subsequent history, one is tempted to invert the original formulation of the appropriated blessing. Just as the wily Jacob was seen as the appropriator, by his own account confirmed by God in possession of the blessing at Bethel, so Christianity could, as we have seen, confirm its own appropriation of the Hebrew tradition by asserting that Esau was the type of the Jews, and identifying itself typologically with the line of Jacob. Yet it might be a better description to say that just as the blessing had appropriated Jacob to its own narrative ends, so it subsequently appropriated Christianity, and now finally it had appropriated the pagan classical tradition as well. From henceforth, though the ancient world remained a constant reference-point for the legitimation of anything from the arts to politics, it had to be mediated through the new religion not the old. All classical narratives had to be sublimated to the great metanarrative provided by the Old and New Testaments. If we can see the greatness of Virgil, the pagan political poet, in the fact

[63] Richard Jenkyns, *The Victorians and Ancient Greece*, Oxford: Basil Blackwell, 1980, pp. 174–5.

that he could be taken up and enhanced, after thirteen hundred years by Dante,[64] that same redeployment is also a measure both of Dante's greatness, and of the final success of the appropriation of the pagan and Hellenistic world begun so clumsily by those Jewish chroniclers of the third century BCE.

As the mention of Virgil already anticipates, that process of cultural legitimation by appropriation of Homer was, of course, most notably to be achieved in the legends of the foundation of Rome. As every classical student knows, it was Aeneas, leader of a band of refugees from the sack of Troy who, after countless setbacks and difficulties, finally reached the coast of Italy to found the Trojan community, and whose descendants, via the cities of Lavinium and Alba Longa, were eventually to found the Eternal City. The story provides the plot of the *Aeneid*, the material for Livy's history, Lucan's *Iliacon*, and for many lesser works – most notoriously, perhaps, Nero's *Troica*, inspired, we are told, by the burning of Rome. But, as Gruen has pointed out, on its way to achieving canonical status the Virgilian version had to overcome some very persuasive competition from other, in some ways more attractive, founding legends.[65] What might be called the retrospective triumph of the Trojans becomes the more remarkable when we consider that the first accounts of the founding of Rome come not from Roman but from Greek historians. In line with normal Hellenic practice, however, these varied stories attributing the origins of Rome to the descendants of Odysseus, or other Achaean warriors adrift after the fall of Troy, mostly tended to assume that it could only have been founded by Greeks. The Trojan variant makes its first appearance among Sicilian Greek writers, in some ways a marginalised group on the edge of the Hellenic world with a special interest in linking the newly emerging power of Rome with the epic stories that defined the common Greek Mediterannean culture.

The interesting question, however, is not so much where the legend originated, but why, among the plethora of what might be seen as more politically flattering accounts, did the Romans *themselves* favour the Trojan version – and thus legitimise their origins not in the stories of the victorious Greeks, of whom the front-runner must be the proverbially cunning Odysseus, but in those of their defeated and exiled opponents? Gruen's answer is twofold:

---

[64] See Curtius, 'Virgil', p. 4.   [65] Gruen, 'Cultural Fictions', pp. 5–6.

It enabled Rome to associate itself with the rich and complex fabric of Hellenic tradition, thus to enter that wider cultural world, just as it had entered the wider political world. But at the same time it announced Rome's distinctiveness from the dominant element in that world ... The celebrated Trojan past lay in remote antiquity, its people no longer extant, the city but a shell of its former self. Troy, unlike Greece, persisted as a symbol, not a current reality. So Rome ran no risk of identification with any contemporary folk whose defects would be all too evident – and all too embarrassing. The Romans could mold the ancient Trojans to suit their own ends. As in so much else, they astutely converted Hellenic traditions to meet their own political and cultural purposes. The Greeks imposed the Trojan legend upon the west as a form of Hellenic cultural imperialism, only to see it appropriated by the westerner as a means to define and convey a Roman cultural identity.[66]

More to our point, this act of historical appropriation provided both a new way of reading the past and a hermeneutic principle to explain the present. It enabled Rome to shake off the label of barbarian and strike 'the pose of heir and standard-bearer of an antique civilization shared by Trojans and Achaeans'. But, of course, the story of Aeneas was not just a historical legend, it had been mediated by the most powerful artist then known to the ancient world: Homer. In creating the *Aeneid* Virgil was not just fulfilling the Emperor Augustus's essentially political commission – important as that was. Nor was it merely a matter of finally securing Rome's entry into 'a wider cultural world'. In appropriating Homer Virgil was actively claiming his role as heir to that world. It is, of course, one thing to claim a role; quite another to fulfil it; but the fact remains that his act of appropriation was also able to liberate the most extraordinary creative energies both within his own culture and far beyond it. Virgil came to enjoy a pre-eminence in the ancient and mediaeval worlds almost inconceivable today, and, through him, the story of the fall of Troy took on a significance for Europe that would have been quite unimaginable had it stayed within the confines of Homer.[67] Nor would the progressive metamorphoses of Troy into Rome, into Augustine's City of God, into Dante's Florence and – as we shall see – even into Shakespeare's London ever have been possible if Virgil's epic had been no more than a paean of propaganda to Rome's greatness. His theme is not so much the glory of war as its destructiveness – what Wilfred Owen in the twentieth century was to call the 'pity of war'. Curtius notes that Virgil's proud boast, *imperium*

---

[66] *Ibid.*, pp. 8–9.
[67] Ernst Curtius, *European Literature and the Latin Middle Ages*, trs. Willard Trask, Oxford University Press, 1946, ch. 1.

sine fine dedi ('[I] have given (Rome) unlimited dominion') only finds its fullest meaning within a context of loss, a sense of vanished greatness, where the vision of restitution and wholeness merges into a wider eschatological vision.[68] If we ignore for the moment the hauntingly 'Christian' Virgil of the Fourth Eclogue, one might be tempted to call it the fulfilment of the Trojan rather than the Homeric vision, were it not, of course, that the Trojans themselves had been so appropriated by their conquerors that they are known to us not from their own accounts but only as constructs of the Greek legends. What mattered was not who the Trojans were, but the sense that they had been. The classical process of legitimation, like the biblical, depended not on covert, but explicit appropriation.

For that reason, of course, we cannot ignore the 'Christian' Virgil – if only because of what Dante was able to create by a further act of appropriation in thirteenth-century Italy. The Middle Ages had created its own version of the story partly through episodes in Ovid's *Metamorphoses* and *Heroides* but principally through two shadowy and apocryphal figures, Dictys Cretensis and Dares Phrygius, whose accounts (now assumed to be fourth- or fifth-century Latin forgeries) were treated as those of eye-witnesses. The former, who was supposedly a companion of Idomeneus, was said to have kept a journal of the Trojan War which was subsequently translated from the Phoenician into Latin in the fourth century. The latter, believed to have been a Trojan priest, is, similarly, the putative author of a history of the siege. From these sources a mediaeval legend of chivalry and romance had already emerged in such works as Benoît de Sainte-Maure's *Roman de Troye* in the twelfth century. But Dante's appropriation is less concerned with creating traditions of chivalric romance than with the tradition of poetry itself.

Of all the many introductions of real historical personages into the *Divine Comedy*, none has the boldness of incorporating Virgil, not just as a character, but as (for almost two-thirds of the poem) prime mover, poet and psychopomp. In claiming Virgil in the way that he does, Dante also lays claim in his turn to the Homeric tradition, with its central motif of wandering and exile which was not merely so important personally to himself, as a banished Florentine, but to a whole cultural world that sought its legitimation and roots in a vanished past. But Dante's use of Virgil goes far beyond any simple

---

[68] 'Virgil', p. 8.

legitimatising manoeuvre. Throughout the *Inferno* the reader, like Dante the character, slowly becomes so accustomed to Virgil's presence that when it is abruptly, and totally unexpectedly, removed in Canto xxx of the *Purgatorio* we are as shocked as Dante himself.

> Tosto che nella vista mi percose
>   l'alta virtù che già m'avea trafitto
>   prima ch' i fuor di puerizia fosse,
> volsimi alla sinistra col rispitto
>   col quale il fantolin corre alla mamma
>   quando ha paura o quando elli è afflitto,
> perdicere a Virgilio: 'Men che dramma
>   di sangue m'è rimaso che non tremi:
>   conosco i segni dell'antica fiamma';
> ma Virgilio n'avea lasciati scemi
>   di sè, Virgilio dolcissimo patre,
>   Virgilio a cui per mia salute die'mi;
> nè quantunque perdeo l'antica matre
>   valse alle guance nette di rugiada,
>   che, lacrimando, non tornasser atre.   (40–54)

As soon as the lofty virtue smote on my sight which had already pierced me before I was out of my boyhood, I turned to the left with the confidence of a little child that runs to his mother when he is afraid or in distress, to say to Virgil: 'Not a drop of blood is left in me that does not tremble; I know the marks of the ancient flame.' But Virgil had left us bereft of him, Virgil sweetest father, Virgil to whom I gave myself for salvation, nor did all the ancient mother lost avail my cheeks washed with dew that they should not be stained with tears.[69]

There follows Beatrice's famous rebuke, when she brings tears to the poet's eyes by accusing him – at this, of all moments – of faithlessness. I have discussed this passage in a different light elsewhere, and it would be tedious to repeat myself.[70] Here I simply want to focus attention on one aspect of this dramatic disconfirmation. Though Virgil's loss is deliberately presented to the reader in poignantly human terms, there is, as always, a subtle and extremely complex allegorical basis for the narrative. His role is not just as the great pre-Christian poet, but as the representative of the poetic tradition on which Dante has hitherto drawn. Virgil is neither simply a friend, nor yet the spirit of poetry – though he is certainly both these things. He is also that which Dante's culture revered more than anything else: the representative of a

---

[69] *The Divine Comedy of Dante Alighieri*, trs. John D. Sinclair, New York: Oxford University Press, 1939, vol. II.

[70] *Words and the 'Word': Language, Poetics and Biblical Interpretation*, Cambridge University Press, 1986, pp. 149–73.

legitimatising tradition going back to Homer and the very roots of European poetry. The idea that the encounter with the divine vision (for Beatrice, though personal, is nothing less) negates or simply expunges that whole tradition is at once brilliant and terrifying. In a way that is difficult for the modern reader fully to understand, it is the tradition that makes Dante the poet. Now that support, that source of creativity, is not merely swept away so suddenly that Dante is not even aware of it happening but he discovers that to mourn for its loss is a sin.

Yet, of course, that tradition is what has brought him to the divine vision. Dante, the character, must learn to accept that it is both his highest earthly treasure and, at the same time, confronted by that which is higher, utterly worthless. It is this ability both to appropriate, and to use that appropriation to show how it must be discarded that makes Dante the supreme European Christian poet, and alters for ever the nature of the European poetic tradition. Just as Virgil had made it impossible ever again to read Homer in the same way, so Dante made it impossible ever to read either Virgil or Homer as they had hitherto been.

Nor does this, now double, appropriation of the classical past cease with the Renaissance. Writing in 1802, from a French perspective, Chateaubriand sees Milton also as part of this Virgilian tradition, not so much in his direct borrowings from Virgil (of which there are many) but specifically in the way that he appropriates the past and, by using it in the present, opens up the past as well:

We shall, moreover, observe that the bard of Eden, after the example of Virgil, has acquired originality in appropriating to himself the riches of others; which proves that the original style is not the style which never borrows of any one, but that which no other person is capable of reproducing.

This art of imitation, known to all great writers, consists in a certain delicacy of taste which seizes the beauties of other times, and accommodates them to the present age and manners. Virgil is a model in this respect.[71]

Here, for the Romantics, we notice, appropriation is immediately linked with its seeming opposite, originality, in such a way that it can be read back into a new interpretation of the past.

For Julius Hare, writing towards the middle of the nineteenth century, such a historical process of appropriation is the key to

---

[71] Chateaubriand, *The Genius of Christianity* (1802), trs. Charles White, Baltimore, 1856, p. 221.

understanding the progressive development of self-consciousness in European poetry.

With regard to modern poetry, when we are looking at any question connected with its history, we ought to bear in mind that we did not begin from the beginning, and that, with very few exceptions, we had not to hew our materials out of the quarry, or to devise the groundplan of our edifices, but made use, at least in great measure, of the ruins and substructions of antiquity. Hence Greece alone affords a type of the natural development of the human mind through its various ages and stages. Owing to this, and perhaps still more to the influence, direct and indirect, of Christianity, we from the first find a far greater body of reflective thought in modern poetry than in ancient. Dante is not, what Homer was, the father of poetry springing in the freshness and simplicity of childhood out of the arms of mother earth: he is rather, like Noah, the father of a second poetical world, to whom he pours out his prophetic song, fraught with the wisdom and the experience of the old world. Indeed he himself expresses this by presenting himself as wandering on his awful pilgrimage under the guidance of Virgil.[72]

Hare's theme, of the biblical tradition as one of a developing and reflecting self-consciousness, is one to which we shall return.

SHAKESPEARE AND HISTORY

On a more provincial scale, when Shakespeare appropriates the chronicles of Hall, Holinshed and Stow as a basis for his history plays, it is clear that he, too, is making of his material something entirely new. A chronicle, by definition, is simply an account of events as they are believed to have happened. It is neither the chronicler's business to provide explanations, nor to give meaning to the sequence of happenings he records. History, on the other hand, starts not so much with events as with problems – which require explanation and interpretation. But for Shakespeare, as for any Elizabethan, history was much more than simply an explanation for the events or problems of the past.

Secular history was a branch of that universal and divine history revealed by God through the Bible. It was, therefore, implicitly charged with divine meaning – meaning which it was the task of the historian to bring out and clarify. History was, in effect, a series of moral *exempla* to illustrate in practice the great unchanging truths of God's judgement. Even in pre-Reformation times such matters could

---

[72] Julius and Augustus Hare, *Guesses at Truth* (2nd edn 1838), Macmillan, 1871, p. 42.

clearly be controversial. But with the Reformation and subsequent wars of religion the interpretation of history acquired a new urgency. Though apparently a conforming Protestant, Shakespeare (like many of his contemporaries) had strong Catholic connections. Much has been written on the question of his possible Catholic or Protestant sympathies without any decisive result; much less on the indisputable fact that anyone in his position would be deeply familiar with the modes of biblical exegesis around which the debate revolved. Not merely was the representation of history an essentially hermeneutic and even polemical activity, such representation was always assumed to be on many levels. It was of the nature of narrative to be so. All mediaeval systems of exegesis, however much they may have disagreed with each other as to whether there were properly four, seven or twelve levels to be found in the Bible, were at least united in their acceptance that the written word was essentially polysemous.[73] Such systems of interpretation were part of the normal habit of mind of most people, even as late as the beginning of the nineteenth century, in a way that has been almost entirely lost today. Thus when, for instance, critics have noted elements of the mediaeval morality play in the plot of *Henry IV* – especially in the relationship of Hal and Falstaff – they have been less quick to add that this is, as in Dante 200 years earlier, classic *figural* typology. A universal moral truth is demonstrated from the lives of real historical people. At the same time, a much wider truth about the nature of order and power is also being disclosed.

Yet in secular literature, chronicle and even in history, the boundaries between 'fact' and 'fiction' were not those that a modern audience would necessarily take for granted. The Latin word *historia* covered both 'history' and 'story' in our modern sense. The Elizabethan chronicles were by no means simply factual accounts of events – raw material, as it were, awaiting the shaping hand of the true historian. They were in many ways as midrashic as the books of the Old Testament. It is no accident that, for instance, Stow's *Chronicles of England* (1580) repeat the story, first related by Joseph of Exeter and Geoffrey of Monmouth, of the foundation of Britain by Brutus, great-grandson of Aeneas.[74] His capital on the Thames, Troynovant (or New Troy) later became London, and among his descendants were

---

[73] See, for instance, Marjorie Reeves, 'The Bible and Literary Authorship in the Middle Ages', in S. Prickett (ed.), *Reading the Text: Biblical Criticism and Literary Theory*, Oxford: Basil Blackwell, 1991, pp. 12–56.

[74] Here, and in what follows, I am indebted to the work of Robert Maslen.

Gorboduc, Cymbeline, Coel (Cole: the 'merry old soul' of nursery rhymes) and Arthur. Something of the story's popularity can be judged from the fact that among Caxton's first printed books was his translation of Raoul Lefèvre's *Recueil des hystoires troyennes*. It would be easy to imagine from this that Stow is convinced that this legendary material is factually accurate; but the truth is probably a good deal more complicated. Most educated Elizabethans were in fact well aware that this was mythological material; its purpose was to produce neither 'history' nor 'chronicle' in our modern senses of the words, but rather a kind of national or political allegory – a form of poetic literary code or conceit by which current events could be judged and commented on. As in the case of Dante's appropriation of Virgil, historical legitimation did not depend so much on a belief in the truth of the sources (even by the criteria of the time) as on the fact that they constituted a *written* tradition. A previous book was, to some extent, its own justification. The Trojan legend provided the background not merely for Shakespeare's *Troilus and Cressida*, but for a British 'history', *Cymbeline*, and the fact that this belongs in time and mood with such late Romances as *Pericles* and the *Winter's Tale* (with its famous 'seacoast of Bohemia'), and not the history plays tells us much about how Shakespeare himself regarded the factuality of this part of Stow.

At the same time, Shakespeare was fully capable of altering the chronicler's more prosaic factual accounts for his own purposes. As Holinshed makes clear, for instance, Hotspur was in reality a good twenty-five years older than Hal, yet in *Henry IV*, Shakespeare, for reasons of dramatic contrast, makes them the same age. Which is 'history' in the Elizabethan sense? The chroniclers' midrash or the dramatist's interpretation? If there is a good case for saying that, for Shakespeare and his contemporaries, *Henry IV* is the real 'history', and that the chroniclers merely provided appropriate raw material to be given significance by the dramatist, what do we make of the Brutus story – which most Elizabethans were well aware was more a form of political allegory than history in our sense? Once we start to think of the problems and questions behind apparently self-evident notions like 'history', we can see how relatively modern too is our seemingly straightforward distinction between 'fact' and 'fiction' – which does not date back much beyond the end of the eighteenth century and the work of such historians as Niebuhr and von Ranke. It is worth remembering that the origin of the word 'fact' lies not in any notion of objectivity but in the Latin *factum*: 'a thing done or performed'. For the seventeenth century, as for our own, a historical narrative was as much something *created* as any work of art; where it differed from ours was not so much in its more ready awareness and acknowledgement of it, but that, in belonging to a pre-critical historical era, the distinction had not yet been clearly demarcated. As a result, the age was also more openly and even conventionally conscious of the polysemous nature of all such constructed narratives.

At first sight we appear to have here well-documented examples of appropriation analogous to those which Volney claimed to have found behind the Old Testament. Shakespeare has given an order and a meaning to history – what Volney's contemporary, Voltaire, would later call 'nothing more than a tableau of crimes and misfortunes'[75] – taking the raw material provided by the chroniclers of the period and making it his own by creating from it a dramatic polysemous historical narrative in much the same way that Volney believed the anonymous Hebrew writers had done with their sources. As they had no doubt altered or modified the events of the earlier stories, where necessary changing the emphasis, and rewriting events so that this 'history' would tell the story of God's relationship with his chosen people as they believed it should be told, so Shakespeare has altered his source-material to tell *his* version of events. Certainly in terms of its durability, this must be one of the most effective appropriations ever made. For everyone who knows the correct ages of Hal and Hotspur, there must be ten thousand who know Shakespeare's version. Similarly Falstaff has taken his place in the mythology of English history; thus we all *know* that Hal had a wild youth; that he tried on the crown while his father lay dying; that he rejected Falstaff to go on to be king, invade France, gain the victory at Agincourt, and die glamorously young. Yet there is one important difference between this and the making of the Old Testament. Though the chronicles of Hall, Holinshed, and Stow, survive and can be read as they always could, they have been effectively obliterated not so much by a new hermeneutic theory (though we should neither under-estimate the comprehensiveness nor the subtlety of Shakespeare's philosophy of history) as by something even more powerful: a change of medium. The shift from chronicle to drama, and the polysemous nature of the latter art-form, makes Shakespeare's History plays – in the immortal words of *1066 And All That* – 'utterly memorable'.

---

[75] *L'Ingénu* (1767), ch. 10.

THE REWARDS OF THEFT

As we might expect, the moment we start to look at such examples of cultural appropriation in any degree of detail a wide variety of individual patterns emerge. Yet our central metaphor of Jacob's theft of his brother's birthright will never be far away, providing both a model and a tradition to which later, especially Romantic, writers repeatedly returned. In particular, time and again it seems to be the case that the two meanings of the word 'appropriation' we noticed at the outset are much more closely linked than might have been expected. The idea of quasi-legal 'theft' that lies just below the surface of the latinate Anglo-French word and the connotations of biological growth behind the German *aneignen* are not just alternative possibilities but appear to be structurally part of the same phenomenon. Finally, it is a tradition not just of legitimation, but of a growing consciousness of the process by which such legitimation is achieved, and of the growing self-consciousness (or even self-construction) that necessarily accompanies it.

It is only when the writer is conscious of his (or her) own difference from what has gone before that he is capable of interpreting or changing it. The scholar who is most fully respectful of his master's ideas is not likely to be the one who makes fullest use of them. This point is by no means a new one – it lies, for instance, behind T.S. Eliot's argument in his essay 'Tradition and the Individual Talent' that the real meaning of the word 'tradition', when applied to the history of European poetry, is not about capacity to imitate, but to change our understanding of what has gone before.[76] The truly 'traditional' work is the one that is really new. The great poet or writer, as distinct from the merely talented one, is the one who can absorb and appropriate the works of the past and *then* create something distinctively different from them. A synthesis such as Dante's involves *both* the dubieties of 'appropriation' and the organic growth of *aneignen*. Similarly Shakespeare transformed the Elizabethan chroniclers from a mass of history, legend and polemic into the story of England – not necessarily the modern historian's version, but a saga of legitimacy, power and order that captured the imagination of a whole people and created a secular myth of origins in some ways only slightly less powerful than that of Virgil or the Old Testament.

[76] T.S. Eliot, 'Tradition and the Individual Talent', in *Selected Essays*, 3rd edn, Faber 1951, pp. 13–22.

It seems to be from this paradoxical matrix that some of the world's most influential ideas had their origins. If the case-defining story of Jacob and Esau, which has a good claim to be the earliest recorded example of appropriation, suggests that Jacob's usurpation of the birthright blessing illustrated a point so crucial to Jewish history that it could overcome any questions of morality, it was because, in the last resort, what was important in the blessing was less its detailed content than the fact that Jacob (or, to be precise, his mother) *saw* it as important. In that act of deceiving a blind old man Jacob stepped out of a traditional tribal structure into the modern world. If henceforth the story of Israel was in a very peculiar sense the story of monotheism, it is no less true, and intimately linked with it, that the tradition was to be carried forward by a series of peculiarly self-conscious individuals who could, in various ways, dissociate themselves sufficiently from their social matrix to prod, criticise or denounce their society. From the new critical principle of monotheism the material of the canon of the Hebrew Bible was shaped not merely out of the existing literature of the Jewish people, but also, it has become clear, out of much of that of the surrounding cultures as well.

Yet even here there are surprises. For instance, what the new hermeneutic principle would seem to suggest is that a material primogeniture is to be replaced by a spiritual one: Jacob is not Isaac's legitimate heir in the physical sense, but the blessing makes him so by adoption. This principle of the 'adoption' of Jacob was one that appealed to a number of early Christian commentators, including Paul himself, when thinking about the legitimacy of the Church (Romans 9: 4–13).[77] It was even applied to Jesus's relationship to God. But though adoption was common enough in the Graeco-Roman world (the word Paul uses in his Epistles is the Greek word *huiothesia*) there is unfortunately no corresponding Hebrew word because the concept itself was unknown in the Old Testament. Since, for the ancient Hebrews, a 'father' was the one who 'protected' or 'nourished' his child, rather than being simply the physical parent, the extra quality of incorporation into the family necessary for the distinctive act of adoption was *already* present in the original concept of fatherhood.[78] The nearest thing to adoption in the later sense was Jacob's decision to give Joseph's two sons, Ephraim and Manasseh, equivalent status to his own – and therefore eventually to be founders of two of the Twelve

[77] Also elsewhere, as in Galatians, 3: 26–7; 4: 4–5; Ephesians, 1: 5
[78] Alan Richardson (ed.), *A Theological Word Book of the Bible*, SCM Press, 1950, p. 15.

Tribes. Despite obvious connections, 'blessing' in the Old Testament was something subtly different again: though spoken by human agency, it carried with it also a mysterious and divine gift.

Nor, if we turn to the curious unfolding of Jacob/Israel's own line of descent, is the sequence so simple as an 'adoption' theory might suggest. It is complicated in the first place by the story of Leah and Rachel, which reads like an odd inversion of Jacob's own trick on Esau. Having run away from Esau's wrath, he goes to work as a herdsman for his uncle, Laban. At the end of seven years Jacob asks for the hand of his cousin Rachel, Laban's beautiful younger daughter, in marriage. This is granted, but after he has taken his veiled bride to bed on the wedding night he discovers that he has in fact been given the elder, and less attractive sister, Leah. For Rachel, his original and best-beloved, he has to work another seven years for Laban. Rachel, however, proves barren while Leah produces child after child. In mediaeval typology much was made of the difference between the two sisters as types of the active and the contemplative life.[79] Of Jacob's 'twelve sons' six are by Leah (Reuben, Simeon, Levi, Judah, Issachar and Zebulun), two by Bilhah, Rachel's maid (Dan and Naphtali), two by Zilpah, Leah's maid (Gad and Asher) and two by Rachel (Joseph and Benjamin). Now as any reader of Genesis knows, it is these last two, the favoured sons of Jacob and Rachel, who are to be the important players in the next stage of the story. So far, the expected sequence based on choice (or, if you happen to be one of the sons of Leah, favouritism) rather than primogeniture holds good. But, as Gabriel Josipovici has pointed out, the story of Joseph and his brothers has an unexpected sting in its tail.[80]

Between the story of Joseph being sold by his brothers to the Midianite slavers (Genesis 37) and Joseph's arrival in Egypt (Genesis 39) is the curious story of Judah and Tamar, in which Judah is tricked into getting his widowed sister-in-law pregnant. The story seems so isolated from its context that even critics of the stature of von Rad have seen it as an interpolated 'local unit of tradition'.[81] Yet Judah, after all, is no incidental figure in the Joseph story. It is he who, though at first conniving at Joseph being cast into the pit, later saves his life by having him sold to the Midianite slavers. In Egypt it is he who pleads for his brother Benjamin's life before the still unrecognised Joseph. His role as

---

[79] See Prickett, *Words and the 'Word'*, pp. 167–8.

[80] Gabriel Josipovici, *The Book of God*, New Haven, Conn.: Yale University Press, 1988, pp. 7–8.

[81] Gerhard von Rad, *Old Testament Theology*, trs. D.M.G. Stalker, 2 vols., Edinburgh: Oliver and Boyd, 1962, vol. I, p. 172.

the reluctant defender of his two younger half-brothers takes on a new significance, however, when we realise that the story of Tamar actually concerns the unlikely course of his own descent. With the death of his sons Er and then Onan he is left childless except for Shelah (of whom it is merely recorded that Tamar is 'not given to him to wife'). In fact, it is *only* because he is tricked into getting Tamar with child, it seems, that his line is perpetuated at all. The full irony of this lies altogether outside Genesis, when we realise that the apparently triumphant and justified Joseph is the only one of his brothers personally *not* to found a tribe, and that it will be from the tribe of Judah, not from Joseph's sons Ephraim or Manasseh, that David and the Hebrew golden age will eventually come. Moreover it is only the tribes of Judah and Benjamin that will survive the Babylonian captivity as a remnant of the faithful.[82] In other words the all-important line of descent that will eventually lead beyond David, through the Babylonian captivity and, perhaps, even to the Messiah, deviates once again in a quite unpredictable and mysterious way.

We are reminded, too, how central a motif displacement and appropriation is in the biblical narrative. It begins with the enigmatic story of Cain and Abel – where the line of descent, once again, runs through the evil, not the virtuous brother. But as Psalm 78 makes clear, it also leads forward to the displacement of Saul (of the tribe of Benjamin, Rachel's descendent) by David (of the tribe of Judah, and as we have just seen, back to the children of Leah, once more):[83]

[The Lord] refused the tabernacle of Joseph, and chose not the tribe of Ephraim:
> But chose the tribe of Judah, the mount Zion which he loved.
> And he built his sanctuary like high palaces, like the earth which he hath established for ever.
> He chose David also his servant, and took him from the sheepfolds:
> From following the ewes great with young he brought him to feed Jacob his people, and Israel his inheritance. (verses 67–71)

---

[82] Even Josipovici omits to mention the further irony that, in both the lineages of Jesus given in the New Testament (Matthew 1 and Luke 3), the descent of Jesus (through Joseph!) is given as via David to Pharez, the child by incest of Judah and Tamar. Matthew, moreover, even lists two further irregularities in the line of Jesus's descent (1: 5f.): the first is that it goes through Rahab, the prostitute of Jericho, who had sheltered the Hebrew spies; and then later through Solomon, the son of David by Bathsheba, the death of whose husband, Uriah the Hittite, he had engineered, and so earned Nathan's denunciation.

[83] Possibly the most detailed discussion of this whole web of election is to be found in Karl Barth's *Church Dogmatics*, ed. G.W. Bromiley and T.F. Torrance, trs. G.W. Bromiley, J.C. Campbell, Iain Wilson, J. Strathearn McNab, Harold Knight and R.A. Stewart. Edinburgh: T. and T. Clark, 1957, vol. II, Part 2, pp. 340–410.

What the biblical story of Jacob and Esau gives us, in short, is not so much answers as questions – but questions of a disturbing new kind. If each movement of that all-important line of descent seems to take us forward to a kind of further hermeneutic understanding, we are as likely to lose it again shortly thereafter. Yet movement is what this story is all about. Through the following chapters we shall also try and trace something of the manner in which ideas are transmitted from one generation, one culture, one religion to another. In the process we shall also learn much about the nature and influence of written texts themselves and the way in which they seem to have a life of their own long after their progenitors are gone. We may even see texts themselves as a kind of 'blessing', a paradigm, as it were, of all narrative whose meanings must often be appropriated by strange and seemingly illegitimate heirs if they are to speak at all. Though the Romantics took the Bible as the foundational text of Western civilisation, we shall be able to see in what follows how, so far from being the unchanging rock on which the sixteenth-century Reformers could found their Protestant Christianity, the successive appropriations of its meaning reflect in microcosm major shifts of political and social power over the last two thousand years, as well as how it both created and inhibited new ideas. If the iconoclastic challenge mounted by Volney was the culmination of half a century of new historical scholarship, it may equally well be seen as only the latest of a progressive series of such rereadings.

We can, perhaps, read the story of Jacob and Esau as part of an alternative tradition of appropriation and constant change that runs throughout the Bible narrative, and parallels in the development of its internal discourse the narrative of the external history of the text. Without it, and the always ambiguous tradition of inheritance and blessing that Jews and Christians alike have believed to run through their scriptures, there would be no sense of that progression or narrative which has always been as central to biblical hermeneutics as it has to the later development of European literature. In various forms that mysterious story of the hijacked destiny of Israel and its accompanying revelation at Bethel is the *leitmotif* of the rest of this book.

CHAPTER 2

The presence of the past

THE BIBLE AS TRANSLATED TEXT

Translation was, and remains, one of the most powerful and effective means of literary appropriation. The transaction involved is rarely, if ever, a wholly innocent one, however; nor does it take place between cultural equals. Moreover, even if we disregard the technical problems caused by the fact that languages never have direct linguistic equivalencies, translation also changes the totality of a work simply by the fact of appropriating it into a new context. Meaning is never complete; never impermeable. To translate is not to put a ready-made and finalised meaning into new words, but to put a meaning as vulnerable as it is variable into well-used words that already have their own history and are already charged with an existing and alien cultural freight of which the native speakers are themselves often unconscious. The more powerfully associative the connotations of a word in one direction, the more possible it is to close off other connotations. 'It is not so much our judgements as our prejudices that constitute our being', writes Gadamer on the universal problem of hermeneutics: 'prejudices, in the literal sense of the word constitute the initial directedness of our whole ability to experience.'[1] If that is true of an individual, it is no less true of a language and its associated culture.

For Europe the Bible has always been a translated book. More than that: it is a book whose translated, and therefore foreign, status has always been a conspicuous part of our whole civilisation's historical identity – in a social, literary and even religious sense. Almost every line of its text serves to remind us that it is about the people of another time and place who belonged to other kinds of societies from our own and who spoke different languages from ourselves. We have grown so

[1] Hans Georg Gadamer, 'The Universality of the Hermeneutic Problem' (1966), in *Philosophical Hermeneutics*, trs. and ed. David E. Linge, Berkeley: University of California Press, 1976, p. 9.

accustomed to this curious fact that it is worth pausing for a moment to call attention to the obvious. Both represent what Ricoeur calls 'keryg-matic' (rather than 'totemic') cultures,[2] yet if we compare the Bible with, say, the Qur'an as holy books, we find at once that there is one very striking difference. Whatever its degree of borrowing from the Bible and other earlier writings, the Qur'an is mediated to the Islamic world in the same Arabic in which it was written by the prophet Mohammed. A Muslim, whether in Baghdad, Glasgow, Jakarta, Khar-toum or Samarkand, is obliged to pray in the original and therefore sacred language dictated to the founder of his faith, it is said, by the Archangel Gabriel for that purpose – and for that reason there must be no tampering with the word of God. Three-quarters of the Christian Bible, by contrast, is acknowledged even by its most fundamentalist adherents to be originally the scriptures of another religion and written in a language never spoken by any Christian community since the first century.[3] Moreover, even that section, originally the Hebrew Bible, was never at any stage a linguistically homogenous whole.

Though what non-Jews now call the Old Testament was mostly written in Hebrew, as has been mentioned substantial parts of the canon are translations or paraphrases from yet other earlier sacred texts – Canaanite, Mesopotamian or Egyptian, for instance. Indeed, since, as we have seen, it appears to have originated as a critical and often hostile commentary on those earlier religious writings,[4] there is a very real sense in which the Bible can be said to owe even its origins to intertextuality. Nor do we need to accept the whole neat pattern of Volney's universal diffusionist thesis to find many well-documented earlier external sources for biblical stories. We have already mentioned the case of the Hurrian version of the Deluge. Indeed the resemblances between some of the early Genesis stories and the Mesopotamian *Atrahasis Epic* and the *Epic of Gilgamesh* have led some critics to argue for the existence of a genre of creation-to-flood epics in the ancient Near East.[5] Similarly if Albright's hypothesised large-scale 'Ugaritic epics' have as yet inconveniently failed to turn up quite as predicted, there is

[2] Paul Ricoeur, 'Structure and Hermeneutics', in Don Ihde (ed.), *The Conflict of Interpretations*, Evanston: Northwestern University Press, 1974 pp. 50–4.

[3] The problem of the Old Testament's relationship to Christianity is, of course, too complex to be so swiftly dismissed. See, for instance, John Bright, *The Authority of the Old Testament*, Grand Rapids, Mich.: Baker Book House, 1980, ch. 2 for a lucid exposition of the 'classical' solutions to this fundamental problem of Christian origins.

[4] This point is well argued by David Damrosch in *The Narrative Covenant: Transformations of Genre in the Growth of Biblical Literature*, San Francisco: Harper and Rowe, 1987.

[5] *Ibid.*, pp. 18–35.

plenty of undeniably Ugaritic and Canaanite material that has – not least in the apparent origins of the 'historical' or 'history-like' events narrated in Exodus.[6] Many biblical terms for household items, including clothing, furniture and perfumes, are demonstrably Ugaritic in origin. There are clear parallels in the use of metaphors: where Psalm 137 ('By the waters of Babylon ...') reads 'If I forget thee, O Jerusalem, let my right hand forget her cunning', an earlier Ugaritic text has 'If I forget thee, O Jerusalem, let my right hand wither.'[7] There are also strong Egyptian influences on parts of the Old Testament. Psalm 104, for example, bears a striking similarity to the 'Hymn to Aten', reputedly written by the heretical monotheistic Pharaoh, Akhenaten, in about 1345 BCE.[8] Similarly the story of Joseph and Potiphar's wife (Genesis 39) first occurs in an Egyptian story called the 'Tale of Two Brothers' dating from at least 1200 BCE.[9] Some stories seem to bear the marks of at least two external sources. Thus, although the name 'Moses' is an authentic Egyptian one, the story of the baby in a floating reed basket caulked with pitch is also told of King Sargon, who, by the Bible's own dating, lived more than a thousand years earlier than Moses, around 2500 BCE.[10] Pitch, moreover, does not occur in Egypt, but was a common material in Sargon's Mesopotamia.

There had almost certainly been strong Mesopotamian influences in Israel before the Captivity, but more than fifty years of exile in Babylon completed the cultural cross-fertilisation. It was in this period too, as Volney was quick to point out, that the Jews in captivity came into close contact with the much older monotheistic religion of the Persians, Zoroastrianism. The post-exilic court of Zerubbabel and his descendants spoke not Hebrew, but Aramaic – the common language of the Persian Empire. There are ironies latent here that even Volney failed to exploit. G.B. Caird, for instance, argues that:

The language of Haran, whence Abraham is said to have come, was Aramaic ... Hebrew was the language of Canaan (Isa. 19: 18) and was taken over by Israel from the Canaanites, along with their knowledge of agriculture and the

---

[6] F.M. Cross, *Canaanite Myth and Hebrew Epic*, Cambridge, Mass.: Harvard University Press, 1973.
[7] John Romer, *Testament: the Bible and History*, Michael O'Mara, 1988, pp. 8–9. One's confidence in Romer is not increased, however, by his description of Jonathan as being David's son – a clear misreading of II Samuel 17. For some implications of this quotation see Harold Fisch, 'Bakhtin's Misreadings of the Bible', *Hebrew University Studies in Literature and the Arts*, vol. 16 (1988), pp. 145–7.
[8] Romer, *Testament*, pp. 51–2.
[9] *Ibid.*, pp. 52–3.   [10] *Ibid.*, p. 55.

pertinent sacrificial rites ... When during the last three centuries B.C. Hebrew gradually fell into disuse and was supplanted by Aramaic as the vernacular of the Palestinian Jews, this was reversion rather than innovation.[11]

Certainly by the time Ezra returned to Jerusalem, some eighty years after Zerubbabel and the first wave of exiles, and the bulk of the writings that now compose the Old Testament were either written or put into their present form, there is a lot of evidence to suggest that Hebrew was no longer the current language of these Jews. When the New Testament came to be written during the first century CE, Hebrew was so unfamiliar to the Palestinian Jews that, even in the synagogues, the Hebrew scriptures had to be read either by means of paraphrases into Aramaic, called *Targums*, or, in Greek-speaking areas, by the Greek translation called the Septuagint. Biblical Hebrew is in many ways a language created for an ideological purpose. It is worth noting, however, that this does not make it unique – the same can be said of Homer[12] or even of Milton's *Paradise Lost*. Moreover, as we shall see, it is not an aberration but actually a recurring characteristic of the Bible that it is written in a language at some remove from that actually spoken by its readers.

If we assume that Jesus and his immediate circle were themselves mostly Aramaic-speakers, we have to note also the fact, so easily ignored, that the written accounts of his life and sayings are themselves, even in their earliest known forms, translations – since the remaining section of our Bible, the New Testament, was written in a different language altogether: *koiné* Greek, a non-literary low-status form of the language spoken mostly by traders and non-Greeks throughout Asia Minor and elsewhere in the early years of the Christian era. This was a sign of the times, for within only a generation or so the early Christians had lost almost all contact with both Hebrew and Aramaic and were using either the Septuagint or the Old Latin and then the Vulgate versions. Thus what was in effect the first truly unified monoglot version of the Bible, was already itself not merely a translation, but a translation of translations. Nor was this the end of the long process of textual

---

[11] 'These facts', he adds, 'ought to have deterred those writers, ancient and modern, who have held that Hebrew was a unique langauge, specially designed by the Holy Spirit for conveying theological truth.' G.B. Caird, *The Language and Imagery of the Bible*, Duckworth, 1980, p. 35.

[12] '[The Homeric epic's] language was not a Greek that anyone had ever spoken in day-to-day life, but a Greek specially contoured through use of poets learning from one another generation after generation' (Walter J. Ong, *Orality and Literacy: the Technologising of the Word*, Routledge, 1982, p. 23). In the same category with Rabbinic Hebrew, Ong lists learned (mediaeval) Latin, classical Arabic, Sanskrit and classical Chinese (*ibid.*, p. 114).

accommodation. Whatever the degree of idealistic fervour for a return to presumed origins that accompanied the first English translations of the Bible, the English King James Authorised Version was as much a political as a religious undertaking, in which the Protestant appropriation and alteration of the Catholic Vulgate was to parallel the earlier Christian appropriation and alteration of the Jewish scriptures.

Whether one views Christianity as an appropriation of Judaism depends on the model one uses to describe the separation between the two religions. Recent scholarship has tended to see early Christianity more in terms of a 'party' or perhaps more formally, even a sect, within Judaism, rather than being an initially new religion.[13] Some have even argued that Christianity was, and indeed still is, a particular form of Judaism.[14] According to this view, there eventually emerged from a highly pluralistic phase in the first century two dominant 'Judaisms': Rabbinic Judaism and Christianity. However much they might vary in the way they interpreted their tenets, we can find in both groups four so-called 'pillars' of belief which constituted in effect a sufficient common core for us to speak of them as belonging essentially to the same religion: the ideas of monotheism, election, the Torah and the Temple.[15] Whereas Rabbinic Judaism inclined towards a more literalistic view of them, Christianity was to develop an elaborate metaphorical interpretation of all four. Thus Hebrew monotheism was eventually to be expanded into the doctine of the Trinity; the idea of the election of a 'chosen people' was made to include the whole human race 'called' to the Church; and the body of law and ritual contained in the Torah was reread in terms of the 'spirit' as pointing to Jesus as the promised Messiah. Perhaps most significant, however, in the light of later developments, was the idea of the Temple – from whence the metaphor of the four pillars was, of course, originally derived. There is evidence to suggest that until CE 70 the Jewish Christians in Jerusalem under James continued, unopposed, to participate in the worship of the Temple, although the prominence given in all four Gospels to Jesus's prophecy of

---

[13] I am indebted here, and in the rest of this paragaph, to Professor Richard Bauckham's paper 'Christianity within Judaism', delivered to the Scottish–Scandinavian Conference on 'Growth Points in Biblical Studies', in Glasgow, April 1993.

[14] See, for instance, G. Boccaccini, *Middle Judaism: Jewish Thought 300* B.C.E. *to 200* C.E., Minneapolis: Fortress Press, 1991; E.P. Sanders, *Judaism: Practice and Belief 63* B.C.E. *to 66* C.E., SCM Press, 1992; M. Casey, *From Jewish Prophet to Gentile God: The Origins and Development of New Testament Christology*, Cambridge: James Clarke, 1991; and J.D.G. Dunn (ed.), *Jews and Christians: the Parting of the Ways, A.D. 70 to 135*, Tübingen: Mohr (Siebeck), 1993.

[15] See J.D.G. Dunn, *The Partings of the Ways Between Christianity and Judaism and their Significance for the Character of Christianity*, SCM Press, 1992.

its destruction might suggest that they saw it as already doomed. At the same time the imagery of the New Testament hammers home the message that the nascent Church was itself to be seen as the new eschatological Temple of God. Once the Second Temple had been destroyed in AD 70 this metaphorical reading of the Jewish tradition in terms of the Church was so reinforced that Christians felt no need to participate in the efforts of Rabbinic Judaism to rebuild the Temple or to take part in the final Jewish revolt early in the second century. Thus we find Irenaeus, for instance, at the end of the second century condemning the Ebionites, a surviving Jewish Christian sect, for still continuing to revere Jerusalem 'as if it were the house of God'.

Whether or not we are prepared to accede to the argument that Christianity and Rabbinic Judaism are better seen as parallel developments from a common source, rather than in more conventional terms of schism and appropriation, it is undoubtedly true that this movement towards reading the Jewish tradition and its scriptures as metaphors of the new universal religion was to have enormously important repercussions on the development of Christianity. It also serves to remind us that there was more to the appropriation of the Jewish scriptures than simply linguistic translation. Indeed, it would in some senses be truer to say that the linguistic translation – which, after all, as we have seen, had already been begun within pre-Christian Judaism with the Septuagint and the *Targums* – was part of the *political* translation from Judaism to Christianity that began in the first century AD and continued until at least the fifth century. Not the least important of the political moves that underlie the formation of the Christian Bible is the *idea* of the Bible itself. As a number of recent writers have stressed, the notion of the Bible as a single entity is itself very misleading.[16] There are many Bibles – and the relationship between the various canons is extremely complex. Indeed, the model of Christianity and Rabbinic Judaism as parallel developments can draw some support from the fact that it is a moot point whether we can say the Hebrew Bible is actually older than the Christian one. Though it clearly drew on a high degree of existing consensus, the work of creating a Hebrew canon did not actually begin until after the destruction of Jerusalem in CE 70 – by which time some of the New Testament books (Paul's letters, for example) were already in existence. Certainly anyone who doubts the political nature of the creation of these rival canons, Hebrew or Christian, needs only to look

[16] See, for instance, Robert P. Carroll, *Wolf in the Sheepfold: the Bible as a Problem for Christianity*, SPCK, 1991, p. 7; and Romer, *Testament*, p. 227.

at the reasons why they were found necessary and how the final choices were made. The first known list of Christian books – in effect a putative New Testament – was made by Marcion, a second-century heretic. That we now so label him is an indication that he was the loser in just one of the many political struggles of the period – as is the fact that all his works were subsequently destroyed. Nevertheless, we know of the Marcion canon from the attacks that were made upon it: it consisted of one gospel (Luke's) and some of Paul's letters. He also took the logical step of dropping the Hebrew scriptures altogether from the Christian canon. It was in response to Marcion that the early Church then had to define orthodoxy by making its own canon and declaring it to be a single, sacred and unalterable corpus. 'Canons are about struggle and community conflict', writes Robert Carroll, 'much persecution helped to create the illusion of uniformity, and the arrow of time allowed the mythology of the victors to write the history books'[17] – but these 'victories' were not always so clear-cut and decisive as such political theories of history might suggest. The process of canon-formation was accompanied by intense and often acrimonious debate, involving fierce conflict between different Christian communities and traditions, and was only more or less completed by Eusebius after the Council of Nicaea – which had been summoned by the Emperor Constantine probably less with an interest in formulating Christian doctrine and defining heresy than with the political objective of defining what role the emperor was to play in the new Christian state.[18]

The process of translating the Hebrew scriptures for Christian purposes also involved a massive metaphorical re-interpretation of their contents – creating what Austin Farrar has called a 're-birth of images'.[19] By its very formation, a canon tends to loosen a text from its particular historical setting and to make it transcend its original purpose.[20] Some of this involved what Ernst Fuchs and Klaus Ebeling have called *Neuheitserlebnis*, or the experience of radical novelty, where the existing cultic language of Judaism was given new life by being redeployed with reference to Jesus as its paradigm example.[21] We see just such a process in the Epistle to the Hebrews, where the Old Testament idea of sacrifice is reread to encompass the crucifixion of Jesus – which is then read back

[17] Caroll, *Wolf in the Sheepfold*, pp. 17; 69.
[18] Romer, *Testament*, pp. 196–7.
[19] Austin Farrer, *A Rebirth of Images*, Dacre Press, 1944.
[20] See Brevard Childs, *The New Testament as Canon: an Introduction*, London: SCM, 1984, p. 16.
[21] See Cornelius Ernst, 'World Religions and Christian Theology', in *Multiple Echo: Explorations in Theology*, Darton, Longman and Todd, 1979, p. 34.

as the supreme example of the ritual. What we see happening very early
in the Christian era is thus, in effect, a two- or even arguably threefold
process of translation and appropriation. At the same time as the
Hebrew, Aramaic and Greek of the Christian Bible were being translated into Latin, the very terms of the translation were also being
transformed with radically new metaphorical meanings. Thus by identifying Jesus with the sacrificial Passover lamb of Jewish ritual, not merely
was the idea of sacrifice being given a new focal point and meaning, but
in addition a rich vein of figurative pastoral typology was simultaneously
being opened up and appropriated from the Hebrew scriptures to link
with similar imagery in the New Testament – as numerous popular
translations of the twenty-third Psalm bear witness.

Many of the books of the Hebrew canon, however, involved
prescriptions for cultic rituals which had little or no relevance to the
practices or beliefs of the new Christian communities scattered around
the eastern Mediterranean. The Hellenistic cities which they inhabited
were, in effect, the world's first pluralistic societies. Unlike previous
cultures, they had no official religion, but entertained a wide variety of
competing cults. Converts to Christianity did not necessarily have a
common background even in paganism. Marcion's open dismissal of
the Hebrew scriptures was one logical, if blunt, response to the obvious
difficulty. In the creation of a canon, where does the fine line between
the legitimacy of appropriation and the heresy of misappropriation
fall? For those like Irenaeus and Eusebius, who nevertheless believed
the Hebrew writings to be divinely inspired, some method had to be
found to harmonise them with what was now believed to be their
fulfilment. Jewish interpreters had already shown with their allegorising
of the Song of Songs how texts could be given other meanings apart
from their obvious literal one, and this existing tradition was now
reinforced by similar methods of exegesis already widespread among
Greek commentators. Both the Homeric poems, for instance, had
already been elaborately allegorised. In the first century AD, Philo, a
Hellenised Jew, foreshadowed the later Christian synthesis of Hebrew
and Greek traditions by claiming that not only were the Hebrew
scriptures compatible with Greek philosophy but that in many cases
the latter had been influenced by them.[22] In so doing he showed how

---

[22] See E.R. Goodenough, *Introduction to Philo Judaeus*, 2nd edn, Oxford: Basil Blackwell, 1962 (1st
edn, New Haven, Conn.: Yale University Press, 1940, and Henry Chadwick, 'Philo', in A.H.
Armstrong (ed.), *Cambridge History of Later Greek and Early Mediaeval Philosophy*, Cambridge
University Press, 1967 pp. 137–57.

Greek allegorical methods could be used on other Hebrew scriptural
books. Soon the general claim that Christianity was the key to understanding the Hebrew scriptures – the message of Philip to the Ethiopian
in Acts 8 – was supported by an increasingly elaborate system of
figurative and allegorical interpretation. Even pagan classical texts
were included by some authorities, who were prepared to see in Virgil's
Aeneid, for instance, a parable of the Christian soul's journey through
life. Later critics, such as Origen and Augustine were to lay the
foundations of a system of exegesis so complex and polysemous that
almost every event of the history of the Old Testament could
simultaneously be read as world history and as the key to contemporary
events.

Different schools of thought differed as to the precise number of
figural interpretations possible to a given passage of scripture. Some
Alexandrian authorities detected as many as twelve, but four was by
far the most widely accepted number.[23] Even this number could itself
be arrived at by typological reasoning. Irenaeus, for example, argued
for the canonical primacy of the four gospels from the fact that God's
world was supplied in fours: as there were 'four zones' and 'four
winds', so there were four gospels; four levels of interpretation followed
easily. According to St John Cassian in the fourth century, these were
a literal, or historical sense, an allegorical, a tropological (or moral)
and an anagogical. Tropological related to the Word, or doctrine
conveyed by it, and therefore carried a moral sense; the anagogical
concerns eternal things. Cassian takes as his example the figure of
Jerusalem. Historically it may be seen as the earthly city; allegorically,
it stands for the Church; tropologically is represents the souls of all
faithful Christians; anagogically, it is the heavenly city of God.[24] As a
later Latin rhyme has it:

> *Littera gesta docet, quid credes allegoria,*
> *Moralis quid agas, quo tendas anagogia.*

[*The letter teaches what happened, the allegorical what to believe, / The moral what to do,
the anagogical toward what to aspire.*[25]

This Christian sense of 'allegory' (from the Greek *allegoria*) came to
carry a quite different sense from the original classical one of a fiction,

---

[23] See John Wilkinson, *Interpretation and Community*, Macmillan, 1963, esp. pp. 119–57.

[24] Marjorie Reeves, 'The Bible and Literary Authorship in the Middle Ages', in Stephen Prickett
(ed.), *Reading the Text: Biblical Criticism and Literary Theory*, Oxford: Basil Blackwell, 1991, p. 16.

[25] A.J. Minnis, *Mediaeval Theory of Authorship*, Scolars Press, 1984, p. 34.

fable or personification with another meaning – of the sort used by Aesop. For the Church the historical reality of the person or event actually served to guarantee its inner spiritual meaning.[26] Erich Auerbach argues convincingly that, far from being merely a hermeneutic fashion, this new Christian interpretative theory was an essential ingredient in its becoming a world religion.

Figural interpretation changed the Old Testament from a book of laws and a history of the people of Israel into a series of figures of Christ and the Redemption – so Celtic and Germanic peoples, for example, could accept the Old Testament as part of the universal religion of salvation and a necessary component of the equally magnificent and universal vision of history conveyed to them along with this religion ... Its integral, firmly teleological, view of history and the providential order of the world gave it the power to capture the imagination ... of the convert nations. Figural interpretation was a fresh beginning and a rebirth of man's creative powers.[27]

It was, in effect, the prime tool of the Christian appropriation of the Hebrew scriptures. As Auerbach also significantly observes, the appropriation was accompanied by a new surge of creative energies – even if some figural interpretations strike the modern reader as little short of grotesque. A sermon among the *spuria* of Chrysostom interprets the Massacre of the Innocents by noting that the fact that children of two years old and under were murdered while those of three presumably were spared is meant to teach us that those who hold the Trinitarian faith will be saved whereas Binitarians and Unitarians will undoubtedly perish.[28] By the Middle Ages the literal meaning of even such writings as Paul's letters took second place to figurative meanings. The fact that such meanings were frequently anti-semitic[29] illustrates with some force the extraordinary double focus that Christian uses of the Bible had acquired by that time.

These origins of the Christian Bible in a tradition of multi-layered and polysemous readings have left it with a very particular, even peculiar, cultural flavour. It is easy to assume, for instance, that the Reformation (which has, with some justice, been described as 'primarily a dispute between translators'[30]) meant also a shift back to a

---

[26] Reeves, 'The Bible and Literary Authorship in the Middle Ages', p. 17.

[27] Erich Auerbach, 'Figura', trs. R. Mannheim, in Auerbach, *Scenes from the Drama of European Literature*, New York: Meridian, 1959, p. 28.

[28] 'The Reasonableness of Typology', in G.W.H. Lampe and K.G. Woollcombe, *Essays on Typology*, SCM Press, 1957, p. 31.

[29] See below, pp. 69 and 115.

[30] Edmond Carey, *Les Grands Traducteurs français*, Geneva: Librarie de l'Université, 1963, pp. 7–8.

literal reading of the Bible, but, as we have already seen with a number of examples in the first chapter, figurative readings were in fact to persist well into the nineteenth century – and are by no means extinct today.[31] Indeed, the idea of a literal reading is itself not unproblematic. More to the point, however, is the fact that just as its openly translated and appropriated quality is more than just part of the 'givenness' of the Bible, but seems to flaunt itself as somehow intrinsic to the way we are expected to read it, so too does a continued sense of it as meaning something more and other than what it appears to say. As has already been suggested, it is possible that the origins of the Hebrew scriptures themselves lie not so much in a particular revelation as in a critical commentary on yet earlier texts or even unwritten traditions of neighbouring societies. A text that, in this sense, gives evidence within itself of the existence of other, prior, texts already also implicitly suggests multi-layered ways of reading. It may also help to account for a curious contradiction in our attitude to the Bible that has had a profound effect on the development of many modern European languages – not least upon English.

Though historically we may have had no difficulty in accepting the Bible's general relevance to our immediate situation – that it is, for example, about the Fall of Man or the Human Condition or the Forgiveness of Sins – we are also simultaneously aware that in some very profound sense that it is *not about us*. It is an indication of the paradox we are engaged with that such a statement immediately sounds as if it is flying in the face of two millennia of often highly rhetorical and emotional polemic to the contrary. Ricoeur's claim, quoted above, that the letters of St Paul were no less addressed to him than to the Romans, the Galatians and the Corinthians, is a modern and deliberately paradoxical restatement of an argument that in origin goes back at least to the days of the Church Fathers. Nevertheless, we all know at the same time how essentially alien to us are the worlds of both the Old and the New Testaments. The immense weight of traditional moralistic and devotional rhetoric urging us to see it as pointing directly to ourselves merely serves to illustrate the almost intractable scale of the original problem.

Until the eleventh or twelfth centuries most people had accepted the Pauline belief that the end of the world was very close and that they were living in the last days. St Augustine had expanded this point by

---

[31] Stephen Prickett (ed.), *Reading the Text: Biblical Criticism and Literary Theory*, Oxford: Basil Blackwell, 1991, chs. 1–4.

arguing that history had reached both its climax and its end in the Incarnation.[32] There only remained a brief period in which nothing significant could be expected to happen except the garnering of souls. Under such circumstances, history had effectively come to an end. It was only following the final failure of the Millennium to appear after the year 1000 that the instinct to discover meaning in post-Incarnational history reasserted itself. A series of mediaeval commentators deduced comprehensive theories of history from typological readings of the Bible. But with the rise of historical interpretations the problem of biblical relevance became correspondingly more acute. One answer appeared to be to cut the Gordian knot and simply assert that the prophecies of the Bible do indeed refer directly and literally to ourselves and our own time. Isaac Newton's application of the prophecies of Daniel to his own times have been mentioned. In the middle of the eighteenth century, another Newton, Thomas (1704–82), produced a three-volume *Dissertation on the Prophecies* which went through many editions. His stated aim was 'not to treat of the prophecies in general, nor even of those prophecies in particular, which were fulfilled in the person and actions of our Saviour; but only such as relate more immediately to these later ages, and are in some measure receiving their accomplishment at this time'.[33] Newton, like many other devout Protestants before him, had no doubts that Papal Rome was the Antichrist of Daniel and Revelation, and he found clear evidence that 'At this present time we are living under the sixth trumpet, and the second woe' (of Revelation 11).[34] The seventh, and last, trumpet, he believed, would sound at the fall of the Ottoman Empire. Such millenarianism, which was to reach a climax at the time of the French Revolution, was by no means the exclusive property of a lunatic fringe. Similar beliefs were shared, for instance, by the eminent scientist and highly rational Unitarian, Joseph Priestley. Thomas Newton himself, incidentally, was Bishop of Bristol.

Yet even for the most thorough-going millenarian, the literal meaning of large tracts of the Bible, especially the narratives, could only be linked to a past as remote historically as it was geographically. Typological and figural readings had hitherto provided an essential

---

[32] Reeves, 'The Bible and Literary Authorship in the Middle Ages', p. 18.

[33] Thomas Newton, *Dissertations on the prophecies, which have been remarkably fulfilled, and at this time are fulfilling in the world,* 3 vols., 1754–8. See Joanna Davson, 'Critical and Conservative Treatments of Prophecy in Nineteenth Century Britain', unpublished D.Phil. thesis, Oxford, 1991.

[34] Newton, *Dissertations* (2nd edn 1759, vol. i), Dedication.

tool in the appropriation and transformation of that remote past in the contemporary present. To lose sight of this is to lose sight of what is happening in all those mediaeval stained-glass windows and illuminated manuscripts where the Patriarchs or Apostles are performing their typological roles in contemporary dress and setting; it is to lose sight of the corresponding deployment of biblical metaphor and typology not merely in religious and moral polemics but in the parallel contemporary discourses of politics, trade, medicine and everyday life. At Ranworth church, near Norwich, a late fourteenth-century manuscript shows Jonah, dressed much as a local parson, being swallowed by a great fish from the nearby Broad.[35] A panel of thirteenth-century stained glass in Canterbury Cathedral shows Jesus raising Jairus's daughter in a curiously perspectived mediaeval merchant's house. To James I of England, thundering against the filthy habit of smoking, it seemed entirely natural to compare the perverted lusts of smokers to the Children of Israel 'lusting in the wilderness after quails'. To Oliver Cromwell, fighting against Catholics in Ireland, it seemed no less appropriate to justify the brutal obliteration of Catholic society and, if necessary, the massacre of his opponents, by supporting the Protestant Plantation in Ulster with images of the Israelites occupying Canaan appropriated from the Book of Joshua. To the Catholic Gaelic Irish of the same period – and later – it seemed equally obvious to compare their sufferings with those of 'the children of Israel in Egypt under the oppression of the enemies of God' – a reciprocity of images that has prompted Conor Cruise O'Brien to comment that Ireland was really inhabited not by Protestants and Catholics but by two sets of imaginary Jews.[36]

Much critical ink has been spilt over the exact nature of mediaeval iconography, and only slightly less on the conventions of seventeenth-century political rhetoric, and it is not my purpose here to enter into such specialist historical controversies. My point is rather to draw attention to the basic hermeneutical problem that underlies all such debates. Though the contemporary relevance of the Bible, its events, imagery and customs, was mediated as being self-evident and indeed as a quasi article of faith to our ancestors, influencing every level in their thinking from the broadest questions of political policy and philosophical speculation down to the minutest detail of their everyday lives, this sense of immediate relevance was achieved not in co-operation

[35] The *Sarum Antiphoner*.
[36] Conor Cruise O'Brien, *States of Ireland*, Hutchinson, 1972, p. 309.

with the actual biblical texts with which they were confronted but rather *in the teeth* of their literal meaning, which, with stubborn consistency, proclaimed not merely their remoteness, but frequently as well their arcane and essentially unrepeatable nature. Indeed, even though by the mid-nineteenth century, neither millenarian nor historicist positions seemed capable of giving the scriptures an immediate relevance in any but a purely moral sense – and to draw direct morals from much of the Old Testament was itself somewhat problematic – the contemporary relevance of the Bible continued to be asserted as an almost unquestioned premiss.[37]

The more we focus on this phenomenon, so familiar to any political, literary or social historian that it normally passes without a second glance, the odder we discover it to be. Not the least odd is the fact that so many of the biblical translators themselves seem to be unaware of it, and to proceed as if there were no cultural or historical gap at all between ourselves and the biblical world. Take, for instance, this quotation from one of our leading experts on the subject, Eugene A. Nida.

Translating consists in producing in the receptor language the closest natural equivalent to the message of the source language, first in meaning and secondly in style ... by 'natural' we mean that the equivalent forms should not be 'foreign' either in form ... or meaning. That is to say, a good translation should not reveal its non-native source.'[38]

This seems to encapsulate what might be described as a modern common-sense approach to biblical translation. Certainly it has been an influential one. Nida was a leading figure in the American Bible Society during the 1960s and 1970s, and the person who, more than any other, was responsible for the theoretical underpinning of the Anglo-American *Good News Bible* – probably still the most successful modern translation on the market.

Translation, for Nida, is basically a matter of 'finding the closest equivalence' in the host language for the message contained by the original source language. In developing this theme in a later book, significantly entitled *Towards a Science of Translating*, he distinguishes between two basic kinds of equivalence, which he terms the 'formal'

[37] For nineteenth-century conservative attempts to find a contemporary relevance in biblical prophecy see Davson, 'Critical and Conservative Treatments of Prophecy'.

[38] Eugene A. Nida, 'Principles of Translation as Exemplified by Bible Translating', in Reuben A. Brower (ed.), *On Translation*, (Harvard Studies in Comparative Literature, no. 23), Cambridge, Mass.: Harvard University Press, 1959, p. 19.

and the 'dynamic'. In his words, formal equivalence 'focuses attention on the message itself, in both form and content. In such translation one is concerned with such correspondences as poetry to poetry, sentence to sentence, and concept to concept.'[39] The purpose of following such structural forms of the original is to reveal as much of the source language as possible. Dynamic equivalence, on the other hand, does not concern itself with forms, but aims to create in the host language an *equivalent effect* to that given in the source language. A classic example in biblical translation is that of the parable of the publican and the Pharisee in Luke 18 (9–14). Now there is apparently a particular tribe in the Congo among whom beating one's breast is a sign of pride and aggression; the corresponding outward sign of humility and repentance is to beat one's head with a club. In such a context, argues Nida, it is no good for the repentant sinner to beat his breast: it is head-clubbing or nothing. Similarly, there is in New Guinea an isolated mountain tribe to whom sheep are quite unknown, but pigs are a much cherished domestic pet. By extension, for such a people, Christ has to become the Pig of God. Coming from a background of missionary translation, Nida is understandably committed to the principle of dynamic equivalence, involving, in his words, the 'interpretation of a passage in terms of relevance to the present-day world, not to the Biblical culture'. Where there is conflict between meaning and style, 'the meaning must have priority over the stylistic forms'.[40] The task of the translator, he writes, is essentially one of 'exegesis', not of 'hermeneutics'.[41]

Now it is understandable why someone coming from Nida's professional concerns should be more interested in exegesis than hermeneutics, but such a translation philosophy, attractive as it may appear in its simple over-riding priorities, is, of course, profoundly simplistic in its assumption of the uncomplicated nature of the 'message' to be conveyed, and no less naive in its approach to linguistic history. So far from being essentially modern in its attitude to language, the principle of dynamic equivalence is in fact a restatement of the classical Ciceronian theory of translation. Of his translations of Demosthenes and Aeschines, whom he believed to be the two greatest Greek orators, Cicero explained that:

[39] Eugene A. Nida, *Towards a Science of Translating*, Leiden: E.J. Brill, 1964, p. 159. See also Nida and C. Taber, *The Theory and Practice of Translation*, Leiden: E.J. Brill, 1969.

[40] 'Principles of Translation', p. 19.

[41] *Ibid.*, p. 15.

I did not translate them as an interpreter but as an orator, keeping the same ideas and the forms, or as one might say, the 'figures' of thought, but in language which conforms to our usage. And in so doing, I did not hold it necessary to render word for word, but I preserved the general style and force of the language. For I did not think I ought to count them out to the reader like coins, but pay them by weight, as it were.[42]

Classical literary theory was essentially a theory of rhetoric; what mattered was not so much the content as the beauty of the expression. It is small wonder, therefore, that the crudeness of the Old Latin Bible and the *koiné* Greek of the New Testament proved especially offensive to those Church Fathers, like Ambrose and Augustine, who had been trained in classical rhetoric.[43] The interesting case, however, is that of Jerome, commissioned in 382 AD by Pope Damasus to begin his great new Latin translation, now known as the Vulgate. Like his contemporary, Augustine, he was a trained rhetorician and an avid Ciceronian. For secular translation there could be no question of not following Cicero's principles. His new task, however, faced him with the problem of how far any translator could be expected to know the full meaning of the words God had originally dictated. Under these circumstances, he had, he felt, no choice but to eschew the smoothness of classical rhetoric, and to allow the oddity and strangeness of the original material to show through. Though it is nevertheless written in characteristically good Latin, this decision behind the translation of the Vulgate was to change the future development of the Latin language and, of course, with hindsight, marks the beginning of the historic division between the antique rhetoric of classical Latin (in effect from then on a dead language) and the form in which it was to survive into the Middle Ages – Church Latin. Something of the personal tensions behind this moral decision to subjugate aesthetics to meaning can be seen reflected in his famous dream of the Last Judgement in which, when he claimed to be a Christian, he was told by an affronted Deity, 'thou liest; thou art a Ciceronian, not a Christian'. For later generations, however, reared not on the Latin of the classics but on that of Jerome's Bible, the problem disappears. The new translation of the Bible had so reconstituted its linguistic context for it to *seem* to be the product of dynamic equivalence even when historically it was not.

---

[42] *De optime genere oratorum 14; De inventione* ..., trs. H.M. Hubbell, Heinemann, 1949, p. 365, cited by David Norton, *A History of the Bible as Literature*, vol. 1, Cambridge University Press, 1993, p. 33.

[43] See Norton, *History of the Bible*, vol. 1, pp. 4–5, and ch. 2.

Jerome provides one of the first illustrations of what was to become a recurring phenomenon in the history of biblical translation: that far from biblical translation being best achieved by finding appropriate 'equivalencies', it has historically had its greatest impact on the host language in precisely those cases where there was *no* existing appropriate equivalent available. As we shall see in the next section, English itself was profoundly reshaped in the course of the sixteenth century by the impact of successive biblical translations; in some ways even more dramatic was the impact of Luther's great translation of the Bible, which virtually recreated the German language into which it was translated. Moreover this same process was already at work in the very biblical languages that Nida is apparently prepared to take as given. Thus the first major example of biblical translation, made around the third century BCE, was the Greek Septuagint. It was to reveal its 'non-native source' in a way that was to have a profound effect on the subsequent development of the Greek language – and ultimately therefore on the *koiné* Greek of the New Testament itself. The Hebrew word *kabod* comes from a root that had originally meant 'weight', but at some point after the time of Ezekiel it had acquired a meaning closer to our word 'glory' – including the visual aspects of light. It was translated in the Septuagint by the Greek word *doxa*, which had originally meant something like 'appearance' or even 'reputation', but now rapidly appropriated these *visual* connotations to mean 'radiance' or 'splendour' – even in other contemporary pagan texts apparently unconnected with religious discourse.

Yet the cultural and linguistic distance between Hebrew and Greek, however great it may be to the historian, is of course as nothing to the temporal and cultural gulf that separates Hebrew from English. Nevertheless the degree to which the latter has been modified by the former is out of all proportion greater. There is a story (possibly apocryphal) that when the translators of the *New English Bible* came to the parable of the Prodigal Son they decided to find out the modern English equivalent of the 'fatted calf'. Accordingly they consulted a butcher at Smithfield Market in London as to what one called a calf that had been specially fattened up for a particular occasion. He explained that the technical phrase was 'fatted calf', and that it came from the Bible. Similarly, astonishingly little critical attention has been paid to the way in which western Europe, with its cool temperate climate and abundant rainfall, was able to assimilate and successfully make use of the everyday imagery of a semi-nomadic Near-Eastern desert people as part of its own cultural and poetic heritage. The same paradox is at work even in what may at first sight have seemed a rather trivial example used earlier. We have already mentioned James I, in his *Counterblast to Tobacco* (1604), thundering against the self-indulgence of smokers 'lusting after' the weed 'as the Children of Israel did in the wilderness after quails'.

The straightforward answer is that he probably had in mind 1 Corinthians verse 6, where Paul makes the famous comparison between the new Christian community that is coming into being and the Children of Israel in the wilderness, and concludes that 'these things were our examples, to the intent we should not lust after evil things, as they also lusted'.[44] Yet Paul's *exempla* nowhere specifically include the quails, and this particular feeding of the Children of Israel in the desert is itself presented quite explicitly as a one-off and not-to-be-repeated miracle (apparently justifying God's promise to Moses in verse 12 that 'at even ye shall eat flesh') in contrast with the other much greater miracle of the consistent daily supply of manna over the forty years sojourn in the wilderness. By way of explanation, the seventeenth-century commentary quoted before follows the hint given by Paul in 1 Corinthians and makes the standard typological connection with the manna:

This *Figure* doth most lively represent to us the *Holy Eucharist*, as *Jesus Christ* himself witnesseth in the *Gospel*; and we may boldly say *That how wonderful soever this Food of the Jews was, yet had not they in this, nor in any other miraculous Favours bestow'd upon them, any Advantage beyond the* Christians, *who do truly feed on the* Heavenly Manna, *and the* Bread of Angels, *which* Jesus Christ *gives to those who are come forth out of Egypt, that is, from the Corruptions and Defilements of the* World, *and wherewith he comforts and supports them in the* Wilderness *of this* Life, *until they enter into the true* Land *of* Promise, *as the* Jews *were maintained with* Manna *till their entering into* Canaan.

The condemnatory note in James' diatribe comes, of course, from the fact that those who tried to horde the manna found that it went bad on them, and this provides the excuse for yet again a little anti-Jewish homily:

Wherefore also Christians *ought to take great Care to acknowledge and improve this divine Grace and Favour better than the* Jews *did, and to tremble at the Thought of falling into a distaste and dislike of this* Heavenly Food, *after their Example; who though at the first View of this* Miraculous Bread, *they were struck with Wonder, yet, being once accustomed to it, they preferred the* Garlick *and* Onions *of* Egypt *before it.*[45]

---

[44] I am indebted to Dr Donald Mackenzie for this suggestion.

[45] *The History of the Old and New Testaments Extracted from the Sacred Scriptures, the Holy Fathers, and Other Ecclesiastical Writers ...* 4th impression, 1712, p. 50.

No seventeenth-century commentary that I have yet discovered makes a special typological case for the quails on their own, and it is not, in any case, part of my theme to speculate too closely on what exactly was in James' mind in referring to them. My point is rather a threefold one: first, that such a reference was second nature both to the king and to his intended audience, for whom it was much more than just an illustration; it was, however inappropriate and baffling we may find it, a typological fixing, locating an excessive love of tobacco within the entire divine scheme of the fall and redemption of humanity. The Bible was a part of the standard referential language of king and people alike, and even the most trivial incident within its pages could thus legitimately be given an immediate contemporary significance.

My second point, of course, is diametrically opposed to this. Nothing could in fact be further removed from the experience of early seventeenth-century London than the story of the wanderings of the Children of Israel in the desert, and the miraculous processes by which we are told they were sustained for forty years. Everything about the narrative of Exodus 16 serves to stress its extraordinary nature and its place as part of the story of an alien and far-off people – even down to the explanation of such weights and measures as *omers* and *ephahs* in verse 36. My third point arises directly from the inherent tension between these two and concerns the way in which by the seventeenth century it is a matter of historical record that the English language found itself shaped and even dominated by the terms and figures of a book inherited from another time, culture and place – and mediated by means of not one translation, but several. In other words, it concerns the very processes of linguistic affinity and change which Nida, and his fellow modern biblical translators, neither understood in their own language nor sought to develop in other languages.

Indeed, neither the debate over the significance of changes in language, nor the parallel one centring around Nida's belief that a translation should not reveal its non-native source, begins to deal with this fundamental cultural peculiarity revealed by the appropriation and successful assimilation of translated material. Behind his – and most other modern – translation theories there seems to lie the unstated and probably unconscious assumption that at any specific time the language of a particular culture in some way constitutes a homogenous whole. To a very large degree this view has its roots in the German Romantics' agenda of creating, in default of political union, a new sense of national identity through their language and literature. For Herder, von

Humboldt, the Schlegels, and Hölderlin the history of a people and its language were so interconnected that one could be taken as a record of the other.[46] Whereas the traditional view of translation was that a particular word existed merely as an index to a concept, it was now insisted that concepts and cultures were shaped by the language.[47] That such a belief could co-exist for many of the leading German Romantics with an equally passionate hellenism[48] points not least to its essentially political motivation; it also helps to explain the extraordinary dream of, among others, von Humboldt, Bunsen and Schleiermacher, that it might be possible to produce an indigenous German hellenised Christianity, stripped of all its 'alien Semitic' features, and pervaded by the 'opener more flexible Indo-European genius'.[49] Such a manufactured synthesis has an uncomfortable ring today, but in nineteenth-century Europe it found a ready and sympathetic audience. In France it was popularised and given a further pseudo-scientific basis by Renan, de Gobineau and Burnouf;[50] it was also widely admired among contemporary scholars in the English-speaking world – not least by such figures as Matthew Arnold, who, in his essay 'On the Study of Celtic Literature' (closely modelled on the work of Renan), explains that

The modern spirit tends more and more to establish a sense of native diversity between our European bent and the Semitic bent, and to eliminate, even in our religion, certain elements, as purely and excessively Semitic, and therefore, in right, not combinable with our European nature, not assimilable by it.[51]

Renan, in his *Life of Jesus*, hints[52] at what Burnouf is prepared to say openly – that Jesus was racially not really a Jew at all, but, like his

---

[46] L.G. Kelly, *The True Interpreter: a History of Translation Theory and Practice in the West*, Oxford: Blackwell, 1979, pp. 26–30.

[47] *Ibid.*, pp. 1–2.

[48] See Richard Jenkyns, *The Victorians and Ancient Greece*, Oxford: Basil Blackwell, 1980; also Stephen Prickett, 'Hebrew Versus Hellene as a Principle of Literary Criticism', and Anthony Stephens 'Socrates or Chorus Person? The Problem of Individuality in Nietzsche's Hellenism', in G.W. Clarke (ed.), *Rediscovering Hellenism: the Hellenic Inheritance and the English Imagination*, Cambridge University Press, 1989.

[49] 'On the Study of Celtic Literature', in *Complete Prose Works of Matthew Arnold*, ed. R.H. Super, Ann Arbor: University of Michigan Press, 1960–77, vol. III, p. 301.

[50] Ernest Renan 'The History of the People of Israel', in *Studies in Religious History*, 1893; Joseph Arthur de Gobineau, *The Inequality of Human Races*, trs. Adrian Collins, Heinemann, 1915; Emile Burnouf, *The Science of Religions*, trs. Julie Liebe, 1888. See also Frederick E. Faverty, *Matthew Arnold the Ethnologist*, Evanston: Northwestern University Press, 1951, pp. 164–72.

[51] 'On the Study of Celtic Literature', p. 26.

[52] Ernest Renan, *The Life of Jesus*, Watts, 1935, p. 118.

fellow Galileans, a displaced Aryan, who succumbed to the Semitic wiles and priestcraft of the Jews of Jerusalem.[53]

What is interesting about this fantasy, of course, is that it represents, not for the first time in European history, a profound resentment of Western civilisation's 'oriental' heritage, and an attempt so completely to appropriate it as to expunge altogether its real origins. In contrast Plumb has pointed out how the literate European has always been conscious that he shared his 'house of intellect' with the active ghosts of the past which were an integral and powerful part of that vast literary tradition in which his society was rooted.[54] He suggests that this very awareness of a multiple past is one of the distinctive features of Western, or European, civilisation that makes it fundamentally different from either its Greek or its Roman forebears, or the parallel historic civilisations of China or India.[55] Indeed, one could extend his point by observing that for the United States or even Australia, Europe itself is only one of multiple pasts. Our concept of 'foreignness', of the presence of other societies very different from our own, is as much an essential part of our sense of cultural identity as it was for Homer. In the case of England – and, with national variations, the rest of the English-speaking world – we can say at the very least that from the Reformation to the First World War, that is, from the early sixteenth to the early twentieth centuries, in so far as it was conscious of itself at all, England's social self-consciousness was in relation to a dominant Other, a sense not merely of surrounding nations and cultures as different from our own, but also of a translated biblical world whose referential past haunted and gave meaning to the present. The most famous patriotic passage of all makes the point very clearly:

> This royal throne of kings, this sceptred isle,
> This earth of majesty, this seat of Mars,
> This other Eden, demi-paradise,
> This fortress built by Nature for herself
> Against infection and the hand of war,
> This happy breed of men, this little world,
> This precious stone set in the silver sea . . .
> This nurse, this teeming womb of royal kings,
> Fear'd by their breed, and famous by their birth,
> Renowned for their deeds as far from home,
> For Christian service and true chivalry,

---

[53] Burnouf, *The Science of Religions*, p. 196.
[54] J.H. Plumb, *The Death of the Past*, Macmillan, 1969, p. 50.   [55] *Ibid.*, pp. 112–18.

As is the sepulchre in stubborn Jewry
Of the world's ransom, blessed Mary's Son.[56]

This eulogy of England had by the eighteenth century become an authoritative definition of Englishness, and its bitter condemnation of its present corruptions by the dying John of Gaunt made it a correspondingly two-edged political weapon.[57] Yet its enduring political appropriations rest on the back of explicit metaphorical reference to the great biblical drama of the Fall and Redemption of humanity. In a tradition that looks forward to Blake's great lyric in *Milton*, 'And did those feet in ancient time / Walk upon England's mountains green' it opens with an Old Testament trope of England as another Eden, or demi-paradise, and leads within fifteen lines to the New Testament and Christ's redemption of the world. That this comparison between the fame of the English kings' valour and that of the Holy Sepulchre verges on the blasphemous is in one sense beside the point – but it is also as revealing in its own way as King James' invocation of the quails. Every event, great or insignificant alike, could be seen bifocally: both in relation to its contemporary setting, and in relation to a quite different biblical context – often conceived of in polysemous and typological ways, even where, as here, the point being made is in no sense a religious one. For the vast majority of people everyday life was perceived through an essentially textual act of appropriation. If in some cases this involved elaborate comparisons, in others it was as basic as primary sense-perception. The part which imagination plays in all human perception has long been recognised.[58] In the case of King James' diatribe against tobacco it would, I suspect, be very difficult for the modern reader to be sure whether the connection between smokers' addiction and the Children of Israel's lust for quails in the desert was an elaborately constructed literary conceit or an instinctive act of double focus. Certainly this bifocal vision of the world was such a universal convention as to seem so normal and so obvious to those within it that on the rare occasions when writers chose to call attention to the peculiarity of what they were doing it could seem a grotesque and even fanciful gesture.

How powerful this convention was can be seen from an example which is almost unique in the way that it places one cultural and

[56] *Richard II*, 2, i, 40–6; 51–6.
[57] See Jonathan Bate, *Shakespearean Constitutions: Politics, Theatre, Criticism 1730–1830*, Oxford: Clarendon Press, 1989, pp. 69–70.
[58] The classic account of this is E.H. Gombrich's *Art and Illusion*, Phaidon, 1960.

translated past in direct conflict with the other – with peculiarly powerful dramatic effect. More than perhaps any other work in the English language, Chaucer's *Troilus and Criseyde* is about Europe's dual heritage. It would seem hard to pick on a more obviously classical story than this of two young lovers caught up in the Trojan War: yet in fact they are only names in Homer. The actual plot appears to be no older than the twelfth century, and to have originated in France with Benoît de Sainte-Maure, and it seems clear that Chaucer's immediate source is from the Italian of Boccaccio.[59] In other words, this is not so much a story about Europe's past, as about its *imagined* past. This is significant if only in the way that it demonstrates both the plot's pan-European sources, and the way in which early Renaissance society constantly looked back to its roots – to the foreignness of the past – for legitimation. What is unusual about it, however, is not its invention of a supposed classical origin, but the way in which the classical world is finally placed under judgement from the biblical – and, even more startlingly, from the New Testament. The ending has long been a matter of critical and scholarly debate:

> O yonge, fresshe folkes, he or she,
> In which that love up groweth with youre age,
> Repeyeth hom fro worldly vanyte,
> And of youre herte up casteth the visage
> To thilke God that after his ymage
> Yow made, and thynketh al nys but a faire
> This world, that paseth soone as floures faire.

> And loveth hym, the which that right for love
> Upon a crois, oure soules for to beye,
> First starf, and roos, and sit in hevene above;
> For he nyl falsen no wight, dar I seye,
> That wol his herte al holly on hym leye.
> And syn he best to love is, and most meke,
> What nedeth feynede loves for to seke?

> Lo here, of payens corsed olde rites,
> Lo here, what alle hire goddes may availle;
> Lo here, thise wrecched worldes appetites;
> Lo here, the fyn and guerdon for travaille
> Of Jove, Appollo, of Mars, of swich rascaille!
> Lo here, the forme of olde clerkis speche
> In poetrie, if ye hire bokes eche.   (1835–55)

---

[59] *Complete Works of Geoffrey Chaucer*, ed. F.N. Robinson, 2nd edn, Oxford University Press, 1957, p. 385.

Without becoming involved here in aesthetic questions of what is going on in this extraordinary ending, it is interesting to note how this awareness of the translated past operates. When, in *Richard II*, John of Gaunt speaks of England as 'this seat of Mars / This other Eden' he is merely invoking parallel systems of reference, not calling attention to the basic incompatibility of the classical and Christian mythologies. It is only when Chaucer sets them *against* each other that we realise both how constant is the presence of these two alternative mythologies in European literary consciousness, and how powerful are the normal conventional boundaries constructed between them.

Europe has always used its two appropriated pasts in quite different ways. If the classical world provided both its cultural heritage and frequently the rules of aesthetic production as well, the biblical world mediated divine truth. The problem of reconciling them was one that had always been controversial. It had deeply troubled many of the Church Fathers, including Jerome, Ambrose and Augustine.[60] In so far as it *was* solved – and there always remained something of a tension between them – it was achieved by mythologising the classical Pantheon, and separating it from the 'true' monotheistic religion of the Bible by a kind of invisible mental glass wall. What makes this ending of *Troilus and Criseyde* so disturbing to a post-Renaissance reader is that this convention, which later generations had entirely assimilated, had not yet become fully unconscious. The way in which Chaucer can still call attention to it shows that it is in a transitional stage in its formation. According to a common mediaeval compromise, the Greek and Roman gods, Mars, Venus and the others were held to be genuine but dim visions or foreshadowings of what were real spiritual powers, such as angels or archangels, whose true natures were yet to be revealed, or had been corrupted by the fallen imaginations of human beings. Two hundred and fifty years later, Milton uses a similar appropriative manoeuvre in *Paradise Lost*, when among his fallen angels he peoples his Hell with the less attractive ancient gods: Moloch, Dagon, Mulciber and their ilk. Chaucer, however, simply points out that the gods who have motivated his story of unhappy love and betrayal are false – indeed, by the Christian standards of his society, little better than a collection of sexual freaks and perverts. For him, one suspects, the two pasts were not remotely comparable, let alone to be safely harmonised. If the classical world represented his cultural origins, the biblical world

---

[60] See Prickett (ed.), *Reading the Text*, pp. 5–6.

was not really a past at all. Christ's crucifixion was an ever-present reality. It belongs, as it were, to a continuous timeless present that intersected with his own world.

But there was another, powerful factor that gave an added contemporary importance to the mediaeval view of the Incarnation and the Crucifixion. As we have seen, the idea of the Bible as presenting any kind of relevant pattern to later history was a relatively new idea. After the failure of the Millennium to arrive in the year 1000 the mediaeval world developed a series of theories of history from typological studies of the Bible by such figures as Gerhoh of Reichersberg, Eberwin of Steinfelden and, perhaps most influentially, Joachim of Fiore. This tradition was to culminate in the fourteenth century with that of Dante himself in the *Divine Comedy* – one of the very few literary works other than *Troilus and Criseyde* to place the characters of classical mythology firmly under Christian moral judgement. Moreover, for Chaucer, as for Dante, all history worthy of the name was of the nature of an *exemplum* – to be treated, if not with the same reverence as scripture, at least as a source of moral instruction. There could be no relativising of the past. On this matter, at least, the fourteenth century more resembled the contemporary world of the New Historicists, than that of the post-Enlightenment idea of history promulgated by, say, von Ranke. There was a sense in which both the classical and the biblical pasts were ever-present, but they were not equal; the one could only be understood in the light of the other. Only with the rediscovery of the classics in the Renaissance was this to change – in so far as it meant that a separate and conventionally secure space was created for them. Thus by the seventeenth century, when Milton was writing, for instance, the supremacy of the Bible was not in doubt, but that moral and spiritual supremacy also involved a tacit and conventional recognition of the space reserved for the *literary* supremacy of the classical models. At the same time the Protestant reformers were as certain as their Catholic rivals that the Bible held all the clues to the meaning of history. Both these assumptions have left their mark on the translation theory of the period.

The inapplicability of biblical moral standards to classical themes has been so carefully drummed into us even as we are introduced to them that it requires a considerable effort of mind even to realise that often both sources concern very much the same kind of story. As Milton has to make clear in *Samson Agonistes*, simply *because* it comes from the Bible, the story of Samson belongs to a fundamentally different mental set from that of Hercules; if both are equally tragic, and to the untutored eye appear to contain much the same mixture of bravado, adventure and lust, the one is nevertheless a tale of pagan mythology, while the other is of God's righteous judgement. But though his meaning is biblical, Milton's form is that of a Greek tragedy. His prologue is at once a perfect example of an educated seventeenth-century awareness of the dual past of his culture, and an object-lesson in how, even in creating such a fusion, they could be kept apart by assigning each to its rightful sphere. 'The Apostle Paul', he carefully reminds us, 'thought it not unworthy to insert a verse of Euripides into the text of Holy Scripture, 1 Cor. xv. 33.' 'Of the style and uniformity', he continues, 'and that commonly called the plot ... they only will be best judge who are not unacquainted with Aeschylus, Sophocles, and Euripides, the three tragic poets unequalled yet by any, and the best rule to all who endeavour to write tragedy.'[61] In other words, one appropriated past provides the form, the other the content. To suggest that the classical world was somehow at fault for not being aware of the moral and spiritual values of the biblical one would by then have been as outrageous as to suggest that the biblical world was at fault for not creating the art-form of tragedy or knowing the classical unities. For Milton, there is a tacit balance, even a creative harmony between his two cultural pasts. To the post-Renaissance sensibility, perhaps the reason why Chaucer seems so indecent in *Troilus and Criseyde* is that he is doing what is so often taken as the cause of indecency: making explicit what is conventionally implicit. Chaucer, in following Dante, is consciously and deliberately infringing that space by calling attention to these unspoken rules for his own aesthetic reasons.

In so doing, he is also revealing something else of which, for obvious historical reasons, he could never have been conscious. Plumb's argument that Europe is uniquely distinguished by having a dual past is in fact no more than a half-truth. If it is correct, as Albright, Damrosch and others claim, that the origins of the Bible lie in the 'problem' presented to the ancient Hebrews by the older literature and cultures of surrounding Near-Eastern peoples,[62] then it is also true that this quality of having a multiple, even a 'translated' past which must then be appropriated, was as true of Old Testament times as of modern Europe. More perhaps: since what we might call the 'cultural

---

[61] *The Poems of John Milton*, ed. John Carey and Alastair Fowler, Longman, 1968, pp. 365, 367.
[62] See pp. 53–4 above.

unease' which characterises so much of the Old Testament provides not merely a model for the later Christian synthesis but was also transmitted to it. If it is true that the section in which that past is explicitly acknowledged, the pre-Patriarchal part of Genesis, is handled very differently from the rest, it is also true that the Bible as a whole is permeated with an awareness of other hostile and inimical cultures that threaten not merely the political existence of Israel, but much more fundamentally, its own unique culture.

For Chaucer and for the mediaeval European world, as we have seen, the two components of its dual past were never equal partners. One past was safe because it genuinely *was* past. Once the triumph of Christianity was assured, and Asgard and Niflheim had gone the way of Olympus, the study of the pagan classical writers, however influential they might prove, was essentially cultural archaeology. In *Samson Agonistes*, Milton is consciously, brilliantly and learnedly reviving a dead form. He even had to write a preface to explain what he was doing. The other past, however, was contemporary and dangerous. Though for Chaucer both were equally translated pasts, the fact that one was still mediated in its original language whereas the other, in the form of the Vulgate, was already a translation of a translation, was, oddly enough, profoundly symptomatic of their unequal status. Whereas a knowledge of the classics was to remain for centuries not merely the mark of the educated person, but also very largely the content of that education,[63] for post-Reformation Protestants a knowledge of the Bible was to become little short of mandatory for salvation.[64] Though it was not the original cause of that difference in status (Chaucer could not have known it when he died in 1400) the fact that the Bible was of its essence a translated work, whereas the classics were only incidentally translated into English, was totally to alter their relationship within a hundred years of the majestic equipoise of Milton's *Samson*. Even though it was never cast in wholly contemporary language, the translated text was to hold its vigour and appeal while the untranslated, but original and therefore 'pure' literature of the classical world, in spite of its role both as definer and supporter of higher education, eventually was to languish. In an ironic reversal of status, by 1800 when the Bible was for the first time coming under fire for its historical authenticity, it was also being widely accepted as the most prolific

---

[63] See Hugh Kearney, *Scholars and Gentlemen*, Faber, 1970.
[64] See Rivkah Zim, 'The Reformation: the Trial of God's Word', in Stephen Prickett (ed.), *Reading the Text: Biblical Criticism and Literary Theory*, Oxford: Basil Blackwell, 1991, pp. 71–6.

source of the sublime and had largely replaced the classics as a model of literary form. Yet that earlier cultural unease was never completely overcome. Dr Johnson, famously, was worried by what he felt was an impious mingling of traditions in Milton's *Lycidas*, and in the mid-nineteenth century Francis Close, in a book entitled *Divine and Human Knowledge* (1841), pointed out how the classically trained Tractarians frequently designated various branches of pagan learning 'the hand-maids of literature'. 'Handmaids', he comments, no doubt with the biblical story of Sarah and Hagar in mind (Genesis 16), 'are sometimes apt to forget their place'.

The tension between the Bible's contemporaneity and its translatedness is so basic to our sense of what constitutes a holy book that only when we contrast it with the doctrine of the verbal stability of the Qu'ran do we begin to realise just how great is the gulf separating Christianity and Islam in their unconscious pre-conceptions about the nature of a text. In spite of a strong fundamentalist tradition in certain parts of evangelical Protestantism, Christianity, by the very eclecticism of its origins, has always been at least dimly conscious of, and correspondingly uneasy about, its own distance from its sacred writings. In other words, it has *always* needed a theory of reading, a hermeneutic system of interpretation – even if, as in some cases, that appears to be largely in the form of an insistence on the inspired nature of the King James Version. In contrast, though English-language versions of the Qu'ran are, of course, now available,[65] it is nevertheless clearly understood by Muslims that these are *not* translations but paraphrases; they do not, and cannot carry the force or beauty of the original inspired Arabic wording – which is at once so arresting and compelling that, we are told, many early conversions to Islam were made simply by hearing passages of it recited.[66] Indeed, so important is the precise original wording of the Qu'ran that some Muslims have evolved a doctrine of the 'uncreated Qu'ran', arguing that, like the Jewish Torah or the Christian Logos, it was in God's mind from before the beginning of time.[67] Certainly, whatever earlier sources or degrees of appropriation modern scholars may detect behind the various Surahs of the Qu'ran, there is, officially at least,

[65] See, for instance, that of Mohammed Marmaduke Pickthall (1930) (Star Books, 1989).
[66] Muhammad ibn Ishaq, *Sira*, 145 quoted in A. Guillaume (trs.), *The Life of Muhammad*, 1955, 160, cited by Karen Armstrong, *A History of God. From Abraham to the Present: the 4000-year Quest for God*, Heinemann, 1993, p. 172.
[67] Armstrong, *A History of God*, p. 188.

no countenancing of the idea that the way in which we understand the past might be conditioned by the cultural circumstances of the present. This has, of course, been made easier by the fact that for contingent historical reasons, until large-scale migration of Islamic communities to Europe and North America began in this century, it was possible for most of the Islamic world not to feel any problematic or disturbing cultural gap between itself and its sacred texts. Though it has spread outward from the countries of its origin in the Arabian peninsula, unlike Christianity, it has never been forced to decamp entirely from its own geographical heartland.

Nevertheless, if the Bible is essentially a book in exile from its original context, we should note how, as we have seen, this has *always* been true – at least of the Christian versions. Though Rabbinic Judaism has also been for most of its history a religion in exile, it has kept the Hebrew Bible and, just as important, the Torah, in the original language. Similarly the Qu'ran, in which aesthetics and theology form an almost seamless web, has had, for that reason, correspondingly less impact on the other vernacular languages of the Islamic world, and ensured that Arabic, thus recreated, was central to Islam. In contrast to the other people of the book, however, what was perceived as the crudity of New Testament Greek meant that Christianity, unlike either Judaism or Islam, was from its beginning without a sacred language of its own. Almost throughout its history its scriptures have been mediated through translation – making them at once peculiarly immediate and peculiarly distant. For this reason (if for no other) the Bible has always been Christianity's problem as well as its inspiration. There is indeed a very real sense in which all theology can be seen as a branch of literary theory: a particular way of appropriating and reading an otherwise difficult or intransigent text so as to explain or counter the problems raised by it. As we have seen, the reversal of fortune whereby for the late eighteenth century the Bible had come to replace the classics as a model of literary form would have staggered the early Church Fathers – Ambrose, Augustine, Jerome or Origen – for whom the scriptures were almost totally devoid of any kind of aesthetic appeal. What had intervened were two things: the major shift in aesthetic sensibility that we now call 'Romanticism', and, no less important, that the Bible the English romantics knew was a particular translation – the Authorised Version – which was itself the product of a particular appropriative method. It will be the subject of our next section.

THEOLOGY AND POLITICS: THE MAKING OF THE
AUTHORISED VERSION

Even before the Reformation biblical translation was recognised to be a serious matter. An anonymous pre-Wyclif translator noted that in embarking on his translation he risked his life.[68] He was probably right. In 1401 the ecclesiatical statute, *De heretico comburendo*, provided that anyone found in possession of an English translation of the Bible should be burned at the stake; in the light of this draconian measure, the 1408 Constitution from the Convocation at Oxford forbidding anyone, on pain of excommunication, to translate any part of the scriptures unless authorised by a bishop, seems comparatively modest and even lenient. Not merely was no authorisation subsequently ever given, however, but Wyclif's followers, the Lollards, were ferociously suppressed. To make the message even clearer, Wyclif's body, which had been buried at Lutterworth, was dug up and thrown into the river Soar. As David Lawton has acutely pointed out, this vehemence of response to the idea of translation may well betray not merely an unwillingness to allow the Bible to be removed from the institutional controls imposed by Latin, but also, at a much deeper level, a feeling that, when applied to holy things, the English language, or indeed any vernacular form, was a kind of blasphemy:[69] or, as we might say, that true to the Latin derivation of that word, the kind of literary appropriation involved in the act of translation into the vernacular represented an intolerable theft and desecration of the sacred. Certainly Tyndale's challenge to the suitability of Latin as against English as a fit medium for the scriptures seems to be responding to just such a tacit assumption.[70] So clear indeed was that message for would-be translators that for more than a century, in spite of the invention of printing in the meantime, no further attempt at translation was made. Nor was the fate of Tyndale, who, against all odds, finished his translation of the New Testament in 1525, any more encouraging. On orders from the emperor he was kidnapped from where he was in hiding in Antwerp, strangled and burned at the stake.

Concentration on the persecution and often grisly fates of the first English translators, however, can easily obscure what is, with hindsight,

---

[68] J.F. Mozley, 'The English Bible before the Authorised Version', in *The Bible Today*, Eyre and Spottiswode, 1955, p. 127.
[69] David Lawton, *Blasphemy*, Hemel Hempstead: Harvester Wheatsheaf, 1993, ch. 3.
[70] See quotation below, pp. 85–6.

one of the most significant features of their work – and that is the essentially appropriative nature of the successive biblical versions themselves. Indeed, there is a curious sense in which the textual history of the English Bible in the sixteenth century seems to reflect in miniature the much larger history of the formation of the Old and New Testaments. Just as they were composed of layer upon layer of textual appropriation and reuse, so from Tyndale onwards the nascent English Bible developed by constant and cumulative use of appropriate earlier translated material. The Authorised Version is in some ways less a translation than a crowning refinement to what is, in effect, a palimpsest of the best of previous translations, corrected and winnowed through almost a hundred years of development. Thus Coverdale's complete English Bible printed at Cologne in 1535 is based not so much on his use of Hebrew or Greek (of which he knew little) but on Tyndale, where extant, plus Latin and German sources. Partly because Coverdale was himself a fine prose stylist, the result was remarkably successful – and though it was not licensed by the newly Protestant Henry VIII, Anne Boleyn had a copy in her chamber.

In 1537, Tyndale's disciple John Rogers, in order to preserve the still unpublished sections of the Old Testament translated by his master, produced at Antwerp under the name of Thomas Matthew another Bible which incorporated all of Tyndale's work, and made up what was lacking from Coverdale. This, in turn, was revised by Coverdale and became the basis of the new official, or, because of its size, so-called 'Great Bible', which Thomas Cromwell in 1537 ordered to be installed in every church for the reading of laymen. With the accession of Mary, however, a large number of the copies of this Bible were burned. Many leading Protestants went into exile, and it was one such, William Wittingham, who began in Geneva what was to be the first truly popular English translation. Among his companions in Geneva was John Knox, and to assist his translation was a team that included John Bodley and his son Thomas (later to be the founder of the library at Oxford). Calvin himself wrote the introduction. Though its notes were held to be objectionable and, indeed, more to the point, politically unacceptable, because of its pocket size and use of roman type it rapidly became the standard for all English Bibles – far outselling the officially sanctioned Bishops' Bible of 1602.

There is a fine line between polemical translation and polemical notes to a translation. Though Tyndale's notes to his New Testament are on the whole terse, and not as inflammatory as is sometimes claimed, he had outraged the authorities by such things as consistently translating the Vulgate's *ecclesia* not as 'church' but as 'congregation' – thereby quite deliberately suggesting that the early Christians belonged to a loose confederation of self-governing local congregations, much on the lines desired by the Puritan reformers, rather than being part of a fully developed episcopal organisation. The Geneva Bible had gone much further – especially in view of what was to be the fate of Charles I – by explaining in a note that 1 Chronicles 16: 22, 'Touch not mine anointed', did not justify the special sanctity of kings, but referred to all God's people, the ordinary church members, who should not therefore be harrassed by the civil authorities.

The accession of James I to the combined throne of England and Scotland in 1603 prompted a renewal of pressure for puritan reforms in the liturgy and discipline of the Church of England. At a conference of divines convened by the king at Hampton Court later that year, John Reynolds, the former Dean of Lincoln and President of Corpus Christi College, Oxford, requested 'that there might be a new translation of the Bible, because those that were allowed in the reigns of Henry the eighth and Edward the sixth were corrupt and not answerable to the truth of the original'.[71] The Bishop of London, Richard Bancroft, was sceptical: 'if every man's humour might be followed, there would be no end of translating'. James, however, proved to be in favour: 'I profess I could never yet see a Bible well translated in English; but I think that of all, that of Geneva is the worst. I wish some special pains were taken for an uniform translation; which should be done by the best learned in both universities, then reviewed by the bishops, presented to the privy council, lastly ratified by royal authority to be read in the whole church and no other.' 'But it is fit that no marginal notes be added thereunto', rejoined Bancroft. Not suprisingly, the king agreed: 'That caveat is well put in; for in the Genevan translation some notes are partial, untrue, seditious, and savouring of traitorous conceits.'

The ground rules for the new translation laid down as a result of this debate indicate very clearly what was to be expected of the projected Authorised Version. It was from the start deliberately conceived of not only as a document of political and theological compromise, but as a text that would openly refer to and incorporate previous translations. Among the instructions given to the translators were:

---

[71] William Barlow, *The Sum and Substance of the Conference ... at Hampton Court January 14 1603* London, (1604), Gainesville: Scholars Facsimilies and Reprints, 1965, p. 45.

i.   The ordinary Bible read in the church, commonly called the Bishop's Bible, to be followed, and as little altered as the original will permit.

ii. The names of the prophets and the holy writers, with other names in the text, to be retained as near as may be, accordingly as they are vulgarly used.

iii. The old ecclesiastical words to be kept, viz. as the word church not to be translated congregation &c.

iv. When any word hath divers significations, that to be kept which hath been most commonly used by the most eminent fathers, being agreeable to the propriety of the place and the analogy of faith.

v.   The division of chapters to be altered either not at all, or as little as may be, if necessity so require.

vi. No marginal notes at all to be affixed, but only for the explanation of the Hebrew and Greek words which cannot without some circumlocution so briefly and fitly be expressed in the text . . .

xiv. These translations to be used when they agree better with the text than the Bishops' Bible, viz. Tindal's, Matthew's, Coverdale's, Whitchurch, Geneva.[72]

Not merely was it intended that, wherever useful or politically expedient, it should be heavily reliant on the collective endeavours of earlier translations, this element of consensus and collectivity was heavily reinforced by an elaborate committee structure which ensured that each of the forty-seven appointed translators had his individual work reviewed by the others in his group before the work of each group was then reviewed by all the other groups. Finally, two members from each of the three centres of translation, Cambridge, Oxford, and Westminster, were chosen to review the entire Bible and to prepare the work for publication in London. There was to be no authorisation of individual idiosyncrasy in this version. It is frequently claimed that committees encourage mediocrity and are inimical to the production of great art or literature, but if, as is sometimes asserted, 'a camel is a horse designed by a committee', then the Authorised Version is the ultimate camel.

This explicit commitment to both tradition and consensus left its mark on the text in two very important ways. Firstly, it meant that the new translation was deeply conservative. There was nothing new in this respect for established verbal forms. We know from the correspondence of Augustine and Jerome that the latter had, against his own rhetorical training, been forced to leave in place in his translation phrases and

---

[72] Cited by Norman Sykes, 'The Authorised Version of 1611', in *The Bible Today*, Eyre and Spottiswode, 1955, pp. 141–3.

even incorrect forms of words which had become so much a part of the consciousness of Christian congregations that they could not be altered without making the whole Vulgate unacceptable.[73] Similarly, the new Authorised Version, if it was to gain popular acceptance, had to begin with little room for manoeuvre. Moreover, such was the earlier association between vernacular translation and blasphemy, that in a period when the English language was changing more rapidly than ever before or since, it was doubly important that the Bible was set in words that were designed to stress the essential continuity of the Anglican settlement with the past by recalling the phraseology not merely of the familar Geneva Bible, but of Coverdale and Tyndale – and beyond that even of the Vulgate itself.

In the Bodleian Library, Oxford, is a copy of the 1602 Bishops' Bible with extensive marginal annotations of the New Testament in the handwriting of three of the appointed translators. It seems to be the only known survivor of the '40 large churchbibles' sold unbound by Robert Barker, the King's Printer, to the translators of the Authorised Version for use as a basis for their revisions.[74] If one compares the text of this Bishops' Bible with that of the Authorised Version line by line and verse by verse, it is striking to see how few are the amendments. When they do occur, however, it follows that they are there for a good reason. But this conservatism goes well beyond the original brief of simply retaining where possible the earlier phraseology. Unlike Tyndale, who had translated the *koiné* Greek of the New Testament into a direct and forceful contemporary vernacular, the language of the new translation was often deliberately archaic and latinised.

Tyndale's own translation theory had been anything but conservative. Though he was as highly trained a classicist as Milton himself, he had, as usual, been flamboyantly intransigent in his resistance to the conventional Latin scholasticism of the day. A hundred years before *Samson Agonistes*, in the 'Preface to the Reader' of his *Obedience of a Christian Man* (1528) he had not merely argued the case for biblical translation, but had insisted that, unlike Latin, there was a natural affinity between the biblical languages and English:

They will say that it [the Bible] cannot be translated into our tongue, it is so rude. It is not so rude as they are false liars. For the Greek tongue agreeth more with the English than with the Latin. And the properties of the Hebrew

[73] Norton, *History of the Bible*, pp. 35–6.
[74] See Edward Craney Jacobs, 'King James's Translators: the Bishops' Bible New Testament Revised', *The Library*, 6th series, vol. 14, no. 2 (June 1992), pp. 100–26.

tongue agreeth a thousand times more with the English than with the Latin. The manner of speaking is both one, so that in a thousand places thou needest not but to translate it in to the English word for word when thou must seek a compass in the Latin & yet shall have much work to translate it well-favouredly, so that it have the same grace and sweetness, sense and pure understanding with it in the Latin as it hath in the Hebrew. A thousand parts better may it be translated into the English than into the Latin.[75]

Reading Tyndale one cannot but agree – at least about the way in which *he* handles the language (this is, after all, also the age of *Euphues*). The bald uncircumstantial style of the New Testament on the whole goes well into colloquial sixteenth-century English. Yet we need to remember that such claims of a natural affinity between Hebrew and the particular language into which it is being translated was a common feature among translators.[76] Here, as in these other cases, Tyndale's superbly arrogant claim also conceals a corresponding act of appropriation – for, of course, the argument that the contexts and modes of thinking of the original and host languages were (either providentially or fortuitously) sufficiently similar for what was being said to sound as normal and natural in English as it was in that particular provincial version of Greek, projects on to the latter assumptions about the Bible that properly belong to the Reformation – and not least to Tyndale's own view of translation. In accordance with their revised ideological brief, it was a view that was bound to be unacceptable to the new translators.

But the conservatism of the new translation was not just a reversion to an older latinised style – though the ready-made associations of Latin with dignity and ecclesiastical authority undoubtedly played their part. Another reason for the deliberate use of archaism may be seen from the revisions to Luke 2: 13 in the Bodleian Library copy of the Bishops' Bible referred to above. The Bishops' Bible had followed Tyndale's translation for verse 13: 'And suddenly there was with the Angel a multitude of heavenly soldiers, praising God, and saying ...' The Greek words for these 'heavenly soldiers' are *stratias ouraniou*. In the plural *stratia* means simply 'soldiers' (of a land army as distinct from a

---

[75] Cited by David Daniell, *Tyndale's New Testament*, New Haven, Conn.: Yale University Press, 1989, p. xxii.

[76] James L. Kugel, *The Idea of Biblical Poetry: Parallelism and its History*, New Haven, Conn.: Yale University Press, 1981, p. 301. See also examples from Norton (*History of the Bible*, vol. 1, pp. 278–9): e.g. Augustinus Steuchus' claim that Hebrew poetry 'is similar to the Italian rather than to the Latin'; and Le Clerc that the 'genius' of Hebrew in its poetic form is 'conformable to that of the French tongue.'

navy); in the singular, as here in Luke, it would be more literally translated as 'army'. The associations of the word not merely with the men but with actual weapons of war can be seen from elsewhere in the New Testament, when Paul, in II Corinthians 10: 4, uses it again, this time metaphorically, to mean the 'weapons of warfare' ('for the weapons of our warfare are not carnal').[77] The Latin Vulgate here follows the Greek very closely with *multitudo militiae caelestis*: 'a multitude of the heavenly army'. The first break in these serried military formations seems to be in Luther's 1534 translation, where the passage appears as *die Menge der himmlischen Heerscharen* – the final word being more or less directly equivalent to the English 'hosts'. Whether or not it owes anything to Luther here, the systematic disarming of these massed ranks of heaven by the Authorised Version is, nevertheless, remarkable. We can see from the successive layers of annotation in the Bodleian Library copy of the Bishops' Bible that Tyndale's blunt phrase 'heavenly soldiers' was first marked down as needing revision, before being provisionally altered to 'heavenly army', and finally changed again to the final well-known Authorised Version reading of 'heavenly host'.[78] Nor is it difficult to guess why the more disciplined and unified word 'army' was at first seen as politically preferable as well as more accurate than Tyndale's unofficered loose egalitarian collectivity of 'soldiers', not to mention why both the contemporary military words were eventually excised in favour of the altogether more archaic and distancing word 'host' (reminiscent of I Kings 22: 19). At a time when religion and politics were not merely inseparably intertwined, but within a generation were to spill over into Civil War, any suggestion of multitudes of heavenly soldiers, whether or not properly organised into armies, was clearly unacceptable – and probably with good reason, for Tyndale's phrase is indeed prophetic of the metaphors of Puritan rhetoric of the 1640s. On the other hand, the words 'heavenly host', which like so many phrases from the Authorised Version, have passed into the language, effectively play down the immediate military connotations – without scholarly falsification. As a whole tradition of subsequent angelic illustrations has made plain, the demilitarising strategy of the new translation was eminently successful. I cannot recall any Nativity picture where the angels rejoicing at the birth of the Prince of Peace are shown carrying weapons. Too close a connection with that other heavenly army, Elisha's 'horses and chariots of fire' in

---

[77] I owe this translation and subsequent illustration to David Jasper.
[78] *Ibid.*, p. 105.

II Kings 6: 17, has been quietly circumvented. The new Bible was not merely a statement of continuity with the past, it was above all a monument to stability and order. It was, in the fullest sense of the words, a political document.

Secondly, there was no room for individual interpretation. Tyndale, we recall, had drawn the wrath of Church and government alike by translating the Latin *ecclesia* as 'congregation' rather than 'Church'. In the volatile atmosphere of the day this was little short of a revolutionary act. Not merely were such interpretations politically inexpedient, moreover, they were also held to be theologically inappropriate and even, in extreme cases, blasphemous. If the Bible was inspired by the Holy Spirit and the source of its own authority, then it was doubly dangerous of man to seek to amend it in any way. Indeed Nicholas von Wyle, a fifteenth-century German translator, had gone so far as to declare that in the case of the Bible even copyist's errors should be faithfully transcribed.[79] The King James translators had the added sanction of the Catholic translators of the Rheims and Douai Bibles – the Douai Old Testament had only just finally appeared after a twenty-seven-year delay in 1609 – who had attacked their Protestant rivals for softening the hard places whereas they themselves, they claimed, 'religiously keep them word for word, and point for point, for fear of missing or restraining the sense of the holy Ghost to our phantasie'. Thus John Bois, a fellow of St John's College, Cambridge, who was both a translator of a section of the New Testament for the Authorised Version, and a member of the final revision panel, recorded in his notes that he and his committee had been careful to preserve ambiguities in the original text. Referring to the word 'praise' in I Peter 1: 7, which might refer either to Jesus or to the members of the church, he commented that 'We have not thought that the indefinite ought to be defined.'[80] Seventeenth-century translators, whether Protestant or Catholic, were under no doubt that whatever the difficulties or peculiarities of the Hebrew or Greek, they were there for a divinely ordained purpose, and were not to be lightly corrected by human agency.

Yet it is clear, even from these examples, that this unquestioning obedience to the text could, and did, produce a certain degree of conflict with the political requirements of the brief. While it might, for

[79] George Steiner, *After Babel: Aspects of Language and Translation*, Oxford University Press, 1976, p. 262.
[80] Ward Allen (ed.), *Translating for King James*, Allen Lane, Penguin, 1970, p. 89.

instance, be possible to argue on scholarly grounds that 'host' is just as accurate a translation of *stratia* as 'army', it would be disingenuous not to acknowledge that the distancing and disarming of this putative military assembly also had other motives than purely scholarly ones. But there is, of course, more to that change than merely a preference for the political connotations of one word as against another. What was at stake here was a very real struggle for the control of language itself. Appropriation, as we have seen, involves not just the reuse of something in a new context, but actual *seizure* – it is as if there were an innate if tenuous link between the creative forces liberated by the act of appropriation and the destruction or obliteration of the previous ownership in such a way as to make the new use seem legal and even natural. Such was the tortuous story of the transformation of the wily shepherd Jacob into Israel, the Patriarch; such, for Christian Europe, was the appropriation of the Hebrew Bible as the Old Testament. In this instance, 'host' was not merely an archaism in the seventeenth-century context, it was a word with a long and already loaded history. The Latin *hostis* originally meant 'stranger' and came, by an obvious route, also to mean 'enemy' – and, by extension, a large number or army of enemies. Via the Old French *hoste* it also took on the opposite meaning of one who entertains strangers in his house. The route to the disarming of the angels at the Nativity can be traced in the successive meanings listed in the *OED*: beginning with 'an armed company or multitude of men' (1290), we pass to its peaceful equivalent, 'a great company; a multitude' (1440), and then, quite specifically, its 'biblical and derived' usage, 'the host, or hosts of heaven (Heb. *ts'ba hashsha-mayim*) applied to a) the multitude of angels that attend upon God, and b) the sun, moon, and stars' (1382). In the Old Testament this was, of course, an *armed* company of angels – and any of King James' translators wishing to defend his choice of words needed only to cite I Kings 22: 19 or II Kings 6: 17 to make his point. But, as we have seen, the New Testament angels were also unequivocally armed; it was, paradoxically, the use of the more archaic word, with its Old Testament associations, rather than the contemporary military term that allowed the subsequent elision of the *OED*'s third meaning from being an adjunct of its first meaning, to that of the second. In achieving this, the appropriation was complete. Not entirely lost, however, was that element of fundamental alienness present in the original Latin. Hosts of angels are very definitely 'other'.

As an examination of the later *OED* citations shows, the word 'host'

was from then on largely inseparable from its third, biblical meaning –
and in this guise the word returns to more popular usage in a totally
demilitarised and largely ceremonial sense of 'an uncountable
number'. Later, apparently secular, usages from Wordsworth's 'host of
golden daffodils' to Fanny Trollope's 'host of trunks just arrived from
France', turn out on closer inspection almost invariably to be figurative,
ironic or comic variants on the biblical theme. By the nineteenth
century the word 'host' had become essentially a biblical term. In
short, the conscious use of an archaism in the Authorised Version,
almost certainly selected originally for political reasons, had the effect
of significantly altering the English language by restoring the use of a
semi-obsolete word in a particular specialised sense – one now, moreover, heavily modified by its biblical resonances.

Nor is this the only such example. David Norton gives a whole series
of examples of words, including 'ate', 'discomfiture', 'eschewed',
'laden', 'nurture', 'ponder' and 'unwittingly', which were current or
familiar archaisms in the sixteenth century but which had dropped out
of use by the eighteenth century, and later revived into common
speech in the nineteenth century.[81] Many, though not all, of these can
be shown to have made their comeback with the increasing popularity
of the Authorised Version. The word 'ponder', for instance, seems to
have survived on the strength of one famous verse, taken by the
Authorised Version straight from Tyndale, Luke 2:19: 'but Mary kept
all these things and pondered them in her heart'. By the mid-eighteenth
century it is listed as being obsolete, and its revived sense reflects all the
solemnity of Luke's Annunciation. The point here is not just that, as
Norton very convincingly argues, the Authorised Version has acted 'as
a kind of uncrowded Noah's ark for vocabulary for perhaps two
hundred years'[82] but also that such words, even where not specifically
coined for the needs of translation, are restored to us from the ark
subtly transformed, and often with added value.

But by no means all the changes made by the King James translators
are cases of politically motivated archaism. It is intriguing to note, for
instance, that in no fewer than three places in the epistles of Timothy
(I 1: 6, I 6: 21, and II 2: 18) Tyndale's word 'erred' was replaced by the
curiously modern-sounding 'swerved'.[83] The word is, however, actually

[81] Norton, *History of the Bible*, vol. II, pp. 80–5.
[82] *Ibid.*, p. 85.
[83] Ward Allen, 'The Meaning of ἀστοχήσαντες at I Timothy 1:6', *Bulletin of the Institute of
Reformation Biblical Studies*, vol. 2, no. 1 (1991), pp. 15–18.

of Anglo-Saxon origin, and, like so many words in use in the early seventeenth century, it carried then both a physical and a metaphorical meaning – captured by Shakespeare in Othello's typically grotesque description of Desdemona as a 'bed-swerver'. The fact that none of the major twentieth-century translations has chosen to keep the word, replacing it by a variety of other metaphors of motion ('falling short' (New English Bible), 'gone off' (J), 'wandered away' (New International Bible), 'deviated' (New American Bible; New Revised Standard Bible)) suggests the degree to which the original ambiguity between intention and accident in 'swerved' has been largely (though not entirely) lost today. Indeed, it is important to note that the translators' declared unwillingness to limit the meaning of the inspired words of scripture by translation did not hamper them linguistically nearly as much as a modern critic might expect. As Ward Allen's pioneering work on the revisions of the King James Bible has shown, in the last resort the choices of the translators seem to have depended less upon any deterministic laws of linguistic history, than on specific principles of translation. The modern translators whose theories were discussed above have doubtless a greater knowledge of the original biblical languages than these revisers of the Authorised Version. But where they differ most radically from their seventeenth-century predecessors is not in their scholarship, but in their translation theory. For the Jacobean translation committees, like the heroic pioneering sixteenth-century figures whom they relied upon so heavily, the Bible was still to be interpreted figuratively as a seamless whole. However much the Protestant and Catholic scholars might have differed over the meaning of individual passages, they were largely agreed over the framework in which that meaning was to be understood. Like the pre-Reformation commentators, they saw the literal meaning as, at best, only one among many layers of figural and typological meaning to be patiently and even prayerfully unravelled. In such a context reading was less a univocal narrative experience – involving the following through of a single story – than a polyvalent one in which many narratives might be simultaneously discerned.

Thus even the shepherds and heavenly host of Luke 2 are not merely a part of the Christmas narrative, but also carry a further weight of meaning for the pious reader. According to St Gregory the shepherds were the types of 'the true pastors of the Church', and the appearance of the angels denoted what the appearance of our Saviour (who is the true pastor) would one day produce in the Church. Similarly the light by which they were accompanied signified the divine light, and its appearance in the world.[84] As to the moral or tropological meaning, another commentary adds that 'we should also imitate the shepherds by glorifying God for the wonderful things he has graciously made known to us; and the thought that the Saviour of the world was born in a state of poverty should prevent any one from murmuring, because God has not thought fit to place him among the rich and great'.[85] The point about such readings is that they are not peculiar to biblical interpretation, but a normal part of the seventeenth-century reading process. A training in allegorical and figural interpretations in any literary work, be it by Dante, Spenser or Herbert, was a standard part of the equipment provided by a contemporary education. Moreover, as we shall see, such systems of polyvalent readings persist well into the nineteenth century in both religious and secular texts.

Polyvalency of meaning was aided by a greater polyvalency of language. As we have suggested, one of the most obvious and notable differences between early seventeenth- and late twentieth-century English is the way in which many words which then carried both a spiritual and a material sense have now been reduced to their purely material sense. In Acts 24: 25, for instance, Paul preaches to Felix and his wife Drusilla: 'And as he reasoned of righteousness, temperance, and judgement to come, Felix trembled, and answered, Go thy way for this time; when I have a convenient season, I will call for thee.' Now 'convenient', like 'convince' and 'comfort', belong to a class of words which have been progressively narrowed down from a wide resonance of meaning in the early seventeenth century to a single sense today. The Latin *convenient,* from the root *con-venio,* meant originally a 'coming together' – hence therefore a moment that was 'fitting' and 'suitable'. According to the *OED,* of the six meanings of 'convenient' available to Renaissance writers, the only one left to us now is 'personally suitable or well-adapted to one's easy action or performance of functions; favourable to one's comfort, easy condition, or the saving of trouble; commodious'.[86] Five other senses, now all obsolete, were available to the translators of the Authorised Version:

---

[84] *The History of the Old and New Testaments Extracted from the Sacred Scriptures, the Holy Fathers, and Other Ecclesiastical Writers . . .*, 4th impression, 1712, NT, p. 17.

[85] Mrs (Sarah) Trimmer, *Help to the Unlearned in the Study of the Holy Scriptures,* 2nd edn, 1806, p. 570.

[86] Again I am indebted to a suggestion of Ward Allen for this example.

Agreeing (in opinion); in accord. Accordant, congruous, consonant (*to*).

Agreeing with or consonant to the nature or character of; in accordance with; in keeping with; befitting, becoming (*to* or *for* a thing or person).

Of befitting size or extent; commensurate, proportionate (*to*). Suitable, appropriate; *to* or *for* a purpose etc.

Suitable to the conditions or circumstances; befitting the case; appropriate, proper, due.

Of time: due proper.

Morally or ethically suitable or becoming; proper.

Felix is not merely looking for a moment of greater material comfort and leisure, he is actually even more confused than his blatant evasion might seem in modern English. He will call Paul again when he is in agreement with him; when Paul's argument seems accordant with reason; when it suits his character; when it is appropriate to his purposes in life; to his circumstances; when he finds it to have a moral and ethical validity; when the time is ripe, and soon. The encoded excuses tumble over each other in confusion – for, of course, none of them is true. The point is that, in selecting a word of such moral as well as material connotations as 'convenient', the unhappily named Felix is laying himself open to a far greater range of ironic self-condemnation than the bare current meaning allows.

The history of the Authorised Version's 'convenient season' is a curious and instructive one here. At first glance it does not seem very much of a change from Tyndale's 'convenient time', which matches the Greek so well that it was followed by both the Geneva Bible and Coverdale's first (1535) version. When, however, Coverdale came to revise his work for the 1539 Great Bible, he introduced a fresh and haunting vocalic echo between 'convenient' and 'season' – the irony enhanced by its suggestion of ripeness, and an organic rhythm to the mysterious movement of the spirit. With its usual sureness of choice, the Authorised Version follows Coverdale's revision. We recall that Felix is here confronting of all people Paul, the man whose own dramatic conversion on the road to Damascus was 'convenient' in every one of the above senses *except* the modern one. Felix, in contrast, has missed the moment of convenience, and the seasons move inexorably on. The phrase has all the complex irony of the mature Shakespeare.

As we have seen here, a structural theory of polyvalency in meaning went hand in hand with a greater resonance of language. The Jacobean translators deliberately matched ambiguity with ambiguity, and exploited to the full both the material and moral meanings of the words available. But if they were apparently providentially aided by the greater range of meanings available to seventeenth-century English, they were also aided by something just as important – their own personal sensitivities to that range. Something of the complexity of this interplay can be seen in another example of the way in which the Authorised Version uses and reworks the original Tyndale translations. In Tyndale's New Testament, John 8: 46 is rendered as 'Which of you can rebuke me of sin?' Instead of following this perfectly intelligible reading, the Authorised Version has chosen the much more obscure and, again, seemingly archaic: 'Which of you convinceth me of sin?' The Greek word in question is *elengcho*, which is translated at different points in the Authorised Version by no fewer than six English words: 'convince', 'convict', 'tell one's fault', 'reprove', 'discover' and (as Tyndale had it here) 'rebuke'. Why then the need to depart from Tyndale's reading at this point? The answer seems to lie with the history of that word 'convince'. Though the *OED* allows only one current meaning of the word, it also lists seven other obsolete senses – all of which were current in the early seventeenth century. Lady Macbeth, for instance, says of Duncan's chamberlains

> Will I with wine and wassail so convince
> That memory, the warder of the brain,
> Shall be a fume, and the receipt of reason
> A limbeck only.   (i, vii, 64–7)

Most Shakespeare glossaries suggest that 'convince' here means 'over-power', but other meanings of the word, such as 'to prove a person guilty ... especially by judicial procedure', or 'to disprove, refute', or 'to demonstrate or prove absurdity' all suggest how Lady Macbeth's mind is racing ahead to visualise how the grooms might be over-powered, their protestations swept aside and refuted as absurd, and finally be convicted. Similarly in the Authorised Version's careful substitution of 'convince' for 'rebuke' we can catch a hint that Jesus is seen to be challenging the whole network of semi-judicial accusations flung against him as absurd – without, of course, allowing the reader to lose sight of the fact that one day soon these will indeed overpower him and bring him to the ultimate absurdity of the Cross.[87] More importantly for our purposes, however, it renders much less credible arguments that would attribute such subtlety of interpretation simply to the state of seventeenth-century English. If that were the case, then

---

[87] *Ibid.*

Tyndale's 'rebuke me of sin' would surely have sufficed. What we are looking at here seems to be clear evidence of informed and educated personal choice.

Something of the care with which these particular words were chosen is indicated by a later passage in John 16: 8: 'And when he is come, he will reprove the world of sin, and of righteousness, and of judgement.' Though the selected translation of *elengcho* here is 'reprove' (again replacing 'rebuke' in Tyndale), the translators have added 'convince' in the margin. Whether or not this indicates some shade of disagreement among them, it also serves to emphasise not merely how closely the words 'reprove' and 'convince' were associated in their minds but yet again the degree of personal selection that was brought to that search for finer shades of meaning. It is not just the language, but such sensitivities both to the nuances of individual words and to their relationship to the larger rhythms of the Bible that make the Authorised Version so remarkable a translation.

This is, of course, something the modern translators are not unaware of. Kenneth Grayston, for instance, one of the leaders of the panel responsible for the New English Bible of 1970, writes with undisguised distaste for the degenerate state of the contemporary English at his disposal in contrast with what he sees as the 'richer denser' language available to Spenser, Sydney, Hooker, Marlowe and Shakespeare – not to mention the translators of the Authorised Version.[88]

Modern English, it seems to me, is slack instead of taut, verbose and not concise, infested with this month's cliché, no longer the language of a proud and energetic English people, but an international means of communication. And 'means of communication' gives the game away: it seems to me a repository for the bad habits of foreigners speaking English. This is how we must speak if people are to listen and grasp what we say.[89]

Here, unfortunately, xenophobia seems to have outrun scholarship: for reasons more to do with changes in the literary and intellectual contexts than the bad habits of anglophone foreigners, English *has* indeed changed – just as, incidentally, it had changed in the sixteenth century between the time of Tyndale and the Authorised Version. As we have seen, in the last four hundred years the language has in fact altered in certain very clearly distinguishable ways. We are less concrete and more abstract; we tend to be more circumlocutory; we are less

---

[88] 'Confessions of a Biblical Translator', *New Universities Quarterly*, vol. 33, no. 3 (Summer 1979), p. 287.
[89] *Ibid.*

ambiguous, and differentiate more clearly between mental and material qualities; above all, we have come to tell our stories in a different
way. This is due in part to the scientific revolution of the seventeenth
and eighteenth centuries, and also in part to the development of the
novel as the dominant art-form. As a result, modern English narration
has tended to lose some, at least, of those natural affinities with the
plain directness of Greek and Hebrew. Put into contemporary speech,
the Gospels or Old Testament histories now often tend to sound oddly
bald and breathless – or, as some critics have been quick to observe,
like childhood fairy stories.

Yet the differences between sixteenth- and seventeenth-century
English and that of the twentieth century are not easily captured by
such grand generalisations. Translation theory is not *just* the product of
the state of the language at any given period, it also contributes to it.
There is, for instance, a beautiful if strange line in Ezekiel 27 (v. 25)
which the Authorised Version (translating, as always, fairly literally)
gives as 'the ships of Tarshish did sing of thee in thy market'. This
Hebrew metaphor of a fleet of cargo ships singing praise to its owner or
nation simply by the wealth and splendour of its merchandise is not a
conceit that would have seemed too far-fetched to the contemporaries
of John Donne; indeed, Kipling in one of his finest short stories actually
attributes it (very slightly amended) to Shakespeare himself:

'But, Ben, ye should have heard my Ezekiel making mock of fallen Tyrus in
his twenty-seventh chapter. Miles sent me the whole, for, he said, some small
touches. I took it to the bank – four o'clock of a summer morn; stretched out
in one of our wherries – and watched London, Port and Town, up and down
the river, waking all arrayed to heap more upon evident excess. Ay! "A
merchant for the peoples of many isles" ... "The ships of Tarshish did sing of
thee in thy markets"? Yes! I saw all Tyre before me neighing her pride against
lifted heaven ... But what will they let stand of all mine at long last? Which?
I'll never know.'[90]

Modern translators, however, have all insisted on explanatory paraphrases – in so doing offering fascinating insights into their unconscious
assumptions. Thus Lightfoot's Revised Version, completed in 1885,
turns it into 'The ships of Tarshish were caravans for thy merchandise'
– an image which, in spite of the desert connotations of the word for
most English-speaking people is pedantically correct in that 'caravan'
may, according to the *OED*, also apply specifically to fleets of 'Russian

---

[90] Rudyard Kipling, 'Proofs of Holy Writ', *Sussex Edition of Kipling's Works*, Macmillan, 1937–9, vol.
XXX, p. 354.

or Turkish' merchant ships. This reading has been retained by both Grayston's New English Bible and its successor, the Revised English Bible. For the twentieth-century Good News Bible, guided by Nida, such Victorian exoticism as eastern caravans is clearly unacceptable since this might presumably suggest a non-native source. The result is strictly prosaic: 'Your merchandise was carried in fleets of the largest cargo ships' – but ironically it does, nevertheless, in its own way, carry a particular eastern Mediterranean flavour: that of Onassis or Niarchos, perhaps. The Roman Catholic New Jerusalem Bible (1985) is, however, less impressed by sheer size than by financial organisation, and declares that 'Ships of Tarshish sailed on your business.'

Other, more questionable, readings from the Authorised Version which the more cautious translators of the Revised Version had left intact are clarified with similar éclat by the Good News Bible. For instance, Psalm 11: 6, in the Authorised Version reads 'upon the wicked He shall rain snares, fire and brimstone and an horrible tempest'. 'Snares' (or 'traps') is again an unlikely (though not impossible) reading and in fact only the most minute alteration of the Hebrew pointing is required to change 'snares' to the more probable 'coals'. The Good News Bible reads 'He sends down flaming coals and burning sulphur on the wicked; he punishes them with scorching winds', adding a footnote to explain how it has amended the Hebrew 'traps'. This is unexceptionable textually, but in addition to altering 'traps' to 'coals', it has introduced its own (quite unauthenticated) 'Hebrew parallelism': setting the 'scorching winds' over against the 'flaming coals and burning sulphur' rather than being the third term in the triad. The effect is to suggest not one kind of cataclysmic event (a reference presumably to the fate of the 'cities of the plain', Sodom and Gomorrah, Genesis 20) but *two* quite separate ones: if not fire and brimstone (on their cities?), then scorching winds (on their crops?). It is difficult to know if this is an example of substituting an equivalent cultural effect – atomic holocausts, perhaps, and dustbowls in the Midwest – or merely the kind of lack of attention to exact wording that we have already noted as characteristic of modern translation theory.

'In translating', wrote Goethe, 'we must go to the brink of the Untranslatable; it is only then that we really become aware of the foreignness of the nation and the language.' When we read the Bible, we do not take on a patchwork of piecemeal concepts to be matched with supposed equivalencies, we enter into a changing yet self-subsistent world that we can only learn to understand from inside.

The language of the Bible forms a uniquely self-referential whole[91] – and it is important to realise that this is not in spite of its palimpsestic and translated origins, but rather *because* of them. The reason why, for instance, the language of the Authorised Version (in spite of its many scholarly errors) is more subtle, more suggestive, more resonant, and in the end (I think history will show) more successful, has little to do with the supposed 'superior' state of Jacobean English, and much to do with respective translation theories and, not least, with the consequent choices of the individual translators. The seventeenth-century translators believed, rightly or wrongly, that they were dealing with a seamless web of divine guidance from the first sentence of Genesis to the last page of Revelation. As we have seen, they also inhabited a world where the events of the Bible were read as both alien and immediately close. Their language was not a monolithic and opaque entity to which the unfamiliar had to be painstakingly accommodated but an essentially translucent medium *through* which other older or alternative layers and meanings could clearly be discerned. As one might expect with hindsight, this meant that though they were much *less* prepared to take liberties with the original texts, they were much *more* prepared to make such innovations as seemed to them appropriate in the English language itself. The Authorised Version was not the product of Calvinistic predestination, nor yet its modern equivalent of blind historical or linguistic forces, it was the outcome of a deliberate piece of social and linguistic engineering. As we have seen, there are many contingent reasons, but no intrinsic historical necessity why it should have been a success.

Indeed, as David Norton has demonstrated, that success was in fact a long time coming. There is nothing to suggest that the victory of the Authorised Version owed anything to its being recognised as a superior translation, and a good deal of evidence to suggest that many early seventeenth-century readers either could not or simply did not distinguish between the Authorised and Geneva Versions at all. Hybrid versions using the King James text and Geneva notes continued to be printed in Amsterdam until 1715, and in London the Bishops' Bible continued to be printed *in toto* until 1617 – and parts until 1639. Stranger still, in spite of its unpopularity with the authorities, the Geneva Bible was never officially proscribed, and even Archbishop Laud, who was to become one of the most powerful agents in the

---

[91] For a further discussion of the self-referential qualities of the Bible see Gabriel Josipovici, *The Book of God*, New Haven, Conn.: Yale University Press, 1988.

eventual decline of the Geneva version, used it himself in printed sermons, often in tandem with the Authorised Version, until the mid-1620s.[92] 'The Church and the State were not so much for the KJB or even for a uniform Bible', Norton concludes, 'as they were against the Geneva Bible' – but the evidence, especially from Scotland, suggests that they did not feel powerful enough to ban it outright.[93] Final acceptance of the Authorised Version does not seem to have been assured until the Restoration of 1660, and there is little to suggest then that this might be due to any superior literary merit.

This has not prevented later critics from seeing that final appropriation in terms of various kinds of historical necessity. Though such acute observers as Coleridge were prepared to find in what he called the process of 'desynonymy', or the formation of new words to convey new shades of meaning, evidence for some kind of 'immanent will' or even Hegelian *Geist* operating through the historical process of human consciousness,[94] later models tended to seek some more respectable scientific shape even when their motivation was no less overtly theological. J.B. Lightfoot, for instance, Hulsean and then later Lady Margaret Professor of Divinity in the University of Cambridge, and finally Bishop of Durham, was, as it were, the Nida of his day. He was one of the prime creators of the Revised Version of the Bible of 1885, and had led the way with revisions of the New Testament during the 1870s. Like most biblical translators, he also wrote about his theory of translation; where he broke new ground was in his modest willingness also to offer a coherent theory for the eventual success and acceptance of his translation over earlier versions. Both Jerome's Vulgate and the Authorised Version, he points out, were originally received with the same 'coldness' that now attends his Revised Version; both in time gained acceptance by a process which he does not hesitate to ascribe to a moral version of Darwinian evolution.

But the parallel [with evolution] may be carried a step farther. In both these cases alike, as we have seen, God's law of progressive improvement, which in animal and vegetable life has been called the principle of natural selection, was vindicated here, so that the inferior gradually disappeared before the superior in the same kind; but in both cases also the remnants of an earlier Bible held and still hold their ground, as a testimony to the past. As in parts of the Latin Service-books the Vulgate has not even yet displaced the Old Latin,

[92] Norton, *History of the Bible*, vol. I, pp. 214–15, 225–6.
[93] *Ibid.*, p. 215.
[94] See Prickett, *Words and the 'Word'*, pp. 133–45.

which is still retained either in its pristine or in its partially amended form, so also in our own Book of Common Prayer an older version still maintains its place in the Psalter and in the occasional sentences, as if to keep before our eyes the progressive history of our English Bible.[95]

Since the Revised Version is in scholarly terms clearly an 'improvement' on the Authorised one, it will eventually triumph by a process of moralised natural selection, where even the vestigial remains of the earlier versions in the prayerbook are given an improving significance.

Such an optimistic theological faith in progress was not, however, allowed to pass unchallenged, even in late Victorian England. The Rev. E.W. Bullinger was no less formidable a scholar than Lightfoot. His *Critical Lexicon and Concordance to the English and Greek New Testament* was the result of nine years' research, and had established him as one of the foremost Greek scholars of his day. In 1898 he published a work called *Figures of Speech Used in the Bible*, which, in spite of the slightly dilettante suggestions of its title, was quite as magisterial a piece of scholarship as anything by Lightfoot – running as it did to over 900 pages. In a section on 'Changes of Usage of Words in the English Language' he notes gloomily 'It is most instructive to observe the evidence afforded by many of these changes as to the constant effect of fallen human nature; which, in its use of words, is constantly lowering and degrading their meaning.'[96]

Nor should we too readily assume that this kind of debate between progressivists and deteriorationists belongs exclusively to the nineteenth century. If Kenneth Grayston believes that the language into which he had helped to translate the Bible was an enfeebled and degenerate instrument in comparison with the patriotic power and resonance of seventeenth-century English, Peter Levi, in *The English Bible* (1974), while agreeing with the deteriorationists about the actual quality of the new translations, is more optimistic. He clings, if not to a progressivist view, at least to a meliorist one, about the total cultural scene: 'it appears that the proper virtues of the language have not altered so much even now, but have simply been disregarded, as happened often in the past, and will reassert themselves as they did then'.[97]

---

[95] J.B. Lightfoot, *On a Fresh Revision of the English New Testament*, 2nd edn, revised, New York: Harper and Rowe, 1873, p. 31. I am indebted here, and in the following illustration, to Professor Ward Allen, who first drew my attention to this passage.

[96] E.W. Bullinger, *Figures of Speech Used in the Bible*, Eyre and Spottiswoode, 1898, reprinted Baker House, 1968, 15th printing 1990, p. 856.

[97] Peter Levi, *The English Bible 1534–1859*, Constable, 1974, p. 13.

Behind their powerful scholarly and historical apparatus, both these diametrically conflicting models are, we note, not just essentially theological in thrust, but specifically predestinarian – overtly in the nineteenth-century examples, more covertly in the case of the twentieth century. Thus the progress or deterioration of the English language, or indeed of human consciousness in general, is not so much a responsibility of individuals, nor even of the race, but of the iron laws of (according to taste) a progressively orientated or a hopelessly fallen universe. Neither view seems to allow for any great degree of human spontaneity and creativity, or for the possibility that the English language, so far from being a monolithic linguistic code, might in fact be better seen as a chaotic historical palimpsest of many cultural codes and dialects together with the influence of multiple layers of translation. Nor do they make any provision for the fact that, as with other forms of literary appropriation, the very illegitimacy – not to mention theoretical impossibility – of translation actually seems to liberate creative forces in the human psyche. Finally, and perhaps most surprisingly, neither of these neo-Calvinisms makes any provision for the success of deliberate and planned human intervention of the kind we have seen at work in the making of the Authorised Version.

What is clear is that in this, as in other things, there is a radical disjunction between the Authorised Version and the various modern versions. Twentieth-century scholarly knowledge of the biblical world and its background is probably infinitely greater than that of the early seventeenth century. It is hardly surprising, therefore, that the many modern translations differ much more from each other and from their predecessors than the Authorised Version did from its immediate forerunner, the Bishops' Bible. Yet, though it was to take several generations, by the last quarter of the seventeenth century the King James translation effectively appropriated the earlier versions of the sixteenth century – the Bibles, lest we forget, actually used by people like Spenser, Sydney, Shakespeare and Donne – in a way that none of the twentieth-century versions has so far done. Moreover, it is as if, vampire-like, such an appropriation feeds off and draws further energy from the very versions that it has so effectively obliterated. With its careful distancing from the immediate and therefore fluctuating present, its open polyvalency of meaning and, at the verbal level, minute attention to the nuances of its words, phrases and even cadences, the Authorised Version was successfully designed to control the language of salvation, and to occupy the linguistic high ground in such a way as to allow its rivals, whether Geneva or Reims, less verbal space, less legitimacy, less power. As we have seen, it was always part of its brief that it should do so. Though there is some doubt as to whether it was ever in fact officially authorised, the King James Version was being referred to as the 'authorised Bible' by the 1620s,[98] and the very notion of such royal 'authorisation' carried with it also the corresponding idea of exclusiveness. At any one time there could only be *one* such version: just as the Bishops' Bible had replaced the Great Bible, so now the new King James Version was to replace the Bishops'. Indeed, as was suggested above, there is a real sense in which the story of the Authorised Version is a microcosm of the story of the Bible as a whole. As we saw in the previous chapter, though the Bible is overtly acknowledged to be one among several great holy books of the world, it also radiates a tacit exclusiveness: a unique status that for the West is reflected by the fact that its title is the same as the generic word for 'book'. Just as the Bible has appropriated the concept of a book, so, for the English-speaking world, the Authorised Version has appropriated the notion of the Bible. All other English versions still exist, as it were, in its shadow. From heavenly host to fatted calf, it has shaped, formed, appropriated the language with which the others must speak. When the Revised Version of the New Testament was published in 1855 the *Edinburgh Review* was one of a number of sources that criticised it for bending the native English idiom to conform with the Greek[99] – the reviewer being apparently unaware that this was precisely the criticism that had, with equally good reason, been thrown by an earlier generation of critics against the Authorised Version itself. In the intervening two and a half centuries, however, those archaic and sometimes tortured phrases produced by literal renderings of Greek and Hebrew had themselves been assimilated into the English language and hallowed by time and custom so that we no longer recognise such phrases as 'the skin of my teeth', 'lick the dust' or 'fell flat on his face' as alien semitic intruders.[100] Similarly Kenneth Grayston's complaint against the perceived inadequacies of modern English perhaps owed less to linguistic history and more to Herder and German Romantic theories of language and nationality than he realised. The theme of the decay

---

[98] See Norton, *History of the Bible*, vol. I, p. 214.
[99] *Ibid.*, vol. II, p.237.
[100] Job 19: 20 ; Ps. 72: 9; Num. 22: 31. (*Ibid.*, p. 342.)

of native linguistic vigour under pressure from the insensitivities of foreign speakers is one that recurs, sometimes with sinister undertones, in many European countries in the nineteenth and twentieth centuries.[101] In Grayston's case, however, it may tell us more about his unconscious assumptions concerning the nature of biblical English, than about the state of the language spoken in the United Kingdom today. I suspect it is not so much that modern English is an unworthy instrument for biblical translation as that the Authorised Version has so dominated his concept of what the appropriate language *should* sound like that it has left him, as it were, no verbal space to create a correspondingly dominant contemporary biblical discourse.

Such a complaint is, of course, itself a product of historicism rather than hermeneutics – and it is worth reminding ourselves how far our modern concept of linguistic change, like our idea of history in general, is essentially an Enlightenment and Romantic phenomenon, dating from no earlier than the second half of the eighteenth century. Oddly enough the belated *recognition* of the Authorised Version's linguistic dominance (which is, of course, not to be equated with the fact of that dominance) is itself a product of the same historical movement that was responsible for the critical revolution in biblical studies which was in the long run to weaken the historical authority of the Bible. Once again, a new appropriation was being prepared. As Henning Graf Reventlow has pointed out in his brilliant and persuasive study of the Bible in early eighteenth-century politics, it was a continuation of precisely this struggle for the control of the high ground of religious discourse which we have seen mirrored in the history of the Authorised Version that was to lead to the development of biblical criticism in seventeenth- and eighteenth-century England. By denying its status as the source of revelation and pointing out the human elements in its composition, the Whig ideologists sought to deprive their opponents among the High Church Tories of their use of the Bible to support their position.[102] The politics that brought the Authorised Version into existence could also undermine it. Far from seeming to provide in its own pages all that was needful for its understanding, as Protestants had hitherto believed, the Bible itself now appeared to need a new theory of how to read it.

---

[101] This is not merely true of France and Germany, but also, for instance, Hungary.

[102] Henning Graf Reventlow, *The Authority of the Bible and the Rise of the Modern World*, trs. John Bowden, SCM Press, 1984, p. 329.

PART II

The Romantic Bible

CHAPTER 3

The Bible as novel

THE CASES OF THE LEVITE'S CONCUBINE

Sometime during the eighteenth century there occurred in England one of those momentous sea-changes in reading that permanently altered the way in which books, whether sacred or secular, were understood and interpreted. The effectiveness of the new approach, and its success in obliterating its predecessor, can be judged by the fact that we are now hardly conscious of it ever having taken place at all. What makes it very different from previous appropriations is that it was not the work of any organised party or faction, and it was only in retrospect that a theory of reading emerged to justify what had happened.

Though one can find examples enough of realistic secular narrative fiction in the seventeenth century, it was probably not until the extraordinary success of Defoe's *Robinson Crusoe* in 1719 that one becomes aware of how the new art-form, the so-called 'novel', was altering not merely standards of realism, but – less obvious, though in the long run perhaps even more important – also the way in which other kinds of narrative were being read and understood. That such a new and, for a long time, low-status form of entertainment could or should affect the reading of God's Word would no doubt have seemed utterly incredible to contemporaries. Only with hindsight can such changes be seen to have happened, and explanations sought. Indeed, only since Hans Frei's pioneering work, *The Eclipse of Biblical Narrative*, appeared some twenty years ago have we learned to see the rise of eighteenth-century biblical criticism in relation to what was happening in the contemporary novel. Though it leaves many unanswered questions, his case is persuasive – not least because it is one of the very few historical analyses to have addressed this hermeneutic change at all. For Frei, the factors which led to a critical and historical approach to the Bible in the first half of the eighteenth century were roughly comparable in both England and Germany; the reason why the ways in which they were to develop were so markedly different, he argues, was primarily due to the relative status of prose fiction in the two countries:

In England, where a serious body of realistic narrative literature and a certain amount of criticism of that literature was building up, there arose no cumulative tradition of criticism of the biblical writings, and that included no narrative interpretation of them. In Germany, on the other hand, where a body of critical analysis as well as general hermeneutics of the biblical writings built up rapidly in the latter half of the eighteenth century, there was no simultaneous development of realistic prose narrative and its critical appraisal.[1]

I have discussed this argument extensively elsewhere,[2] and it is not my intention to repeat that discussion here; instead, I want to make two different but related points. The first is that though Frei, of course, is primarily interested in the way in which what we now call, from the German, the 'higher criticism' failed to be influenced by the development of the English novel as much as he believes it might have been, and why English literary criticism correspondingly failed to influence biblical criticism; his argument can just as well be turned upside down. In other words, I believe that he is probably correct in asserting that there was a close connection between theories of biblical and literary criticism in this period, but that he is mistaken in assuming that criticism of the novel would naturally lead towards the higher criticism of the Bible. In fact, as we shall see, the rise of the novel in the eighteenth century *did* have a profound effect on the way in which the Bible was read in England – though it did not, as Frei assumes, lead to the higher criticism. What happened, rather, was that the Bible – and in particular the Old Testament – ceased to be read as though it spoke with a single omniscient dogmatic voice, and began instead to be read as dialogue, with a plurality of competing voices. At the same time, what had been universally accepted as an essentially polysemous narrative, with many threads of meaning, was narrowed into a single thread of story, which was almost invariably interpreted as being 'historical'. My second hypothesis follows from this: namely that,

---

[1] Hans Frei, *The Eclipse of Biblical Narrative: a Study in Eighteenth and Nineteenth Century Hermeneutics*, New Haven, Conn.: Yale University Press, 1974, p. 142.

[2] See Stephen Prickett, *Words and the 'Word': Language, Poetics and Biblical Interpretation*, Cambridge University Press, 1986, pp. 82–4.

contrary to Frei's assumption, in the nineteenth century it was the English novel tradition that was influenced by the rise of biblical criticism rather than *vice versa*. As we shall see, the two developments were intimately linked.

For both these to become possible, however, there had first to be a fundamental shift away from the seventeen-hundred-year-old system of polysemous and figurative hermeneutics that had been the principal engine of the original Christian appropriation of the Hebrew scriptures. As a critical theory, it had proved itself immensely sophisticated, subtle, flexible – and incredibly durable. With its aid every passage of the Bible, however incongruous or unseemly, from the story of the Levite's Concubine to the Song of Songs could be interpreted as equally important – if not in its literal meaning, then perhaps all the more so in its moral, allegorical or anagogical meanings. It had survived more or less unchanged from late antiquity to the Middle Ages; it had even proved itself adaptable enough to take in its stride the radical Protestant appropriation of the scriptures at the Reformation. Conventional wisdom has it that it was the rise of historical criticism, taking its cue from such philosophical writers as Spinoza,[3] and by the eighteenth century emanating principally from Germany, that was to deal the mortal blow to this hallowed tradition of polysemous hermeneutics. Yet when we look in detail at the way in which this new critical method was introduced into England, and how it was adapted there, the situation begins to look rather more complicated.

Certainly it is true that, for an English-language reader, the absence of a well-developed tradition of realistic prose fiction in eighteenth-century Germany is striking. As we shall see in a later chapter, the so-called 'Jena' Romantics at the end of the eighteenth century developed extensive and influential theories about the novel. But perhaps in keeping with their belief that criticism was properly a constitutive element of literature, it is noticable that, if we exclude poetry, even such a highly creative group as this was much more productive of criticism than actual literature. Moreover, once we move from theoretical principles to detailed textual criticism, it is clear how much their view of prose fiction suffered from the lack of contemporary German models. It is symptomatic that when Goethe, in *Wilhelm Meister* (1796),[4]

---

[3] See, for instance, Stuart Hampshire, *Spinoza: an Introduction to his Philosophical Thought*, Penguin, 1951, p. 151.

[4] It was in fact begun as early as 1777, and the passage quoted was written sometime between then and 1785.

needed examples of leading characters from novels, his entire selection was drawn not from German but from English literature: 'Grandison, Clarissa, Pamela, the Vicar of Wakefield, Tom Jones'.[5] It is also significant that, in spite of a whole book of the novel being devoted to a religious consciousness with great stress, in the Moravian tradition, on reading the Bible,[6] there is little or no indication that the metafictional structure of the novel at this stage owes anything directly *either* to the new biblical critical theories *or* to traditional modes of polyvalent typology. On the contrary, like Fielding in *Tom Jones*, Goethe takes his principal literary model from drama – and from *Hamlet*: English poetic drama at that. *Wilhelm Meister*, in fact, is often seen in retrospect as the first great German novel,[7] and when Friedrich Schlegel wished two years later, in 1798, to add his critical praise to the book, in spite of his abstract eulogies of the new genre of prose fiction in the *Athenaeum*,[8] he found it natural to do so not in terms of the novel at all, but to turn to what was for him a much more real model: the classical form of epic poetry – for him the origin of the 'narrative genre'. 'It is all poetry, high, pure poetry', he writes. 'Everything has been thought and uttered as though by one who is both a divine poet and a perfect artist.'[9] As Amelia, one of the characters in Schlegel's own *Dialogue on Poetry and Literary Aphorisms* (1800), says: 'If it goes on like this, before too long one thing after another will be transformed into poetry. Is everything poetry then?'[10]

In such a critical climate it is small wonder that we find that the connotations of 'prose' and 'poetry' were acquiring very different flavours in the two countries, and that, as in the Jena group, German theoretical discussions of literary creativity and 'poetics' tended to see prose narrative more as an extension of poetry than a new medium in its own right, and to assume correspondingly different conventions of reading. The German word *Roman*, normally translated into English by

---

[5] *Wilhelm Meister's Apprenticeship and Travels*, trs. Thomas Carlyle. 2 vols. (Centenery edn, Carlyle: *Works*, Chapman and Hall, 1896–1903, vols. XXIII and XXIV), vol. I, p. 345.

[6] Book VI, 'Confessions of a Fair Saint'.

[7] The only earlier contender might be Wieland.

[8] See, for instance, Friedrich Schlegel, *'Lucinde' and the Fragments*, trs. Peter Firchow, Minneapolis: University of Minnesota Press, 1971, Critical Fragment 26. Also Philippe Lacoue-Labarthe and Jean-Luc Nancy, *The Literary Absolute: the Theory of Literature in German Romanticism*, trs. Philip Barnard and Cheryl Lester, Albany: State University of New York Press, 1978, pp. 88–94.

[9] 'On Goethe's *Meister*' (1798), *German Aesthetic and Literary Criticism: the Romantic Ironists and Goethe*, ed. Kathleen Wheeler, Cambridge University Press, 1984, p. 64.

[10] *Ibid.*, p. 75.

the word 'novel', is for the Schlegels more a theoretical term than simply the name of a yet almost non-existent genre – corresponding closer to our (slightly uncomfortable) phrase 'creative writing'.[11] 'It must be clear to you', writes Antonio, one of Schlegel's mouthpieces in the *Dialogue*, 'why, according to my views, I insist that all poetry should be romantic and why I detest the novel insofar as it wants to be a separate genre.'[12]

As Frei, of course, is well aware, though the higher criticism of the Bible is popularly associated with its rapid development in Germany in the second half of the eighteenth century, its roots lay a hundred years earlier in France and subsequently in England. Its failure in the former country in contrast with its success in the latter has been plausibly ascribed to the political rather than the scholarly climate. But in the seventeenth century, in both France and England, religion *was* politics. In 1678 a French Oratorian, Richard Simon, had published a book with the innocent-sounding title of *Histoire critique du Vieux Testament*. Its aim was to counter the Protestant principle that scripture alone was necessary for salvation. By applying the kinds of scholarly techniques then being developed for classical texts, Simon set out to demonstrate that so far from being the direct dictation of the Holy Spirit, the biblical writings had origins no less human, complex and varied, and that only with careful guidance from the Church could the pious reader begin to grasp their real meanings. To this end he challenged such traditional views of the scriptures as that Moses was the author of the Pentateuch, arguing that these books were more likely to be a composite creation of scribes and what he called 'public writers'.[13] Ironically, such suggestions aroused the immediate wrath of the Catholic hierarchy, the book was promptly banned in France (where it never circulated), and Simon expelled from his Order.

As a further irony – in view of Simon's polemical intentions – it was a French Huguenot librarian, Henri Justel, who was responsible for smuggling two copies of the *Histoire critique* to England, where a

---

[11] Kathleen Wheeler describes it as more 'a *tendency* in modern literature away from classical styles and towards prose of an intensely poetic type, encompassing a wide range of content and styles as well as genre' (*German Aesthetic and Literary Criticism*, p. 4).

[12] Friedrich Schlegel, *Dialogue on Poetry and Literary Aphorisms*, translated, introduced and annotated by Ernst Behler and Roman Struc, University Park: Pennsylvania State University Press, 1968, p. 101.

[13] See Françoise Deconinck-Brossard, 'England and France in the Eighteenth Century', in Stephen Prickett (ed.), *Reading the Text: Biblical Criticism and Literary Theory*, Oxford: Basil Blackwell, 1991, 136–43.

translation was published in 1682. Simon's second book had a slightly
more tactful title, a *Critical History of the Text of the New Testament*, and
appeared in English in 1689 – the same year as the first French
edition.[14] As one might have expected, both volumes received a mixed
reception in Europe's foremost Protestant country. Edward Stillingfleet, the Dean of St Paul's and later Bishop of Worcester, attacked
Simon's work on much the same grounds as had the Catholic
authorities in France – that it tended to undermine the authority of
holy scripture. On the other hand both Locke and Dryden – the one a
Protestant of Deist leanings, the other shortly to become a Roman
Catholic – while not necessarily accepting all Simon's conclusions,
were both deeply impressed by his methodology and scholarship.
Locke had no fewer than two annotated copies of the *Critical History of
the Old Testament* in his library, and corresponded with Justel, whom he
had known in France. Similarly Dryden devotes much of the second
half of his *Religio Laici* to discussing 'this weighty Book, in which
appears / The crabbed Toil of many thoughtful years' (234–5).
Whether reading Simon did in fact contribute to his conversion to
Catholicism a few years later is not clear, but certainly a growing
scepticism about the value of religious disputes based on particular
interpretations of ambiguous biblical texts played its part.

Whatever the causes of Dryden's conversion, however, it was clear
that Simon's work offered anyone who took it up a two-edged sword.
As mentioned above, Henning Graf Reventlow has argued that Whig
apologists in England saw the new biblical criticism as a political
weapon to destabilise the High Church Tories.[15] Similarly, opponents
of the Anglican establishment, whether Roman Catholic or Deist, were
in general agreement with Stillingfleet that the new critical scholarship
did offer a way of undermining the authority of the Bible – and
welcomed it accordingly. There is a curious, if tragic, parallel between
the career of Simon in seventeenth-century France and Alexander
Geddes (1737–1802), an eighteenth-century Scottish Catholic priest, in
Britain, who embarked upon his own new translation of the Bible. He
was at first encouraged both by Protestant critics, such as Benjamin
Kennicott and Robert Lowth, and by his own hierarchy, who took the
familiar view that anything that tended to weaken Protestant reliance
on biblical authority could only be good for Catholicism. As Simon

---

[14] Various possible translators have been named, including John Hampden and Henry Dickinson.
See *ibid.*, p. 143.
[15] See chapter 2, above p. 103.

had found, however, Catholic tolerance of a genuinely historical approach to the Bible was as fragile as the Protestant. Geddes' *Critical Remarks upon the Hebrew Scriptures* (1800) rapidly led to his suspension, and he would almost certainly have been excommunicated had he not died first.[16]

But it would be a mistake to see the centres of the new biblical criticism in England as being largely motivated by opposition to the Anglican establishment. However their work was later to be exploited by others, both Kennicott[17] and Lowth were not merely staunch but exceptionally well-regarded Anglicans – the latter becoming successively Bishop of St David's, Oxford, and London. Robert Lowth's father, William, himself a biblical commentator, had been one of Simon's few English defenders, and it is inconceivable that his son did not also know the Frenchman's work. Nevertheless, he made no direct reference to it when, in May 1741, as the newly elected Professor of Poetry in the University of Oxford, he gave the first of the series of lectures on *The Sacred Poetry of the Hebrews* that by common consent seems to have triggered off the critical revolution in England.[18] Though this may well represent a degree of political caution, it may on the other hand merely reflect the somewhat makeshift conditions under which the lectures were begun.[19] With almost no time to prepare the scholarly apparatus which conventionally accompanied such a prestigious lecture series, it is possible that his insistence on a proper understanding of the historical background of the Old Testament was more pragmatism than a statement of principle, and that what we now read as the programme for his new historical criticism of the Psalms was more an off-the-cuff reflex than a considered agenda:

He who would perceive the peculiar and interior elegancies of the Hebrew poetry, must imagine himself exactly situated as the persons for whom it was written, or even as the writers themselves; he is to feel them as a Hebrew ... nor is it enough to be acquainted with the language of this people, their manners, discipline, rites and ceremonies; we must even investigate their inmost sentiments, the manner and connexion of their thoughts; in one word, we must see all things with their eyes, estimate all things by their opinion: we

[16] R.C. Fuller, *Alexander Geddes*, Sheffield: Almond Press, 1983.

[17] Benjamin Kennicott's massive edition of the Old Testament, *Vetus Testamentum Hebraicum* (1776–80) involved consulting and collating some 683 manuscript versions. It is still used today.

[18] For a more detailed discussion of Lowth's influence on criticism in England and Germany see Prickett, *Words and the 'Word'*, ch. 3.

[19] *Ibid.*, p. 105.

must endeavour as much as possible to read Hebrew as the Hebrews would have read it.[20]

If in retrospect this was to prove the clarion-call to a critical revolution, it is clear that for Lowth there was never any question of undermining the authority of scripture. In the Preliminary Dissertation to his *New Translation of Isaiah*, written some thirty years after the above, he states the modest aim of historical criticism as simply to produce a better, more scholarly working text for exegesis:

All writings transmitted to us, like these, from early times, the original copies of which have long ago perished, have suffered in their passage to us by the mistakes of many transcribers, through whose hands we have received them; errors continually accumulating in proportion to the number of transcripts, and the stream generally becoming more impure, the more distant it is from its source.[21]

A correct text was an essential prerequisite for translation. But though any translation necessarily had to concentrate primarily on understanding the literal meaning in its historical context, for Lowth this did not by any means imply subsequently being tied down to a single interpretative level. His list of essential priorities begins like Nida and ends like Augustine.

The first and principal business of a Translator is to give us the plain literal and grammatical sense of his author; the obvious meaning of his words, phrases, and sentences, and to express them in the language into which he translates, as far as may be, in equivalent words, phrases, and sentences ... This is peculiarly so in subjects of high importance, such as the Holy Scriptures, in which so much depends on the phrase and expression; and particularly in the Prophetical books of scripture; where from the letter are often deduced deep and recondite senses, which must owe all their weight and solidity to the just and accurate interpretation of the words of the Prophecy. For whatever senses are supposed to be included in the Prophet's words, Spiritual, Mystical, Allegorical, Analogical, or the like, they must all entirely depend on the Literal Sense.[22]

This is not so much a stress on the literal sense for its own sake,[23] as a belief that all figurative interpretation must be grounded in an accurate

---

[20] Robert Lowth, *Lectures on the Sacred Poetry of the Hebrews*, trs. G. Gregory, 1787, vol. 1, pp. 113, 114.

[21] Robert Lowth, *Isaiah: a New Translation* (1778), 5th edn, 2 vols., Edinburgh, 1807, vol. 1, p. lxxv.

[22] *Ibid.*, p. lxviii.

[23] A long tradition of Reformation divines had stressed the importance of the literal meaning, e.g. William Perkins: 'there is only one sense and that is the literal' (*The Art of Prophecying*, 1592).

text. In discussing Isaiah 35: 5–6 ('Then shall the eyes of the blind be opened, and the ears of the deaf shall be unstopped. Then shall the lame man leap as an hart, and the tongue of the dumb sing ...') Lowth is at pains to link it with its standard New Testament antetype: Matthew 9: 4–5 ('that the lame walked and the deaf heard'). Indeed, his commentary suggests more a typical mediaeval fourfold reading than simply the kind of two-level typology more common in eighteenth-century commentaries.

To these [the words of Matthew] the strictly literal interpretation of the Prophet's words direct us ... According to the allegorical interpretation they may have a further view: this part of the prophecy may run parallel with the former, and relate to the future advent of Christ; to the conversion of the Jews, and their restitution to their land; to the extension and purification of the Christian Faith; events predicted in the holy Scriptures as preparatory to it.[24]

Small wonder that such apparent conservatism did not ring the kind of alarm bells or arouse the opposition that Simon had done. Nor, indeed, is it easy at first glance for the modern reader to see how this very traditional-sounding interpretation could ever be taken as offering a new way of approaching the Bible at all, or, even more unlikely, could provide the historic opportunity for yet another appropriation in a long series of appropriative readings. Yet such it was to prove.

As has been mentioned, the conventional explanation points to Germany. When Lowth's work (still in Latin) was introduced there by Michaelis, it was to help change the whole development of biblical criticism. His influence on such figures as Herder, Reimarus, Lessing and Eichhorn is well documented.[25] Nevertheless, as an explanation it leaves a number of important questions unanswered. Why, as Frei has asked, in spite of Lowth, did the historical criticism never in fact catch on in England, the country that had taken it so far, and where the ground seemed to be so well prepared for its further development? The problem is an obstinate one that has never yet been satisfactorily dealt with by historians of biblical criticism. This may partly be a matter of focus. Lowth's only modern biographer, Brian Hepworth, looking primarily at his massive influence on the development of German historical criticism, understandably sees him first and foremost as a

---

[24] *Isaiah*, vol. II, p. 232.
[25] See Prickett, *Words and the 'Word'*, p. 49.

'materialist' and one of the prime agents of secularisation.[26] Yet, in fact, Lowth was never, like the later German critics, a 'historian' in the modern materialist sense at all. Though he was certainly concerned with the material conditions under which the ancient texts were produced, he nevertheless tended to take the biblical narratives at their face value, did not question miracles, and, in the 1740s he was still in no doubt that the Hebrew scriptures shared 'one common author' in the person of the Holy Spirit. In a significant aside, Hepworth notes that, in his 1758 Preface to the Göttingen Latin edition of the *Lectures*, Michaelis 'saw Lowth not as a Churchman *or* even as a professor, but as a poet speaking about poetry'.[27] Bearing in mind that, as we have seen, the concept of 'poetry' had a much wider significance in eighteenth-century Germany than it had in England, and embraced what in English would include prose, this is still a highly suggestive remark. It is certainly supported by the way in which during the thirty years or so between the publication of the *Lectures* and the translation of *Isaiah*, Lowth shows himself if anything *more* rather than *less* interested in the poetic and polysemous nature of the biblical texts. According to one's point of view, Lowth is either already showing in his own work symptoms of what we have already noticed as a national failure to advance the historical criticism, or he was always *more* interested in the poetic and polysemous possibilities of the biblical prophecies than their historical context. Is it possible that for Lowth historical criticism was never more than a part of what was essentially a linguistic and aesthetic quest?

Now it is certainly possible to argue that Lowth himself was unaware of the full implications of what he was doing, and that, like many other pioneers of new methodologies, he himself was not prepared to take it to the lengths of his successors. He would have been unlikely to recognise in Eichhorn, let alone Feuerbach, logical extensions of his own work and would clearly have been more in sympathy with, say, Herder's *Spirit of Hebrew Poetry* – which openly acknowledges its debt to him. The difference in tone between Lowth's interest in the potential range of meanings that he takes for granted are encoded in the text of Isaiah, and the sceptical reductionism of Eichhorn's *Einleitung in das Alte Testament* is striking. Certainly Coleridge, who had read both, while admiring the boldness of Eichhorn's questioning, was profoundly alienated by what he saw as the sheer crudeness of his yardstick for

---

[26] Brian Hepworth, *Robert Lowth*, Boston, Mass.: Twayne, 1978, p. 36.
[27] *Ibid.*, p. 39.

historical veracity.[28] Given this fundamental difference in emphasis, it would be unwise not to examine much more closely what Lowth himself believed were the implications of his work before seeing him completely appropriated by the later German higher critics. The alternative possibility is that Lowth, even while he pioneered an interest in the historical context that was to change the face of European scholarship, was, as he explicitly claims, mainly interested in that context as a way into a deeper study of the subtleties of the text itself. By his own account, his interest is *neither* that of the Jacobean translators, like John Bois, of a hundred and fifty years before, *nor* that of the historical critics who (as he was well aware) were rapidly developing his work in Germany between the time of his *Lectures on the Sacred Poetry of the Hebrews* and his *New Translation of Isaiah.* If Lowth's reading of the Bible was the seminal development behind the German historical critics, it was equally important to certain contemporary English novelists. It is time, therefore, that we looked at some of those novelists in more detail – and, not surprisingly, Laurence Sterne, one of the favourite novelists of the Schlegels and the *Athenaeum* group, is going to be one of our key witnesses.

Before we reach Sterne, however, I want to look briefly at a passage from another writer who had also greatly influenced him: Henry Fielding. One of the most interesting features of *Tom Jones* from a narratological point of view is the way in which Fielding claims to be constantly searching for models to describe the role of the novelist. As a successful playwright before he turned to prose fiction, it is hardly surprising that he constantly refers to the action of his story as if it were a drama, but intermingled with his theatrical metaphors is a constant flow of other analogies, sometimes bizarre, sometimes comic. After comparing himself as author, with a dramatist, a pastry cook, a judge and a governor, Fielding turns at last to the most obvious creator of all: the Author of the great Book of Nature. Like God himself, he writes, the novelist *creates* his own universe, with its own peculiar inhabitants, laws and events. The reader is thus warned: 'Not too hastily to condemn any of the Incidents in this our history, as impertinent and foreign to our main design, because thou dost not immediately conceive in what manner such incident may conduce to that design. This work may, indeed, be considered as a great creation of our

---

[28] See E.S. Shaffer, *'Kubla Khan' and 'The Fall of Jerusalem'*, Cambridge University Press, 1975, p. 88; Stephen Prickett, *Romanticism and Religion: the Tradition of Coleridge and Wordsworth in the Victorian Church*, Cambridge University Press, 1976, pp. 66–7.

own.'[29] The novelist here is not so much story-teller as Calvinistic God. The reader, like fallen humanity, cannot be expected to know everything that is going on in the plot, and thus cannot judge the great design. The Creator's word is final. If at one level this is theological parody, the point that is being made about the nature of narrative fiction is a perfectly serious one – Dante would have understood and appreciated it.

But there is another point here that would have been more difficult for a contemporary reader to observe. The description of God as author of the *liber naturae*, the 'book of Nature', was by the eighteenth century already not so much an active conceit as a hallowed cliché that stretched back to mediaeval times.[30] Its origins belong to a world where there was essentially only *one* book – the Bible itself. For Christians, therefore, Nature could be seen as God's 'other book', guiding them towards Natural Religion just as the Bible pointed to Revealed Religion. As Sir Thomas Browne put it in 1643: 'Thus there are two Books from which I collect my Divinity; besides that written one of God, another of his servant Nature, that universal and publick manuscript, that lies expans'd unto the Eyes of all, those that never saw him in the one, have discovered him in the other.'[31] But the second book, like the first, however 'universal and publick' it might appear, was nevertheless difficult to interpret without a guide. Like the first, therefore, it required a theory of interpretation. If we try to understand seventeenth-century science in this light, the obsessions of such members of the Royal Society as Newton, Boyle, Wilkins and others with biblical prophecy and interpretation become more comprehensible. By 1749, when Fielding published *Tom Jones*, the context of the metaphor had been subtly changed from when Shakespeare's Soothsayer, in *Anthony and Cleopatra*, could claim to read a little 'in Nature's infinite book of secrecy'.[32] 'Nature' meant no longer the relatively cosy mysteries of the Ptolomaic universe, but the more vast and mathematically quantifiable system of Newton. Though this universe, governed by apparently immutable Natural Laws, was in an obvious sense much less secret than it had been, its Creator was in some ways more arbitrary and inscrutable than ever before. At the same time, with the

---

[29] Henry Fielding, *Tom Jones*, ed. R.P.C. Mutter, Penguin, 1966, p. 467.

[30] See Ernst Robert Curtius, *European Literature and the Latin Middle Ages*, trs. Willard R. Trask, Routledge, 1953, pp. 319–26.

[31] *Religio Medici*, section 16, in *The Works of Sir Thomas Browne*, ed. Charles Saye, 3 vols., Edinburgh: Grant, 1927, vol. I, p. 25.

[32] Act I, scene ii, 11.

rise of the novel and a novel-reading public had come a whole variety of books, and a whole new genre of fictional prose narrative. As Fielding of all people knew very well, the author, too, was a very different animal. Grub Street had arrived. Though it would have been more difficult for a contemporary than for ourselves to see it, by the middle of the eighteenth century the existence of *Tom Jones*, and its fellow novels, meant that the way in which the Bible itself was being read was part of a general process of cultural change, affecting not merely prose narrative, but even that largely lost secondary art-form, the prose sermon.

There have not been many studies of Sterne's sermons, and those there are have largely concentrated either on their relationship to his fiction, or on their historical context within the ecclesiastical politics of the Diocese of York. The only full-length monograph on them deals almost exclusively with their sources – and with the later charge that they were largely plagiarised.[33] Whether his scripts were plagiarised or not, however, we know that by the 1740s Sterne had established himself as an outstanding preacher. His fund-raising sermon at St Michael le Belfry, the parish church for York Minster, in aid of two local charity schools in 1747 had raised the astonishing sum of £64. 11s. 8d.[34] That particular sermon, 'The Case of Elijah and the Widow of Zarephrath', (Sermon 5), is unusual in being easily datable. All we can be sure of concerning most of the rest is that those eventually published as *The Sermons of Mr Yorick* between 1760 and 1766 were probably written sometime during the 1740s and 1750s[35] – in other words that they pre-date *Tristram Shandy* and the *Sentimental Journey*. As such, they have been quarried by literary critics seeking – and often finding – clues to the development of the mature novelist's style. So far as I know, only Françoise Deconinck-Brossard's magisterial study of mid-century sermon-writing in the north of England, has attempted to set Sterne's work in the context of other contemporary sermons, and even she spares only a few pages for the seemingly highly uncontroversial question of contemporary biblical hermeneutics.[36]

Yet to the reader who is familiar with English eighteenth century

[33] Lansing van der Heyden Hammond, *Laurence Sterne's 'Sermons of Mr Yorick'*, New Haven, Conn.: Yale University Press, 1948, pp. 127–8, 145, 168, 180.

[34] Arthur H. Cash, *Laurence Sterne: the Early and Middle Years*, Methuen, 1975, p. 216.

[35] Hammond argues almost all the sermons were in fact written before 1751, but this view is challenged by Cash. See Cash, *Laurence Sterne*, p. 221.

[36] Françoise Deconinck-Brossard, *Vie politique, sociale et religieuse en Grande-Bretagne d'apres les sermons prêchés ou publiés dans le nord d'Angleterre 1738–1760*, Paris: Didier Erudition, 1984.

biblical interpretation, what is most striking about the *Sermons of Mr Yorick* is not what they contain, but what they do *not* contain. Even a cursory knowledge of eighteenth-century biblical commentaries and homilies reveals the degree to which theories of biblical hermeneutics were still overwhelmingly dominated by traditional typological and figural readings. Though the work of Kennicott and Lowth might be affecting small groups of avant-garde intellectuals, such groups typically tended to be Nonconformist or Unitarian rather than Anglican. Even Lowth, we recall, makes clear in the notes to his *New Translation of Isaiah*, that in the last resort the prime purpose of textual criticism, with its concentration on the literal and historical sense of the passage, is not to produce a univocal reading, but rather to permit figural and allegorical readings to be placed on a sounder scholarly basis. Similarly Joseph Butler's sermons, which are atypical in their heavy reliance on philosophical reasoning from first principles, make it equally clear that the prime purpose of the Old Testament is to point figuratively to the New.[37] A standard exegesis of Elijah and the Widow of Zarephath, for instance, reveals that it signified 'the holy Mystery of the Incarnation, wherein the Divine living Body was applied to our dead Bodies, to quicken them from the Death of Sin'.[38] Yorick's Sermon 22, 'The History of Jacob Considered', has as its text Genesis 47: 9: 'And Jacob said unto Pharoh, The days of the years of my pilgrimage are an hundred and thirty years: few and evil have the days of my life been.' As was the Elijah story, this verse is a favourite one for contemporary typological commentaries. A seventeenth-century gloss, for instance, focuses on the future consequences of Jacob's move to Egypt, citing both St John Chrysostom (so named on account of his 'golden-mouthed' eloquence) and St Bernard to the effect that 'Egypt ... that is to say, the World, ought always to be apprehended and suspected by true Israelites; whatsoever Caresses she might seem to make them, they ought not to trust her: For it is evident, That the People of GOD have always been forced (sooner or later) to acknowledge, that their entering into it has been of troublesome Consequence.'[39] One of the most popular mid-eighteenth-century Bibles is so keen to draw the appropriate moral in its notes

---

[37] See his sermon for the SPG, 16 February 1738: *Fifteen Sermons Preached at the Rolls Chapel to which are added Six Sermons Preached on Publick Occasions*, 4th edn, 1749, pp. 324–5.

[38] *The History of the Old and New Testaments Extracted from the Sacred Scriptures, the Holy Fathers, and Other Ecclesiastical Writers ...* 4th impression, 1712, p. 136.

[39] *Ibid.*, p. 42.

that it manages at a stroke to blot out all the more dubious episodes in Jacob's past life:

The life of man cannot be more properly represented than as a pilgrimage; we have all but a short time to stay upon earth, and should endeavour to make the best use of it, in order to secure to ourselves a place in the mansions of everlasting bliss ... If Jacob, who had lived in the most exemplary manner during an hundred and thirty years, called his days few and evil, how much more reason have men in these degenerate days, to lament that their days are few and evil, being shortened both by their own excesses, and by diseases transmitted to them by their parents.[40]

It is hard to imagine how anyone who had actually read the biblical saga of Jacob as a narrative, rather than as a series of types and figures, could describe him as having 'lived in the most exemplary manner', but even as late as the early nineteenth century we find Mrs Trimmer drawing the same essentially figural moral from Jacob's gloomy retrospective on his life: 'Christians have such a pilgrimage to take, and their hopes and views should be directed to the same heavenly country.'[41]

Against this background Sterne's sermons come as something of a shock. Nowhere in his discussion of Elijah and the widow does he even gesture towards a tradition of typological interpretation going back to the Church Fathers. The whole weight of his discussion is, in his own later sense of the word, sentimental: on the affecting nature of the widow's plight and Elijah's pity for her. In place of the traditional fourfold interpretation of scripture or the kind of philosophic disquisition based on reason that we find in Butler, Sterne reads his Bible as he might a novel. Even more striking is his approach to Jacob. Sterne takes the cue for his interpretation from Jacob's own words to his father-in-law, Laban:

These twenty years that I have been with thee, – thy ewes have not cast their young; and the rams of thy flock have I not eaten. That which was torn of the beasts I brought not unto thee; I bear the loss of it; – what was stolen by day, or stolen by night, of my hands didst thou require it. Thus I was: in the day the drought consumed me, and the frost by night; and my sleep departed from my eyes. Thus have I been twenty years in thy house: – I served thee fourteen years for thy two daughters, and six years for thy cattle: and thou hast changed my wages ten times. (Genesis 31: 38–41)[42]

[40] *The Royal Bible or a Complete Body of Christian Divinity*, with notes and observations by Leonard Howard, 2nd edn, 1761.

[41] Mrs Sarah Trimmer, *Help to the Unlearned in the Study of the Holy Scriptures*, 1806, p. 45.

[42] *The Works of Laurence Sterne*, ed. James P. Browne, 2 vols, 1885, vol. II, p. 252.

This is not Jacob the trickster, who had cheated Esau out of his birthright for a mess of pottage, nor yet Jacob the Patriarch, the man who was to become Israel, and the visionary whose descendants were to become a great people, whose every action and utterance is therefore fraught with typological meaning for Jews and Christians alike, but rather a disappointed and saddened, if not embittered man – in many ways much closer to the Jacob of Thomas Mann than it is to any contemporary eighteenth-century biblical exegesis.

Even more dramatic is Sermon 18, on the Levite and his concubine (Judges 19). Here the tendency to break into dialogue is so powerful that it completely runs away with the traditional form of the sermon. It opens in a way that, however startling it might have been to the congregation, is instantly familiar to anyone coming to it with the hindsight of *Tristram Shandy*:

A CONCUBINE! – but the text accounts for it; 'for in those days there was no king in Israel'; and the Levite, you will say, like every other man in it, did what was right in his own eyes; – and so you may add, did his concubine too, – 'for she played the whore against him, and went away.'

– Then shame and grief go with her; and wherever she seeks a shelter, may the hand of Justice shut the door against her!

Not so; for she went unto her father's house in Bethlehem-judah, and was with him four whole months. – Blessed interval for meditation upon the fickleness and vanity of this world and its pleasures! I see the holy man upon his knees, – with hands compressed to his bosom, and with uplifted eyes, thanking Heaven that the object which had so long shared his affections was fled!

The text gives a different picture of his situation; 'for he arose and went after her, to speak friendly to her, and to bring her back again, having his servant with him, and a couple of asses; and she brought him unto her father's house; and when the father of the damsel saw him he rejoiced to meet him'.

– A most sentimental group! you'll say; and so it is, my good commentator, the world talks of everything. Give but the outlines of a story, – let Spleen or Prudery snatch the pencil, and they will finish it with so many hard strokes, and with so dirty a colouring, that Candour and Courtesy will sit in torture as they look at it ...

... Here let us stop a moment, and give the story of the Levite and his concubine a second hearing. Like all others, much of it depends upon the telling; and, as the Scripture has left us no kind of comment upon it, 'tis a story on which the heart cannot be at a loss for what to say, or the imagination for what to suppose; the danger is, Humanity may say too much.[43]

If we listen attentively, there are actually several dialogues going on

---

[43] *Ibid.*, p. 218.

here at once. The most obvious is that between 'I' and 'you': the preacher and his hearers, who are not passive listeners, but are made to interject with comments of their own. But that dialogue is, in turn, subverted by another voice, seemingly that of conventional wisdom, presumably the so-called 'good commentator' whose commentary begins 'Then shame and grief go with her'. Even this shadowy voice is not the end of these phantom speakers, for no sooner has the speaker 'I' indulged in the wonderful fantasy of the Levite on his knees thanking God that the woman in his life has at last left him than we get the dry corrective: 'The text gives a different picture ...' By the end the very qualities of the reader's mind are crowding in as separate personifications: Spleen and Prudery, Candour and Courtesy, the heart and imagination are all offering us their own unasked-for opinions, not to mention squabbling among themselves.

The obvious critic to invoke at this stage is, of course, Bakhtin. This is heteroglossia in the strict sense of a dialogue between an official 'centripetal' voice and a variety of anarchic 'centrifugal' voices criticising and undermining that central authoritative narrative.[44] In his treatment of the stories of Elijah and the widow, or Jacob and Laban, Sterne takes a third-person biblical narrative and turns it, as it were, into a novel with elaborate characterisation and direct dramatic speech. His Bible is no longer a monolithic unitary text, but a richly dialogic one. But this is something different again. Here, it is true, is dialogue a-plenty, but the dialogue here is not just that of the participants, but of the various critics, including our own varied responses and prejudiced opinions: Sterne has now turned the biblical commentators *themselves* into dramatic participants in his biblical epic.

But perhaps we should pay closest attention to that 'good commentator' with whom so much of Sterne's debate seems to be conducted. As we have seen, it is the succession of such biblical commentators that can give us a sense of the ever-changing interpretations of passages like this. Though it is impossible to be sure in such an impressionistic dialogue, it would seem that it is the voice of the 'commentator' that shifts its ground to a new cliché each time Sterne undermines the last with a further textual detail. As Sterne scornfully concludes, 'the world talks of everything'. Even that key word 'sentimental' is casually thrown to the commentator, though whether in irony or not is left to us. Sterne's own reading, however, is very revealing. It depends not upon

[44] M.M. Bakhtin, 'Discourse in the Novel', in *The Dialogic Imagination*, ed. Michael Holquist, trs. Caryl Emerson and Michael Holquist, Austin: University of Texas Press, 1981, pp. 272–3.

knee-jerk conventional moralistic judgements, but upon a careful
'second hearing', for, like all other stories, 'much of it depends upon
the telling'. Since, as so often in the Bible, the text does not give us any
clue as to how we should read it, we must turn to the response of our
own inner feelings, or, in the phraseology of the period, our 'sentiments' for a lead: ''tis a story on which the heart cannot be at a loss for
what to say, or the imagination for what to suppose'. We have already
seen enough of the history of biblical interpretation to realise just how
dramatic a break with the past such an approach represents. In place
of traditional fourfold polysemous readings is Sterne's dramatic dialogue – as multivocal in its own way as a passage of Shakespeare.
Moreover, so far from trying to eliminate individual or idiosyncratic
responses, Sterne takes it for granted that, subject to internal textual
authority, it is the personal response of heart and imagination that is
all-important – or even more, that it is in some sense the *purpose* of holy
scripture to awaken the emotions and the imagination to their proper
function. Indeed, 'Humanity may say too much': there is a point
beyond which commentary is not merely superfluous, but even
counter-productive, in that it can get in the way of the immediacy of
our own human responses.

What begins to emerge here is less like Thomas Mann than
Kierkegaard in *Fear and Trembling*, who takes a single biblical story –
that of Abraham and Isaac – and tells and retells it, showing in turn
how each obvious interpretation is wrong, and forcing the reader
progressively away from each easy paraphrase back to the mysterious
awkwardness of the text itself. Though, as one might expect, it is unlike
anything else that is going on at this time in eighteenth-century
sermon-writing, there are parallels in at least one contemporary
commentary (in *The Royal Bible*) that suggest the method itself would
not be totally unfamiliar to his audience. This, though it still bases itself
on earlier tradition, turns not to the Fathers, but to Josephus, and
centres itself on the feelings of the characters involved rather than their
typological significance. He, however, is no authority, and is criticised
for suggesting that the concubine's death results from her shame at the
gang-rape rather than its innate violence. What is significant about this
gloss, of course, is not so much that it rejects his internalised version, on
the grounds that he is trying to excuse her abductors, as that it selects
this particular, what one might call, narratalogical, aspect of Josephus
for comment in the first place. The nearest parallel in terms of dialogue
might perhaps be with Bunyan, but he, of course, is seventeenth

century and, as we all know, belongs to a pre-critical world that is still locked into an ahistorical and allegorical frame of reference.

Yet, as with the commentary on Josephus, we might do well to ponder the case of Bunyan more carefully. Typological reading did not so much exclude plain narrative as assert that it was only one among many possible layers of meaning in a text. Lowth's stated purpose of not denigrating polysemous readings, but of subordinating them to what he saw as the primary historical narrative, was fully consonant with this tradition. Similarly, it would be a modern anachronism to read *Pilgrim's Progress* simply as an 'allegory' – if by that term one meant that it possessed a single univocal level of meaning. There is in any such work an inherent tension between surface narrative and hidden meaning. Each provides a commentary on the other. Part of the peculiar richness of *Pilgrim's Progress* comes from this deceptive ambiguity in its form. The story is presented as a highly traditional work, standing in a long line of such Christian apologetics, that make it closer in spirit to the mediaeval world of *The Pearl* and *Everyman* than to novels such as *Tristram Shandy* or *Mansfield Park*. Yet, even though every name reiterates and even flaunts its allegorical status, insisting that the reader should constantly interpret the story at another level from the overt narrative, the fact remains that the characterisation and action of the narration equally insistently pull the reader back to the surface story. A comparison with a modern allegory, C.S. Lewis' *Pilgrim's Regress*, highlights the difference. Lewis' novella, which is very funny in places, is, of course, overtly modelled on Bunyan – but it is more truly univocal in the sense that the surface story holds little intrinsic interest for the reader unless it is linked with the underlying philosophical schema. *Pilgrim's Progress* is, as it were, a novel in spite of itself – in a sense that *Pilgrim's Regress* is not. There is a tension between plot and meaning in the former quite absent in the latter – and apparently flat cardboard figures, such as Faithful, achieve a life of their own. Even more important, for our purpose, the effect of such characterisation is less polysemous than polyphonic. The gap between Bunyan and Sterne is much less than might appear at first glance.

But Bunyan, Kierkegaard or Mann do not turn their accounts into metacritical debates in quite this way. We are exploring not merely the psychological eccentricities of the biblical protagonists, but also of their critics as well. It is as if the conventional commentators Sterne has so carefully expelled from his interpretation of the biblical text have now been re-admitted in their proper role as chorus to his new drama,

before being finally discarded in favour of the silence of the human
heart. I suspect that there is only one proper adjective to apply to all
this, and that, of course, is 'Shandian'.

This brings us to the curious question of Sterne's formative
influences. A.D. Nuttall notes that it is not uncommon to speak of
Tristram Shandy as if it were a reaction to, or parody of, the linear novel,
'despite the mild historical difficulty that Sterne was writing at a period
at which Thackeray, George Eliot and Henry James had not yet
happened, but Rabelais, Cervantes and Swift *had* (the old problem of
the eccentrics outnumbering the normals).' Nuttall continues: 'It really
is more fruitful, I suspect, to see *Tristram Shandy* not as an explosion
from *within* the narrative mode, but as dramatizing an act of invasion
from outside. In this novel the serial order of narration is continually
invaded by the order of explanation.'[45] Replace the word 'novel' in
that last sentence by the words 'biblical story' and we have an almost
exact description of what has been going on in that sermon on the
Levite's concubine. Not merely is the biblical narrative dramatised, but
so keen is Sterne here, as in *Tristram Shandy*, to deal with *all* levels of
explanation, and that nothing shall be left out, that those externally
invasive critics are invited on to the stage to join in the dialogue. It is
hard to say if this is an example of the Bible influencing Sterne,
however, or Sterne rewriting the Bible.

Certainly the result is fraught with ironies of which Sterne could
hardly have been aware. It is difficult, for example, to imagine that he
was as conscious as we are of the degree to which the Bible, as it was
mediated to him in the cultural climate of eighteenth-century Protestant England, was the product of more than a thousand years of such
dialogue – in which the critics were indeed very much on-stage. In *The
Long Search*, the BBC television series on comparative religion, the
presenter, Ronald Eyre, interviews a rabbi, and comments that
whereas all the other religious authorities he had interviewed began by
expounding their particular creeds, the Jewish ones had always begun
by asking questions. The rabbi smiles at him and says, 'Now I wonder
why you say that?' Judaism, Eyre concludes, can be described as
essentially a three-thousand-year-old dialogue with God. It is that
dialogic element, so long neglected by the more authoritarian and
centralised traditions of Christian exegesis, that Sterne's ear has uner-
ringly picked up.

[45] A.D. Nuttall, *Openings*, Oxford University Press, 1992, pp. 157–8.

For England, the latest passage in that critical dialogue had occurred less than twenty years before Sterne's sermon. We recall the implicit programme of Lowth's *Lectures*:

nor is it enough to be acquainted with the language of this people, their manners, discipline, rites and ceremonies; we must even investigate their inmost sentiments, the manner and connexion of their thoughts; in one word, we must see all things with their eyes, estimate all things by their opinion: we must endeavour as much as possible to read Hebrew as the Hebrews would have read it.[46]

Just because of the extraordinary appeal of this agenda to German biblical historians such as Michaelis, Reimarus and Eichhorn, it has been all too easy to miss other, and quite different, resonances. The call for the exegete to become acquainted with the ancient Hebrews' 'manners, discipline, rites and ceremonies' is indeed a demand for historical research – and in the context of Oxford in the 1740s it was revolutionary enough; but to 'investigate' what Lowth calls 'their inmost sentiments, the manner and connexion of their thoughts', implies not so much historical knowledge as empathy, even psychology. In fact, we can be more precise: the use of 'sentiment' in this context is a direct appeal to a word that, even before Sterne had used it in the title of his second novel, had become a key to eighteenth-century feeling. It carried connotations not merely of the way a community thought, but also how it felt, and, in particular, about how it thought about what it felt. Though the word had been in the language since the fifteenth century, the context very clearly suggests that Lowth is edging his way towards this relatively new eighteenth-century meaning – shortly to be popularised by Sterne. The 'manner and connexion of their thoughts' is no less precise in its reference – immediately invoking Locke on the association of ideas. Locke had observed how cultural particularities – especially those of religious sects – are created and reinforced by habitual association of ideas.[47] So, the creator of Uncle Toby might have added, are most human obsessions. As Nuttall has suggested, much of Sterne's comedy stems from the fact that he saw the innate absurdity of Lockean psychology while believing implicitly in its truth.[48] What has not been noted is that Sterne's psychological and

---

[46] Robert Lowth, *Lectures on the Sacred Poetry of the Hebrews*, trs. G. Gregory, 1787, vol. I, pp. 113, 114.

[47] John Locke, *Essay Concerning Human Understanding*, 1690. See in particular Book II, ch. 33: 'Of the Association of Ideas'.

[48] A.D. Nuttall, *A Common Sky: Philosophy and the Literary Imagination*, Chatto, 1974, ch. 1.

novelistic treatment of the Bible is actually directly sanctioned by no less an authority than Bishop Lowth himself.

We cannot, of course, know for certain that Sterne had read Lowth. Sterne was a Cambridge not an Oxford man, but he was well read none the less. Lowth published, as he had lectured, in Latin, and he was not translated into English until 1783. Nor, it is true, do all Sterne's sermons work in this dialogic manner. But Sterne was not merely a good preacher; he was, at least in the York area, a famous one.[49] The way in which, when his imagination does catch fire, he turns biblical narrative not merely into dialogue, but into what is essentially metacritical dialogue, is one of the most extraordinary spectacles of the eighteenth century. It suggests that *Tristram Shandy* is far more rooted in the Bible than one might have any reason to suspect at first reading; no less significantly, it also suggests an answer to the problem that was puzzling Hans Frei in the quotation with which we began. Historical criticism of the Bible did not take hold in England as it was to do in Germany precisely *because* England had a more highly developed novel tradition and theory of prose fiction. As we see very clearly with the next generation of English critics, such as Coleridge, it is not the scholarly distancing of historicism so much as the psychological intimacies of hermeneutics that were to fascinate them. When Coleridge, who certainly *had* read Lowth, says that he takes up the Bible to read it for the first time as he would 'any other work',[50] I suspect his view of what constitutes that 'other work' is much more shaped by the tradition of the English novel than he knows. I suspect also that his assumptions about the nature of the Bible were shaped less by Eichhorn and more by Sterne than he had any idea of.

Though one can hardly argue the case for a fundamental shift in the reading habits of a nation on the originality of one highly eccentric novelist, however influential he was to prove, it is possible to see in Sterne both the beginning and a symptom of a much larger trend. We see it again in the early nineteenth century in Lamb's parallel desire to appropriate Shakespeare into prose narrative: internalised, psychologised and novelised. If Sterne had begun by choosing to turn certain passages of the Bible into dialogue, Byron, for instance, could follow by turning others into a play. His *Cain* is one of the first of a whole series of nineteenth-century dramatisations

---

[49] Cash, *Laurence Sterne*, p. 216.
[50] S.T. Coleridge, *Confessions of an Inquiring Spirit*, 2nd edn, 1849, p. 9.

of biblical stories.[51] More significantly, by the early years of the nineteenth century that hermeneutic sea-change had affected the nature of even the most conservative biblical commentaries. Though Mrs Trimmer, for instance, makes gestures in the direction of traditional polysemous interpretations, she has no real stomach for any but the literal meaning – and the most obvious of morals to be deduced from it. Moreover, as we have seen, unlike earlier commentators, her reaction to the behaviour of Jacob in stealing his brother's birthright, is one of barely concealed embarrassment. We can trace a similar development in the case of the Levite's concubine. Seventeenth-century commentaries can still quote Ambrose with equanimity, and find in the story a typological condemnation of the laxity of the time;[52] as we have seen, one eighteenth-century commentary examines and rejects a crudely psychologised version from antiquity. Mrs Trimmer, however, finds the whole episode so disturbing that she can only comment on Judges 19, 20 and 21 that:

These chapters give an account of some shocking and dreadful things that happened in Israel in the days of Phineas the high priest ... when the Israelites had in a great measure forsaken the LORD, particularly the tribe of Benjamin, and committed all kinds of abominable deeds, which at last occasioned a civil war, and almost all the tribe of Benjamin was cut off.[53]

All opportunity for typology has been abandoned and her response is now entirely dominated by the historical narrative. This is entirely in keeping with her own introduction to the Bible, which, without denying the possibility of figural interpretations, insists on their strictly secondary status:

it has pleased GOD to cause the HOLY SCRIPTURES to be written with such clearness and plainness, that all who will study them with humility and diligence may understand, as much at least of them as is necessary for their comfort in this world, and their salvation in the next. Those who have but little leisure, therefore, have no occasion to puzzle themselves to find out *hidden meanings* in difficult passages..[54]

A casual reading might suggest that this rejection of hidden meanings and polysemous interpretations represents the triumph of the historical method, but that would, I think, be to perpetuate the confusion that we

---

[51] Coleridge had, of course, earlier attempted a 'dramatic poem' on the same theme – much of the material of which was later to appear in *The Rhyme of the Ancient Mariner*.

[52] *History of the Old and New Testaments*, p. 72.

[53] Trimmer, *Help to the Unlearned*, p. 144.

[54] *Ibid.*, p. v.

have already seen in Hans Frei's analysis. Mrs Trimmer's criterion is not historical verisimilitude; nor does she even apparently suspect for a moment that there might be textual problems with any of her material. On the contrary, she is totally engrossed in the narrative before her and reads it with the same attention to character and plot as she might any secular novel. But, of course, as she reminds us, this is self-evidently much *more* than any secular novel – and hence, in part, her horror at the story once it is read in purely human terms. Here is her introduction to the historical narratives themselves.

The Books that follow, as far as the BOOK OF ESTHER, are called the HISTORICAL BOOKS. The Histories they contain differ from all the other histories that ever were written, for they give an account of the ways of GOD; and explain *why* GOD *protected and rewarded* some persons and nations, and *why* he *punished* others; also, *what led* particular persons mentioned in Scripture to *do* certain things for which they were approved or condemned; whereas writers who compose histories in a common way, without being *inspired of God*, can only form guesses and conjectures concerning God's dealings with mankind, neither can they know what passed in the hearts of those they write about; such knowledge as this, belongs to *God* alone, whose ways are *unsearchable and past finding out*, and *to whom all hearts are open, all desires known!* [55]

Fielding's author as Calvinistic God pales into insignificance beside this extraordinary portrait of a Calvinistic God as author. Gone indeed are the 'hidden meanings', the fourfold readings of scripture and the figural interpretations of an Ambrose or an Augustine. This is, rather, Sterne's novelised and internalised version of the scriptures read back into the Bible as a commentary. Its narratives are treated as those of a novel, peopled by characters with recognisable psychological motivations and feelings. The only difference is that these are *not*, of course, fictional characters, but *real* ones, described for us by the only truly omniscient Author.

The significance of Mrs Trimmer is that so far from being an original in the sense that Sterne was, she is consciously addressing the 'unlearned' and adapting her remarks to 'common apprehensions'. Indeed, she stresses that her account of the Bible is no more than a collection of the observations of the most learned and 'approved' authorities. She may, nevertheless, be rather more original here than her modesty implies. Though David Norton recognises that there was a revolution in taste concerning the literary qualities of the Bible in exactly the period we are considering, between about 1760 and 1790,

[55] *Ibid.*, p. iii.

his evidence suggests that claims for the Bible in terms of its character-isation (as distinct from its literary style) were still comparatively rare. Indeed, among his examples only Samuel Pratt's *The Sublime and the Beautiful of Scripture* (1777) comes anywhere near such a discussion.[56] But of course Mrs Trimmer's claim is not about the creation of character as a literary artifact, but a much more literalistic one that God understood the characters of the Old Testament as no human historian or novelist possibly could. And here her admission to second-handedness is itself of interest. If her commentary is indeed no more than popular distillation of the conventional wisdom of the time, then it is possible to argue that what we are looking at is, in effect, the results of a highly successful appropriation. That there *was* such a fundamental and permanent change in the way in which the Bible was read around the end of the eighteenth century is not, I think, in question. To see Lowth, together perhaps with Richard Simon, as father of the higher criticism is certainly accurate as far as it goes, but that does not exclude an opposite effect: that the ways of reading the Bible begun with him, so far from leading *only* towards the higher criticism, had also created a new dialogic fiction – eventually so powerful and all-pervasive that those coming afterwards are scarcely conscious that there might have been other ways of reading the sacred history. Without anyone apparently being aware of what had been happening, the new 'sentimental' and novelistic way of reading the Bible had by the early nineteenth century become the accepted norm. The problem is whether the new way of reading was, as has been generally assumed, fundamentally 'historical', and concerned first and foremost with questions of narrative veracity, or whether it involved something that at first glance looked very like this, but was in fact much more concerned with seeing the biblical protagonists as individual characters of the kind made familiar through the new literary genre of the novel and possessed of a quite new kind of inner consciousness.

THE IRON GATE TO THE NARRATIVE GARDEN

It would, no doubt, have pleased Sterne inordinately had he been able to know both the extent and the unpredictability of his posthumous influence on later writers. Jane Austen, for instance, is not always seen as owing much to him – but consider, for instance, the following

---

[56] David Norton, *History of the Bible as Literature*, Cambridge University Press, vol. II, pp. 116–17.

passage in chapter 10 of the first book of *Mansfield Park*, where the various protagonists approach the iron gate that leads from the wilderness to the main park in the grounds of Sotherton, the house of Rushworth, Maria Bertram's fiancé. Since Maria has set her heart on going through it, Rushworth goes to get the key; Henry Crawford, who comes upon her moments later, comments on the contrast between her immediate dissatisfaction and the beauty of the scenery before them: 'Your prospects, however, are too fair to justify your want of spirits. You have a very smiling scene before you.' Maria at once takes him up on the still-innocent double meaning, her language now alerting the reader to the possibility of further layers of significance in what follows:

'Do you mean literally or figuratively? Literally, I conclude. Yes, certainly, the sun shines and the park looks very cheerful. But unluckily that iron gate, that ha-ha, give me a feeling of restraint and hardship. "I cannot get out", as the starling said.' As she spoke, and it was with expression, she walked to the gate; he followed her. 'Mr Rushworth is so long fetching this key!'

The reference to the caged starling is from Sterne's *Sentimental Journey* – and it strikes a whole series of further literary and figurative resonances.[57] It reminds us, to begin with, how familiar Jane Austen was with Sterne, and how in making such an overt reference she could apparently appeal to a readership that would immediately follow her. It also suggests how, despite the obvious dissimilarities, she could model certain aspects of her style on his. The caged bird was a commonplace metonym for the soul or *anima* locked in the carnal prison of the body; even before the French Revolution it had acquired further connotations of restraint versus *liberté*; finally, and most pertinent here, being caged had become a familar metaphor for the condition of trapped women[58] – specifically, Maria's 'feeling of restraint' encapsulates succinctly her dilemma that the price of becoming mistress of the very desirable estate of Sotherton is marriage to the obnoxious and patently silly Rushworth. The implied appeal to Crawford to 'rescue' her takes on a further irony from the fact that the hero of the *Sentimental Journey*, though he presents himself as a modern-day knight errant (albeit a self-deprecating and comic one), proves

[57] Among others is the episode in Richardson's *Clarissa* where she initiates her 'expulsion from the garden' (seen in Edenic imagery) by agreeing to meet Lovelace at the gate – where there is also much play with locks, keys, etc. (See Alistair Duckworth, *The Improvement of the Estate: a Study of Jane Austen's Novels*, Baltimore, Md.: Johns Hopkins University Press, 1971, p. 18.)

[58] See Lorenz Eitner, 'Cages, Prisons, and Captives in Eighteenth Century Art', in K. Kroeber and W. Walling (eds.), *Images of Romanticism*, New Haven, Conn.: Yale University Press, 1978. I am indebted to Rivkah Zim for this illustration.

himself in practice only too willing to take advantage of his damsels in distress when occasion offers. Crawford's response is immediate and in the light of his later seduction of her, only too clear. He persuades Maria to squeeze round the gate, saying:

And for the world you would not get on without the key and without Mr Rushworth's authority and protection, as I think you might with little difficulty pass round the edge of the gate, here, with my assistance; I think it might be done if you really wish to be more at large, and could allow yourself to think it is not prohibited.[59]

Critics have long observed the so-called 'symbolism' of the visit to Mr Rushworth's estate in *Mansfield Park*. It is not an accident of the novel's spiritual topography that Mary Crawford has a long discussion with Edmund, the hero, who is about to be ordained, on the role of a clergyman while the party is strolling in the part of the garden technically known as 'the wilderness' – nor that her attempts to dissuade him should be on a serpentine path deviating from the main axis. Nor, similarly, is it any accident that when they eventually come to the little iron gate that leads from the wilderness to the main park each member of the party acts in such a way as to foreshadow their eventual approach to marriage. Mr Rushworth, the legal owner of the estate, and the legally betrothed fiancé of Maria, goes to get the legal 'key', but this, like the marriage it represents, takes time – time enough for the unscrupulous Crawford to suggest an easier route to instant gratification and release. Julia Bertram, Maria's sister, who later elopes with Mr Yates, simply scrambles across the ha-ha in their wake, while Fanny, ever the passive if virtuous heroine, remains on the right side, waits for Edmund (whom she is eventually to marry) – and complains of a headache.

Much of this has been noted before – as 'symbolism'.[60] But, of course, it is not. It is, however ironic in its employment, old-fashioned biblical typology of the sort that Parson Austen's daughter was accustomed to hearing every Sunday from the pulpit. The fourfold senses of the text are as much present here as they might be in any traditional commentary on Genesis – however much the spirit behind them may have changed. The reference to the caged starling itself suggests a spiritual, a moral/political and a personal reference ('what shall it profit a man, if he shall gain the whole world and lose his own

---

[59] *Mansfield Park*, ed. R.W. Chapman, 3rd edn, Oxford: Clarendon Press, 1934, p. 99.
[60] For instance Tony Tanner, *Jane Austen*, Macmillan, 1986, pp. 160–2.

soul?', Mark 8: 36). Similarly, in encountering the gate the literal sense of the narrative is complemented by the typological: each character foreshadows his or her later sexual behaviour, and consequently their ordained fate, within the novel. Morally we see that waiting for legal marriage, as the 'key' to future happiness, though it takes more time and denies immediate gratification, is the correct course. In mediaeval typology the anagogical sense normally was taken to foreshadow a future state beyond time – the type of a spiritual paradise. Here what is being decided is who is to eventually inherit the 'estate' itself – and the double meaning, now archaic, of both 'land' and 'position' is significant. By eloping with Crawford, Maria violates at once both propriety and property,[61] thus forfeiting not merely her social status but (in jilting Ruthworth) also Sotherton; Fanny gains not just Edmund's love, but also (spiritually, as the wife of the incumbent) Mansfield Park itself, even the name of which ('Mans-field') in the novel has a clearly allegorical reference to the human condition.

But even this typological rereading of the incident is in danger of missing much of its significance unless we observe the degree to which, historically, it faces two ways. On the one hand, as we have seen, with its explicit reference to Sterne and his new inward characterisation based on the contingencies of personal motivation, it takes the development of character in the novel a stage further; on the other, with its redeployment of multilayered biblical typology, it looks back to, and effectively appropriates, a two-thousand-year-old tradition of textual exegesis. Moreover, as we read the Sotherton chapter we realise that this act of appropriation is not simply a matter of redeploying a traditional technique; it is an essential part of the scene that it sits at the centre of a finely reticulated web of association and influence reaching out to every part of the framework of human history as it was then understood.

As a title, *Mansfield Park* appears at first sight to be an exception to Austen's general practice of naming her novels after a theme. *Sense and Sensibility*, *Pride and Prejudice* and *Persuasion* are all named after abstract qualities that immediately alert us to crucial aspects of their plots; if we accept that the study of a single character may also constitute such a theme, even *Emma* may be held to adhere to this general rule. *Mansfield Park*, however, like *Northanger Abbey*, is the name of a place – not merely

---

[61] As Coleridge points out, the separation in meaning (or desynonymy) of these two words was comparatively recent (*Biographia Literaria*, ed. J. Shawcross, Oxford University Press, 1907, vol. I, p. 61).

a house, but quite literally a house-and-garden; an estate. The name of the latter novel, Austen's first, is clearly a pointer to its status as a satire on the conventions of the gothic novel. 'Abbeys' can be old, mysterious, even sinister – and, as the fifteen-year-old author of a 'History of England' had surmised, part of Henry VIII's effort to 'improve' the landscape by scattering so many elegant ruins across it. But we must be careful here: Donwell Abbey in *Emma*, Knightly's home, is patently none of these things. Mansfield, however, drew its wealth not from the appropriation of former monastic lands, but, we are told quite explicitly, from slavery in Antigua. Moreover, it is a park, not an abbey. A number of critics have convincingly argued that the emphasis on place in this novel is an expression of Austen's political conservatism in face of the French Revolution, and a way of stressing the positive conservative values of order, harmony and continuity represented by a large country estate as it is handed down over the generations.[62] Yet that does not fully explain why the story of the sufferings and eventual triumph of Fanny Price should be called after a garden – or, indeed, why the key incident described above should take place in another garden. Gardens, it would seem, have a central and particular significance in this novel.

Interestingly enough, we are told more about the garden and grounds of Sotherton in the course of that one, outwardly uneventful visit, than we are about Mansfield Park itself in the whole novel. What we learn about it is that, though it is large and well kept, it is essentially old-fashioned in design and layout. But as a historical presence it is dead: neither Rushworth, nor his mother, who shows the visitors around, has any real sympathy for what tradition represents; the chapel is disused and no longer the centre of a living community. The house itself has large lofty rooms, 'amply furnished in the taste of fifty years back, with shining floors, solid mahogany, rich damask, marble, gilding, and carving, each handsome in its way'.[63] Since *Mansfield Park* was written between 1811 and 1813 and published in 1814 that would effectively place Sotherton's style in the early 1760s – at a period when 'Capability' Brown and his successor, Humphry Repton, were busy transforming the parkland of England from the earlier more formal

---

[62] Duckworth, *The Improvement of the Estate*; see also Lionel Trilling, 'Jane Austen and *Mansfield Park*', in Boris Ford (ed.), *From Blake to Byron*, Harmondsworth: Pelican, 1957; Marilyn Butler, *Jane Austen and the War of Ideas*, Oxford University Press, 1975; and Park Honan, *Jane Austen*, Weidenfield and Nicolson, 1987.

[63] *Mansfield Park*, Book I, ch. 9, p. 84.

layouts to the open, 'natural' look that was to become famous throughout Europe as the 'English Garden'. It is clear, however, that though Rushworth would dearly love to employ Repton to 'improve' them, Sotherton's grounds are shaped in the style of Bridgeman and Kent. We know from other novels that Austen preferred this earlier eighteenth-century style as being even more 'English' than the open parkland favoured by Brown. Indeed, Knightly's Donwell Abbey, in *Emma*, is specifically described as having all the characteristics that Rushworth and the Crawfords so scorn at Sotherton.

[Emma] felt all the honest pride and complacency which her alliance with the present and future proprietor could fairly warrant, as she viewed the respectable size and style of the building, its suitable, becoming characteristic situation, low and sheltered – its ample gardens stretching down to meadows washed by a stream, of which the Abbey, with all the old neglect of prospect, had scarcely a sight – its abundance of timber in rows and avenues, which neither fashion nor extravagance had rooted up. – The house was larger than Hartfield, and totally unlike it, covering a good deal of ground, rambling and irregular, with many comfortable and one or two handsome rooms. – It was just what it ought to be, and it looked what it was – and Emma felt an increasing respect for it, as the residence of a family of true gentility, untainted in blood and understanding.[64]

Like Sotherton, Donwell is in a valley and, though that gives it more shelter, lacks 'prospect' – in contrast with the elevated setting of more modern country houses; like Sotherton, its timber is in straight rows and avenues – in contrast, again, with the more studiedly 'natural' groupings of trees favoured by Brown and Repton. Above all, the house has not been refaced or modernised into regularity: it shows a kind of honesty and integrity through the age and history of its architecture.

Rushworth, confronted at Sotherton by what is evidently a very similar kind of house and garden to Donwell has a predictably adverse reaction. He has no knowledge of or feeling for its history and what it might stand for. For him, the contrast with Repton's modernising of his friend Smith's estate at Clopton, makes Sotherton looks 'like a prison – quite a dismal old prison ... It wants improvement ... beyond anything. I never saw a place that wanted so much improvement in my life: and it is so forlorn, that I do not know what can be done with it.'[65] That word 'prison' ironically prefigures Maria's later speech about the iron

---

[64] *Emma*, ch. 42.
[65] *Mansfield Park*, Book I, ch. 6, p. 53.

railing and the gate, and has – as we shall see – several layers of significance. It also tells us indirectly much about the way in which the garden is arranged, in both a physical and a figurative sense. Physically, it is still divided up, in the old-fashioned manner, into walled gardens, enclosed spaces and tree-lined avenues, but the revulsion of Rush-worth, the Crawfords and the Bertram sisters against the rigidity and formal enclosure of this older type of garden is not merely a revulsion of fashion, it is also, at a much deeper level a rejection of the figurative and metaphysical meaning inseparable from such a traditional garden.

Until the mid-eighteenth century the creation of a garden was seen as not merely a cultural, but quite explicitly a historical and even a religious exercise. It recreated the sanctuary of an ancient Arcady or the Paradise of Adam and Eve; a hermitage, a haven of solitude or a setting for theatre and display.[66] Pagan associations with classical mythology, filtered through the Latin literary tradition of writings on villa and rural life which included works by Virgil, Pliny and Cicero, were balanced by biblical and Christian imagery. Thus the first modern book on garden design, *Hypnerotomachia Poliphili* (Venice, 1499), was adorned with woodcuts of temples and other classical ornaments suitable for the embellishment of what was, in effect, a philosophical or even metaphysical statement about its owner and his lineage – 'the temple with the pyramid', 'the tomb of Adonis' and so on.[67] This was the beginning of a long tradition of allegorical garden architecture that celebrated not merely the joys of intellectual seclusion, but also, to the initiated, even esoteric ideas of the progress of the soul. It also contained another monument not irrelevant to the events at Sotherton: a statue of Priapus 'under a canopy of foliage' – for Priapus was not merely the Roman deity of sexual prowess, he was also specifically the tutelary god of gardens. This classical association of gardens with sexual desire was reinforced in the Middle Ages when the enclosed walled garden, the *hortus conclusus*, was also sometimes given overtly female, even vaginal, associations.

For many Renaissance gardeners Christian and classical motifs could co-exist without strain. 'God Almightie first planted a Garden', wrote Bacon at the beginning of his essay *Of Gardens* (1625). Erasmus' *Convivium religiosum*, a dialogue in an idealised garden, though modelled

---

[66] J. Baltrusaitis, cited in Monique Mosser and Georges Teyssot (eds.), *The History of Garden Design: the Western Tradition from the Renaissance to the Present Day*, Thames and Hudson, 1991, Introduction, p. 17.

[67] *Ibid.*, p. 12.

on a Ciceronian dialogue, has St Peter as porter at the garden gate, and Christ as Priapus.[68] Similarly, few of the many eighteenth-century English discussions of gardens could escape appropriate references to the description of Eden in Milton's *Paradise Lost*. The two traditions of figurative imagery contributed to the neo-classical topos of *beatus ille*: the happy man, whose contentment was attributed to his rural dwelling and (given the elision of Christian with Roman ideas) his virtuous, even pious, appreciation of the harmonious scheme of nature and its benevolent Creator.[69] The topography of gardens became mirrors of the moral life. At the Villa d'Este the visitor had to choose between taking the easy path to the grotto of Venus, or a steep uphill climb to the grotto of Diana.[70] An English sampler of 1799 takes the allegory one stage further by picturing the 'happy man' walking in his garden, each part of which is made to correspond to a particular Christian virtue.

Much of this urge to turn a garden into a philosophic statement can be traced to Petrarch. As one historian of garden design puts it:

The link, amounting at times almost to an obsession, between his two enthusiasms, for gardens and for antiquity, may serve to remind us that Renaissance *imitatio* was not mere copying. Gardening became the privileged model for a species of imitation that seeks not to reproduce its object mechanically but to make it grow: to seize those fruitful principles by which the humanity of the ancients might be cultivated within the space of one's own world and one's own sensibility.[71]

For Petrarch and his many successors the garden was peculiarly the place where not merely the ideas of the past might be appropriated and brought, as it were, to bloom in fresh soil, but where the *idea* of the past itself might be appropriated. What makes Petrarch, in Schlegel's terminology, a 'modern' rather than a 'classic' is that he is aware of the past and his roots in it, in a way that the classical civilisation that preceded his, was not. We recall again Plumb's characterisation of European civilisation in terms of its awareness of its multiple pasts.[72] The past is the single most dominating presence in Renaissance art.

---

[68] Terry Comito, 'The Humanist Garden', in Monique Mosser and Georges Teyssot (eds.), *The History of Garden Design: the Western Tradition from the Renaissance to the Present Day*, Thames and Hudson, 1991, p. 37.

[69] John Dixon Hunt and Peter Willis (eds.), *The Genius of the Place: the English Landscape Garden 1620–1820*, 2nd edn, Cambridge, Mass.: MIT Press, 1988, Introduction, p. 11.

[70] Comito, 'The Humanist Garden', p. 41.

[71] *Ibid.*, p. 38.

[72] See Introduction above, p. 5.

But gardening was not a matter of slavish imitation. Just because it was something living and growing, it provided the perfect metaphor for the way in which the new humanists sought to appropriate and use the wisdom and culture of that earlier civilisation. It was, not least, a way of exorcising that huge shadow of antiquity under which they perceived their own labours as taking place.

It is this concept of the garden as a means of appropriating history, not as a dead catalogue of past events, but as a living and dynamic culture in perpetual dialogue with the present, that underlies and gives significance to so many of the seemingly trivial events and conversations in *Mansfield Park* – or rather, as we shall see, what underlies them is the *failure* of almost all the protagonists, with the exception of Fanny, to understand this traditional meaning of a garden, and therefore of both Sotherton and of Mansfield Park itself. To grasp the context and extent of this failure, and its symbolic consequences, we must turn to the history of English garden design in the eighteenth century – before the time of Brown and Repton.

Following the Renaissance tradition, many early eighteenth-century writers and artists saw in gardening a kind of synaesthesia. Addison, Shaftsbury and Pope are quick to compare the artifice of the garden with that of painting. 'All gardening is landscape-painting', writes Pope; 'Just like a landscape hung-up.' But he is equally quick to establish the links between painting and poetry: *ut pictura poesis*, 'as in a picture, so in a poem'.[73] Dryden's essay on the *Parallel of Poetry and Painting* was re-issued in 1719 with Pope's own 'Epistle to Jervas'. Nor did this nexus of gardening, painting and poetry complete the complicated pattern of cross-reference, for garden design was also explicitly compared with that other meeting-point of painting and poetry, the theatre. As the *OED* shows, the words 'scene' and 'scenery', applied to a garden or landscape, came into use during the eighteenth century as direct metaphors from the language of the theatre. It is significant that William Kent, perhaps the greatest garden-designer of the early part of the century, had, like Vanburgh a generation earlier, come to horticulture from being a successful stage-designer. Contemporary descriptions of gardens treat them in terms of 'scenes' as the visitor comes round a corner or approaches a fresh vantage-point. Just as the landscape of

---

[73] Cited by John Dixon Hunt, ' "Ut Pictura Poesis": the Garden and the Picturesque in England (1710–1750)', in Monique Mosser and Georges Teyssot (eds.), *The History of Garden Design: the Western Tradition from the Renaissance to the Present Day*, Thames and Hudson, 1991, p. 231.

history-painting provided the 'scenery' for the 'actors' in some great event, so the scenery of a landscape garden provided the backdrop against which visitors might themselves become actors as well as spectators.[74]

Kent was one of the pioneers of the thematic garden. As an associate of Lord Burlington, creator of the great garden at Chiswick, he was a member of a circle which included the poet Pope – who not merely wrote on the theory of the landscape garden in verse and prose, but also created his own garden, on a miniature scale, at his villa in Twickenham, complete with a much-admired grotto. One of Kent's surviving sketches is of an imaginary landscape illustrating the progress of culture from ancient Rome to contemporary England.[75] His design for Rousham in Oxfordshire brought the Renaissance ideal of an allegorical garden into the eighteenth-century landscape. Here not merely the buildings, but the order in which they were encountered became important. The same was true at Stowe, where Kent made extensive alterations to Bridgeman's layout of the gardens, and at Stourhead, a joint composition of one of Kent's associates, Henry Flitcroft, and of the owner himself, Henry Hoare. Phrases from Milton, Pope, Akenside, Virgil and Ovid sprinkle Hoare's letters on the planning of the garden to his nephew and heir, Richard.[76] On the Temple of Flora at Stourhead, where the visitor begins the circular walk, is the portentous inscription, from Book VI of the *Aeneid*: *Procul, O procul este profani* ('Begone, you who are uninitiated! Begone!) and a number of recent scholars have argued that it was intended as a clue to an esoteric meaning to the whole garden.[77] Others, noticing the presence not merely of the gothic cottage, but of the parish church and of Alfred's Tower, have preferred to see the garden more in terms of a dialectic between classic and Christian values.[78] Certainly any such original Virgilian scheme seems to have been diluted or weakened by later oddities like the (now vanished) 'Turkish tent', which suggest a more dilettante eclecticism. What is not in doubt, however, is that Burlington, Hoare and Pope, like the professionals Bridgeman, Kent

---

[74] *Ibid.*

[75] *Ibid.*, p. 233.

[76] See Kenneth Woodbridge, *The Stourhead Landscape*, The National Trust, 1991, p, 17.

[77] See Kenneth Woodbridge, 'The Sacred Landscape: Painters and the Lake Garden at Stourhead', *Apollo*, vol. 88 (1968), pp. 210–14; Edward Malins, *English Landscape and Literature 1660–1840*, Oxford University Press, 1966; Christopher Hussey, *English Gardens and Landscapes 1700–1750*, *Country Life* 1967; Ronald Paulson, *Emblem and Expression: Meaning in English Art of the Eighteenth Century*, Thames and Hudson, 1975, ch. 2.

[78] See, for instance, Malcolm Kelsall, 'The Iconography of Stourhead', *Journal of the Warburg and Courtauld Institutes*, vol. 46 (1983), pp. 133–43.

and Flitcroft, saw a garden primarily in terms of allegorical meaning, or meanings. As in a history painting, or a stage set, a landscape garden was part of a continuous cultural and moral dialogue with the past: at once an affirmation of belief and a questioning of the relationship of that belief to the past so conjured up. Indeed, even the gothic cottage at Stourhead might well have belonged to such a dialogue. At Stowe, Lord Cobham's so-called Gothic Temple was also the Temple of Liberty, expressing the political principles which formed the main theme of the garden. For Cobham, a leading Whig, the gothic stood for the ancient Anglo-Saxon liberties – including Magna Carta, trial by jury and parliamentary representation. When it was first constructed in 1741 the temple was surrounded by a semi-circle of Saxon deities, while over the door was inscribed (in French) 'I thank the Gods that I am not a Roman' – the implication being that, by benefit of his political institutions, the eighteenth-century Englishman enjoyed greater liberty and happiness than any ancient Roman. The example of Kent's work at Stowe is a reminder, too, that though classical motifs might appear to predominate over biblical, it was always a Christian ('public-school' or, to use a later example, Gladstonian) classicism; the Gothic Temple is not merely a reminder of Saxon liberties, but also of the superiority of Christianity over classical paganism. Even before Dante, Virgil had, of course, long been sanctified as a Christian forerunner, and a properly educated eighteenth-century gentlemen had little difficulty in eliding Anglican and classical rural virtues.

Everything we are told of the grounds at Sotherton makes it clear that they belong in plan and style to this tradition of implicit meaning. The grand avenue, the lawn, bounded on each side by a high wall, the bowling-green, the long terrace walk and the wilderness, containing both a straight vista and narrower serpentine paths, are all common features of the gardens of the 1730s and 1740s laid out by Kent, Flitcroft and other members of the Burlington circle. Though we may recall, as doubtless Austen intended us to, the sexually charged couplet from Marvell's Coy Mistress urging the lovers to 'tear' their 'pleasures with rough strife / Through the iron gates of life', even the iron palisade and gate leading from the wilderness to the park at Sotherton, to which so much typological importance is attached, is a common, indeed a highly recommended, feature of gardens of this period.[79] Similarly the

---

[79] See for instance, Timothy Nourse, *Campania Foelix* (1700); A.J. Dézallier D'Argenville, *The Theory and Practice of Gardening*, trs. John James (1712); Stephen Switzer, *Iconographia Rustica* (1718 and 1742); in *The Genius of the Place*, pp. 105, 127, 160.

'wilderness', which was a standard feature of any sizeable garden of this period, here takes on a double meaning as both a more 'natural' area, in the current vocabulary of gardening, and, morally, in the novel, as an area free of the normal legal constraints of society where people (the 'actors' in this 'play') express their feelings in ways they otherwise might not. For Fanny, perhaps there is also a biblical resonance: like the Children of Israel wandering in the wilderness before being permitted to enter the Promised Land, she must keep her integrity during this period of trial before coming into her reward. The point is that just as the 'initiated' visitor to a garden like Stourhead would be expected to recognise and understand the multilayered meanings of the classical references in the landscape, so here the initiated reader would be expected to understand how this 'scene' in the novel is part of a dialogue that is at once historical, aesthetic and moral.

This idea of the garden as theatre leads directly on to Mr Yates' proposal to enact Mrs Inchbald's *Lovers' Vows* – a free translation from the German of Kotzbue's play, *Natural Son*.[80] The real irony, of course, is that whereas this plan for a 'false' representation of reality is frustrated by the return of Sir Thomas Bertram, all its actors, including Fanny, have already (though unknown to them because they cannot understand the symbolism of their surroundings) taken part in a 'true' piece of theatre in the grounds of Sotherton. The action of *Lovers' Vows* is thus transformed from a sentimental drama into a work of typological significance. As Baron Wildenheim, Henry Crawford is, once again, Maria Betram's seducer; Rushworth is still a fop; Mary Crawford, as Amelia, is once more in a position to throw herself at Edmund. The link is made even more explicit when in volume III, chapter 5, Mary Crawford quotes the opening lines of the speech of the parson, Anhalt, who was to have been played by Edmund, on the happy marriage – which is framed within an allegorical garden. The full passage is as follows:

When two sympathetic hearts meet in the marriage state, matrimony may be called a happy life. When such a wedded pair find thorns in their path, each will be eager, for the sake of the other, to tear them from the root. Where they have to mount hills, or wind a labyrinth, the most experienced will lead the way, and be a guide to his companion. Patience and love will accompany

---

[80] There were in fact no fewer than four different English translations of *Natural Son* published between 1798 and 1800, all, somewhat confusingly, with the title *Lovers' Vows*; but only Mrs Inchbald's seems to have been performed, and, as Mary Crawford's quotation in vol. III, ch. 5, makes clear, this is the version Austen is using. It was enormously popular, and by 1799 it had gone through no fewer than twelve editions.

them on their journey, while melancholy and discord they leave far behind. – Hand in hand they pass on from morning till evening, through their summer's day, till the night of age draws on, and the sleep of death overtakes the one. The other, weeping and mourning, yet looks forward to the bright region where he shall meet his still surviving partner, among trees and flowers which they themselves have planted, in fields of eternal verdure.

In contrast, the corresponding portrait of the unhappy marriage is framed within an allegory of imprisonment:

When convenience, and fair appearance joined to folly and ill-humour, forge the fetters of matrimony, they gall with their weight the married pair. Discontented with each other – at variance in their opinions – their mutual aversion increases with the years they live together. They contend most, where they should most unite; torment, where they should most soothe. In this rugged way, choaked with the weeds of suspicion, jealousy, anger, and hatred, they take their daily journey, till one of these *also* sleep in death. The other then lifts up his dejected head, and calls out in acclamations of joy – Oh, liberty! dear liberty![81]

To readers as familiar with *Lovers' Vows* as Jane Austen clearly expects hers to be, there is no further need to spell out the connection between gardens and imprisonment.

But it was precisely this allegorical language of place, with its typological unfolding of meaning, that the present occupants of Sotherton and their friends are both ignorant of, and determined to ignore. Brown and Repton had not merely swept away the last vestiges of the formal garden, with its enclosed parterres, its walls and avenues, they had also deliberately made this new 'open' landscape free of all allusion and meaning. By 1770 Thomas Whately, in his *Observations on Modern Gardening*, could distinguish between what he called 'emblematic' and 'expressive' gardens.[82] Whereas the former used the complex syntax and grammar of history painting, the latter provided vacant spaces into which visitors could insert their own personal meanings. In describing Sotherton as a 'prison' Rushworth is not merely feeling oppressed by the walls and enclosed spaces of the older emblematic garden, he is also (unconsciously no doubt) feeling imprisoned by a weight of implicit significance and a tradition that he is incapable of understanding. He is therefore profoundly alienated from what is, in both literal and figurative terms, his own inheritance. During the tour of the building it becomes clear that neither his

---

[81] Mrs Inchbald, *Lovers' Vows*, reprinted in *Mansfield Park*, pp. 504–5.
[82] Hunt, 'Ut Pictura Poesis', p. 235.

mother nor he have any sympathy with or understanding of the house and its history – a point typologically encapsulated by the disused chapel. Their relationship to their past and the attitude of the visitors is summed up in the guided tour:

Mrs Rushworth began her relation. 'This chapel was fitted up as you see it in James the Second's time. Before that period, as I understand, the pews were only wainscot; and there is some reason to think that the linings and cushions of the pulpit and family seat were only purple cloth; but this is not quite certain. It is a handsome chapel, and was formerly in constant use both morning and evening. Prayers were always read in it by the domestic chaplain, within the memory of many; but the late Mr Rushworth left it off. 'Every generation has its improvements', said Miss Crawford, with a smile, to Edmund.[83]

For Mrs Rushworth their house is essentially a museum. No wonder it has become a 'prison' for her son. The fact that Mary Crawford does not yet know of Edmund's plans to be ordained is only one of the ironies of that last sentence; her use of the same term, 'improvement', for the cessation of prayers that has been used shortly before for the metaphysical stripping of meaning from a garden is part of the debasement of language associated with the destruction of a living tradition.[84] For Austen, Repton would be the perfect 'improver' for a landowner such as Rushworth who wished to sweep away both the culture and the meaning of the past encoded in what was, for her, the traditional English garden.

This attitude of what one might term typological conservatism in *Mansfield Park* is in keeping with other aspects of Austen's conservatism. Critical studies and biographies have alike stressed the innate and even at times polemical conservatism of her views. Two of her brothers became admirals in the Royal Navy fighting against Revolutionary and then Napoleonic France – and she is even recorded as having confessed that her favourite reading was military history. Yet her use of what is at first sight a highly conservative, not to say old-fashioned, system of polysemous biblical interpretation is anything but conservative in its effects. On the contrary it was to give the novel a new kind of depth and narrative resonance at the very time that the biblical narratives, from whose exegesis it was derived, were increasingly seen in other,

---

[83] Book I, ch. 9, p. 86.
[84] For the way in which this word had become a key term of the period, see, for instance, B.C. Southam, '*Sanditon*: the Seventh Novel', in Juliet McMaster (ed.), *Jane Austen's Achievement*, Macmillan, 1976.

more linear, terms. For example, we have so far been reading the 'scene' in the wilderness at Sotherton purely in terms of its traditional and typological resonances. But it is possible now to dispense with such aids and reread the scene in terms of a psychology that was only slowly being explored in Jane Austen's time, and whose language belongs properly to the late nineteenth and twentieth centuries. Earlier I suggested that Rushworth's desire to 'improve' his patrimony was in part an 'unconscious' resistance to a system of ideas and beliefs he neither understood nor wished to know about. If such an anachronistic word is meaningful in this context, it is because the author has already put in place a vocabulary of her own for revealing aspects of her characters' personalities that are concealed even from themselves and therefore could only be shown indirectly. Thus, if we read attentively, the reiterated 'prison' metaphors of this part of the book tell us much more about the protagonists' states of mind than they themselves would be aware of. If at one level it gives clues to the enclosed nature of the formal gardens at Sotherton, at another, more personal level, it suggests the degree to which Rushworth, in spite of his wealth, feels his lack of any real autonomy or freedom in his life. As his name suggests, he is a lightweight, and the tool of others – manipulated by his mother, the calculating Crawfords, even by Maria Bertram, who secretly despises him.

Maria, however, is 'imprisoned' for a different set of reasons. She has been trapped into what her mother is convinced is a 'good marriage' with Rushworth, but the fact is that, as her brother Edmund (who, we must remember, was Anhalt in *Lovers' Vows*) enigmatically puts it, 'if this man had not twelve thousand a year, he would be a very stupid fellow'. Her appeal at the gate to the much more interesting and attractive Henry Crawford can be read at two levels. Maria wants to be freed, as she puts it, from the 'feeling of restraint' by the society which has entrapped her into the prospect of a loveless marriage, but at the same time there is a suggestion that she is almost over-eager for sexual experience ('Mr Rushworth is so long in fetching this key') – as the ever-attentive Crawford is quick to notice and exploit.

In spite of her Anglican roots and upbringing, and indeed the survival of three prayers in her own handwriting, some critics have argued on the grounds of theme that Jane Austen is the herald of a new secularity in the novel.[85] Others have pointed to the alleged meaning

---

[85] See, for instance, Lawrence Lerner, *The Truthtellers*, Chatto, 1967.

of a remark of Jane Austen's in a letter to her sister, Cassandra, that
Mansfield Park is about 'ordination', as evidence of a strong religious
motivation behind her work.[86] Whatever her personal convictions,
however, it is clear from the texture and allusiveness of her writing that
her religion is not an individualistic Evangelical piety but is inseparable
from a whole cultural and historical nexus.[87] If Fanny does not reflect
the tastes of her creator in anything else, she does in this: her views are
unequivocally High Church. She would have found Keble and
Newman much more to her taste than members of the Clapham Sect
like Simeon or Venn. Moreover, though Austen's novels may appear at
first sight to be entirely naturalistic and secular, if we start to look
beneath the surface, we discover that this secularity forms only the
thinnest of veneers over a narrative structure still heavily dependent on
traditional modes of biblical exegesis. Implicit in the gardens of
Mansfield Park is a typological universe of 'correspondences' remarkably
similar to that of the popular verse of John Keble's *Christian Year*.[88]

From our point of view, however, the question of Austen's private
religious beliefs is irrelevant. What is important is that she clearly
opposes an aesthetic which drains meaning from her fictional landscapes. Her own art, in contrast, rests on systematic appropriation –
extending the synaesthesia of gardens, painting, poetry and drama
beloved of Pope and the Burlington circle to include the novel. Even
the name of her heroine, Fanny Price, is that of the maiden 'chaste and
lovely' in Crabbe's *The Parish Register* who rejects an 'amorous knight' in
favour of the humble and untitled youth she really loves. But the self-
conscious literariness of the novel is only the tip of an iceberg of
submerged meanings that underlies every part of the action and
setting. The 'improvement' of landscape associated in *Mansfield Park*
with Repton is the gardening equivalent of sweeping away the tradition
of visual iconography in painting or the reading of a literary work at
only one level of meaning. Whether that work be a modern novel or
the Bible is here irrelevant; by virtue of being a written narrative, both
are subject to what her contemporary, Coleridge, would have called
'the same laws of association'. What is at stake for her here is the
difference between the educated and the uneducated mind. It is true
that too great a sense of the past can lead to its own absurdities.

---

[86] Honan, *Jane Austen*, p. 336.
[87] The best commentary on this context is probably Oliver MacDonagh, *Jane Austen: Real and Imagined Worlds*, New Haven, Conn.: Yale University Press, 1991, ch. 1.
[88] For Keble's notion of correspondences see Prickett, *Romanticism and Religion*, pp. 105–6.

Fanny's sense of history is sometimes almost as romantic as Catherine Moorland's: in her disappointment over the chapel at Sotherton she exclaims 'This is not my idea of a chapel. There is nothing awful here, nothing melancholy, nothing grand. Here are no aisles, no arches, no inscriptions, no banners. No banners, cousin, to be blown by the night wind of Heaven.' No signs that a 'Scottish monarch sleeps below'.[89] But if she has been reading too much Scott, the alternative is the essentially one-dimensional world of the Rushworths, the Bertram sisters and the Crawfords.

And that one-dimensional world is not merely one of intellectual and spiritual impoverishment; it is, as the ending of the novel makes clear, one of self-destructive sin and error. As the gardening typology subtly makes clear, appropriating the past does not mean being dominated by it, but, on the contrary, providing oneself with the possibility of wholeness and growth; not to be able to appropriate it is to live in the isolation of the moment, and in the end to be at the mercy of forces that can be neither comprehended nor controlled. But there is an important difference here between Rushworth and Crawford. The former, a minor character in the novel, is simply stupid; Crawford is a much more important and subtle creation, as he has to be for there to be any tension in Fanny's rejection of him. The earlier 'theatres' of Sotherton and the aborted rendering of *Lovers' Vows* at Mansfield are balanced by a third moment of 'theatre' when, in Book III, Henry Crawford falls in love with Fanny. This time the play is Shakespeare's *Henry VIII*. When Edmund and Henry enter the room, Lady Bertram explains with her usual precision what she and Fanny have been doing:

'We have not been silent all the time ... Fanny has been reading to me, and only put the book down upon hearing you coming.' – And sure enough there was a book on the table which had the air of being very recently closed, a volume of Shakespeare. – 'She often reads to me out of those books; and she was in the middle of a very fine speech of that man's – What's his name Fanny? – when we heard your footsteps.

Crawford took the volume. 'Let me have the pleasure of finishing that speech to your ladyship', said he. 'I shall find it immediately.' And by carefully giving way to the inclination of the leaves, he did find it, or within a page or two, quite enough to satisfy Lady Bertram, who assured him, as soon as he mentioned the name of Cardinal Wolsey, that he had got the very speech. – Not a look, or an offer of help had Fanny given; not a syllable for or against.

[89] Book I, ch. 9, pp. 85–6. The references appear to be (inexact) quotations from Walter Scott's *Lay of the Last Minstrel*, Canto 2, stanzas XII, and XVI. The 'Scottish monarch' would therefore be Alexander II.

All her attention was for her work. She seemed determined to be interested by nothing else. But taste was too strong in her. She could not abstract her mind five minutes; she was forced to listen; his reading was capital, and her pleasure in good reading extreme. To *good* reading, however, she had long been used; her uncle read well – her cousins all – Edmund very well; but in Mr Crawford's reading there was a variety of excellence beyond what she had ever met with. The King, the Queen, Buckingham, Wolsey, Cromwell, all were given in turn; for with the happiest knack, the happiest power of jumping and guessing, he could always light at will, on the best scene, or the best speeches of each; and whether it be dignity or pride, or tenderness or remorse, or whatever it were to be expressed, he could do it with equal beauty. – It was truly dramatic. – His acting had first taught Fanny what pleasure a play might give, and his reading brought all his acting before her again; nay, perhaps with greater enjoyment, for it came unexpectedly, and with no such drawback as she had been used to suffer in seeing him on the stage with Miss Bertram.[90]

The passage provides several answers to those who express surprise at the gap between Austen's own known love of the theatre and her apparent endorsement of Sir Thomas's ban on amateur theatricals at Mansfield. Crawford, it seems, was 'truly dramatic'. Drama here, for Fanny, does not depend on staging; it can be rendered equally well by reading – 'good reading'; – and, by implication, Shakespeare is in a different class from the trite sentimentalities of Mrs Inchbald. She is here in good company: both Lamb and Coleridge had serious doubts both about whether Shakespeare could, or should, be acted upon the stage, or was actually better in the privacy of the imagination.[91] But, of course, from the reader's viewpoint, another little drama is in progress. We are seeing another of those dramatic epiphanies, those moments of character revelation when both the best and the worst of Henry Crawford are exposed. His confidence – apparently justified – that he can find the exact place (exact enough, at least, for Lady Bertram), his skill at reading and acting a part, his 'happiest knack ... of jumping and guessing' to reach the best bits, are at once part of his charm and an indication of his ultimate shallowness, for, as in *Lovers' Vows*, he is being measured against another, unquoted but omnipresent text, this time that of Shakespeare himself. Crawford is, as he admits himself, a dilettante; his skill is not based on any kind of real knowledge or appreciation of what he is reading. 'That play must be

[90] Book III, ch. 3, pp. 336–7.
[91] Jonathan Bate, *Shakespearean Constitutions: Politics, Theatre, Criticism 1730–1830*, Oxford: Clarendon Press, 1989, pp. 129–34.

a favourite with you', says Edmund; 'You read it as if you knew it well.'

'It will be a favourite I believe from this hour,' replied Crawford; – 'but I do not think I have had a volume of Shakespeare in my hand before, since I was fifteen. – I once saw Henry the 8th acted. – Or I have heard of it from somebody who did – I am not certain which. But Shakespeare one gets acquainted with without knowing how. It is part of an Englishman's constitution. His thoughts and beauties are so spread abroad that one touches them every where, one is intimate with him by instinct. – No man of any brain can open at a good part of one of his plays, without falling into the flow of his meaning immediately.[92]

That last remark, for all its plausibility, is so stunningly silly as almost to obliterate its actual purpose of discreet self-praise. This is Crawford the garden 'improver' all over again. Even the covert imagery of his verbs might be horticultural: 'thoughts and beauties are spread abroad', 'one touches them' and falls 'into the flow' of their meaning. Only this time he is flipping his way through Shakespeare. And yet, of course, as in his response to the grounds at Sotherton, this superficial delight in the language of the plays is totally divorced from any appreciation of either the typological meaning or even simply the plot. Just as he had no idea of what a traditional garden meant, so he has here, by his own confession, no knowledge of Shakespeare's plays, and still less of their underlying morality. There is no accident, one suspects, in the irony that ensures that Crawford begins his reading with Cardinal Wolsey, who 'was ever double / Both in his words and meaning' (*Henry VIII*, 4, ii, 38–9). Henry Crawford, we may suppose, sees himself in the role of Shakespeare's Henry, who (in the play) has to persuade the reluctant and unambitious Anne Bullen to accept the honours thrust upon her. Such figurative deployments of Shakespeare were part of a long tradition of eighteenth-century satire.[93] But if we recall the judgement of the fifteen-year-old Jane Austen in her 'History of England' that 'the crimes and cruelties of this monarch were too numerous to mention' (and that his daughter Mary was little better) it is not surprising that her heroine, Fanny, sees *both* Henrys as self-deceiving and capricious, moving from woman to woman as fancy dictates.

But all this discussion of Shakespeare, it turns out, is merely a preamble to the more serious conversation which follows with Edmund

---

[92] *Ibid.*, p. 338.
[93] Walpole as Wolsey was a stock identification of the 1720s; Fox with Falstaff (the misleader of the Heir Apparent) in the 1790s. See Bate, *Shakespearean Constitutions*, ch. 3.

once again on the topic of 'improvement' – but this time that of sermons. Once again, too, Crawford is eloquent on the superficies of a subject on which he knows nothing of the inner meaning – and once again there are ironies of which he cannot be aware.

A sermon, well delivered, is more uncommon even than prayers well read. A sermon, good in itself, is no rare thing. It is more difficult to speak well than to compose well; that is, the rules and tricks of composition are oftener an object of study. A thoroughly good sermon, thoroughly well delivered, is a capital gratification. I can never hear such a one without the greatest admiration and respect, and more than half a mind to take orders and preach myself. There is something in the eloquence of the pulpit, when it is really eloquence, which is entitled to the highest praise and honour. The preacher who can touch and affect such an heterogeneous mass of hearers, on subjects limited, and long worn thread-bare in all common hands; who can say any thing new or striking, any thing that rouses the attention, without offending the taste, or wearing out the feelings of his hearers, is a man whom one could not (in his public capacity) honour enough.[94]

In other words, Sterne is Crawford's favourite clergyman. That he was also, along with Crabbe, very likely Jane Austen's favourite as well is irrelevant. What Crawford wants to see in his ideal sermon is precisely what Sterne had very deliberately achieved in his. As we have seen, Yorick's sermons show an unrivalled capacity for taking biblical stories, whose typology had been worn thread-bare by generations of commonplace biblical commentaries, and arousing the sentiments of his audience by dramatising the characters, and giving them 'a new or striking' treatment. That the effect of such a 'improvement' was, at least in the case of Crawford, more one of aesthetic 'gratification' than piety cannot be entirely blamed on Sterne. Moreover, the only person in the novel who is recorded as having any reaction to a sermon is actually Lady Bertram, who, upon hearing one, immediately cries herself to sleep.[95]

The point is that Crawford's tastes and sensibility and outlook are those of a thoroughgoing romantic. Whether in religion, literature, gardening or sexual relations, he stresses personal response over convention, private association over traditional typology, feeling over meaning. As a result, just as Rushworth was unaware of the significance of his own horticultural landscape, so Crawford is unaware of the implicit moral judgement passed upon him by his entering into a reading of Shakespeare. If Crawford is not actually aware of Sterne's

[94] *Ibid.*, p. 341.   [95] Book III, ch. 16, p. 453.

sermons – and his remarks on the subject suggest he might well be – his conversation with Edmund makes it clear he has been swept up in the revolution of sensibility which Sterne helped to initiate. Even his wooing of Fanny is self-consciously romantic.

This is not to say that Jane Austen cannot also herself be classified in some senses as romantic. The term is loose and baggy enough to contain many different tastes. Nor, incidentally, was she a stranger either to the meaning of the word 'appropriation' or to the current debate about its practice.[96] She was well aware of Sterne's innovations to the novel, and had studied and put to good use both *Tristram Shandy* and *A Sentimental Journey*. But if aspects of her technique are adapted from Sterne, she also appropriates something equally substantial from the Bible, architecture and garden design of the early eighteenth century, in effect underpinning the new romantic sense of individual character with a traditional, but, by her own time, almost defunct, system of referential meaning. Just at the time when Hegel was suggesting that the failure of the traditional religious underpinning of objective meaning in the world was creating a new subjectivity that spelt 'the end of art',[97] Austen was creating a new literature out of precisely that failure. As Walter Ong has observed, she was virtually the first writer to give the hitherto episodic novel form the tightness of plotting and organisation previously found only in the drama.[98] It is not typology in its traditional sense any more than it is symbolism in its modern sense: typology was never related to individual character in this way; modern symbolism is rarely so precise in its reference. By the time *Mansfield Park* was written, the revolution in reading created by the novel that we traced earlier had changed for ever the way in which the Bible was understood; Austen has not put the clock back, but she has appropriated the traditional polysemous framework of biblical interpretation and incorporated it into the novel in such a way as for us to be scarcely conscious of it happening. As we shall see, in this her nearest twentieth-century equivalent is probably Thomas Mann.

[96] See, for instance, Emma Woodhouse's remark to Harriet Smith of Mrs Elton's charade: 'But take [the couplet] away, and all *appropriation* ceases' (*Emma*, vol. I, ch. 9; Austen's italics). (See also Bate, *Shakespearean Constitutions*, p. 3.)

[97] See Andrew Bowie, *Aesthetics and Subjectivity from Kant to Nietzsche*, Manchester University Press, 1990, p. 9.

[98] Walter J. Ong, *Orality and Literacy: the Technologising of the Word*, Routledge, 1982, p. 144.

CHAPTER 4

The Bible and history: appropriating the Revolution

ROMANTICISM AND REVOLUTION

As Jane Austen had suspected, at the heart of romantic liberation there lurked a devastating sense of loss – the more poignant for being so often unconscious and inarticulate. Henry Crawford's own inner emptiness, which helps to explain his attraction to Fanny, also makes him an ideal candidate for romanticism. Its whole mood has been characterised by a 'sense of longing' for something lost or for ever unattainable or incomplete.[1] In the major poets, this sense of loss – at once personal and cultural – could become a mainspring of their art. For Wordsworth in the *Immortality Ode*, and no less in the autobiographical *Prelude*, it takes the form of a controlled nostalgia for a state of childhood ecstasy that cannot quite be recalled or recreated, but remains liminal, as it were, just *beyond* the threshold of consciousness. Similarly Coleridge's Ancient Mariner is haunted by the idea of a state of innocence that is unrecoverable – and the more desirable for its very impossibility. Keats' Odes betray something of the same nostalgia for a state of health as much psychological as physical. Even Byron's sturdy mockery of such effete sensibilities has at times more than a hint of whistling in the dark. Perhaps most startling of all, however, is Blake's discovery that in order to recapture the prophetic sense of meaning in current events that he believed was available to both biblical and classical worlds, he has to invent a completely new mythology of history.

What had been lost was religion. Not, that is, religion in the sense in which the word has largely been understood ever since the Evangelical revival of the early nineteenth century, of an individual belief in and relationship with a personal God, but rather a general and collective

---

[1] Thomas McFarland, *Romanticism and the Forms of Ruin: Wordsworth, Coleridge, and the Modalities of Fragmentation*, Princeton University Press, 1981, p. 7.

world-picture in which there was no boundary between the sacred and the secular, in which supernatural or divine power was everywhere apprehended through type, symbol and sacrament – and through a language where such apprehension was implied and taken for granted. Thus this is not to deny that in their own, sometimes very idiosyncratic, ways, Blake, Wordsworth and Coleridge, at least, were devout Christians. The point is rather that, unlike Chaucer, Spencer or Browne, in order to be devout, they *had* to be idiosyncratic. The union of personal piety and collective sensibility so evident in, for instance, Donne, Herbert, Crashaw or Marvell, not to mention Milton, was simply no longer a viable option for them. Though the evidence we have been considering suggests that this religious dissociation was both more comprehensive and more gradual in scope than the purely literary 'dissociation of sensibility' proposed by T.S. Eliot,[2] the phenomenon he was attempting to describe in his controversial essay was arguably a product of this process. If, as some have maintained, this progressive separation of the sacred and the secular stems originally from the Reformation, it is nevertheless true that the conflicts and controversies of the sixteenth century still belonged to a world where religious belief was an instinctive part of the whole landscape of human affairs, affecting every part of life. In contrast, however much the newer forms of religious revival in the eighteenth or nineteenth centuries, Methodism, Evangelicalism or the Oxford Movement, may have differed from one another, what they had in common was that they were a conscious response to a perceived sense of loss – often expressed in the new Evangelical terminology as 'a sense of sin'.

Closely parallel feelings of loss, and a similar quest for a new wholeness of experience, can be detected at the root of both French and German Romanticism. Nor were even leading romantics immune from the associated need to re-invent their own religion rather than turn to the established forms. The paradox of Chateaubriand's *The Genius of Christianity* (1802) is that his intensely conservative Catholicism draws him into proposing what is, in effect, a quite new romantic religious synthesis. For him too, 'What particularly distinguishes Christian eloquence from the eloquence of the Greeks and the Romans is, in the words of La Bruyère, *that evangelical sadness which is the soul of it, that majestic melancholy on which it feeds*' (his italics).[3] Friedrich von Hardenberg (better known as Novalis) wrote of what he called 'the

---

[2] See 'The Metaphysical Poets', in *Collected Essays*, Faber, 1933.
[3] Chateaubriand, *The Genius of Christianity*, trs. Charles White, Baltimore, 1856, p. 438.

infinite sadness of religion'. Schleiermacher has a similar sense of what he calls a 'holy sadness' in religious feeling 'which accompanies every joy and pain'.[4] For all of them, the answer involved, among other things, a quite new relationship with a past where, it was felt, such a loss had not yet occurred. Ludwig Tieck's friend, Wilhelm Heinrich Wackenroder, turned back in history to his own imaginary golden age of the Italian Renaissance in the persona of a friar in his *Confessions from the Heart of an Art-Loving Friar* (1797). The mysticism of Novalis looked backwards to the world of Jacob Böhme and the seventeenth century, and beyond that to the other-worldly mysteries of Gnosticism and Neo-platonism.[5] Though Novalis lived only to the age twenty-nine, this attempt to return to a unified world-picture made a deep impression on his friend Friedrich Schlegel, who was with him when he died in 1801. Schlegel had been initially contemptuous of the institutional Lutheranism of his upbringing, but partly under the posthumous influence of Novalis' essay *Die Christenheit oder Europa* – which he had refused to publish in the *Athenaeum* when it was first written because of what he saw as its Catholic bias – Schlegel himself converted to Catholicism in 1808.[6] As his wife, Dorothea, who converted at the same time, wrote 'If only because it is so ancient, I prefer Catholicism. Nothing new is of any use.' Schleiermacher's Protestantism, though very different in outlook from his friend Schlegel's later Catholicism, had in common with it a distaste for contemporary Lutheranism so strong as to force him almost to recreate a romantic Christianity of his own.[7]

The causes of this shift from a collective to an individualistic religious sensibility, like the parallel movement from an externalised to an internalised apprehension of feelings, are complex and much-debated; in what is perhaps the best modern study of social and religious attitudes during the period, J.C.D. Clark has argued that in England this change was a much slower and less perceptible process than literary critics have sometimes allowed.[8] The evidence of the last chapter would seem to support this. Yet there is, I believe, little doubt that the

---

[4] Friedrich Schleiermacher, *On Religion: Speeches to its Cultured Despisers*, trs. Richard Crouter (1799), Cambridge University Press, 1988, p. 217. See also Mark C. Taylor, *Disfiguring: Art, Architecture, Religion*, University of Chicago Press, 1992, pp. 21–2.

[5] Jack Forstman, *A Romantic Triangle: Schleiermacher and Early German Romanticism*, Missoula, Mont.: Scholars Press, 1977, pp. 47–63 *passim*.

[6] Hans Eichner, *Friedrich Schlegel*, New York: Twayne, 1970, pp. 106–11.

[7] *On Religion*, 'First Speech: Apology'.

[8] J.C.D. Clark, *English Society 1688–1832*, Cambridge University Press, 1985, *passim*, but esp. ch. 5.

need for personal salvation which was to become so characteristic of Enlightenment and post-Enlightenment religious movements, and which we can see beginning perhaps even as far back as Bunyan, was an implicit recognition of the breaking-up of the old world-picture and a corresponding sense of an incompleteness, a lost innocence, a disjunction between feeling and reality that was mirrored in the new forms of narrative reading that we observed in the last chapter. In the interpretation of scripture a God-given polysemousness was replaced by a man-made polyphony.

A shift in reading the Bible is a shift in reading the universe. However gradual and even unconscious may have been the changes in biblical interpretation noted in the last chapter, their wider consequences were to prove momentous – although a necessary process of secularisation was not one of them. Behind the Romantic sense of loss and the corresponding attempt to rediscover a wholeness perceived as missing from the contemporary world, lay a radical re-appropriation of the past as 'history' for the first time in the modern sense. Enlightenment historians, however militantly secular, had been at one with their religious predecessors in their view of the *methods* of history. For Hume, Voltaire and even for Gibbon, the purpose of studying the past was to provide *exempla* of timeless truths. In contrast von Ranke's sense of the difference of the past, and the inapplicability of contemporary rules to societies that were fundamentally alien in outlook was the product of a sensibility which was (in this respect at least) essentially a Romantic one.

The movement from typological to narrative readings of the Bible was also a movement from a static to a dynamic world-view. 'In my end is my beginning.' The effect of reading Genesis or Exodus in terms of their supposed prefiguration of the life of Christ had been to give a seamless simultaneity to the entire cycle of Fall and Redemption represented by the Old and New Testaments. That story has sometimes been described by post-Romantic commentators as a great 'cosmic drama', but in truth for the seventeenth-century typological reader of the Bible it was probably anything but dramatic. To read the mediaeval Miracle Plays or even the story of *Paradise Lost* as 'dramatic' in the sense of a story whose plot unfolds in surprising or mysterious ways is to read into those works a narrative suspense that is quite anachronistic. As the *OED* makes clear, the word was not even used in this metaphorical sense of 'actions or course of events having a unity like that of a drama, and leading to a final catastrophe or consummation' until the early eighteenth century. Miracle Plays were essentially acted homilies, not thrillers. As Milton, the Calvinist and predestinarian, constantly reminds us through the very structuring of his narrative, the story of man's first disobedience and the fruit of that forbidden tree is foreknown and previsioned from the beginning of time. Yet a hundred years later Fielding's *Tom Jones*, where the author is similarly likened to a Calvinistic God, is, in contrast, permeated by metaphors from drama and the stage. To recapture the stories of Abraham and Isaac, or of Joseph and his brothers, as in any way suspenseful and contingent it is necessary to read them not as polysemous pieces of a universal jigsaw in which every piece interlocks with almost every other, but, like Sterne and Mrs Trimmer, as univocal, linear and successive scenes from a play or chapters of a novel.

Moreover, as Jane Austen was well aware, such a densely patterned figural way of reading the Bible was exactly paralleled by the emblematic and allegorical gardens of Kent, Burlington, Hoare and Flitcroft, where, for all their apparent freedom and irregularity in comparison with the formal geometry of French eighteenth-century plans, a total pattern of meaning was implicit in every fountain and grotto, vista and serpentine path. In contrast, the open and 'expressive' landscapes created by Brown, Repton and Payne Knight proclaimed the existence of a much more subjective and indeterminate meaning, which, like beauty, was in the eye and sensibility of the beholder. Here indeed was the possibility of drama in that new sense almost for the first time – as the elision of the 'scene' at the iron gate with the role-playing of *Lovers' Vows* suggests. Even the title of Kotzbue's play becomes a further 'play' on the meaning of the words. In this new subjective landscape, the once solemn religious vows of lovers no longer have fixed and determinate meaning, but will be interpreted by them according to circumstances and feelings. Faced with his abandoned mistress and illegitimate child, Baron Wildenheim must himself illuminate the vegetative metaphors strewing the path of life.

Once again, changes in the meanings of words reflect changes in sensibility and outlook. The first recorded usage of the word 'drama' to describe the Bible in this new narrative sense comes from a sermon of John Sharp, Archbishop of York, published in the year of his death, 1714, where he refers his congregation to 'the great drama and contrivances of God's providence'. Not surprisingly Gilbert Burnet records that Sharp was a great lover of poetry and the theatre, and was wont to say that the Bible and Shakespeare had made him arch-bishop.[9] It is significant also that, as we have seen, this new meaning of the word 'drama' coincides with the introduction of the theatrical metaphors 'scene' and 'scenery' to describe landscape. In 1789 Boydell opened his Shakespeare Gallery in Pall Mall with the avowed object of promoting an English School of history-painting – and, though the war frustrated much of his plan to export prints and eventually bankrupted him,[10] his attempt to appropriate history as theatre caught a popular trend. August Schlegel comments sarcastically: 'If the English taste in painting is going to spread even further into the continent, as the mechanical excellence of their engravings gives reason to fear, then one would like to propose that we abandon the name "historical painting," which in any case is rather unsuitable, and introduce in its stead "theatrical painting".'[11] But such a metaphorical shift not merely accompanied changes in sensibility but, as we can see at least with hindsight, implicitly foretold and even influenced their development. The application of metaphors from drama generally, and, in the case of Sharp (we may suspect), Shakespeare in particular, to either biblical narrative or landscape gardening already presupposes in some form that 'final catastrophe or consummation' characteristic of the theatre itself. Encapsulated and embryonic within the new reading was an idea of change, even of total transformation, that by the end of the 1780s was about to overflow from the confines of the playhouse to the stage of history itself.

Thus for Edmund Burke the events in France constituted nothing less than 'the awful drama of Providence now acting on the moral theatre of the world'.[12] In a world where Calvinism was common and the Bible was held to portray the beginning and foretell the end of all things, Providence would hitherto have seemed an unlikely drama-turge. In so far as the social and political upheavals of the seventeenth century had been seen in terms of biblical paradigms, they had tended to be directly allegorical, and so possessed of a fixed and determinate meaning. In contrast, though English images of the French Revolution are frequently biblical, drawing on tropes of liberation from bondage,

[9] Burnet, *History of his own Time*, 1725, vol. III, p. 100.
[10] Jonathan Bate, *Shakespearean Constitutions: Politics, Theatre, Criticism 1730–1830*, Oxford: Clarendon Press, 1989, pp. 45–57.
[11] *Athenaeum* Fragment 311, in Friedrich Schlegel, *Philosophical Fragments*, trs. Peter Firchow, Minneapolis: University of Minnesota Press, 1991, p. 62.
[12] Edmund Burke, *Letters ... on the Proposals for Peace with the Regicide Directory of France* (1795), *Works*, 1797, vol. VIII p. 78.

or later on the uncertainty and violence of nature, in tempests, hurricanes, and eruptions,[13] they are symbolic and impressionistic rather than precisely referential.

A typical construction of a biblical metanarrative is to be found in Richard Price's sermon of 4 November 1789, published as a *Discourse on the Love of our Country* the following year – the work that was to provide the occasion for Burke's *Reflections*. Part of the final peroration of this eminently liberal piece goes as follows:

Be encouraged, all ye friends of freedom, and writers in its defence! The times are auspicious. Your labours have not been in vain. Behold kingdoms, admonished by you, starting from sleep, breaking their fetters, and claiming justice from their oppressors! Behold, the light you have struck out, after setting AMERICA free, reflected to FRANCE, and there kindled into a blaze, that lays despotism in ashes, and warms and illuminates EUROPE![14]

This is certainly dramatic – and, given Price's background, it is hard to imagine that this image of prisoners starting from sleep to a blaze of light and finding their chains broken does not draw on Charles Wesley's well-known lines on spiritual conversion:

> Long my imprisoned spirit lay
> Fast bound in sin and nature's night;
> Thine eye diffused a quickening ray –
> I woke, the dungeon flamed with light;
> My chains fell off, my heart was free,
> I rose, went forth, and followed Thee.[15]

But the source for both is, of course, Acts 12: 7, where Peter is released from Herod's prison by an angel. The vividness of the image may owe something to conflation with the parallel story of Paul and Barnabas in Acts 16: 23–33, as well as to the fact that Wesley himself had visited prisoners in Newgate.[16] What is interesting here, however, is the way in which the biblical miracle was conceived in terms of personal drama, first as a trope of individual evangelical salvation from the bondage of sin in a way that parallels similar incidents in Bunyan's *Pilgrim's Progress*, and then as a metaphor for the political release of the French people from the Bastille of tyranny. What it has gained by such

---

[13] See Ronald Paulson, *Representations of Revolution (1789–1820)*, New Haven, Conn.: Yale University Press, 1983, p. 53, and Melvin J. Lasky, *Utopia and Revolution*, University of Chicago Press, 1976, p. 275.

[14] Richard Price, *Discourse on the Love of our Country*, 1799. p. 49.

[15] Charles Wesley, 'Free Grace' (better known as 'And can it be …') verse 4, in *Hymns and Sacred Poems*, 1739.

[16] H. Martin, *The Baptist Hymn Companion*, Psalm and Hymns Trust, 1953, p. 292.

a path is, of course, the additional notion of *conversion* that is missing from the original New Testament story. The people of France have not just had a miraculous release from bondage: that release has come through their 'conversion' (as Price assumes) to liberty and democracy through the 'admonishment' and preaching of the 'friends of freedom'.

Only some years after the Revolution, and then often in retrospect, do images from the Apocalypse come to the fore.[17] In a sermon of 1795, James Bicheno, Baptist Minister in Newbury, in the confidence that the long-expected signs of the Last Things were coming to pass, quotes the words of Increase Mather of eighty years before: 'May the kingdom of France be *that tenth part of a city* which shall fall! May we hear of a mighty revolution there!'[18] For English contemporaries of the French Revolution, biblical, and especially apocalyptic, prophecy took on a new urgency and relevance for those who believed themselves personally caught up in those events. Indeed, as Bicheno says,

the subject becomes vastly more interesting and affecting, if we ourselves, are acting a part in the great drama, witness the scenes of the fulfilment of the divine predictions, and are able to ascertain, with any tolerable degree of precision, their instant progress. In prophecy we discern not the policy of men, but the councils of God. We behold the Supreme Being himself opening the volume of his divine decrees, and disclosing futurity to the world.[19]

He and his auditors are no longer merely seeking to interpret words on a page, but have become 'actors' in the unfolding drama, 'witnesses' to events, and 'beholders' of God's awsome disclosure. Nor was such a feeling of participation in events greater than their comprehension confined to millenarians.

The example of Price is also interesting in the way that, as a sermon on contemporary events, it can use the past simultaneously in two quite different ways. On the one hand it recognises and rejoices in a process of historical change; on the other, it uses and reuses biblical tropes to create an idea of seamless moral or spiritual continuity. As we shall see repeatedly, both methods of appropriation co-exist throughout the Romantic period – at least until the 1830s. What was at stake was the way in which the writings handed down from previous generations could be appropriated and deployed in the present. Dante had used

---

[17] See Stephen Prickett, 'Wordsworth's Apocalypse: Robespierre and the Tribe of Moloch', *Graphé*, no. 3 (1994), pp. 87–99.

[18] Increase Mather, *Exhortations to Faith* (1710), p. 97; quoted by James Bicheno, *A Word in Season* (1795), p. 19. I am indebted to Christopher Burdon for this reference.

[19] *A Word in Season*, p. 18.

Virgil, as Virgil before him had used Homer and the Trojan myths: as a form of legitimation, an assurance that the present work stood in canonical relationship to the past. Though Milton, interestingly, believed he had lived too late in time to be truly canonical, he, like Dante, had drawn on Christian and pagan classical works alike to assert his continuity with the existing tradition. Such an assertion of continuity was the unspoken corollary to a belief in a particular kind of static universe.

When, in 1750, Thomas Gray begins his famous 'Elegy in a Country Churchyard' with an unacknowledged quotation (lines 20–4[20]) from Lucretius' *De rerum natura* (Book III, lines 894ff.[21]), his appropriation was a recognised cultural gesture parallel to that of Hoare's placing of a Virgil quotation over the door of the Temple of Flora at Stourhead. The educated reader was not merely meant to recognise the phrase, but to see the relationship between its original context and its new one. Indeed, in a very real sense that was what 'education' was about. The solidly classical diet of the English public school (and, to only a slightly lesser extent, the unreformed German *Gymnasium* or French *lycée*) was not, as it has often been interpreted, so much a way of preserving class barriers as a way of ensuring that the class which was being educated had entry into a world which was replete with such significations. For Gray the churchyard was a reminder of the unchanging permanences of village life: our modern 'historical' suspicion that whatever the actual conditions of farm labourers in Stoke Poges in 1750, they were unlikely to bear any relation to those in the Campagna around Pompeii, where Lucretius may (according to one theory) have had his estate in the first century BCE, is beside the point. Gray's appropriation of Lucretius is designed to place and legitimise his own meditation on human mortality in a long and rich tradition of such lucubrations; the atomistic Epicureanism of Lucretius is also a clue to the marked absence of any Christian reference to an after-life or the immortality of the soul in the 'Elegy'.

Yet Gray's own relationship to his material is actually more problematic than this conventional exposition might suggest. At first sight his

---

[20]
> For them no more the blazing hearth shall burn,
> Or busy housewife ply her evening care:
> No children run to lisp their sire's return,
> Or climb his knees the envied kiss to share.

[21] *De rerum natura*, ed. Cyril Bailey, 3 vols. Oxford: Clarendon Press, 1947, vol. I, p. 349; vol. II, p. 1143.

celebration of village permanencies is entirely consonant with an immutable social order:

> Perhaps in this neglected spot is laid
> Some heart once pregnant with celestial fire;
> Hands that the rod of empire might have sway'd,
> Or wak'd to extasy the living lyre.
>
> But Knowledge to their eyes her ample page
> Rich with the spoils of time did ne'er unroll;
> Chill Penury repress'd their noble rage,
> And froze the genial current of the soul.

But for all its gestures towards a conventionally deferential social structure, something uncomfortably new has surfaced here. In spite of the Lucretian trappings, the idea of death as a great social leveller, which is a frequent motif of neo-classical writings from Addison to Volney, is *not* in fact a common one in the slave-owning societies of antiquity. It is, rather, a distinctive feature of the eighteenth-century appropriation of the classical past. Moreover, in line with his general avoidance of supernatural references, Gray specifically orders his class-structure in strictly human terms. In the last resort this is not a God-ordained hierarchy, but an economic one. Human potential is languishing unrecognised simply through 'penury'. But once a problem has been articulated as being a product of human poverty rather than divine will, human solutions become not merely acceptable, but even a moral duty. A call for universal primary education lurks within the Lucretian stasis. Whether Gray himself recognised the significance of his economic reformulation of the social order is not a profitable question; in view of the later stanzas, very likely not. But lurking beneath that stanza is the revolutionary slogan: *la carriére ouverte aux talents.*

There is, in the last resort, an unresolvable contradiction between the past as a living source of legitimation and the past as history. Both assume an essential continuity between past and present, but whereas the former sees that continuity in terms of fundamental similarity, the latter sees it in terms of fundamental difference. For Gray, the appropriation of Lucretius is an appeal to eternal verities – not so much that 'some things don't change', but rather a signal that, for a world entirely governed by the mechanical and random flux of atoms, the idea of meaningful change does not enter into the matter. For Wordsworth, on the contrary, the past is a narrative of change.

Autobiography is thus an inescapable duty of the romantic poet. Struggling in *The Prelude* to construct himself as a poet, his childhood memories are a vital link in explaining who he is, and – which is for him the same thing – how he became as he is. Like the blind beggar in Book VII of *The Prelude*, the poet has a self-defining role. He is one who must, as it were, wear upon his chest 'a written paper to explain / His Story, whence he came, and who he was.' (lines 641–2) Nor was Wordsworth merely a spectator caught up in Burke's 'awful drama of Providence' in France; in telling the story of his own involvement he is part historian, part dramaturge. For him, as never for Gray, the poet is essentially a historical being. Between the two poets and their respective positions lies a new idea of revolution.

It is hard for the modern reader to grasp that the title of Burke's most famous work, *Reflections on the Revolution in France*, is intended as ironic. But Burke's point is that there has not been a 'revolution' in any proper sense of the word at all. What has emerged from this 'awful drama' was not a return to a previous state, but something totally new – and that, as he correctly points out, is not a 'revolution' at all. Johnson's dictionary of 1755 had defined the word 'revolution' primarily in terms of its astronomical meaning, which described the circular motion of an object such as a planet which returned always to its starting point. When applied metaphorically to politics it had hitherto retained this original notion of circularity.[22] Thus the English Civil War of 1649 was called 'the Great Rebellion', while the Restoration of Charles II was referred to as 'the Revolution of 1660' because it meant a *return* to the Stuart monarchy and the *status quo*. Those Britons like Price and Mackintosh who hailed the events in France of 1789-90 with enthusiasm did so because they drew an immediate parallel with the so-called 'Glorious Revolution' of 1688, where the word now signified that the expulsion of James II and the succession of William and Mary, so far from being a change of political direction, was in reality a restoration of ancient liberties threatened by the tyrannical actions of James. Though the *OED* admits earlier examples of what looks like the new sense scattered throughout the eighteenth century – often applied to earthquakes and other natural disasters – Burke is right, if rhetorically pedantic, in drawing attention to the circular origins of the word. Even the revolution of the American colonists in 1776 drew heavily on a 'Whig' rhetoric of the infringement and

---

[22] Paulson, *Representations of Revolution*, p. 50.

subsequent restoration of traditional English liberties. It was this, still circular and astronomical, use of the word 'revolution' by Price in his sermon of November 1789 to the Society for Commemorating the Revolution in Great Britain – an eminently respectable body of historically minded citizens – that called forth the fiery rhetoric and scorn of Burke's title, *Reflections on the Revolution.*[23]

Not unnaturally, the French word underwent a similar, if more rapid, transformation. It is said that when the Duke of La Rochefoucauld-Liancourt informed Louis XVI, on the evening of 14 July 1789, of the storming of the Bastille, the astonished king replied 'That is a revolt!' 'No Sire', the Duke replied, 'c'est la révolution!'[24] It may well be, as Iain McCalman has convincingly argued,[25] that Burke's astonishing fury against the events in France was fuelled more by memories of the anti-Catholic Gordon riots in London of 1780 than by any prophetic vision of horrors to come, but the fact remained that whatever might have been the intentions of some of those who took the Tennis Court Oath in Paris in 1789, or of their many English sympathisers, by 1793 there was no way in which either French participants or foreign observers could pretend that what was in progress was a restoration of anything. The word 'revolution' had acquired its new meaning of a clean break with the immediate political past. From henceforth the nature and language not merely of political but of social, aesthetic and philosophic thought had been irrevocably altered all over Europe. The theatrical metaphors that had increasingly become part of the eighteenth-century vocabulary before 1790 had at last found, in the new meaning of revolution, a word adequate for the catastrophe and consummation they had always tacitly suggested.

In October 1798 the novelist Fanny Burney wrote to her father, Dr Burney, a well-known musicologist and historian: 'There is nothing in old history that I shall any longer think fabulous; the destruction of the most wonderful empires on record has nothing more wonderful, nor of more sounding improbability, than the demolition of this great nation, which rises up against itself for its own ruin – perhaps annihilation.'

---

[23] For a fuller account of the Price–Burke controversy see Stephen Prickett, *England and the French Revolution*, Macmillan, 1989, pp. 31–61.

[24] Cited by both Geoffrey Best and Eugene Kamenka, in Geoffrey Best (ed.), *The Permanent Revolution*, Fontana, 1988, pp. 1 and 86. See also Arthur Hatto, 'Revolution: an Inquiry into the Usefulness of a Historical Term', *Mind*, vol. 58 (1949) pp. 495–517.

[25] Iain McCalman, 'Prophesying Revolution: Edmund Burke, Mad Lord George and Madame La Motte', in *Learning and Living: Essays in Honour of J.F.C. Harrison*, ed. Malcolm Chase and Ian Dyck, Scolars Press, 1995.

For Burke, writing only a few months later, 'The French Revolution is the most astonishing that has hitherto happened in the world.' Nor was this feeling of sheer amazement lessened by the passing of time. Looking back at the end of his long life, the radical publisher William Hone, born during the Gordon Riots of 1780, began his memoirs with the statement: 'In the course of my brief life the most astounding events of modern times have happened.' If the revolution was the most formative and lasting influence on Wordsworth and Coleridge, then only in their early twenties, it was hardly less so for Shelley, Carlyle and Dickens, who were not yet born.

Nor, as has been suggested, was this feeling of the uniqueness of the revolution confined to it in a political sense. What Ronald Paulson calls the 'paradigm' of revolution created in France in the 1790s[26] rapidly came to carry much wider connotations. As early as 1791, the revolution has been aestheticised by James Mackintosh, who argued in his *Vindicaie Gallicae* that art requires a breakage in order that beauty may be produced. Similarly the metaphor of 'Industrial Revolution' was first coined in France in the 1820s not just as a description of the radical changes in contemporary means of production, but as a polemical pointer to the way in which those changes should be seen and understood: as a complete and irresistible break with the past. The history of the phrase is itself a classic example of the process of appropriation – with all the ambiguity between theft and renewal we have seen always attached to the word. It was taken up by Blanqui in the 1830s, translated into German by Marx and Engels, and only popularised in English by Arnold Toynbee in the 1880s.[27] For a whole tradition of European thought, from Rousseau to Althusser,[28] the idea of a recaptured human wholeness was henceforth inseparable from the idea of revolution.

VOLNEY VERSUS CHATEAUBRIAND

As we have seen, Volney's *Ruins* can be seen as part of a concerted campaign to undermine the credibility of French Catholicism, with its strong associations with the monarchy and *ancien régime*. As in English

---

[26] *Representations of Revolution*, p. 4.
[27] See Clark, *English Society*, p. 65.; and Sir George Clark, *The Idea of the Industrial Revolution* (Glasgow University Publications, no. 95), Glasgow: Jackson, 1953.
[28] See Dennis Porter, *Rousseau's Legacy: Emergence and Eclipse of the Writer in France*, Oxford University Press, 1995.

Whig attacks on Tory High Church positions, an essential part of this strategy was a way of reading the Bible in relation to its historical context that would destroy its claims to uniqueness, special revelation and divine inspiration. Volney was well equipped for the task. In 1781 he had published an examination of Herodotus' chronology that had given him an international scholarly reputation. His next book, *Voyage en Syrie et en Egypt* (1793) had confirmed his status as an Orientalist and earned him a decoration from Catherine the Great. To prepare for that expedition he had spent some time in a Coptic monastery and learned Arabic. Like Herodotus, his first subject, he had been over-whelmed by his first-hand experience of the historical *difference* of past cultures from his own culture and society. From the first pages of the *Ruins* it is clear that there is a connection in his mind between the ruins of countless Near-Eastern civilisations lost in the desert and those of the (metaphorically) still-smouldering Bastille nearer home. 'Who knows', says his anonymous traveller, 'Who knows but that hereafter some traveller like myself will sit down upon the banks of the Seine, the Thames, or the Zuyder See ... who knows but that he will sit down solitary amid silent ruins, and weep a people inurned, and their greatness changed into an empty name?'[29] It was an image that was to haunt the historically minded nineteenth century, from Macaulay's vision of some New Zealander of the future standing on Ludgate Hill contemplating the ruins of St Paul's, to the pessimism of Kipling's *Recessional* where 'all our pomp of yesterday' is 'one with Nineveh and Tyre'.

The modern reader is unlikely to find Volney's tone of hostility to all forms of supernatural or revealed religion either as exhilarating or as disturbing as the original audience. Indeed, the *Ruins* is likely to seem an oddly puzzling and oblique work – in many ways less like an intellectual argument than a gothic novel. Volney opens with an invocation to 'Solitary ruins, sacred tombs, ye mouldering and silent walls', before warming to his theme of death, whose terminal egalitar-ianism would have been thoroughly familiar to Addison or Gray:

Tombs, what virtues and potency do you exhibit! Tyrants tremble at your aspect; you poison with secret alarm their impious pleasures; they turn from you with impatience, and, coward like, endeavour to forget you amid the sumptuousness of their palaces. It is you that bring home the rod of justice to the powerful oppressor; it is you that wrest the ill-gotten gold from the merciless extortioner, and avenge the cause of him that has none to help; you

[29] C.F.C. de Volney, *The Ruins: or a Survey of the Revolutions of Empires*, T. Allman, 1851, p. 7.

compensate the narrow enjoyments of the poor, by dashing with care the goblet of the rich; to the unfortunate you offer a last and inviolable asylum: in fine, you give to the soul that just equilibrium of strength and tenderness which constitutes the wisdom of the sage and the science of life.[30]

The first chapters, where the author contemplates the ruins of Palmyra, provide the metaphor for the spiritual and metaphysical ruins of all creeds that will follow. The word 'revolution' of the title is used throughout in its full modern sense to suggest that not merely is it a universal phenomenon, but that, by implication, this book is the herald of an accompanying intellectual revolution. After a brief allegory of the events of the Revolution itself Volney proceeds to demolish the remnants of ancient superstition in the form of the Catholic Church by a curious crabwise movement of anecdote and philosophical disquisition linked by a series of extended allegories – of which the opening, with its dramatic invocation of the ruins of time as the leveller of tyrants, is only one among many. Rather than using more conventional modes of philosophical exposition, Volney's method of narration may be described as essentially allegorical, dramatic and, in its own strange way, even mythological. Indeed, this 'gothick', even mystical, quality to his writing often makes it seem less like a demolition of all existing religions than a prelude to a new one based on what he calls the Law of Nature. Here, for instance, is Volney's unnamed first-person narrator meditating on the ruins of Palmyra:

The solitariness of the situation, the serenity of the evening, and the grandeur of the scene, impressed my mind with religious thoughtfulness. The view of an illustrious city deserted, the remembrance of past times, their comparison with the present state of things, all combined to raise my heart to a strain of sublime meditations. I sat down on the base of a column; and there, my elbow on my knee, and my head resting on my hand, sometimes turning my eyes towards the desert, and sometimes fixing them on the ruins, I fell into a profound reverie.[31]

The romantic setting of ruins in the dusk; the sense of age and cultural remoteness of the vanished glories of the oasis city; the 'religious thoughtfulness' of the narrator who has, in the ancient tradition of Near-Eastern prophets, retired into the desert to meditate; all combine to give the *Ruins* a prophetic and even mystical rather than a rationalistic flavour. Indeed, it was, I believe, precisely this suggestion (never quite substantiated) that Volney's readers, so far from being sent

---

[30] *Ibid.*, pp. ix, x.   [31] *Ibid.*, p. 3.

out from the darkness of superstition into the cool light of Reason, were about to be initiated into the ineffable mysteries of a new age of the Spirit, that gave Volney a quite different kind of appeal from other rationalist writers of the period. Whether or not there is in the well-documented influence of the *Illuminati* of Avignon the shadowy vestiges of the Joachimite idea of the 'third age', the so-called 'Age of the Spirit', is still a matter of scholarly debate, but its presence is well enough attested in other contemporary anti-religious writers from Lessing to Marx for there to be nothing inherently improbable in the idea.[32] In this sense Volney forms a bridge between the dry scepticism of Enlightenment historiography and the more inward psychological questioning of the next generation of critics, such as Feuerbach and Schleiermacher. Comte's transformation of Volney's key to all mythologies into a positivist religion of humanity[33] is, as George Eliot saw, less a perversion than a logical extension of qualities implicit not only in his argument itself, but also in the rhetoric of its presentation.

In a later work, called *The Law of Nature* (1793), we get a further glimpse into this rhetorical technique through Volney's definition of 'law': 'The word *law*, [i.e. the French *loi* from the Latin *lex*] taken in its literal sense, signifies *reading*; because in early times ordinances and regulations principally composed the readings delivered to the people.'[34] One does not need to be much of a deconstructionist to find here an indication of the way in which Volney's idea of law involves a 'reading' (or, perhaps, even a rereading) of the 'book of nature' which from mediaeval times had been held to offer an alternative and complementary source of knowledge of God to that provided by the Bible. Nor does the rhetoric here deviate from that tradition as much as the content of the *Ruins* might have led us to expect. We learn, for instance, that a proper understanding of Nature leads humanity towards universal justice, peace and benevolence.[35] We also learn that such an understanding points not towards atheism, but to the existence (however shadowy) of 'a supreme agent, a universal and identical mover' thus illustrating 'that the law of nature is sufficient to raise us to the knowledge of God'.[36]

---

[32] See Marjorie Reeves and Warwick Gould, *Joachim of Fiore and the Myth of the Eternal Evangel in the Nineteenth Century*, Oxford: Clarendon Press, 1987.

[33] See T.R. Wright, *The Religion of Humanity: the Impact of Comtean Positivism on Victorian Britain*, Cambridge University Press, 1986.

[34] C.F.C. de Volney, *The Law of Nature*, T. Allman, 1851, p. 1.

[35] *Ruins, ibid., The Law of Nature*, p. 6.

[36] *Ibid.*, pp. 6–7.

Not surprisingly such vague Deism was hardly strong enough to absolve Volney from the general charge of atheism. His 'supreme agent' was close enough to an idea of absolute reason for him to be used by the French Theophilanthropists in the early 1790s as part of their attempt to promote a cultic worship of a goddess of Reason. From the first publication of the *Ruins* in England there was a series of pamphlets attempting to refute his arguments, and his assumed atheism. When, after a period in prison during the Reign of Terror, he made his way to America, he was denounced by another immigrant and victim of religious persecution, the Unitarian Joseph Priestley, who called him among other things 'an atheist, an ignoramus, a Chinaman, and a Hottentot'.[37]

Nevertheless, what was to be in many ways the most powerful and lasting reply to Volney came from a fellow French aristocrat, François René Auguste de Chateaubriand, who in 1802 published his *Genius of Christianity*. It enjoyed an immediate success not unlike that of the *Ruins* eleven years earlier. By 1804 it had gone through seven editions and had been translated into German, Italian and Russian. Though it was essentially a Catholic royalist response to Volney's republican Deism, in fact the two writers' careers and even their eventual views were less far apart than this summary might suggest at first glance. A liberal-minded officer in the army of the *ancien régime*, some ten years younger than Volney, Chateaubriand had made his way to America two years before him and so escaped the Reign of Terror. While in America, both men had been well received by Washington himself.[38] Both returned to France after Napoleon came to power and accepted posts and honours while remaining critical of the authoritarianism of the new Empire. Chateaubriand at first tried to ingratiate himself with Napoleon,[39] and served briefly in a number of diplomatic posts under him; in 1811 Napoleon even offered him a place in the *Académie*, but this was then indefinitely postponed because of his growing criticism of the regime. An ardent royalist, he accepted a ministerial post under the restored Charles XVIII, and was later ambassador to Berlin and then London, but he grew increasingly disenchanted with post-

[37] E.L. de Montluzin, *The Anti-Jacobins, 1798–1800*, New York: St Martin's Press, 1988, pp. 155–6.

[38] The evidence for Chateaubriand's meeting with Washington rests solely on his own *Mémoires d'outre-tombe* (1849–50) and may belong more to the rhetorical category of invented conversations with great figures than to historical fact.

[39] See his sycophantic *Epître dédicatoire au premier consul Bonaparte* to the 1803 edition of the *Genius of Christianity*.

Revolutionary politics altogether and withdrew once more into private life. Volney became a senator (1799), a commander of the *Legion d'Honneur* (1804) and continued with scholarly work on ancient history and Oriental languages. After 1815 he was able to make his peace with the restored Bourbon monarchy and took his seat (metaphorically, if not literally) side by side with Chateaubriand as a fellow member of the House of Peers.

The crucial difference between them lay in neither their politics nor their scholarship, but in their religion. Until almost the age of thirty Chateaubriand had held no particular religious convictions, but at the death of his mother and sister in 1797 he experienced a conversion that was to last the rest of his life: 'Those two voices coming up from the grave, and that death which had now become the interpreter of death, struck me with peculiar force. I became a Christian. I did not yield to any great supernatural light: my conviction came from the heart. I wept, and I believed.'[40] If, as some critics have argued,[41] there was more than a touch of political opportunism in this conversion, the unashamed emotionalism is also a key to Chateaubriand's strategy in the *Genius of Christianity*.

Though not content eventually to leave unchallenged a single point in Volney's diffusionist argument, his main thrust was not aimed at facts at all, but at changing the reader's entire perspective on history. The very qualities of traditional religion which had earned Volney's contempt and which he had seen as its weakest points for attack were now seized upon by Chateaubriand and extolled as its most essential qualities. The irrationality and emotion of Christianity, its ancient mythology, its capacity to inspire the most childish and naive devotion were all now adduced as proof of its imaginative and psychological depth – its unique capacity to satisfy the whole person, in contrast to what was portrayed as the shallow intellectualism of the Enlightenment sceptics. 'It was', wrote Chateaubriand, 'necessary to summon all the charms of the imagination, and all the interests of the heart, to the assistance of that religion against which they had been set in array.' His thesis was original, bold and comprehensive. It was nothing less than to prove that

the Christian religion, of all the religions that ever existed, is the most humane, the most favourable to liberty and to the arts and sciences; that the modern world is indebted to it for every improvement, from agriculture to the

[40] *Genius of Christianity*, p. 27.
[41] Notably Pierre Barbéris, *A la Recherche d'une écriture: Chateaubriand*, Tours: Mame, 1974.

abstract sciences – from the hospitals for the reception of the unfortunate to the temples reared by the Michael Angelos and embellished by the Raphaels ... that nothing is more divine than its morality – nothing more lovely and more sublime than its tenets, its doctrine, and its worship; that it encourages genius, corrects the taste, develops the virtuous passions, imparts energy to the ideas, presents noble images to the writer, and perfect models to the artist; that there is no disgrace in being believers with Newton and Bossuet, with Pascal and Racine.[42]

Nor should we be for a moment satisfied with mere intellectual conviction of the truth of Christianity, nor even to admire its manifold achievements; this is above all a religion to be loved. Here Volney, Voltaire and their fellow *philosophes* have totally misunderstood what religion is about. 'Sublime in the antiquity of its recollections, which go back to the creation of the world, ineffable in its mysteries, adorable in its sacraments, interesting in its history, celestial in its morality, rich and attractive in its ceremonial, it is fraught with every species of beauty.'[43]

Chateaubriand's agenda, in short, is nothing less than a total re-appropriation of world history. The richness of the past, with its arts, literature, philosophy and science is all, even down to the pagan world of antiquity, if properly understood, the domain of Christianity as the presiding 'genius' of the universe – in the new and emotive Romantic sense of that word. Once this total revisionist perspective has been established, the individual points of Volney's argument can be picked off with comparative ease. Nor is it even necessary to mention Volney by name: he is by no means as big a target as, say, Voltaire, and any reader who knows Volney will soon be alerted to the pattern of allusions – as when Chateaubriand turns to the topic of ruins himself. But these are not the ruins of the old world, but of the new.

Within these few years, extraordinary monuments have been discovered in North America, on the banks of the Muskingum, the Miami, the Wabash, the Ohio, and particularly the Scioto, where they occupy a space of upward of twenty leagues in length. They consist of ramparts of earth, with ditches, slopes, moons, half-moons, and prodigious cones, which serve for sepulchres.[44]

In keeping with his general strategy of upstaging Volney on all occasions, these ruins are at once larger and more mysterious than

---

[42] *Genius of Christianity*, pp. 48–9.
[43] *Ibid.*, p. 50.
[44] *Ibid.*, p. 126.

anything that Orientalists could discover in the Syrian desert. Unlike the ruins of Palmyra, we have no idea who built these colossal remains, nor what sort of cities they can have been. The meditations they induce are not upon the inevitable failure of priestcraft and absolutism, but simply on the inevitable depredations of time. In what is almost a direct parody of Volney, Chateaubriand conducts his own meditation.

For my part, a solitary lover of nature and a simple confessor of the Deity, I sat once on these very ruins. A traveller without renown, I held converse with these relics, like myself, unknown. The confused recollections of society, and the vague reveries of the desert, were blended in the recesses of my soul. Night had reached the middle of her course; all was solemn and still – the moon, the woods, the sepulchres, – save that at long intervals was heard the sound of some tree, which the axe of time laid low, in the depths of the forest. Thus everything falls, everything goes to ruin![45]

Volney had also, we recall, been to America. But unlike Volney, Chateaubriand claims to bring to his meditations not just an enquiring mind, but, as a lover of nature and of God, a unified sensibility. For someone who brings their whole soul to the experience there is no need to develop a threadbare political allegory. If Volney's ruins are in some sense those of the Bible, Chateaubriand's are those of that other book: of Nature. In this true universal history, he implies, Nature herself provides an answer more profound than any cheap philosophising. Ruins are not just the product of revolutions or caused by human mismanagement and tyranny, they are the inevitable, even majestic, consequence of time alone.

Volney's cultural diffusionism, similarly, presents Chateaubriand with little difficulty once we accept his premiss that, just as the Old Testament finds its true fulfilment in the New, so earlier religions only find their fulfilment and explanation in Christianity. The argument is a familiar one, from at least mediaeval times, but it can rarely have been presented with such panache and verve as here. Thus the mythologies of other, earlier religions, are not the source of later Christian doctrines, but instead point towards them. The most obvious examples are ideas concerning the future life and the immortality of the soul. Many of these, Chateaubriand is happy to admit, are in truth taken from older religions and philosophies, but in their Christian form they are no longer selective or culture-specific. 'The heaven and hell of the Christians are not devised after the manners of any particular people,

---

[45] *Ibid.*, p. 127.

but founded on the general ideas that are adapted to all nations and to all classes of society.'[46] Unlike the classical Elysium, for instance, the Christian heaven admits children, slaves and 'the lower classes of men'; unlike the Norse Valhalla it does not specify either the weather or social activities. Moreover, unlike the mystery religions on which it has no doubt drawn, Christianity has no esoteric secrets. 'What the brightest geniuses of Greece discovered by a last effort of reason is now publicly taught in every church; and the labourer, for a few pence, may purchase, in the catechism of his children, the most sublime secrets of the ancient sects.'[47]

But Chateaubriand's appropriation of pagan mythologies does not stop there. Even such post-biblical and distinctively Christian doctrines as that of the Trinity can, he claims, be found in earlier philosophies. The Trinity was, it seems, known to the Egyptians, alluded to by Plato, and familiar in Tibet and the East Indies.[48] But he is careful not to allow greater antiquity to imply superior wisdom. Though the biblical (or Mosaic) cosmogony has much in common with those of Zoroaster, Plato, the ancient Chinese or the Scandinavians, it is nevertheless vastly superior to them.[49] 'Voltaire somewhere asserts that we possess a most wretched *copy* of the different popular traditions respecting the origin of the world, and the physical and moral elements which compose it. Did he prefer, then, the cosmogony of the Egyptians, the great winged egg of the Theban priests?'[50] As for the chronology of these same ancient Egyptians, which Volney uses to undermine the credibility of Genesis, the supposed eighteen-thousand-year span of their records is based on a misunderstanding, since Plutarch – 'who cannot be suspected of Christianity' – tells us that an Egyptian 'year' was in some cases no more than a month.[51] The Egyptians were in general useful pawns in contemporary polemic since, after Napoleon's expedition there in 1798, they were very much in fashion. Hieroglyphics, on which any accurate dating depended, remained indecipherable until the discovery of the Rosetta stone in 1822. In the 1790s and 1800s, in the absence of any possibility of translation, the word 'hieroglyphic' had itself become a synonym for arcane mystery.

[46] *Ibid.*, pp. 203–4.
[47] *Ibid.*, p. 204.
[48] *Ibid.*, pp. 54–5.
[49] *Ibid.*, pp. 107–10.
[50] *Ibid.*, p. 107.
[51] *Ibid.*, p. 122.

Undoubtedly the weakest part of Chateaubriand's whole argument, and probably the least relevant to his own thesis, is his commitment to defend the chronology of Genesis. But he clearly cannot bear to lose even a single trick to his opponent. Recent scientific discoveries are pressed into service selectively – remains of Indian elephants found in Siberia prove the comprehensiveness as well as the truth of the Deluge[52] – but, even in 1802, it was difficult to ignore the mounting scientific evidence that the earth was considerably older than the five thousand years or so produced by a literal adherence to the biblical dating.[53] Chateaubriand's answer anticipates the thesis of Philip Gosse's notorious *Omphalos* by more than fifty years: 'God might have created, and doubtless did create, the world with all the marks of antiquity and completeness which it now exhibits.'[54]

More central to his main argument is Part II, entitled 'The Poetic of Christianity'. This brings us much closer to the central appropriative thesis of the *Genius*, which is to show how far Christianity has outshone the pagan world in its capacity to inspire the arts – especially poetry. From the start there are only two possible contenders for the bay-leaf crown: 'A poetic voice issues from the ruins which cover Greece and Idumaea, and cries afar to the traveller "There are but two brilliant names and recollections in history – those of the Israelites and of the ancient Greeks".'[55] After what has gone before, it comes as no great surprise to learn that, whatever may be the beauties of Homer and his fellow Greeks, they are occluded by the grandeur and sublimity of the Bible. It is, however, interesting to discover that Chateaubriand is here following 'the deep and various learning of Bishop Lowth, and his elegant and refined taste' in 'his work on the sacred poetry of the Hebrews'.[56] In comparison with the Christian moderns, moreover, the ancients fare no better, even in the one area where they might be expected to excel: 'whatever may be the genius of Homer and the majesty of his gods, his *marvellous* and all his grandeur are nevertheless eclipsed by the *marvellous* of Christianity.'[57]

But Chateaubriand is less concerned with simple comparisons than with developing a critical theory which would account for the

[52] *Ibid.*, p. 130.
[53] One of the best accounts of the debate over the age of the earth and the existence of vanished species is in Adrian Desmond, *The Hot-Blooded Dinosaurs*, Blond, 1976, ch. 1.
[54] *Genius of Christianity*, p. 136.
[55] *Ibid.*, p. 210.
[56] *Ibid.*, p. 349.
[57] *Ibid.*, p. 330.

superiority of the Christian moderns – and here his argument becomes much more subtle.

Christianity is, if we may so express it, a double religion. Its teaching has reference to the nature of intellectual being, and also to our own nature: it makes the mysteries of the Divinity and the mysteries of the human heart go hand-in-hand; and, by removing the veil that conceals the true God, it also exhibits man just as he is.

   Such a religion must necessarily be more favourable to the delineation of *characters* than another which dives not into the secret of the passions. The fairer half of poetry, the dramatic, received no assistance from polytheism, for morals were separated from mythology.[58]

For Chateaubriand the French word *caractère* carries here a double meaning not easily conveyed by its English counterpart. Not merely does it suggest 'character' in the novelistic sense, but also a person's social role: such as that of a father, brother, daughter, etc. Chateaubriand's point is that the modern sense of individuality, even self-consciousness, is enhanced by the individual's consciousness of their moral function within society. This is a point with which Jane Austen could scarcely disagree. Not merely did the new art-form of the 'novel' depend above all on such an exploration of character, but, as we have seen, the eighteenth-century revolution in the way in which the Bible was read also depended on a corresponding empathy with the powerful but latent characterisation of the biblical narratives in just this double sense. If Chateaubriand is one of the first critics to articulate what has now become something of a critical commonplace: that whereas eighteenth-century and neo-classical criticism laid great stress on the generality and uniformity of human experience, Romanticism tended to stress its particularity and even idiosyncrasy, he is no less conscious of the moral and social dimensions of that new sense of individuality. 'Christianity ... by mingling with the affections of the soul, has increased the resources of drama, whether in the epic or on the stage'.[59] Thus since pagan antiquity had little interest in an after-life, classical tragedy ended simply with death. In contrast, in a play like Racine's *Phèdre* the tragic tension is increased by the fact that, as a Christian wife, Phèdre is also jeopardising her immortal soul. It is, perhaps, not surprising that the Romantics should have increasingly turned away from classical towards biblical literary models in their search for legitimation from the past.

---

[58] *Ibid.*, p. 232.   [59] *Ibid.*, p. 299.

But there is another, no less important, sense in which Christianity may be said to have unveiled the secrets of human character. In our introductory discussion of Jacob and Esau we noted that what was being handed down in the blessing was in the end the story of the theft itself, and that in a very real sense what was to distinguish the children of Israel and, no less, their Christian rivals in so far as they were also the people of the Book, was a heightened self-awareness, or self-construction, as heirs and beneficiaries of that tradition. Chateaubriand is here sowing a seed that, as we shall see in our final chapter, was to take deep root in nineteenth-century consciousness, profoundly affecting the development of twentieth-century literature.

It is this new sense of individuality and inner space produced by Christianity which, Chateaubriand claims, has transformed poetry. In spite of the praise heaped by neo-classicists upon the evocativeness of classical mythology, instead of embellishing nature, in reality, claims Chateaubriand, it had the effect of destroying her real charms. 'Mythology diminished the grandeur of Nature – the ancients had no descriptive poetry, properly so called.'[60]

No sooner had the apostles begun to preach the gospel to the world than descriptive poetry made its appearance ... Nature ceased to speak through the fallacious organs of idols; her ends were discovered, and it became known that she was made in the first place for God, and in the second for man ... This great discovery changed the whole face of the creation.[61]

Though this argument is very much a corollary to the previous one, in that it sees Christianity as the prime agent of a demythologising of nature, in so far as it gave rise to the modern (Romantic) concept of nature, it is of central importance to Chateaubriand's strategy of aesthetic appropriation. It is not merely the great religious poems that owe their aesthetic sublimity to the Bible. Chateaubriand makes far less play with Dante than one might expect, and, though he devotes more time to Milton, even with *Paradise Lost* he is unhappy with the overtly religious theme of the poem.[62] What saves it, in his eyes, is rather its depiction of the human and the natural. In short, he is claiming that the entire aesthetic behind Romanticism is neither contingent nor merely a movement of fashion, but is a necessary and inevitable outcome of a Christian and biblical civilisation.

Moreover, the development of such a sensibility enables us to look

---

[60] *Ibid.*
[61] *Ibid.*, p. 305.
[62] *Ibid.*, p. 215.

back on the past and appropriate from it qualities which could not have been appreciated, or even necessarily seen at all, in earlier or non-Christian societies. 'The growth of descriptive poetry in modern times enables us to see and appreciate the genius of the poets of Job, Ecclesiastes and the Psalms.'[63] Such a view of the past as requiring a modern and specifically Christian perspective for a proper appreciation even of its aesthetic qualities is an essential part of the theoretical underpinning of Chateaubriand's whole appropriative strategy – paralleling Schleiermacher's hermeneutic ambition to understand the figures of the past better than they understood themselves.

Chateaubriand also claims another privilege essential to his strategy. He has all along insisted that Christianity forms a complete and coherent philosophical and social system, and that the nature of Christian society is not directly dependent upon the actual beliefs of particular individuals within it. This is important in two ways. Firstly, it allows for the doctrine of Original Sin.[64] In any Christian society there will always be, he maintains, a profound gap between its ideals and its actual practices. Given the fallen state of humanity, such a gap is only to be expected, and the failure of its practitioners, lay or clerical, to live up to their aspirations does not in any way invalidate those ideals. On the contrary, it makes them of even greater value. Secondly, it enables him to appropriate within his scheme sceptics and infidels who would personally be opposed to any classification as 'Christian'. His prime example of this is – as ever – Voltaire.

It is, perhaps, ironic that he is convinced that Voltaire's great contribution to posterity is his poem *The Henriad*, which was too important a work to leave out in an account such as this, and that his sceptical writings and philosophy would soon fade from memory. Nevertheless, it could not be denied that Voltaire was actively opposed not merely to the Church, but to Christianity *per se*. To this Chateaubriand has two answers. The first consists of a series of deft historical side-swipes: 'This great man had the misfortune to pass his life amid a circle of scholars of moderate abilities, who, always ready to applaud, were incapable of apprising him of his errors.'[65] Or again: 'We have no doubt that Voltaire, had he been religious, would have excelled in history. He wants nothing but seriousness.'[66]

---

[63] *Ibid.*, p. 308.
[64] *Ibid.*, p. 60.
[65] *Ibid.*, p. 228.
[66] *Ibid.*, p. 431.

The second is a much more powerful one that has gained increasing currency in the twentieth century. Whether he likes it or not, Voltaire must be seen among the ranks of the Christian poets because he had grown up within a society whose values had been formed by the Bible and generations of Christian teaching. In so far as Voltaire criticised the Church in particular or society in general on moral grounds, he was acting in the tradition of a long line of Christian social and moral reformers. To see just how different a non-Christian society might be, we have only to look at the pagan classical societies whose values were as alien to us as their customs were abominable.[67] To some extent this is a matter of the cultural shift noted above. A world where the love of Paris and Helen, or the wrath of Achilles, is the work of gods rather than an internalised sense of human character is one whose values are of action rather than thought, sentiment or moral choice. An integrated and morally responsible individual in the new Romantic sense belongs essentially to the psychology of a biblically based society. But in addition to this psychological revolution there has also been a real revolution in values with the coming of Christianity. 'Christianity has changed the relations of the passions, by changing the basis of vice and virtue ... Among the ancients, for example, humility was considered as meanness and pride as magnanimity [sic: French = *grandeur*]; among Christians, on the contrary, pride is the first of vices and humility the chief of virtues.'[68] It is, moreover, characteristic of the values of a Christian society that it is impossible, even for those who reject its metaphysical foundations, to return to earlier pagan values. The stern neo-classicism of the early years of the Revolution, with its admiration for Brutus, who condemned his sons to death, was bound to fail. Similarly, for Voltaire, who criticised the God of the Old Testament on moral grounds, it would have been unthinkable to return to the gladiators and beasts of the Colosseum.

This is not to say, of course, that Chateaubriand's view of history is necessarily one of progress. For one in sympathy neither with the Revolution nor with Napoleon, that would be an unlikely position in 1802. What he does believe is that, in contrast with either the pagan historians of antiquity or the infidel historians of the present, Christianity provides a theoretical framework for the explanation of all human history. Moreover, such a history is at once dynamic and typological. Thus, just as we find that the revelation of God's divine

---

[67] *Ibid.*, p. 668.   [68] *Ibid.*, p. 269.

purpose in the Bible is also a revelation of human character, so we find that biblical history is also a revelation of the collective character of mankind.

When we reflect that Moses is the most ancient historian in the world, and that he has mingled no fabulous story with his narrative ... we cannot forbear feeling the highest astonishment. But when, with a reference to Christianity, we come to reflect that the history of the Israelites is not only the real history of ancient days, but likewise the type of modern times; that each fact is of a twofold nature, containing within itself an *historic truth* and a *mystery*; that the Jewish people is a symbolical epitome of the human race, representing in its adventures all that has happened and all that ever will happen in the world; that Jerusalem must always be taken for another city, Sion for another mountain, the Land of Promise for another region, and the call of Abraham for another vocation ... we are at a loss for words, and are ready to exclaim, with the prophet, 'God is our king before ages!'[69]

To combine an idea of history, in its post-revolutionary sense as a process of verifiable and meaningful change, with the older view of history as a series of transparent *exempla* of timeless truths may be intellectually dubious by later standards, but Chateaubriand was here in respectable company, extending from Lowth to Coleridge. As so often in *The Genius of Christianity*, we feel that in his efforts to retain what he passionately believes to be endangered qualities of traditional Christianity, he has been side-tracked and distracted from his main goal. Yet, even here, there is another quite distinctive and original strand that immediately distinguishes it from earlier statements of the same theme. The purpose of this passage in context is neither to insist solely upon the accuracy of Moses' history, nor its typological meaning, but rather to stress the profundity and emotionalism of the reader's response. The divine meaning of history is not something to be considered by the intellect alone, but one that demands integration and self-conscious participation of the whole personality. For Chateaubriand, this is what true history is about. In contrast pagan historians were mere chroniclers; Voltaire and his ilk mere speculators. Christianity does not just provide a theoretical framework for the understanding of history, important as that is, it also provides warmth and feeling in our approach to the past, a sense of its grandeur and pathos.[70] Over and over again Chateaubriand returns to this theme of the psychological wholeness of Christianity in contrast with the

---

[69] *Ibid.*, p. 346.   [70] *Ibid.*, pp. 428–32.

fragmented nature of Enlightenment philosophy or pagan antiquity. If (in some ways strangely like his contemporary, Hegel) he insists that the comprehensiveness of his system, and its metaphysical grounding in the absolute, prevent historical relativism and allow a privileged hermeneutical viewpoint, it is because he is convinced that only Christianity can offer such a totally integrated vision.

CHAPTER 5

The Bible as metatype: Jacob's ladder

SCHLEIERMACHER, HERMENEUTICS AND JENA ROMANTICISM

In Germany, the impact of the French Revolution had led to a quite different appropriation of the past from that of either England or France. If the higher criticism of Reimarus, Lessing and Eichhorn had already created by the latter part of the eighteenth century a historicist perspective on the Bible that in many ways pre-dated that of Volney in France, the revolutionary Romanticism of the Jena circle was to lead towards a new hermeneutical approach to the scriptures. Unlike Chateaubriand, whose rereading of the history of Christianity was motivated primarily by a desire to preserve the *status quo*, this version of Romanticism was from the very first both radical and theoretical.

The reasons were in part intellectual, in part political. Though France had created the Revolution as a political fact, there is a sense in which the *idea* of revolution was created and sustained by Germany long after the event itself had passed into history. There, as nowhere else, the idea of revolution was generalised and philosophised.[1] In spite of peasant revolts in Saxony and Silesia and the annexation of the Rhineland to France, by popular petition, the political impact of the Revolution had been relatively slight. The lack of political unity or any common social issues between the three hundred or so German states, meant that from the first the French Revolution was experienced more as a state of mind than as a political option. Though there was strict censorship in some states, including Austria, this did little to inhibit the intellectual vigour of German cultural life which supported the publication of more books and periodicals at this period than anywhere else in Europe.[2]

[1] See Ehrhard Bahr and Thomas P. Saine (eds.), *The Internalized Revolution: German Reactions to the French Revolution, 1789–1989*, New York: Garland, 1992.

[2] R.R. Palmer, *The World of the French Revolution*, Allen and Unwin, 1971. p. 233.

As a result the metaphor of revolution in its new sense, implying a radical and dramatic transformation of ideas, quickly became a critical commonplace in German writing, and formed, in various ways, the keystone of the philosophies of Fichte, Schelling and Hegel. All three had been intermittent members of the group of young self-consciously styled 'Romantics' in Jena that centred on the Schlegel brothers, August and Friedrich, together with Caroline Michaelis, August's mistress (later to marry Schelling) and Dorothea Mendelssohn, who was later to marry Friedrich. Closely associated with this core were Novalis (Friedrich von Hardenberg), Schleiermacher, Fichte, Schelling, Tieck and, somewhat more distantly and intermittently, Brentano, Hölderlin, Hegel and Steffens. Though they were initially drawn to the university at Jena by the proximity of Herder and Goethe at Weimar, with the publication of their journal, the *Athenaeum*, they rapidly, if briefly, acquired a powerful intellectual and critical momentum of their own – and it is in the pages of the *Athenaeum* that we find some of the first evidence of the new literary and religious theories that were to change the course of German thought.

Yet if one wished to see the secondary effects of the Humboldtian separation of theology from the other humanities in Germany[3] one need look no further than the subsequent reception of the ideas of Friedrich Schleiermacher. Perhaps the only thing on which Wilhelm Dilthey, his nineteenth-century disciple and biographer, and Heinz Kimmerle, the twentieth-century editor of his hermeneutics lecture notes, would have agreed is that his thought is best understood by dividing it into distinct periods, and that in his maturer theological work Schleiermacher moved steadily away from his early Romanticism. Even Karl Barth, while insisting in theory on the peculiar unity of Schleiermacher's sensibility, draws such a sharp distinction between his early role as apologist and his later dogmatics as to make in practice what amounts to an equally strong divide between the Romantic and the theologian.[4] A similar reluctance to see Schleiermacher as a whole can be found among modern philosophical commentators. 'In looking at Schleiermacher', writes Andrew Bowie, 'I shall not be dealing with his theology, impressive though it often is, because most of his philosophy can stand without his theology.'[5] For Bowie, it is axiomatic

[3] See above, p. xii.
[4] Karl Barth, 'Schleiermacher', in *Protestant Theology in the Nineteenth Century*, Valley Forge: Judson Press, 1973, p. 441.
[5] *Aesthetics and Subjectivity from Kant to Nietzsche*, Manchester University Press, 1990, p. 146.

that 'aesthetic theory from Kant onwards faces the problem of finding a whole into which the particular can fit in a meaningful way, once theological certainties have been abandoned'. It is, on the contrary, central to the thesis of this present book that Schleiermacher's theological writings – that is, not merely *On Religion*, but even his late hermeneutics – are of a piece with his philosophy, and are 'Romantic' in the quite specific sense that they owe their origin to the crisis in aesthetics provoked by Kant and the resulting formulations of the Jena group.

Moreover, so far from the new German Romantic philosophy being based on a rejection of religion, it is clear that much of its agenda was devoted to a reconstruction of it in the aftermath of the loss of the divinely guaranteed world order we noted at the beginning of chapter 4. Any new synthesis, however, could no longer be rooted in what was seen as the reimposition of traditional dogma but in the subjectivity of individual experience. A slightly mysterious document known as the 'Oldest System Programme of German Idealism' (1796) illustrates very clearly the degree of common thinking in the Jena group around the time of the *Athenaeum* in the late 1790s. Though this manifesto for a new religious philosophy appears to be in the hand-writing of the young Hegel, it has also been attributed to Schelling and to Hölderlin, or possibly a collaboration of both.[6] In addition, many of its postulates foreshadow the later pronouncements of Friedrich Schlegel. For instance: 'the highest act of reason, which embraces all Ideas, is an aesthetic act ... The philosopher must possess just as much aesthetic power as the poet.' This is not merely a philosophic programme, however, but despite its scorn for priesthood and super-stition, a putative bible for a new religion:

we hear so often that the masses should have a sensuous religion. Not only the masses but also the philosopher needs monotheism of reason of the heart, polytheism of imagination and of art ... we must have a new mythology, but this mythology must be in the service of the Ideas, it must become a mythology of *reason*.

Before we make the Ideas aesthetic i.e. mythological, they are of no interest to the people and on the other hand before mythology is reasonable the

---

[6] See Philippe Lacoue-Labarthe and Jean-Luc Nancy, *The Literary Absolute: the Theory of Literature in German Romanticism*, trs. Philip Barnard and Cheryl Lester, Albany: State University of New York Press, 1988 pp. 27–37; and Bowie, *Aesthetics and Subjectivity*, p. 45. H.S. Harris, however, defends Hegel's authorship, arguing that it fits in with the general development of Hegel's thought very well. *Hegel's Development: Toward the Sunlight 1770–1801*, Oxford: Clarendon Press, 1972, p. 249.

philosopher must be ashamed of it. Thus enlightened and unenlightened must finally shake hands, mythology must become philosophical and the people reasonable, and philosophy must become mythological in order to make the philosophers sensuous. Then eternal unity will reign among us. Never the despairing gaze, never the blind trembling of the people before its wise men and priests. Only then can we expect the *same* development of all powers, of the individual as well as all individuals. No power will then be suppressed any more, then general freedom and equality of spirits will reign! – A higher spirit sent from heaven must found this new religion among us, it will be the last, greatest work of mankind.[7]

At the heart of this 'new religion' is the familiar ideal of a balanced yet total development of every individual's powers. With it a new and unforeseeable relationship between philosophy and aesthetics will become possible. Something of this desire to turn the subjectivity of Kantian aesthetics into the germ of a new religion is also present in both Schlegel's and Schleiermacher's attitude to the Bible, that proto-type of 'an eternally developing book', in which 'the gospel of humanity and culture will be revealed'.[8] For Novalis, too, the Bible is an essentially subjective and unfinished work. 'The history of every man is intended to be a Bible; will be a Bible ... A Bible is the highest task of authorship.'[9] In one of his letters to Novalis, Schlegel suggests, not entirely flippantly, that they should themselves found a new religion – proposing that he could play the role of Paul to the former's Christ.

I am planning to institute a new religion, or rather, to help in its annunciation ... If Lessing were still alive, I would not need to begin this work ... It seems to me that this new Evangelium already begins to stir itself. Besides those indications of philosophy and action in general, there is a stirring of religion in individuals who are particularly our contemporaries and belong to the few fellow citizens of the dawning period. A few examples. Schleiermacher (who if no apostle, is a born critic of anything having to do with the Bible, and, given the word of God, would preach mightily for it) is writing a work on religion ... and does the synthesis of Goethe and Fichte amount to anything other than religion? ... the seeds for the achievement of such a synthesis already lie in Lessing ... not to mention Schelling and Hülsen, whom I think of as antennae on the snail of this new philosophy, stretching forth toward the light and warmth of the new day.[10]

---

[7] Bowie, *Aesthetics and Subjectivity* (own translation) pp. 265–6.

[8] *Ideas*, 95.

[9] *Fragments* III, 202. Cited by Karl Barth, 'Novalis', in *Protestant Theology in the Nineteenth Century*, Valley Forge: Judson Press, 1973, p. 361.

[10] Novalis, *Schriften*, ed. Paul Kluckhohn and Richard Samuel, Leipzig: Bibliographisches Institut, 1929, trs. Thomas McFarland. See *Coleridge and the Pantheist Tradition*, Oxford: Clarendon Press, 1969, pp. 103–4.

If, at one level, this is half a game, it is also at least half serious. As
Schleiermacher also seems to have believed at this stage, any revival of
religion in the context of late eighteenth-century Germany would have
to be so revolutionary as almost to constitute a 'new' religion.
Significantly, even Novalis, fascinated as he was by mediaevalism, was
not unwilling to play with the idea of the role, if not play it outright,
and in his own notes on the *Ideas* he refers to Schlegel as 'the Paul of
the new religion'.[11] Within two years, however, he was dead, and the
torch of this first phase of German Romanticism had passed to
Schleiermacher.

In the *Athenaeum Fragment* 350 Schleiermacher had written:

No poetry, no reality. Just as there is, despite all the senses, no external world
without imagination, so too there is no spiritual world without feeling, no
matter how much sense there is. Whoever only has sense can perceive no
human being, but only what is human: all things disclose themselves to the
magic wand of feeling alone. It fixes people and seizes them; like the eye, it
looks on without being conscious of its own mathematical operation.[12]

To unpack something of the extraordinary theological freight of this
statement and to relate it to the new conception of the Bible emerging
from Jena will involve a lengthy excursion into the entire philosophic
and literary matrix from which it comes.

To begin with, like much of the rest of the aesthetic soundings of the
Athenaeum, it is addressing the philosophic and intellectual crisis provoked by the Romantics' interpretation of Kant's attempt to replace
divine revelation by the human mind as the ground of truth. Hence the
Critique of Pure Reason (1781), was devoted to showing how our perceptions, so far from conforming to the objects themselves, can only
conform to the conditions imposed by our own minds – which include
even such apparently objective external conditions as space and time.
For Kant, the 'real' world of 'things-in-themselves' is both unknown
and unknowable. We inhabit a universe of our own constructs.

This was Kant's own intellectual 'Copernican revolution', which
coincided so closely in time with the political upheavals in France that
it seemed to many of those (mostly German) observers who were aware
of his work that it partook of the same irresistible force. Moreover it
was clear from the start that Kant's philosophy of subjectivity posed a
special problem to theories of literature. Almost from the appearance

[11] Novalis, *Schriften*, p. 23.
[12] Friedrich Schlegel, *Philosophical Fragments*, trs. Peter Firchow, Minneapolis: University of
Minnesota Press, 1991, p. 71.

of the First Critique, philosophers have been deeply divided whether it necessarily implied an unbridgeable gap between mind and the real world.[13] But certainly most Kantians, then and now, have seen the purpose of Kant's Third Critique, *The Critique of Judgement* (1790), as being to discover a bridge between the realms of the two earlier Critiques – pure and practical Reason (or Understanding).[14] For Kant, reflective judgement is the power by which we discover and distinguish between the sublime and the beautiful. In the Third Critique these qualities were reflected alike in nature and art, but subsequent philosophers, following Schiller, in *The Aesthetic Education of Man*, tended to see art rather than nature as central in the construction of the human world. With Hegel the Kantian priorities are explicitly reversed: beauty in art has higher status than natural beauty.[15]

For Kant aesthetic ideas differ from other kinds in that they are products of the imagination. By freeing itself from the strict law of association, and yielding to principles that 'occupy a higher place in reason' imagination works the material of nature up 'into something which surpasses nature.'[16] The problem so posed, that though beauty is in the sphere of sensibility it can in some sense be regarded as objective, has proved equally controversial: seeming to offer a special place to the arts, even while apparently denying the validity of its perceptions. Anyone who has tried to struggle with the inherent gaps and paradoxes of the Kantian position in the Third Critique will sympathise with Friedrich Schlegel's tart observation in *Athenaeum Fragment* 104: 'a Kantian is only someone who believes that Kant is the truth, and who, if the mail coach from Königsberg were ever to have an accident, might very well have to go without the truth for some weeks'.

Thus 'No poetry, no reality' is by no means the Wildean hyperbole that it might appear, but a quite sober statement of the implications of the Third Critique, where Kant takes poetry as the representative of the aesthetic for the purposes of his argument.

Of all the arts poetry (which owes its origins almost entirely to genius and will least be guided by precept or example) maintains the first rank. It expands the mind by setting the imagination at liberty and by offering, within the limits of a given concept, amid the unbounded variety of possible forms accordant

[13] See, for instance, Henry E. Allison, *Kant's Transcendental Idealism*, New Haven, Conn.: Yale University Press, 1983.
[14] See Hazard Adams, *Philosophy of the Literary Symbolic*, Tallahassee: Florida State University Press, 1983, ch. 2: 'The Kantian Symbolic'.
[15] Bowie, *Aesthetics and Subjectivity*, p. 133.
[16] *Philosophical Fragments*, pp. xiv–xxv.

therewith, that which unites the presentment of this concept with a wealth of thought to which no verbal expression is completely adequate, and so rising aesthetically to ideas.[17]

This new role assigned, however tentatively, by Kant to the realm of the aesthetic was to change radically the whole theory of literature and the arts. This area has again recently become a matter of debate with Philippe Lacoue-Labarthe and Jean-Luc Nancy's book, *The Literary Absolute: the Theory of Literature in German Romanticism*. Originally published in French in 1978, it achieved wider currency in the English-speaking world when it was translated in 1988. As the summary of the original French edition puts it:

Because it establishes a period in literature and in art, before it comes to represent a sensibility or style (whose 'return' is regularly announced), romanticism is first of all a *theory*. And the *invention* of literature. More precisely, it constitutes the inaugural moment of literature as *production of its own theory* – and of theory that thinks of itself as literature. With this gesture, it opens the critical age to which we still belong.[18]

Hegel's assertion that 'in our time' the theory of art is much more important than any actual examples of its practice was only a reiteration of one of the fundamental tenets of the Jena group.[19] Indeed, one of the features that rapidly became common to Romanticism right across Europe at this period is a concept of 'Literature' as of inherent value in itself over and above its ostensible subject.[20] The *OED* lists this value-added variant as the third, and most modern, meaning of the word, defining it as 'writing which has a claim to consideration on the ground of beauty of form or emotional effect' – adding the rider that it is 'of very recent emergence in both France and England'. In Germany this Kantian philosophic crisis meant that the idea of literature was to take on an even higher status than in those countries since it could be seen as in some sense *the* mediator of reality. Indeed, it was possible for extreme Kantians to hold that poetic or literary descriptions, as aesthetic constructs, were actually *more* real than direct sense-data, which, in the last resort, have no access at all to things-in-themselves. The distinctive addition made by the Schlegels and their circle, however, is that it was, or should be, impossible to distinguish between

---

[17] Immanuel Kant, *Critique of Judgement*, trs. J.H. Bernard, New York: Hafner, 1951, pp. 170–1.
[18] Lacoue-Labarthe and Nancy, *Literary Absolute*, pp. xxi–xxii.
[19] *Ästhetik*, ed. Friedrich Bassenage, Frankfurt-on-Main 1965, vol. 1, p. 20. Cited by Bowie, *Aesthetics and Subjectivity*, p. 135.
[20] *Literary Absolute*, p. xiv.

such a theory of literature and its actual practice. This produces in much of the Romantic writing of the period a kind of theoretical synaesthesia which links poetry, the novel, philosophy and frequently theology as well. Discussing Schelling's philosophy in *Athenaeum Fragment* 304, for example, Friedrich Schlegel writes:

Philosophy ... is the result of two conflicting forces – of poetry and practice. Where these interpenetrate completely and fuse into one, there philosophy comes into being; and when philosophy disintegrates, it becomes mythology or else returns to life. The most sublime philosophy, some few surmise, may once again turn to poetry.

Similarly, the most famous 'definition' of Romantic poetry in the *Athenaeum Fragment* 116, is astonishingly all-embracing:

Romantic poetry is progressive, universal poetry. Its aim isn't merely to unite all the separate species of poetry and put poetry in touch with philosophy and rhetoric. It tries to and should mix and fuse poetry and prose, inspiration and criticism, the poetry of art and the poetry of nature; and make poetry lively and sociable, and life and society poetical ... It embraces everything that is purely poetic, from the greatest systems of art, containing within themselves still further systems, to the sigh, the kiss that the poeticising child breathes forth in artless song ... It alone can become, like the epic, a mirror of the whole circumambient age ... It is capable of the highest and most variegated refinement, not only from within outwards, but also from without inwards; capable in that it organises – for everything that seeks a wholeness in its effects – the parts along similar lines, so that it opens up a perspective upon an infinitely increasing classicism ... Other kinds of poetry are finished and are now capable of being fully analysed. The romantic kind of poetry is still in the state of becoming; that, in fact, is its real essence: that it should forever be becoming and never be perfected. It can be exhausted by no theory and only a divinatory criticism would dare to try and characterise its ideal. It alone is infinite, just as it alone is free; and it recognises as its first commandment that the will of the poet can tolerate no law above itself. The romantic kind of poetry is the only one that is more than a kind, that is, as it were, poetry itself: for in a certain sense all poetry is or should be romantic.

Romanticism here is not so much a thing as an Aristotelian *entelechy*, a process of becoming.

The fragmentariness is as deliberate as the evasion of definition. As Thomas McFarland has shown, the fragment (or ruin) is the endemic form of Romanticism.[21] Drawing on Lacoue-Labarthe and Nancy's pioneer work, Rodolphe Gasché has convincingly argued that the Schlegels' use of aphoristic fragments is also best understood as part

[21] Thomas McFarland, *Romanticism and the Forms of Ruin*, Princeton University Press, 1981.

of an evolving concept of fragmentation as a philosophic response to the problems raised by Kant.[22] For Kant, aesthetic ideas produce an excess of supplementary representation, so that they invoke 'more thought than can be expressed by words'. Because no aesthetic idea can be fully expressed or presented, they can only be perceived as fragments. Thus, Gasché argues, they are not to be seen as leftover, broken or otherwise detached pieces, but represent the only way in which the supersensible can become present.[23] They stand for an incompleteness that is universal, essential and which has nothing to do with the contingent incompleteness traditionally associated with fragments.[24]

In the case of Friedrich Schlegel, Kant's arguments certainly fell on immediately fertile ground: the aphorism became for him such a compulsive medium that by the time of his death he had filled some 180 notebooks with jottings, aphorisms and fragments, revealing a veritable torrent of ideas as they were 'written on the spur of the moment'. Even the hundreds with which he filled the *Athenaeum* – often against the advice of the other members of the group – represent only a tiny fraction of the whole. In addition to creating them, he – as ever – theorised about them. *Athenaeum Fragment* 24 comments enigmatically, 'Many of the works of the ancients have become fragments. Many modern works are fragments as soon as they are written'; 206 adds: 'A fragment, like a miniature work of art, has to be entirely isolated from the surrounding world and to be complete in itself like a porcupine.' Slightly less gnomically, *Fragment* 77 declares that:

A dialogue is a chain or garland of fragments. An exchange of letters is a dialogue on a larger scale, and memoirs constitute a system of fragments. But as yet no genre exists that is fragmentary both in form and content, simultaneously completely subjective and individual, and completely objective and like a necessary part in a system of all the sciences.

The quest for a new genre that would be adequate to all the theoretical requirements being heaped upon it by the fertile aphoristic genius of Schlegel and his friends becomes a familiar one in the pages of the *Athenaeum*. The famous 'definition' of 'Romantic poetry' in *Fragment* 116, quoted above, is, of course, as its constant elision of the present and conditional tenses suggests, not so much a description as a call to action – a theoretical programme. Given the declared impossibility of

---

[22] Rodolphe Gasché, 'Foreword' to *Philosophical Fragments*, pp. x–xi.
[23] *Ibid.*, pp. xxv–xxvii.
[24] *Ibid.*, p. xxx.

achieving such multitudinous goals with any degree of completeness, the fragment makes not merely philosophic but practical sense as well.

Though the *Athenaeum Fragments* make up the main bulk of the fragments published in the *Athenaeum* between 1798 and 1800, there are two other significant sequences: the *Critical Fragments* (also sometimes known as the *Lyceum Fragments*) and another group simply known as *Ideas*. But what is significant about *Fragment* 350, with which we began this long excursus, is that it is *not* by Friedrich Schlegel, who, with his brother, produced the vast majority of the *Athenaeum Fragments*, but by Schleiermacher. It is one of a small group that appear towards the end of the *Athenaeum Fragments* which, while closely consonant with their general aesthetic programme, also show with hindsight particular concerns that were to be distinctive to Schleiermacher's later work.

The first thing to notice about *Fragment* 350 is how Kantian it is in a thoroughly orthodox sense. It was a fundamental tenet of Kant's philosophy that the ideas of the reason were 'regulative' only, and could not be 'constitutive': that is, though the ideas of God, freedom and immortality were innate, and not acquired through experience, such ideas were strictly without content, and would therefore take different forms according to the particular contingencies of cultural context. Thus a Christian growing up in Heidelberg might have one very clear idea of God; a Muslim in Samarkand would have a different one. Among Kant's Idealist successors, Jacobi, Fichte and Schelling, however, there was a constant tendency to turn these regulative ideas into constitutive ones, and so make possible some kind of direct intuitive vision either of the absolute or of things-in-themselves. Here Schleiermacher's rigorous Kantianism is the more noticeable because it was not shared by other members of the Jena circle, which, we recall, included both Fichte and Schelling. Fichte, for instance, was quite explicit about his rejection of Kant on this point. Whereas the French had only 'liberated man from external chains', his philosophy – 'the first system of liberty', as he proudly termed it – liberated man 'from the chains of the Thing-in-itself, or of external influence, and sets him forth in his first principle as a self-sufficient being'.[25] This was a point that clearly appealed to Friedrich Schlegel, who, in 1795, had declared that there was no question that Fichte was the 'greatest metaphysical thinker now alive'.[26] It was, however, Fichte's revolutionary politics, rather than his metaphysics, that so alarmed a counter-revolutionary

---

[25] Cited by Palmer, *World of the French Revolution*, p. 247.
[26] Hans Eichner, *Friedrich Schlegel*, New York: Twayne 1970, p. 75.

secret society, the Eudämonists, that they forced him to resign his chair at Jena.

Just as Schleiermacher has followed Kant's idea of the aesthetic in the Third Critique, so he also follows Kant in insisting that 'there is, despite all the senses, no external world without imagination'. His suggestion that, similarly, we construct our own spiritual worlds by feeling, is, of course, his own – and, as we shall see, it is a key idea in the construction of his later theology. But another sentence of his, from *Fragment* 336, shows how close also to Friedrich Schlegel his thought is at this period:

A human being should be like a work of art which, though openly exhibited and freely accessible, can nevertheless be enjoyed and understood only by those who bring feeling and study to it.

This is both like and unlike Schlegel. At first sight the comparison between a human being and a work of art looks like the familiar Schlegelian synaesthesia, but the human centre of interest is more typically Schleiermacher – as are the implications for Kantian philosophy of placing a human being rather than a work of beauty to bridge the abyss. Religion is to be found in an organic sense of the wholeness of things. In the Second Speech of *On Religion* we are enjoined to 'Think of the genius of humanity as the most accomplished and universal artist.'[27] Here too, is an almost exact parallel to Chateaubriand's assertion of our need to experience people as a totality, rather than piecemeal – a totality that, paradoxically, can here only be presented through the medium of fragments.

It is in this new literary and philosophic form, the fragment, that we find unfolding the first hints of a genuinely hermeneutic understanding of the past. *Athenaeum Fragment* 153, by Friedrich Schlegel, sets the theme:

The more popular an ancient author, the more romantic. This is the governing principle of the new anthology that the moderns have in effect made from the old anthology of the classics, or, rather, that they are still in the process of making.

Though Schlegel is not referring to any particular anthology here, his phrase the 'old anthology' recalls the famous so-called 'Greek Anthology' – western Europe's most important single collection of Greek poetry that had found its home in Heidelberg University Library. His

---

[27] Friedrich Schleiermacher, *On Religion: Speeches to its Cultured Despisers*, trs. Richard Couter (1799), Cambridge University Press, 1988, pp. 120ff.

general point, however, concerns our perspective on the past. To appropriate it we construct – or rather, are constantly constructing: the unfinished nature of the process is important – our own 'anthology' of what is significant to us from the literature of antiquity. Romanticism is thus, in effect, a particular selection or anthology of classical works.

This was, of course, true in a literal sense, in that the Romanticism represented by the *Athenaeum* and its circle began as an attempt to break away from modern literature and recapture the spirit of the classical world. The Schlegels started not with a revolutionary programme for the future, but a new vision of the poetry of antiquity inspired by Winckelmann – and, in the footsteps of Goethe, a search for ways of recreating the classical moment in modernity. From this quest came the distinction between Apollonian and Dionysian modes of art, later to be taken up and elaborated by Nietzsche, and with it, however unwittingly, the beginnings of a philosophy of history.[28] Ironically, it was Friedrich Schlegel's own distinction between the classic and the Romantic that led him towards classicism. For him modern literature emphasised the miraculous, fictitious, purely imaginative and unrealistic to an extent that was incompatible with the kind of true classical objectivity that he so much admired in, for instance, Goethe's *Wilhelm Meister*.[29]

This indicates something of the paradox that lies at the heart of Jena Romanticism. Any modern reader of *Wilhelm Meister* – especially in Carlyle's influential English translation of 1824 – can be forgiven for thinking that it represents the epitome of the Romantic novel.[30] Though, on the one hand, Schlegel's definition of the 'Romantic' includes all post-Renaissance literature, and therefore embraces the entire modern period, there is a second implicit definition contained, as it were, within the main one that defines it more by the way it seeks to appropriate the past than by its representation of the present. Indeed we might say that German Romanticism uses the idea of revolution, and therefore its sense of the historical difference between past and present, as a way of assimilating and coming to terms with the works of the past. Such a mode of appropriation is, of course, utterly at odds with the kind of ahistorical appropriation of the past that we see in, for instance, Dante's use of Virgil.

---

[28] *Literary Absolute*, p. 10.

[29] Eichner, *Friedrich Schlegel*, pp. 22, 65.

[30] See Stephen Prickett, 'Fictions and Metafictions: *Phantastes, Wilhelm Meister* and the idea of the *Bildungsroman*', in William Reaper (ed.), *The Gold Thread: Essays on George MacDonald*, Edinburgh University Press, 1991, pp. 109–25.

We have another example of the relation between the fragment and the anthology of appropriations in one of Schlegel's last groups of aphorisms, the *Ideas*, written in response to Schleiermacher's *On Religion*, where the Bible is seen as the supreme example of such an anthology.

The new eternal gospel that Lessing prophesied will appear as a bible: but not as a single book in the usual sense. Even what we now call the Bible is actually a system of books. And that is, I might add, no mere arbitrary turn of phrase! Or is there some other word to differentiate the idea of an infinite book from an ordinary one, than Bible, the book per se, the absolute book? And surely there is an eternally essential and even practical difference if a book is merely a means to an end, or an independent work, an individual, a personified idea. It cannot be this without divine inspiration, and here the esoteric concept is itself in agreement with the exoteric one; and, moreover, no idea is isolated, but is what it is only in combination with all other ideas. An example will explain this. All the classical poems of the ancients are coherent, inseparable; they form an organic whole, they constitute, properly viewed, only a single poem, the only one in which poetry itself appears in perfection. In a similar way, in a perfect literature all books should be only a single book, and in such an eternally developing book, the gospel of humanity and culture will be revealed. (*Ideas*, 95)

In spite of being one of Schlegel's closest friends at this period Friedrich Schleiermacher was in many ways an odd man out in the Jena circle. The only other active Christian in the group in the 1790s was Novalis, who had initially studied in Jena, but whose work in Freiburg from 1797, and later in Saxony, meant that he never met Schleiermacher before his death in 1801. His mystical and backward-looking religion was, in any case, at an opposite pole from Schleiermacher's determined engagement with the modern world.[31] Although it was known among a group who were predominantly either agnostic or anti-Christian, that Schleiermacher, too, had little time for the conventional Enlightenment Lutheranism of the day, he had nevertheless already chosen to be ordained as a Lutheran clergyman. On the morning of 21 November 1797, Schleiermacher's birthday, a group of his friends, including Schlegel, burst into his flat in Berlin, where he was working, to hold a surprise party, during which they repeatedly urged him to justify to them his position as a Christian by writing a book.[32] To encourage him, Schlegel moved in with him for the next eighteen months. Though it was to be some time before Schleiermacher took up the

---

[31] Jack Forstman, *A Romantic Triangle: Schleiermacher and Early German Romanticism*, Misoula, Mont.: Scholars Press, 1977, pp. 115–22.
[32] *Ibid.*, pp. 65–6.

challenge, in August 1798, there was never any doubt in his mind – or in theirs – that this was to be a *Kampfschrift*, a 'fighting book', that was directly to address his hitherto enigmatic relationship with his avant-garde friends.

The result, *On Religion: Speeches to its Cultured Despisers*, appeared in 1799. The title was an open enough code: the 'cultured despisers' were, of course, the other members of the Jena circle. For them he develops and expands the philosophical and theological position hinted at in the fragments both he and Schlegel had contributed to the *Athenaeum*:

Religion's essence is neither thinking nor acting, but intuition and feeling. It wishes to intuit the Universe ... Thus religion is opposed to these two in everything that makes up its essence and in everything that characterises its effects. Metaphysics and morals see in the whole universe only humanity as the centre of all relatedness, as the condition of all being and the cause of all becoming; religion wishes to see the infinite, its imprint and its manifestation, in humanity no less than in all other individual and finite forms ... Religion shows itself to you as the necessary and indispensable third next to those two, as their natural counterpart, not slighter in worth and splendour than what you wish of them.[33]

Though later editions, in 1806 and 1821, were to soften and to some extent disguise the radical nature of this address to his Romantic friends, what we have here is theologically very uncompromising indeed. In spite of the fact that the words 'God' and 'divinity' appear in the text with some frequency (56 and 36 times respectively), religion, as he tells us explicitly in the Second Speech, does not depend on there being a God at all.[34] Expanding on *Athenaeum Fragment* 350, written more or less at the same time, he continues that 'belief in God depends on the direction of the imagination' which is 'the highest and most original element in us ... it is your imagination that creates the world for you, and ... you can have no God without the world ... In religion, therefore, the idea of God does not rank as high as you think.' Nor is religion a matter either of right knowledge (which is what Schleiermacher means here by 'metaphysics') or right action (or 'morals'), but primarily a matter of 'intuition'. Unlike either metaphysics or morals, intuition seems to consist of 'pure receptivity'. For Schleiermacher in 1799, religious self-awareness begins with the familiar Romantic dialectic between what was conceived of as a spontaneous act of individual intuition and the more objective action of the universe upon us. We

---

[33] *On Religion*, p. 102.   [34] *Ibid.*, pp. 65 and 136.

begin with what he calls an 'intuition of the infinite' (*Anschauung des Unendlichen*).

This is, by definition, a deeply personal and even, to some degree one suspects, incommunicable experience. Later in the same speech, he explains that 'intuition is and always remains something individual, set apart, the immediate perception, nothing more ... Others may stand right behind you, right alongside you, and everything can appear differently to them.'[35] 'To intuit the infinite' in this sense of apprehending the wholeness of things would have been familiar alike to Blake and Chateaubriand.

The universe exists in uninterrupted activity and reveals itself to us in every moment. Every form that it brings forth, every being to which it gives a separate existence according to the fullness of life, every occurrence that spills forth from its rich, ever-fruitful womb, is an action of the same upon us. Thus to accept everything individual as part of the whole and everything limited as a representation of the infinite is religion.[36]

Like Chateaubriand, Schleiermacher was passionately convinced that civilisation, the triumph of spirit over nature, was a peculiarly Christian quality,[37] and like Chateaubriand too he shows a rhetorical flair for taking apparent problems in tracing this argument and declaring them as strengths. Thus he counters the unspoken objection that his idea of intuition is dangerously subjective by stressing the personal immediacy of religious experience against almost all forms of mediation.

What one commonly calls belief, accepting what another person has done, wanting to ponder and empathise with what someone else has thought and felt, is a hard and unworthy service, and instead of being the highest in religion, as one supposes, it is exactly what must be renounced by those who would penetrate into its sanctuary. To want to have and retain belief in this sense proves that one is incapable of religion; to require this kind of faith from others shows that one does not understand it.[38]

'In Kant', said Dilthey, 'Schleiermacher learned how to think', and we have already seen how Kantian – even stubbornly so – were many of his early fragments. Indeed, there is a sense in which the *Speeches on Religion* can be read as Schleiermacher's commentary on and disagreement with Kant.[39] His choice of words gives a clue. When he talks of

[35] *Ibid.*, pp. 105, 106.
[36] *Ibid.*, p. 105.
[37] See Barth, 'Schleiermacher', p. 435.
[38] *On Religion*, p. 134.
[39] *Ibid.*, p. 19.

'imagination' as the 'highest and most original element in us' he uses not the Kantian *Einbildungskraft* (a term used by Schleiermacher only once early in the Second Speech) but the commoner and more poetic *Phantasie*. Nevertheless, his comments on the subject drew an almost immediate echo of approval from Schlegel:

The mind, says the author of the Talks on Religion, can understand only the universe. Let imagination [*Phantasie*] take over and you will have a God. Quite right: for the imagination is man's faculty for perceiving divinity. (*Ideas*, 8)

The verbal shift is interesting, in that, true to the Romantics' agenda of poeticising philosophy, the creativity of the imagination has been made more immediately subjective, personal and aesthetic. Such a revision would almost certainly not have been to Kant's liking: in 1796 he had attacked another philosopher, Friedrich Heinrich Jacobi, in an article entitled 'On a Certain Genteel Tone which has of late appeared in Philosophy'; Jacobi, he complained, was 'poeticising' his system by stressing intuition and feeling. Whereas, on the contrary, Kant declared, 'philosophy is fundamentally prosaic; and to attempt to philosophise poetically is very much as if a merchant should undertake to make up his account-books not in prose but in verse'.[40]

Nevertheless, Schleiermacher's word for 'intuition', *Anschauung*, is, of course, also a key Kantian term, referring to 'a singular representation' (as distinct from a 'concept', which is a general representation) of which we are immediately aware[41] – that is to say, our awareness is not mediated by any other agency. Such intuitions are the origins of 'aesthetic ideas' – the very things that Kant somewhat hesitantly suggests in the Third Critique might bridge the 'abyss' between pure and practical reason. Moreover, though commentators are (as usual) divided over the question of whether Schleiermacher differentiates art from religion, even if we accept that (unlike Friedrich Schlegel) he *did* draw a clear distinction between the two, he also explicitly admits that there can be what he calls a 'passing over' from one to the other.[42] Certainly it seems clear that Schleiermacher at this stage was a sufficiently un-Kantian Romantic to see religion as being, at any rate, *like* art, in that it provides an intuitive bridge between pure and practical Reason, and so might even be said to offer a closer approximation to reality than sense-perception itself. There is support

[40] A.O. Lovejoy, *The Reason, the Understanding, and Time*, Baltimore, Md.: Johns Hopkins Press, 1961, p. 11.
[41] Ralph C.S. Walker, *Kant*, Routledge, 1978, pp. 42–3.
[42] *On Religion*, p. 48.

for this in the stress he lays on religious intuitions as particular and unmediated forms of experience.

Though not always consistent, the idea of art was to remain central to Schleiermacher's thought. Indeed, if his use of the word *Kunst* varies between its older sense of a 'craft' and its new post-Kantian meaning of 'art' in the high-status aesthetic sense, that in itself is a good illustration of his hermeneutic conviction that words belong irreducibly to specific contexts that cannot be altogether transcended by abstract concepts or definitions.[43] As in the System-Programme, 'art' in this latter sense is a touchstone of human freedom and individuality – a demonstration of the uniqueness of each person's viewpoint. But for Schleiermacher this aesthetic assertion of individual uniqueness is not necessarily a source of social division: 'interpretation is art'[44] and 'all people who make a work of art their own are to be regarded as artists'.[45] Though always subjective, art is always a two-way communication.

One of the principles set forth by August Schlegel and underlying the *Athenaeum*'s final group of fragments, the *Ideas*, was that the true artist is someone who needs no mediator. Indeed, the 'absoluteness' of the artist lies precisely in this ability to dispense with the mediation: 'Only someone who has his own religion, his own original way of looking at infinity can be an artist' (*Ideas*, 13); but 'everyone is an artist whose central purpose in life is to educate his intellect' (*Ideas*, 20). Yet, of course, mediation is not merely necessary, but inescapable – and indeed, it is the central function of the artist.

Artists make mankind an individual by connecting the past with the future in the present. Artists are the higher organ of the soul where the vital spirits of all external humanity join together, and where inner humanity has its primary sphere of action. (*Ideas*, 64)

Mediation, under such circumstances, as Schlegel argued, is so internalised as to become 'appropriation' in the distinctively German and organic sense we encountered in the Introduction to this book.[46] Thus *Idea* 5 reads:

The mind understands something only insofar as it absorbs it like a seed into itself, nurtures it, and lets it grow into blossom and fruit. Therefore scatter holy seed into the soil of the spirit, without any affectation and any added superfluities.

---

[43] See Bowie, *Aesthetics and Subjectivity*, p. 149.
[44] *Hermeneutik und Kritik*, ed. Manfred Frank, Frankfurt-on-Main: Suhrkamp, 1977, p. 80.
[45] Bowie, *Aesthetics and Subjectivity*, pp. 159–60.
[46] *Literary Absolute*, pp. 67–8.

Here the almost untranslatable idea of *Bildung*, or self-development, is once again directly linked with hermeneutics: understanding is not an instant process, but one that involves the whole personality, taking time and requiring nurture and growth.

Not least among the problems of relating Schleiermacher's pioneering work in hermeneutics to his early Romanticism is that with the exception of two addresses to the Prussian Academy of Science in Berlin, and the so-called *Kompendienartige Darstellung* of 1819,[47] all that remains of his work in this field is a collection of lecture notes. Nothing of these was available to the scholarly public until as late as 1959 when a selection was edited and published by Heinz Kimmerle. Until that time what reputation Schleiermacher had in the history of hermeneutic theory was almost entirely dependent on the advocacy of Wilhelm Dilthey (1833–1911). With the publication of Kimmerle's manuscripts and subsequent work by such scholars as Manfred Frank,[48] it has now become apparent how much Schleiermacher had been appropriated by Dilthey for his own purposes, and made to serve his primarily philosophical approach to hermeneutics.[49]

Dilthey's programme was, however, fundamentally different from Schleiermacher's in that he wanted the humanities to discover for themselves a critical foundation that would put them methodologically on a par with the natural sciences.[50] For him, the task of the sciences was to *explain* natural phenomena, whereas that of the humanities was to *understand* human life and all the complex forms of expression it had created.[51] Though both might deal with the same phenomena, it would be with different perspectives and methodology. He saw man as essentially a 'hermeneutical animal' whose self-understanding came from interpreting the heritage and shared

---

[47] The only edition of which was published by Friedrich Lüke in 1838 and has never been reprinted.

[48] See Werner G. Jeanrond, 'The Impact of Schleiermacher's Hermeneutics on Contemporary Interpretation Theory', in David Jasper (ed.), *The Interpretation of Belief: Coleridge, Schleiermacher, and Romanticism*, Macmillan, 1986, pp. 81–95. Also Bowie, *Aesthetics and Subjectivity*, pp. 148ff.

[49] Werner G. Jeanrond, *Theological Hermeneutics: Development and Significance*, Macmillan, 1991, pp. 51–7.

[50] Ironically, a very different – and in some ways more accurate – version of Schleiermacher's hermeneutics had long been available in the lectures of Philip August Boeckh (1785–1867) at the University of Berlin. See Kurt Mueller-Vollmer (ed.), *The Hermeneutics Reader*, Oxford: Basil Blackwell, 1986, pp. 136–8.

[51] Richard E. Palmer, *Hermeneutics: Interpretation Theory in Schleiermacher, Dilthey, Heidegger and Gadamer*, Evanston, Ill.: Northwestern University Press, 1969, p. 115.

world he inherited from the past, and which was a constant influence on his present actions and decisions.[52] With this passionate lifelong interest in the development of the human sciences (*Geisteswissenschaften*) it is hardly surprising that Schleiermacher and his hermeneutical theories should have been such a major influence on Dilthey's work – so much so that he not merely wrote about his great predecessor, but he also produced a major biography of him.

Yet, ironically, Dilthey's scholarly, even reverent, appropriation of his master exposes the hermeneutical dilemma perhaps more clearly than anywhere else. Schleiermacher's conviction that 'the hermeneutical procedure is to understand the author better than he understood himself' should, if anywhere, have revealed itself most clearly in Dilthey's own hermeneutical understanding of him. Though Dilthey recognised that, because we all come to any given problem from a background of different life-experiences, every interpreter must necessarily understand a given object differently, he nevertheless also seemed to have believed (by analogy with the physical sciences rather than from idealism) that some kind of 'objectively valid knowledge' was possible. As a number of recent commentators have pointed out, this, in itself, presents a fundamental contradiction at the heart of Dilthey's work.[53] Moreover Kimmerle and Frank have made it clear that Dilthey's understanding and use of Schleiermacher was, at best, one-sided, and at worst distorted and even limiting. In particular, the lecture notes make it clear that Dilthey's stress on psychological reconstruction of the historical contexts of the past had obscured what Schleiermacher had called the 'grammatical' side of textual reconstruction – that is, an understanding not merely of the individual and personal situation of the author of a given piece of writing, but also of the more general linguistic conditions that applied at that particular historical moment.[54] Contrary to Gadamer's accusation that Schleiermacher's hermeneutics had a theological bias, Frank has convincingly argued that though Schleiermacher began with his natural need to interpret specific theological texts, he never insisted that the theologian has any prerogative of understanding – and certainly not in the technical question of understanding language.[55]

[52] *Ibid.*, p. 118.

[53] *Ibid.*, p. 106; Jeanrond, *Theological Hermeneutics*, p. 56.

[54] Friedrich Schleiermacher, 'Introduction to General Hermeneutics', in Mueller-Vollmer (ed.), *Hermeneutics Reader*, pp. 86–93.

[55] Jeanrond, 'Impact of Schleiermacher's Hermeneutics', pp. 83–7.

Once again we encounter fundamental and almost subliminal tensions between a model where theology is seen as constituting a 'bias' to hermeneutics, and one where any understanding that leaves out a part is seen as distorted by being incomplete. The latter is exemplified in the thesis of Philippe Lacoue-Labarthe and Jean-Luc Nancy that what was being forged among the Jena group in the final years of the eighteenth century was an essentially new concept of literature as a particular form of valorised writing that necessarily included its own literary theory. Several aspects of what Lacoue-Labarthe and Nancy call the 'literary absolute' are relevant to this debate about Schleiermacher's hermeneutics. The first takes us back to Schlegel's idea of the way in which the modern world, of necessity, interprets the ancient. *Athenaeum Fragment* 393 reads:

In order to translate perfectly from the classics into a modern language, the translator would have to be so expert in his language that, if need be, he could make everything modern; but at the same time he would have to understand antiquity so well that he would be able not just to imitate it but, if necessary, re-create it.

We recall Borges' short story, *Pierre Menard: Author of the 'Quixote'*, where the eponymous hero is so steeped in Cervantes that he is able to recreate *Don Quixote* word for word not from memory, but, as it were, *ab initio* from his own creative faculties. Nevertheless, as we have already seen in the second chapter, Borges' humorous paradox also raises a perfectly serious point not merely about the nature of translation, but also about the process of appropriation that inevitably accompanies it. It was a fundamental tenet of German, as of English, Romanticism that translation was both impossible and necessary. The question of how far any translation from the past could avoid being modern was not, however, an entirely theoretical question in 1800. It had already been raised in England with the case of Chatterton's 'forgery' of the Rowley poems. As has been mentioned, Wackenroder had produced his *Confessions of an Art-Loving Friar* in 1797, and a few years later, in 1818–19, Konrad Friedrich Schulze's *Cäcilie*, a 'mediaeval' epic poem dealing with the conquest and conversion of heathen Denmark in the tenth century, would be published posthumously. Both of these, however, pale into insignificance beside Rudolf Borchardt's early twentieth-century *Dante Deutsch*, which attempted to rectify the unpardonable omission of Dante from German literature (where he clearly belonged) by belatedly providing a translation of the *Divine*

Comedy into a suitably embellished and eclectic fourteenth-century German.[56]

Another fragment by Schlegel, no. 401, picks up this theme of historical understanding and turns it into the classic hermeneutical paradox:

In order to understand someone who only partially understands himself, you first have to understand him completely and much better than he himself does, but then only partially and precisely as much as he does himself.

It is at this point that we begin to realise the degree to which the development of Schleiermacher's later hermeneutics is already present, as it were in embryo in these fragments of Schlegel. Thesis 17 of the Introduction to *General Hermeneutics* (1819), for instance, contains the famous injunction already cited above:

'To understand the text at first as well as and then even better than its author.' Since we have no direct knowledge of what was in the author's mind, we must try to become aware of many things of which he himself may have been unconscious, except insofar as he reflects on his own work and becomes his own reader.[57]

It is characteristic of the Romantic idea of the literary absolute to integrate theory and artifact. The act of appropriation is at once possessive and reflexive in the classic hermeneutic circle.

Allied with this internalised and organic model of appropriation is another feature we have already seen as characteristic of German Romanticism: the sense of a moving target. The model of revolution, with its beguiling suggestions of some new and hitherto undreamed-of organisation of affairs about to burst forth is never far beneath the surface. Schlegel's farewell to the readers of the *Athenaeum* in the second and last issue of 1800 is a typical mixture of revolutionary and apocalyptic prophecy:

Another reason for consolation about the acknowledged unintelligibility of the *Athenaeum* rests in the acknowledgement itself, because it teaches us that the evil will be temporary. The new era proclaims itself to be fleet-footed and winged-soled. The sunrise has donned seven league boots. – For a long time it has been lightning on the horizon of poetry. In one powerful cloud all the thunderous power of heaven was compressed. For a time it thundered mightily, now it seems to lighten only in the distance, but soon it will return with more horrible force. Soon we will speak no longer of a single

---

[56] George Steiner, *After Babel: Aspects of Language and Translation*, Oxford University Press, 1976, pp. 338–41.
[57] *Hermeneutics Reader*, p. 83.

thunderstorm because the whole heaven will burn in a massive flame, and then all your puny lightning rods will be of no use at all. Then will the nineteenth century actually begin, and then also will that little riddle of the unintelligibility of the *Athenaeum* be resolved. What a catastrophe! Then there will be readers who can read. In the nineteenth century everyone will be able to read the fragments with ease and pleasure as an after-dinner diversion, and even for the hardest, most indigestible ones no nutcracker will be required. In the nineteenth century every man, every reader will find *Lucinde* innocent, *Genoveva* a Protestant piece and the didactic elegies of A.W. Schlegel entirely too easy and transparent . . .

The great divide between understanding and not understanding will become more universal, stronger and clearer. Much more hidden unintelligibility will inevitably break forth, but also the understanding will show its omnipotence. He who honours the soul of character and the talent of genius sounds abroad the feeling and the intuition of art. He himself will be understood, and everyone else will finally have to comprehend and admit that each can require the highest and that till now humanity was neither malicious nor dumb but only clumsy and new.[58]

For all its irony and bluster, such an apocalyptic apprehension of what Ruskin was, from the other end of the century, also to call 'the storm cloud of the nineteenth century', was firmly rooted in history – in two almost diametrically opposite senses of the phrase. Firstly, it shows a thorough internalisation of the idea of revolution as an inevitable historical process leading towards unforeseeable change. Not that the fact that it *is* essentially unforeseeable, of course, inhibits Schlegel for a moment from uttering a string of gnomic and ironic predictions. But, more significantly, there is also an idea of inevitable progress here. Ideas that seem difficult or esoteric to one generation are accepted easily by the next as a matter of course. A world where everyone finds *Lucinde*, his semi-autobiographical erotic novel, innocent, or his poetry easy, is one that enshrines a model of intellectual progress (or *Bildung*) and anticipates by forty years Feuerbach's more famous aphorism: 'What yesterday is still religion is no longer such today; and what today is atheism, tomorrow will be religion.'[59]

Similarly, just as Romantic poetry is never completed, but in a constant state of becoming, so the process of constructing an anthology out of the works of the past is a never-ending, never-to-be-completed process. Even categories themselves shimmer and change before our eyes:

---

[58] *Athenaeum*, vol. III, pp. 350–1.
[59] Ludwig Feuerbach, *The Essence of Christianity* (1841), trs. George Eliot, New York: Harper, 1957, p. 31.

Poetry and philosophy are, depending on one's point of view, different spheres, different forms, or simply the component parts of religion. For only try really to combine the two and you will find yourself with nothing but religion. (*Ideas*, 46)

This sense of understanding not as a state, but as a process of constant flux and change, is, of course, the other side of the insistence both by the Schlegels and by Schleiermacher on the unmediated particularity of our intuitions. It leads directly forward to the Introduction to the *General Hermeneutics*:

each person represents one locus where a given language takes shape in a particular way, and his speech can be understood only in the context of the totality of the language. But then too he is a person who is a constantly developing spirit, and his speaking can be understood as only one moment in this development in relation to all others.[60]

If illustration were needed to this principle we need look no further than the way in which Schleiermacher himself revised *On Religion* in the 1806 and 1821 editions. In his admirably lucid discussion of these revisions Richard Crouter subscribes neither to the theory that Schleiermacher shifted radically away from his early Romanticism, nor that he remained essentially true to his original view, but rather points to a whole group of unrelated factors behind the alterations, ranging from changes in the German intellectual landscape, to shifts in the audience he is addressing, and, not least, the subsequent conversions of Friedrich Schlegel and Dorothea Mendelssohn to Catholicism.[61] According to this view, Schleiermacher's appropriation of religion (unlike, say, that of Chateaubriand) was not so much an attempt to present eternal truths in a way that would stand for all time, but represents a singularity: a particular moment in history when he felt that certain things were best expressed in one way rather than another.

Whether it is also true, as Forstman argues, that Schlegel's movement towards religion was also one away from Schleiermacher in the direction of the mysticism of Novalis seems to me less clear.[62] Karl Barth, for instance, sees no essential divergence, but a direct line of theological development from Novalis to Schleiermacher.[63] Certainly though what Schlegel called his 'Bible project' hardly resembled his

---

[60] *Hermeneutics Reader*, p. 75.
[61] *On Religion*, pp. 55–73.
[62] *Romantic Triangle*, pp. 25–7.
[63] Karl Barth, 'Novalis', p. 361.

later Catholicism in any way, it served to make the Bible the central and organising metaphor for the last group of aphorisms to appear in the *Athenaeum*: the *Ideas*. Many of these were composed at the time when Schlegel and Schleiermacher were sharing the same flat in Berlin. Though a smaller number of the *Ideas* than the *Athenaeum Fragments* can be directly attributed to Schleiermacher, it is also true that Schleiermacher seems to have set the agenda for the *Ideas* in a way that he did not in the earlier group. *Fragment* 112 is surely also a significant pointer to Schlegel's state of mind at the time:

In our age or any other, nothing more to the credit of Christianity can be said than that the author of the *Speeches on Religion* is a Christian.

It is here, in this final group of aphorisms, that we find made explicit for the first time the idea which we touched on in the Introduction, that the Bible is not merely the central book of Western civilisation, but that in its subsequent history it encapsulates and in some way stands for the development of literature as a whole.

Poetry and philosophy are, depending on one's point of view, different spheres, different forms, or simply the component parts of religion. For only try really to combine the two and you will find yourself with nothing but religion. (*Ideas*, 46)

In the world of language or, what is much the same, the world of art and culture, religion necessarily assumes the guise of a mythology or a bible. (*Ideas*, 38)

Here, at last, it seems, Schlegel has found the channel through which all his torrent of Romantic ideas can be brought together. The Bible combines poetry, philosophy, the novel and mythology in an inextricable profusion. Religion can here be fused into art. The fragment can hint at unrealisable sublimity and infinite wholes. The Bible constitutes the ultimate anthology from which we constantly shape and reshape our self-understanding. Though it can be generalised and read typologically, it nevertheless speaks always in singularities, with a prophetic voice to the elect throughout history. The history of that self-understanding is essentially revolutionary and dynamic, changing individuals and societies in unforeseen ways. Above all, it fulfils that final requirement of the Romantic absolute, in that it not merely constitutes a unique art-form, but that it also has always been believed to contain its own critical theory, by which it must be read and understood.

JULIUS HARE: *GUESSES AT TRUTH*

The immediate influence of the *Athenaeum* was muted, even inside Germany. Outside Germany it remained virtually unknown. For most of the first fifteen years of the new century Britain remained isolated from continental thought as much by language as by the contingency of the Napoleonic wars. German was read even less than French. Yet there were a few who knew German: among the first romantics most prominently Coleridge. The real question of the extent of Coleridge's German influences has been overlaid and muddied by the secondary question of his plagiarisms, and in the past it has served the interests of some of his defenders to play down the extent of his knowledge of German writers and theologians.[64] Yet in the last twenty years of his life there is ample evidence of his extensive acquaintance with almost all the major German Romantics. *The Statesman's Manual* (1817), for instance, despite lacking any overt reference to other sources, British or foreign, incorporates to a surprising degree not merely the Schlegels' sense of the Bible as at once having an internal dynamic and providing a moving target, but even Chateaubriand's broad cultural sweep:

they [the Scriptures] are the living educts of the Imagination; of that reconciling and mediatory power, which incorporating the Reason in Images of the Sense, and organising (as it were) the flux of the Senses by the permanence and self-circling energies of the Reason, gives birth to a system of symbols, harmonious in themselves, and consubstantial with the truths, of which they are the *conductors* ... Hence ... the Sacred Book is worthily intitled the WORD OF GOD. Hence too, its contents present to us the stream of time continuous as Life and a symbol of Eternity, inasmuch as the Past and the Future are virtually contained in the Present ... In the Scriptures therefore both facts and persons must of necessity have a two-fold significance, a past and a future, a temporary and a perpetual, a particular and a universal application. They must be at once Portraits and Ideals.[65]

Much of Coleridge's later work centred around giving substance to this pregnant summary. In addition to *Aids to Reflection* and the posthumous *Confessions of an Inquiring Spirit* (1846), there remained a mass of other manuscript and notebook material destined to remain unpublished

---

[64] In many ways McFarland's magisterial *Coleridge and the Pantheist Tradition* is still the best account of both the German influences on Coleridge and his plagiarisms, but see also G.N.G. Orsini, *Coleridge and German Idealism*, Carbondale and Edwardsville: Southern Illinois University Press, 1969, and Norman Fruman, *Coleridge: The Damaged Archangel*, Allen and Unwin, 1972.

[65] S.T. Coleridge, 'The Statesman's Manual', in *Lay Sermons*, ed. R.J. White, Routledge, 1972, pp. 28–30.

until the late twentieth century. Besides the so-called 'Magnum Opus' and the *Philosophical Lectures*, Coleridge's notebooks of the later 1820s are almost exclusively devoted to biblical commentaries of one kind or another. I have written extensively on these elsewhere,[66] and, with so much other material available, it would be redundant to repeat it here. As was hardly surprising, both the *Aids* and, even more, the *Confessions* achieved notoriety as well as success, and what some felt was a cowardly unwillingness to reveal the extent of his indebtedness to his German sources, especially in the *Confessions*, often made his arguments more obscure than was necessary.[67]

If the next generation was quicker to acknowledge its sources, it was hardly better equipped to understand them. The Germanophilia of Carlyle and De Quincey was still the exception rather than the beginning of a new trend. When, for instance, in 1823 E.B. Pusey decided to find out more about recent developments in Lutheran theology he could find only two men in the whole University of Oxford who knew any German.[68] Cambridge was only slightly better off. Herbert Marsh, the translator of Michaelis' *Introduction to the New Testament* (1793–1801) had become Lady Margaret Professor of Divinity there in 1807, and had introduced some knowledge of German scholarship. More influential in the long run, however, was Julius Hare, a Fellow of Trinity and later rector of Herstmonceux, who was to become one of the finest German scholars in England. His rectory at Herstmonceux was said to contain more than 2,000 books in German alone.[69] It

---

[66] On *Aids to Reflection* see Stephen Prickett *Coleridge and Wordsworth: the Poetry of Growth*, Cambridge University Press, 1970, ch. 6; for *Confessions of an Inquiring Spirit*, see *Romanticism and Religion* (ch. 1) and *Words and the 'Word': Language, Poetics and Biblical Interpretation*, Cambridge University Press, 1986, pp. 4–5; for the late notebooks, see *Romanticism and Religion*, ch. 2.

[67] See, for instance, John Sterling's comment: 'Great part of the obscurity of the Letters arises from his anxiety to avoid the difficulties and absurdities of the common views, and his panic terror of saying anything that bishops and good people would disapprove. He paid a heavy price, viz. all his own candour and simplicity, in hope of gaining the favour of persons like Lady—; and you see what his reward is! A good lesson for us all. Thomas Carlyle, *Life of John Sterling*, Chapman and Hall, 1893, p. 364.

[68] David Newsome, *The Parting of Friends*, Murray, 1966, p. 78.

[69] 'You entered and found the whole house one huge library, – books overflowing in all corners, into hall, on landing-places, in bedrooms, and in dressing-rooms. Their number was roughly estimated at 14,000 volumes, and, though it would be too much to say that their owner had read them all, yet he had at least bought them all with a special purpose, knew where they were, and what to find in them, and often, in the midst of discussion, he would dart off to some remote corner, and return in a few minutes with the passage which was wanted as an authority or illustration. Each group of books (and a traceable classification prevailed throughout the house) represented some stage in the formation of his mind, – the earlier scholarship, the subsequent studies in European literature and philosophy, the later in patristic and foreign theology' ('Memoir of Julius Hare', *Guesses at Truth*, Macmillan, 1871. p. xlv).

was he, if anyone, who finally anglicised the Schlegelian fragments, and brought together the German and English Romantic aesthetic traditions.

Hare had been introduced to German at the age of ten, when his parents spent the winter of 1804–5 in Weimar. Though, like most of his fellow students (including Wordsworth and Coleridge a generation earlier) he started by reading mathematics at Cambridge, he switched to classics, and in 1818 was elected to a fellowship in classics at Trinity College – where he was to be tutor to both John Sterling and F.D. Maurice. By the 1820s he had come to know most of the leading English romantics personally, including both Coleridge and Wordsworth, and he made himself responsible for overseeing the publication of Landor's *Imaginary Conversations* while the latter was convalescent in Italy. At the same time he produced a series of translations from German, including Fouqué's novel, *Sintram*, some of Tieck's poems, and most important of all, with Connop Thirlwall, Niebuhr's massive *History of Rome* (1827). He was also reading German theology with the same enthusiasm as the literature and history, and a visit to Bonn at the end of the decade brought meetings with Tieck, A.W. Schlegel and Schleiermacher. In 1827 he was ordained as an Anglican clergyman, and in 1832 became rector of Herstmonceux, the family home in Sussex. In 1840 he became Archdeacon of Lewes.[70]

Though he was the author of a number of distingished theological works, including the so-called 'Cambridge discourses', *Children of Light* and *The Law of Self-Sacrifice* (which were compared by contemporaries with Schleiermacher's *Speeches on Religion*) and *The Mission of the Comforter* (1846), the work that was to have the widest literary and aesthetic influence was *Guesses at Truth*, a collection of literary, philosophic and religious fragments, jointly composed with his brother, Augustus, and published anonymously in 1827. In spite of its distinctly unarresting title it was to show astonishing durability, going through a second, much enlarged edition in 1838, a third in 1847, and thereafter being reprinted in 1867, 1871 and 1884. It was a well-known

---

[70] See the unusually perceptive and frank 'Memoir' attached to the 1871 edition of *Guesses at Truth*. The author, who merely signs himself 'E.H.P.', was in fact Edward Henry Palmer (1840–82), whose own life was as dramatic as any Victorian adventure story. Coming from a humble background, he was a self-taught linguist who started by learning the Romany language of the local gypsies and eventually became Professor of Arabic, Hindustani and Persian at Cambridge. He was shot by Arab brigands in Egypt while on a secret service mission for the British government.

book of its time.[71] Though most English contemporaries were reminded of the more familiar *Pensées* of Pascal, or La Bruyère's
Caractères, to anyone familiar with the *Athenaeum*, the much greater
debt to the Schlegels and the Jena circle is obvious. In fact there is
circumstantial evidence of his knowledge of the *Athenaeum* as early as
1816. To Whewell's comment that Hare was too ready to adopt the
philosophy of 'certain writers' (from the context, one suspects Wordsworth and Coleridge) because he admired their poetry, Hare is
reported to have replied with an argument apparently as startling to
his Cambridge audience as it will be familiar to present readers: 'But
poetry is philosophy, and philosophy is poetry.'[72]

Though it seems clear that Julius and Augustus Hare (together
with a third brother, Marcus) saw themselves as in some way the
English counterpart of the Schlegel brothers, that does not imply any
slavish imitation of the Jena model. Indeed, it would be much better
to describe the various editions of *Guesses at Truth* as an extended
critical dialogue with the fragments of the *Athenaeum*, and with
Friedrich Schlegel in particular. From contemporary accounts of his
inordinately lengthy sermons, both at Herstmonceux and Cambridge,
it may be that fragments were peculiarly well-suited to Hare's
particular gifts. Interspersed with one-liners on religious and aesthetic
topics are much longer essays on specific points of history, philology
and literary criticism. These essays are augmented and increase in
number in later editions, constituting perhaps the best source of
second-generation romantic critical theory in the English language,
and developing ideas that are only latent or embryonic in the more
famous *Four Ages of Poetry* by Peacock or Shelley's *Defence of Poetry*.
Though Hare shows himself better aware of current German theory
than any of his contemporaries, with explicit references to and
quotations from Goethe, Novalis, Schiller, the Schlegels, Schleiermacher and Tieck, the theoretical emphasis is subtly different. In part
this is reflected by the 1838 dedication, repeated in all subsequent
editions, to Wordsworth and to

a name which ... will for ever be coupled with yours in the admiration and
love of Englishmen – the name of Coleridge. You and he came forward
together in a shallow, hard, worldly age, – an age alien and almost averse

---

[71] It was, for instance, one of a parcel of books ordered by Charlotte Brontë from her publishers
in November 1849, along with a translation of Goethe's Conversations with Eckermann and
Soret.

[72] *Guesses at Truth* (1871), p. xxii.

from the higher and more strenuous exercises of imagination and thought, – as the purifiers and regenerators of poetry and philosophy.[73]

Nevertheless, Hare was his own man, and any expectation that *Guesses at Truth* is to be a kind of condensed version of J.H. Green's explicitly Coleridgean *Spiritual Philosophy* is doomed to disappointment. Indeed, Hare was not uncritical of Coleridge as a scholar, and saw him more as an inspiration than as an authority on either biblical criticism or philology. In *The Mission of the Comforter* (1846), he writes that Coleridge's role,

> was to spiritualize, not only our philosophy but our theology, to raise them both above the empiricism into which they had long been dwindling, and to set them free from the technical trammels of logical systems ... [he] had a few opinions on points of Biblical criticism, likely to be very offensive to persons who knew nothing about the history of the Canon. Some of these opinions, to which Coleridge himself ascribed a good deal of importance, seem to me of little worth; some, to be decidedly erroneous. Philological criticism, indeed all matters requiring a laborious and accurate investigation of details, were alien from the bent and habits of his mind; and his exegetical studies, such as they were, took place when he had little better than the meagre Rationalism of Eickhorn [*sic*] and Berthold to help him.[74]

In keeping with his specifically English – and, indeed, Anglican – theme, Hare's tone in *Guesses at Truth* is at once more practical and specific and, above all, more explicitly religious than anything produced by the Jena circle. Though it is no less theoretical in its own way, the result is less idealistic, less generalised and more historical, more engaged with actual literature and society and more pietistic than its German models.

Thus, whereas the traditional separation of the German urban intellectuals from both the ruling class and the peasantry meant that politics and social problems never figure in the Jena aphorisms, and the only social awareness displayed is in side-swipes at the 'shopkeeper mentality' of the bourgeoisie, or occasionally at the English for showing collectively the same commercial traits, in *Guesses at Truth* questions of literature and philosophy are interspersed with sometimes lengthy discussions about the state of the poor and even the penal system. The future rector and magistrate can never forget his social and class responsibilities. 'It is an odd device', writes Hare at one point, 'when a

---

[73] *Ibid.*, p. i.

[74] Reprinted in a 'Biographical Supplement' to *Biographia Literaria* (1847), vol. II. Cited by Basil Willey, *Samuel Taylor Coleridge*, Chatto, 1972, p. 253.

fellow commits a crime, to send him to the antipodes for it.'[75] Behind
this attempt to engage with the total cultural and economic fabric of a
country lies also a much more powerful sense of an existing and socially
engaged literary tradition. Whereas Friedrich Schlegel's views on the
novel are derived from only a handful of examples, Hare has a sense
not merely of the enormous range and diversity of his own literary
heritage, but also of how far it had developed and changed over the
years. This shift in perspective is very clear in a lengthy piece devoted
to a topic close to Schlegel's heart, a comparison between ancient and
modern poetry:

Goethe in 1800 does not write just as Shakespeare wrote in 1600: but neither
would Shakespeare in 1800 have written just as he wrote in 1600. For the
frame and aspect of society are different; the world which would act on him,
and on which he would have to act, is another world. True poetical genius
lives in communion with the world, in a perpetual reciprocation of influences,
inbibing feeling and knowledge, and pouring out what it has inbibed in words
of power and gladness and wisdom. It is not, at least when highest it is not, as
Wordsworth describes Milton to have been 'like a star dwelling apart'.
Solitude may comfort weakness, it will not be the home of strength ... In
short, Genius is not an independent and insulated, but a social and
continental, or at all events a peninsular power ... Now without entering into
a comparison of Shakespeare's age with our own, one thing at least is evident,
that, considered generally and as a nation, we are more bookish than our
ancestors ... While the conflict and tug of passions supplied in Shakespeare's
days the chief materials for poetry, in our days it is rather the conflict of
principles ... This appears not only from the works of Goethe and others of
his countrymen, but from the course taken by our own greatest poets, by
Wordsworth, Coleridge, and Landor. They have been rebuked indeed for not
writing otherwise: but they have done rightly; for they have obeyed the
impulse of their nature, and the voice of their age has been heard speaking
through their lips.[76]

Hare is as concerned as the Schlegels with a philosophy of literature,
but it is a historical rather than an idealist aesthetic.

This is equally noticeable in the aphoristic theory behind the work
itself. The first edition of *Guesses at Truth* carries a prefatory motto from
Bacon's *Advancement of Learning:*

As young men, when they knit and shape perfectly, do seldom grow to a
further stature; so knowledge, while it is in aphorisms and observations, it is in
growth; but when once it is comprehended in exact methods, it may

[75] *Guesses at Truth* (1827), vol. I, p. 98.
[76] *Ibid.*, vol. II, pp. 136–40.

perchance be further polished and illustrated, and accommodated for use and practice; but it increaseth no more in bulk and substance.

The similarities and differences between the Hares' and the Schlegels' aesthetics is nowhere better illustrated than here. The key to the Hares' theory is biological: a theory of the mind where organicism has become less a conscious analogy than part of a system of parallels and correspondences operating throughout the natural world.[77] 'Some thoughts are acorns', writes Julius, 'Would that any in this book were.'[78] The idea of thoughts as seeds is part of a theory of aesthetics in which the book has become a symbol or surrogate of life itself:

Life may be defined to be the power of self-augmentation, or of assimilation, not of self-nurture; for then a steam-engine over a coalpit might be made to live.[79]

The debt to the Goethean tradition of appropriation (*Aneignung*) is obvious, and though this was later to become a major theme of both the Schlegels' aesthetic theories, this organicist strain is by no means absent even as early as the *Athenaeum*. The series of aphorisms published by Novalis in the 1798 issue is entitled *Blütenstaub* ('Pollen') and is prefaced by a reference to Christ's parable of the sower: 'Friends, the soil is poor, we must sow a lot of seed properly in order to achieve a reasonable harvest.'[80] Four of the 'grains' that follow are by Friedrich Schlegel himself. Nevertheless, the Schlegelian theory of the fragment is as much philosophical as organic: as we have seen, it stands for the essential incompleteness both of human knowledge and our powers of articulating that knowledge in words. In contrast, the word 'fragment', though familiar even from the German title *Athenaeum Fragmente*, is not one that the Hares wished to use in this context. The contrast between the organic 'seed' and the random broken quality of the inorganic 'fragment' is absolute:

'Second thoughts ... are only fragments of thoughts; that is, they are thought by a mere fragment of the mind, by a single faculty, the prudential understanding ... Now man ... should studiously preserve the unity of his being ...'[81]

Perhaps also aimed at the author of *Lucinde* is this comment:

---

[77] For a fuller account of organic theories of mental growth, see Prickett, *Coleridge and Wordsworth*.
[78] *Guesses at Truth* (1827), vol. II. p. 79.
[79] *Ibid.*, p. 16.
[80] My translation. *Athenaeum 1798–1800*, Stuttgart: J.G. Cotta'sche Buchhandlung Nachf., p. 70.
[81] *Guesses at Truth* (1827), vol. II. p. 96.

Amours are fragments of loves; and by heaping one upon another the dissolute expect apparently to make up love at last. But accumulation is not union: a thousand bits of glass are not a mirror: and though a man may have almost everything else in a seraglio, he cannot have a wife.[82]

But the same principle can be used to distinguish between parts and the whole in mental qualities:

A man may have a talent of a particular kind; he may have several talents of particular kinds ... but he can no more have talent or be a man of talent, than he can have a pound or be a man of pound, than he can have a letter or be a man of letter.

Genius on the other hand is whole and indivisible. We cannot say that a man has geniuses, as we ought not to say that he has talent. Shakespeare was a man of genius; but even Shakespeare was not a man of geniuses. Genius is the excellence of the soul itself as an intelligence. It is that central pervading essence which modifies and regulates and determines all the particular faculties; it is above the soul and one with it; as the talents are its executive ministry and may be many, so genius being its legislative principle can only be one.[83]

Yet the unity of genius is not to be confused with completeness. A thing may be complete and yet unfinished; finished and yet incomplete. This distinction serves as the basis for a further distinction, that between the classic and gothic spirit:

Is not every Grecian temple complete even though it be in ruins? just as the very fragments of their poems are like the scattered leaves of some unfading flower. Is not every Gothic minster unfinished? and for the best of reasons, because it is infinite ...[84]

Hare returns to his obsession with the difference between the ancients and the moderns, but now less at a historical than at a theoretical and aesthetic level, and the similarity with the Schlegels is correspondingly more pronounced. Here, too, perhaps his theory of organic form comes closest to engaging with the Schlegels' philosophical sense of the incompleteness of all language. Yet, typically, the debt he chooses to acknowledge at this juncture is not so much to them as to Coleridge:

so frequently have I strengthened my mind with the invigorating waters which stream forth redundantly in Mr Coleridge's works, that, if I mistake not, many of my thoughts will appear to have been impregnated by his spirit. If they do, may they not shame their parentage![85]

---

[82] *Ibid.*, p. 218.
[83] *Ibid.*, p. 160.
[84] *Ibid.*, p. 250.
[85] *Ibid.*, pp. 279–80.

Whether it be Coleridgean or Schlegelian, certainly a sense of organic unity pervades the whole structure of *Guesses at Truth*, random as the actual juxtaposition of pieces often appears to be. In one of the more engaging asides of the first edition (omitted in later ones) he links two paragraphs with the observation: 'Thought sprouts from thought, as toadlet from toad.'[86] The same organic unity provides, too, the theoretical underpinning for the mixture of literary theory and natural observation that make up so much of the content:

The commentator guides and lights us to the altar erected by the author, although it is at the flame upon that altar that he must have kindled his torch. And what are Art and Science, if not a running commentary on Nature? what are poets and philosophers but torch-bearers leading us toward the innermost chambers of God's holy temples, the sensuus and the spiritual world? Books, as Dryden has aptly termed them, are spectacles to read nature. Homer and Aristotle, Shakespeare and Bacon, are the priests who preach and expound the mysteries of the universe: they teach us to decypher and syllable the characters wherewith it is inscribed. Do you not, since you have read Wordsworth, feel a fresh and more thoughtful delight whenever you hear a cuckoo, whenever you see a daisy, whenever you play with a child? Have not Thucydides and Dante assisted you in discovering the tides of feeling and the currents of passion by which events are borne along in the ocean of Time? Can you not discern something more in man, now that you look on him with eyes purged and unsealed by gazing upon Shakespeare and Goethe? From these terrestrial and celestial globes we learn the configuration of the earth and the heavens.[87]

Central to this accommodation of literature to nature, and *vice versa*, is the *Athenaeum* Romanticism of the synaesthetic role of poetry: 'Poetry is to philosophy what the sabbath is to the rest of the week.'[88] Or, in more graphic detail:

The difference between desultory reading and a course of study may be well illustrated, by comparing the former to a number of mirrors placed in a straight line so that each of them reflects a different object, the latter to the same number so artfully arranged as to perpetuate one set of objects in an endless succession of reflexions.

If we read two books on the same subject, the contents of the second bring under review the statements and arguments of the first; the errors of which are

---

[86] *Ibid.*, p. 88. The reference is, of course, to Coleridge: 'Pretty little additionals sprouting out from it like young toadlets on the back of a Surinam toad.' ('Satyrane's Letters', II, *Biographia Literaria*, ed. James Engell and W. Jackson Bate, Routledge, 1983, vol. II, p. 178.)

[87] *Guesses at Truth* (1827), vol. I, p. 80.

[88] *Ibid.*, p. 26.

little likely to escape this kind of *proving*, if I may so call it; while the truths are more strongly imprinted on the memory . . .

High therefore and precious must be the worth and benefit of poetry: which taking men as individuals, and drawing into strong light the portions and degrees of truth latent in every human feeling, reconciles us to our kind . . .[89]

The juxtaposition of ideas is important here. Books themselves constitute, as it were, an organic unity: such is their relationship to one another, their intertextuality, that their collective power is far greater than the sum of their parts. Meaning is enhanced by context. In a move that anticipates T.S. Eliot's thesis in *Tradition and the Individual Talent* by almost exactly a century, Hare argues that the poet is the rightful interpreter to his own age of this written tradition. This is a point he repeats in a more general context a few pages further on:

Every age has a language of its own; and the difference in words is oftentimes far greater than the difference in the thoughts. The main employment of authors, in their collective capacity, is to translate the discoveries of other ages into the language of their own: nor is it an useless or unimportant task; for this is the only way of making knowledge either fruitful or influential.[90]

More than this, however, he is the representative consciousness of the time. Just as he possesses a greater than usual individual self-consciousness, so he will also have a greater sense of what is common to humanity. It is this tension between what is common and what is individual that gives the artist his unique balance and insight into his own times.

Yet such insight can never be more than at best partial or incomplete.

from the nature of man, no age has ever been able to comprehend itself: a Thucydides or a Burke may discern some of the principles which are working, and may guess the consequences they are bringing on: but they who draw the car of Destiny cannot look back upon her: they are impelled onward and ever blindly onward by the throng pressing at their heels. Far less then can any age comprehend what is beyond it and above it . . . It surprises me not, to be told that Euripides was a greater favourite at Athens than Sophocles: what surprises me is that any audience should ever have been capable of listening with pleasure to the intensely high and deep notes of Sophocles. Neither is it surprising that Jonson and Fletcher should have been more admired than Shakespeare: the contrary would be far more surprising. I have been told that Schiller must be a greater poet than Goethe, because he is more popular in

---

[89] *Ibid.*, pp. 93–4.   [90] *Ibid.*, p. 134.

Germany: were he less popular, I might be led to fancy that there is something in him, besides what thrusts itself so prominently on the public gaze.[91]

At times Hare is so much aware of Schlegel that he engages with him directly – as with this gloss on *Athenaeum Fragment* 395:

'In good prose (says Schlegel) every word should be underlined!' that is every word should be the right one; and then no word would be righter than another. There are no italics in Plato.[92]

What distinguishes Julius Hare's aphorisms from those of Friedrich Schlegel, however, is a greater sense of the practical problems of literature. We are not allowed to forget that Hare's generalisations about linguistic precision are based on extensive experience – especially of translation:

A literal translation is better than a loose one, just as a cast from a fine statue is better than an imitation of it: for copies, whether of words or things, must be valuable in proportion to their exactness. In idioms alone, as a friend remarked to me, the literal rendering cannot be correct.

If theory leads to praxis as toad to toadlet, here the toadlet turns out to be somewhat larger than the toad.

It is almost peculiar to the Bible, that it loses little of its force or dignity or beauty, by translation into any language, whenever the translation is not erroneous. One version may indeed surpass another, inasmuch as its language may be more expressive and majestic: but in all, the Bible contains the sublimest thoughts clothed in the simplest and most fitting words. It was written for the whole world, not for any single nation or age.

One peculiarity of the translations, is, that the translators have been induced by their reverence for the original, to render it with the utmost faithfulness. They were far more studious of the matter, than of the manner; and there is no surer preservative against writing ill, or more potent charm for writing well.[93]

In the light of the debate on biblical translation in chapter 2, it could be regretted that some of the modern biblical translators had not studied Hare. But be that as it may, as we shall see in our final section, this notion of the Bible as being not merely the representative book, but in some overtly platonic sense, the ideal, or archetypal form of a book, is one that was increasingly to dominate certain kinds of Romantic thought.

[91] *Ibid.*, p. 262.
[92] *Ibid.*, p. 256.
[93] *Ibid.*, p. 317.

SWEDENBORG AND BLAKE: THE PRIVATISATION OF ANGELS

No one who has read thus far will be looking for a precise definition of that wayward phenomenon of the spirit we call Romanticism. Nor should we over-generalise responses which were often as personal and idiosyncratic in practice as Schleiermacher claimed they should be in theory. Whether or not we accept A.O. Lovejoy's conclusion that there was no such thing as Romanticism, only many discrete 'romanticisms',[94] there is evidence of enormous diversity. To say, for instance, that in England, still at this period pre-eminently the country of the novel, there was an increasing tendency to read the Bible primarily in narrative and dramatic terms does not for a minute exclude the stubborn persistence of typological readings at all levels of sophistication;[95] nor does it exclude Shelley's use of Volney nor the more detailed philosophical and biblical studies of Coleridge under the influence of German historicist and Romantic critics.[96] To make Chateaubriand's aesthetic and cultural claims for historical Christianity and the Bible central to French Romanticism is not to exclude the anticlericalism of Stendhal or the melancholic nihilism of de Vigny, both of which are also characteristic of the turmoil of the early nineteenth century in France. Similarly, if we have made the efforts of the Schlegels and their circle to see the creation of a 'new' Bible in philosophic and theoretical terms represent Germany, that is not to discount the works of more creative writers, among them Goethe, Schiller and Hölderlin at the same period – all of whom knew the Schlegels, and not all of whom had yet quarrelled with them. Nevertheless, despite the very different intellectual and social conditions prevailing in England, France and Germany at the end of the eighteenth century, it is interesting to note how similar were so many of the responses to the Bible. Not merely were writers in all three countries increasingly preoccupied with a quest for wholeness, and a literary form that permitted discussion of the human condition in all its cultural, intellectual, social and religious complexity, the gradual recognition of the essential subjectivity of human experience placed an increasing premium on the literary and poetic qualities of the

---

[94] A.O. Lovejoy, 'On the Discrimination of Romanticisms', *Essays in the History of Ideas*, Baltimore, Md.: Johns Hopkins Press, 1948.

[95] See, for instance, George P. Landow's studies in typology: *Victorian Types, Victorian Shadows*, Routledge, 1980.

[96] Prickett, *Romanticism and Religion*, chs. 1 and 2.

scriptures. Though in different ways, in all three the Bible was rediscovered as representing an aesthetic ideal. From offering a typological insight into contemporary affairs, it was increasingly seen in terms of what one might call a 'metatype': not so much a form with limited and specific meanings, as a universal and absolute category giving meaning and shape to the rest of literature.

Nor should we ignore the degree to which each country was influenced by ideas from the other two. Volney and Chateaubriand were quickly translated into English. Just as Chateaubriand (fresh from exile in London) was powerfully influenced by English literary models, so the Jena circle frequently turned to English examples either to castigate or to illustrate its evolving literary theory. Schleiermacher's first published works were actually translations from English.[97] Similarly, it is only with some appreciation of what was happening in Europe that we are in a position to realise the degree to which Coleridge's response to the Bible, quoted earlier,[98] was not so much an individual insight as at once a compendium and a summation of contemporary continental Romanticism.

It is from this cross-cultural perspective that I want finally to turn to a particular rendering of the metaphor that has set the theme for this whole book: Jacob's Ladder. Blake's water-colour, variously known as *Jacob's Dream* or *Jacob's Ladder*, was painted in 1808 and exhibited at the Royal Academy of that year.[99] Not much seems to be known for certain about the symbolism, and what little has been written is necessarily speculative in the extreme.[100] Certainly no one, so far as I know, has ever suggested that it was intended as an allegory of Kant's, or even Schleiermacher's, idea of the aesthetic – though, as we shall see, the notion is by no means as far-fetched as it may sound. But, following Schleiermacher's principles, we shall start by trying to understand, as it were, the 'grammar' of the picture before speculating as to its meaning.

Jacob lies asleep at Bethel, his shepherd's crook still in his hand, against a night of starry infinity. Above him the spiral staircase winds

[97] Fawcett's *London Sermons*, 1798, and David Collins' *Account of the English Colony of New South Wales*, 1802.
[98] See above, p. 204.
[99] See G.E. Bentley Jr, *Blake Records*, Oxford: Clarendon Press, 1969, p. 189.
[100] The only discussion of this picture that I can find is in a footnote to John E. Grant's 'Envisioning the First *Night Thoughts*', in David V. Erdman and John E. Grant (eds.), *Blake's Visionary Forms Dramatic*, Princeton University Press, 1970, p. 332. From his reference, Grant appears to have seen only the rather poor black-and-white plate in Anthony Blunt's *The Art of William Blake*, New York: Columbia University Press, 1959.

upwards into realms of light – apparently the sun itself – while an assortment of angels ascend and descend as described in Genesis 28: 12. Blake as always, however, has added his own touches. To begin with, his angels appear to be of both sexes, and are accompanied by a large number of children. Since angels were by most traditional earlier accounts asexual, there seems a strong case for assuming that these particular angels are of the Swedenborgian variety. Swedenborg's *Heaven and Hell* is highly unusual in that he specifically describes angels as of both sexes with marriages between them,[101] as well as details of their clothing and everyday life that seem also to figure in this picture. How long Blake was a Swedenborgian is unclear, but he and his wife, Catherine, were certainly founder-members of the London New Jerusalem (Swedenborgian) Church and much of his work is permeated with Swedenborgian imagery – sometimes apparently serious, sometimes ironic. The Swedenborgian hypothesis is given further support from the presence of numerous children of various sizes in the picture. According to Swedenborg, though the angelic marriages, being spiritual, are childless,[102] the numbers of angels are none the less continually augmented by dead human children who are brought up as angels by surrogate mothers.[103] This would account not merely for the fact that all the children in Blake's painting are ascending the stairway, as it were from earth towards heaven, but also why one alone is winged. For Swedenborg heaven is divided into two kingdoms: the 'celestial' and the 'spiritual'. These seem to correspond in some ways to the traditional mystical distinction between the contemplative and the active life: the former is the more exalted, and also the more inward, introverted and intuitive; the latter more social and outgoing in their love. Thus when dead children are received in heaven some are found to have a 'celestial' genius, others a 'spiritual' one. They can be easily distinguished, Swedenborg tells us, by the fact that the latter have 'a sort of vibration, as if of wings'.[104]

Thus immediately behind the lowest angel, who is dressed in diaphanous brown or gold and carrying a basket on its head, is

---

[101] Emanuel Swedenborg, *Heaven and its Wonders and Hell: from Things Heard and Seen* (1758), New York: Swedenborg Foundation, 1978, p. 224.

[102] *Ibid.*, p. 233.

[103] 'every child, wherever he is born, whether within the church or outside of it, whether of pious parents or impious, is received when he dies by the Lord and trained up in heaven, and taught in accordance with Divine order, and imbued with affections for what is good, and through these with knowledges of what is true; and afterwards as he is perfected in intelligence and wisdom is introduced into heaven and becomes an angel' (*ibid.*, p. 192).

[104] *Ibid.*, p. 196.

another, in blue, with a large pitcher. They appear to be a pair – indeed it looks as if they bear the bread and wine of the future Eucharist – and we may assume that since the former angel has wings and the latter is without, they may also represent a pairing of spiritual and celestial genii. Unlike her angelic companion, who stares purposefully ahead, the second angel has turned her head sharply to get a better look at the gold-clad one coming the other way with a child perched on her shoulder – presumably the latest addition to the angelic communion. Swedenborg may also help to explain the reason why the stair winds away from the earthly night into the sun: chapter xiv of *Heaven and Hell* follows the hint given in Dante by explaining that 'the Lord is actually seen in heaven as a sun' and that the ardour of his love is 'tempered' by 'radiant belts about the sun'.[105]

The symbolism of the rest of the picture, though certainly detailed and specific, is also far from clear – not least because the sex of some of the angels is difficult to determine. John E. Grant writes:

At the lowest turning of the vortex a Newton with a compass and scales looks at the great scroll being returned by a female spirit to the source of light. And descending below them, just behind the gifts of spiritual food, are a male and female angel, the first carrying a scroll and showing it to the other, that is as yet sealed. When she has learned her everlasting lesson these seals will become, not a device for binding down the Word, but instruments for gathering the scattered leaves in a single meaningful volume.[106]

That Grant does not give evidence for these insights does not necessarily mean they are incorrect, but they are demonstrably incomplete. Just before the winged infant, for example, is an angel with a lyre apparently in full song. Its presence suggests that there may be an alternative aesthetic pattern in which music, science, literature and painting may all be represented as various manifestations of what Blake, like his German counterparts, saw as the quality of the true artist: 'vision or imagination'.

What is certainly also true is that, if Blake has been using Swedenborgian imagery, here, as so often, he has altered it for his own purposes. To take but one example: Swedenborg's angelic class-distinctions are immutable. Celestial angels cannot normally even meet spiritual ones.[107] But Blake's ladder from heaven to earth, in a post-Revolutionary version of Jacob's dream, brings fraternity and equality

[105]   *Ibid.*, pp. 65, 67.
[106]   Grant, 'Envisioning the First *Night Thoughts*', p. 334.
[107]   *Heaven and Hell*, p. 16.

to the angelic hierarchies themselves. Such a possibility brings us back to my initial suggestion that the stairway linking earth and heaven might be read as having other, much more philosophical, potential.

It has long been observed, for instance, that Swedenborg anticipated a number of Kant's conclusions, and may well even have influenced the development of his thought. The two certainly corresponded, and Swedenborg sent Kant a number of his works. For Swedenborg, as for Kant, space and time are conditions of human knowledge rather than properties of things themselves, and his angels are very properly free of such limitations.[108] Similarly their 'wisdom' (though it, too, is not altogether free of class distinctions) corresponds in some ways to pure reason, in that its conclusions are directly intuitive, while human reason based on experience, is much more akin to Kant's practical reason. Here, too, there is an abyss between earth and heaven that must in some manner be bridged. Though it can only remain a speculative reading, it is entirely in keeping with what we know of Blake and his intellectual context if we take this version of Jacob's Ladder as representing the visionary or imaginative bridge between the mundane and the transcendent that all the Romantics were seeking in their own ways.[109] In such a reading the eucharistic elements of religion would be purveyed by the ministering angels alongside the arts of music, literature, and science in the kind of intellectual synaesthesia also central to the literary absolute of so many forms of Romanticism. Such a spiral of arts and sacraments, leading from the sleeping earthbound shepherd to the divine radiance, would also be a very precise image of the new metatypical status of the Bible itself.

It was suggested in the first chapter that historically the kind of appropriation we are considering would characteristically prove to be at once a process of organic development and at the same time an act of theft, to be justified afterwards by a new hermeneutic theory. Organicism is so much a part of the Romantic appropriation and theorising of the Bible as an aesthetic metatype that it is easy to miss the way in which the process also involved wrenching it free of traditional ecclesiastical control and, in effect, *privatising* it. One can see the process beginning even in Sterne's sermons, but with the Protestant reading of the Bible as novel-like narrative becoming widespread in

---

[108] *Ibid.*, p. 143.

[109] See, for instance, G.E. Bentley Jr: 'It only remains for Jacob and all men who see it to follow the ladder in imagination to heaven' (*Blake Records Supplement*, Oxford: Clarendon Press, 1988, pl. IV, xxxiv).

Britain and Germany by the end of the eighteenth century a quite new kind of reader–text relationship was developing.

This was much more than simply a matter of the traditional Protestant emphasis on allowing people to read the Bible for themselves. As Bakhtin has observed, the novel is inherently an anarchic and uncontrollable form at the best of times. Unlike the theatre, it presupposes solitary rather than collective experience, with correspondingly more unpredictable consequences. But the new Romantic theory, with its stress on the personal and singular quality of all experience, relating it to particular times and occasions, elevated the normal subjectivity of reading into what amounted to a series of raids on the absolute, in which moments of special intuition or grace – 'spots of time' in the Wordsworthian terminology – seemed to offer the reader at any rate the *possibility* of unmediated spiritual experience. In extreme cases, like that of Blake, we find texts removed from the public sphere of ecclesiastical discourse not to be demystified, but in effect to be remystified.

To the degree that institutional control was retained, it tended increasingly to be in the hands of universities rather than churches. Regina Schwartz has noted that 'just as the Reformer's displacement of mediaeval exegesis tells a story about shifting power', so too does the contemporary displacement of interpretation from specifically denominational centres to the universities.[110] She is, of course, right: but to call it 'contemporary' is to misread the history of that process. In Europe it was already well advanced by the end of the eighteenth century. The career of Schleiermacher, and his subsequent appropriation by Dilthey, illustrates very clearly how official biblical exegesis in Germany was passing from Church to university. In England Anglican control of the two main universities meant that the process was delayed until the mid-nineteenth century, but the result in the end was much the same.[111] Even coming from Catholic France it is significant that *The Genius of Christianity* is, in effect, a *lay* sermon. Though Chateaubriand proclaims not merely his orthodoxy but his conservatism, the very imperialism of his claims for Christianity over history and art alike has the curious effect of making Christianity sound primarily like a

---

[110] *The Book and the Text: the Bible and Literary Theory*, ed. Regina Schwartz. Oxford: Basil Blackwell, 1990, Introduction.

[111] See Stephen Prickett, 'Church and University in the Life of John Keble', in Geoffrey Rowell (ed.), *The English Religious Tradition and the Genius of Anglicanism*, Wantage: Ikon Press, 1992, pp. 208–10.

theory of culture rather than a theology in the traditional Catholic sense.

Like all successful appropriations, this shift in control has been made to seem with hindsight more a liberation than a theft. But that should not blind us to the extent of the transformation. From being a book of uncertain provenance, doubtful authority and dubious veracity, the Bible had, in the space of a generation, been re-appropriated by the Romantics as a source of cultural renewal, aesthetic value and literary inspiration. It provided a model of the literary transcendent, by which art might bridge the abyss between sense-perception and mystical intuition. Even more significantly, the Bible had, in the process, become a metatype, the representative literary form, and the paradigm by which other works were to be understood and judged. Though like all other human constructs, in its constituent parts it was no more than a rubble of fragments and ruins, it was also increasingly seen in this overarching sense as the 'type' of wholeness – and so a theoretical counterpart to the essential incompleteness of the fragment. As we shall now see, the effects of this on other writing were to be profound.

CHAPTER 6

Hermeneutic and narrative: the story of self-consciousness

KINGSLEY AND NEWMAN: EROTICS OF INTUITION

As so often with scandalous books of the past, it is difficult for the modern reader to understand the degree of outrage that greeted the publication of Friedrich Schlegel's novel, *Lucinde*. Though its prose is wearisomely, indeed unrelievedly, purple, the suffusion of vague ecstatic adjectives makes the action so unspecific that it is difficult to make out what (if anything) is actually going on – indeed, what narrative can be discerned is so distanced and subjective that it would take considerable critical ingenuity to find anything conventionally erotic in it. Nor is this simply a matter of period: *Moll Flanders* and *Fanny Hill*, both written more than half a century earlier, can still hold an appreciable erotic power for the twentieth century – as their continued presence in paperback testifies. More immediately to the point, Goethe's *Wilhelm Meister*, published four years before *Lucinde*, in 1795, is much more explicit sexually, and was hailed by critics of the day, including Friedrich Schlegel himself, not merely as a masterpiece, but as a book of profound moral insight.

This may, of course, be due in part to the fact that *Wilhelm Meister* is an incomparably better novel than *Lucinde*, but to some extent the question of its 'morality' in the terms of German bourgeois culture of the 1790s can be separated from the more considered literary judge-ment of history. Though sex and religion are by no means unconnected in his novel, Goethe goes to some trouble to separate the young Wilhelm's love-affair in the first book from his discussion of religion (principally Moravian pietism) in the 'Confessions of a Fair Saint' in Book VI. In contrast Schlegel, in *Lucinde*, goes out of his way to blur the distinction between the two: so much so, in fact, that Peter Firchow, his English translator, argues that we misunderstand the book if we fail to realise that it is fundamentally a religious work – 'religious' that is, in the very specific sense that it is elevating sexual love into a religion.[1] It was, I suspect, that crossing of an implicit taboo category-boundary, rather than any explicit eroticism that was to prove so disturbing to its (not very numerous) early readers.

Yet, in retrospect, the crossing of that boundary between eroticism and religious experience, however clumsily done by Schlegel, was to prove one of the most distinctive (and intriguing) qualities of the new Romantic sensibility. At its heart was yet another act of biblical appropriation, which, like so many earlier acts, appears at first both startlingly illegitimate, and, when understood in context, deeply persuasive within that period and cultural setting. Like previous rereadings, it was accompanied by what amounted to a radical change in interpretative theory. At first sight, however, it might seem nothing new. Both Christian and Rabbinic Jewish traditions, however much they differed in detail, had always agreed on reading the Song of Songs, for instance, as an allegory of religious devotion, and in the later Middle Ages the whole cult of the Virgin Mary had, similarly, acquired an elaborate penumbra of often explicit eroticism. But in both cases it was highly controlled and conventionalised; in the Christian tradition, moreover, it was essentially part of a cult of chastity and celibacy. In contrast, and in keeping with the romantic quest for naturalness and lack of external constraint, Romantic religious eroticism was instinctive, subliminal and unconfined. This is very clear, for instance, in the case of Schleiermacher's *Speeches on Religion*, originally written, we recall, at Schlegel's request and while the two men were sharing an apartment in Berlin.

For Schleiermacher the religious ground of our being stems from the fact that all sense-experience is holy. Before we can begin to analyse our own sensations there is an initial moment of total unity with all creation. The passage in which he attempts to describe this moment is a remarkable one, and it is worth paying attention to it in its entirety.

That first mysterious moment that occurs in every sensory perception, before intuition and feeling have separated, where sense and its objects have, as it were, flowed into one another and become one, before both turn back to their original position – I know how indescribable it is and how quickly it passes away. But I wish that you were able to hold on to it and also to recognise it again in the higher and divine religious activity of the mind. Would that I could and might express it, at least indicate it, without having to desecrate it! It is as fleeting and transparent as the first scent with which the dew gently

[1] *Friedrich Schlegel's Lucinde and the Fragments*, trs. with an Introduction by Peter Firchow, Minneapolis: University of Minnesota Press, 1971, p. 23.

caresses the waking flowers, as modest and delicate as a maiden's kiss, as holy and fruitful as a nuptial embrace; indeed, not *like* these, but it *is itself* all of these. A manifestation, an event develops quickly and magically into an image of the universe. Even as the beloved and ever-sought-for form fashions itself, my soul flees toward it; I embrace it, not as a shadow, but as the holy essence itself. I lie on the bosom of the infinite world. At this moment I am its soul, for I feel all its powers and its infinite life as my own; at this moment it is my body, for I penetrate its muscles and its limbs as my own, and its innermost nerves move according to my sense and my presentiment as my own. With the slightest trembling the holy embrace is dispersed, and now for the first time the intuition stands before me as a separate form; I survey it, and it mirrors itself in my open soul like the image of the vanishing beloved in the awakened eye of youth; now for the first time the feeling works its way up from inside and diffuses itself like the blush of shame and desire on his cheek. This moment is the highest flowering of religion. If I could create it in you, I would be a god; may holy fate only forgive me that I have had to disclose more than the Eleusinian mysteries.[2]

As so often with Schleiermacher, the language is as extraordinary as it is deliberate. Eighteen years before Coleridge's description of a symbol as always partaking 'of the reality which it renders intelligible',[3] we find this fleeting quality of immediate (that is, unmediated) experience represented by a 'maiden's kiss' and a 'nuptial embrace' not because of any metaphorical similarity, but because, he claims, it is *actually present* in them. But though Schleiermacher insists, this is therefore not to be taken as imagery in any normal sense, the sexually charged nature of the examples chosen leads the reader on to what, if they are also *not* metaphors, must be among the most erotic accounts of religious experience ever recorded by a Lutheran pastor. If that sounds a feebly qualified statement, we need to recall just how erotic the Catholic mystical tradition, not to mention its pagan Greek precursors, could often be. Despite a rhetorical style which suggests he is freeing his language from all traditional religious associations, Schleiermacher, for his own specific purposes, is drawing here on a very ancient system of erotic symbols for spiritual experience. As a former translator of Plato, he was well aware of the Socratic myth of the soul in the *Phaedrus* – which he believed was the earliest of the platonic writings, setting the pattern for the later ones.[4]

[2] Friedrich Schleiermacher, *On Religion: Speeches to its Cultured Despisers*, trs. Richard Couter (1799), Cambridge University Press, 1988, pp. 112–13.

[3] S.T. Coleridge, *Lay Sermons*, ed. R.J. White, Routledge, 1972, p. 30.

[4] *Ibid.*, p. 112; *Introductions to the Dialogues of Plato*, trs. William Dobson, New York: Arno Press, 1973, pp. 48–73.

The accompanying description, in which he (or his soul) lies upon the bosom of the infinite world, penetrating it in a sexual embrace, manages to combine two of the most apparently diverse philosophical systems ever created – Platonism and Kantianism. On the one hand, it is re-enacting the union of the divided soul figured in the myth of Cupid and Psyche, on the other, it is, once again, suggesting that religious, like aesthetic, intuition has the power to bridge the abyss between pure and practical Reason. I used the phrase 'apparently diverse' of the two systems because, of course, Schleiermacher's own 'myth of the soul' here also illustrates what the two have in common: a belief in an invisible world of (Reason or Forms) which can only be reached by some (spiritual or aesthetic) intuition. That Kant would doubtless have been even less impressed by this attempt to eroticise his system than he was by Jacobi's attempt to poeticise it is beside the point. The fact remains that this presentation of religious intuition as quasi-sexual or erotic in some way that transcended ordinary metaphor was to become one of the most powerful – indeed, potent – images of nineteenth-century fiction.

At the heart of this new eroticising of religious experience lay questions which, in various forms, came to haunt the Victorian novel: what is the connection between *eros* and *agape*, sexual love and heavenly? Can the one lead to the other, or even be mistaken for it? Sometimes, indeed, the process seems short-circuited. Many of Dickens' child-heroines, Esther Summerson or Little Dorrit, for instance, seem more saints than women, by-passing human sexuality in favour of divine grace. As a good Feuerbachian, George Eliot is fascinated by the same theme in its rather more subtle reverse form. If Dinah Morris mistakes her awakening sexuality for divine grace, she has the good fortune to end up in Adam Bede's arms; Dorothea Brooke, on the other hand, against her more practical sister's advice, allows her spiritual intuitions to guide her into earthly matrimony, and has the misfortune to end up if not exactly in Casaubon's arms, at least as his wife. Neither author, however, suggests for a moment that such experiences might involve a rereading of the relevant biblical texts, or turns explicitly to the Bible as justification for this spiritualisation of sexual experience in the way that Charles Kingsley does in *Hypatia* (1853).

Kingsley is relatively unusual among early nineteenth-century writers in that, like George Eliot, he was well aware of many of the new ideas in German aesthetics and theology – even if he shows little corresponding understanding of their relation to Kantian and post-Kantian Idealist philosophy. He had been educated at Helston Grammar School, in Cornwall, under Coleridge's son, the Reverend Derwent Coleridge, and, perhaps even more important in the development of his ideas, by the 1840s, through his Christian Socialist activities, he had become a friend of Julius Hare. During the 1848 Chartist riots in London Kingsley was one of a group including Maurice, Hughes and Ludlow, who would regularly meet at Hare's London house. He would certainly have known *Guesses at Truth*. There are frequent references to German writers in his letters and essays and by the time he first went to Germany in 1850, he was already a passionate Teutonist. The germ of *Hypatia* itself seems to have come during that trip from a visit to the Roman amphitheatre and other remains at Trier.[5]

His plot is taken directly from Gibbon:

Hypatia, the daughter of Theon the mathematician, was initiated in her father's studies; her learned comments have elucidated the geometry of Apollonius and Diophantus; and she publicly taught, both at Athens and Alexandria, the philosophy of Plato and Aristotle. In the bloom of beauty, and in the maturity of wisdom, the modest maid refused her lovers and instructed her disciples; the persons most illustrious for their rank or merit were impatient to visit the female philosopher; and Cyril beheld with a jealous eye the gorgeous train of horses and slaves who crowded the door of her academy. A rumour was spread among the Christians that the daughter of Theon was the only obstacle to the reconciliation of the praefect and the archbishop; and that obstacle was speedily removed. On a fatal day, in the holy season of Lent, Hypatia was torn from her chariot, stripped naked, dragged to the church, and inhumanly butchered by the hands of Peter the reader and a troop of savage and merciless fanatics: her flesh was scraped from her bones with oyster-shells, and her quivering limbs were delivered to the flames.'[6]

Such a combination of sex, violence and religion could hardly fail, and Kingsley brings to this heady brew other ingredients all his own. The sub-title, *New Foes with an Old Face*, is enough to alert the reader to possible contemporary resonances in this bloodthirsty tale of fifth-century Alexandria, while the preface reinforces this impression:

I cannot hope that these pages will be altogether free from anachronisms and errors. I can only say that I have laboured honestly and industriously to discover the truth, even in its minutest details, and to sketch the age, its manners, and its literature, as I found them – altogether artificial, slipshod,

[5] Susan Chitty, *The Beast and the Monk*, Hodder, 1974, pp 147–58.
[6] Edward Gibbon, *The Decline and Fall of the Roman Empire*, Everyman, 1910, vol. v, pp. 14–15.

effete, resembling far more the times of Louis Quinze than those of Socrates and Plato.[7]

This is a scarcely coded address to two major Victorian concerns: classicism and fear of the revolutionary mob – the conflict between eternal values and their violent overthrow. By a brilliant inversion, in which paganism is identified with classicism and Christianity with mob-violence, both are presented as aspects of a civilisation in its death-throes. The atmosphere of decay is introduced on the first page, which opens in what is, literally, a classical twilight in the Egyptian desert. It is littered with Volneyan ruins and fragments:

Here and there, upon the face of the cliffs which walled the opposite side of the narrow glen below, were cavernous tombs, huge old quarries, with obelisks and half-cut pillars, standing as the workmen had left them centuries before; the sand was slipping down and piling up around them; their heads were frosted with the arid snow; everywhere was silence, desolation – the grave of a dead nation in a dying land.[8]

The physical ruins of the landscape are matched by the intellectual decay of classical paganism represented by the beautiful but deluded Hypatia. The classicism that inspired the Schlegels' Romanticism and Schleiermacher's myth of the soul is reduced either to sterile formality or to an introverted complexity understood only by its initiates – if at all. Hypatia lectures to crowded halls of students in Alexandria on the mysteries of Neo-platonism, spinning from Homer ever more elaborate mystical and allegorical interpretations. But, as it rapidly becomes clear, her audience consists of fops and dilettante young men (Kingsley at one point uses the word 'gay' in almost its modern sense to describe them) and the more heterosexual among them are there not so much for her spiritual message as for her sexual charisma.

Here, for the first time is introduced, as if in a minor key, the theme that is to reverberate through the rest of the novel – sexual love as a prelude to spiritual. At this point, though, it is no more than a dangerous delusion. Orestes, the Roman Prefect, though nominally a Christian, and the representative of a nominally Christian imperium, is drawn to Hypatia's paganism partly through sexual attraction, partly because he sees in marriage with her a possible route to further political advancement. Raphael Ben-Ezra, a wealthy young Jew, is openly cynical about playing along with her philosophy, partly because he

[7] Charles Kingsley, *Hypatia, or New Foes with an Old Face*, Everyman, 1907, p. 11.
[8] *Ibid.*, p. 13.

cannot entirely shed his Jewish background, but also because he recognises how much of his interest in her ideas is activated by the sexual attractions of their proponent. Lastly, Philammon, a handsome young monk, fresh from his desert monastery and never having apparently seen a woman before, is also overwhelmed as much by Hypatia's virginal charms as by the sophistication of her doctrines.

Because the Victorian novel was conventionally one of character and manners, most critics have tended to read *Hypatia* in these terms, and to be more impressed by its general vitality than by the subtlety of its characterisation. Indeed, for many observers, then and later, it has seemed a rather adolescent book. An article in *The Church of England Review* for 1858, for instance, noted (not unfairly) that the Goths (who, having sacked Rome, have come on to Egypt, for what the twentieth-century military would call 'R&R') spoke 'a language which, in spite of the archaic Teuton tint washed over it, sets you thinking of the crew of the winning boat at Cambridge any time last summer'.[9] Una Pope-Hennessy observes equally patronisingly that it 'is one of those books that are easier to read in early rather than later life' and that on rereading it presents 'a confused, overcrowded canvas of exceptional artificiality of treatment'.[10] Nevertheless, like a number of Victorian novels that have been found wanting by more fastidious critics, *Hypatia* remains a novel of peculiar power and has been kept more or less continuously in print over the past century and a half. Miss Mitford, always a sensitive barometer of early Victorian middle-brow taste, admired Kingsley's courage in tackling the subject at all: 'He animates that whole mob of Alexandria, animates and individualises Greek, Roman, Egyptian, Goth and Jew. He puts life into the very sands of the desert. But there are some strange things and I half dread what the Bishops may say'[11] Her immediate comparisons are with two other long-forgotten novels, Lockhart's *Valerius* and Ware's *Palmyra*. Both are worthy of brief exhumation, if only to remind us of the variety already present in what was, by the 1850s, a well-recognised genre.

Valerius (1821) by John Gibson Lockhart, Walter Scott's son-in-law and biographer, is an early example of this category of 'classical' historical novel – a genre which was soon to achieve lasting popularity with novels like Bulwer Lytton's *Last Days of Pompeii* (1834). In one sense this desire to recreate the world of antiquity as contemporary fiction is

[9] Margaret Farrand Thorp, *Charles Kingsley 1819–1875*, New York: Octagon, 1969, p. 113.
[10] Una Pope-Hennessy, *Canon Charles Kingsley*, Chatto, 1948, p. 121.
[11] *Ibid.*

part of a much wider early nineteenth-century classicism,[12] but whereas the charge levelled by Pugin, and others, against the classical style in architecture was that it was essentially 'pagan', no such accusation could be made against this category of novel. Indeed, part of its fascination for contemporary readers was clearly the portrayal of the emergence of Christianity from a background of pagan lusts and barbarities. *Valerius* goes further, and is overtly religious in intention. The eponymous hero is converted to Christianity by falling in love with a beautiful but properly reticent upper-class maiden who turns out to be a secret follower of the new religion, and, aided by relatives and friends, they escape to Britain to avoid the persecution of Trajan.

William Ware's *Zenobia, or the Fall of Palmyra* (1837) looks at first sight as if it belongs to the same category. Indeed, with its cumbersome epistolary form, it seems in some ways an old-fashioned work, more like an eighteenth- than a nineteenth-century novel. Yet, though the elements of imperial ruins and Christian persecutions are, by now, familiar novelistic themes, their handling turns out to be startlingly radical. *Zenobia* is more than simply an early religious novel; it is also in certain quite surprising ways a very un-Victorian, even a feminist, one. Not merely is the Palmyrene Empire (correctly) seen as largely Zenobia's own creation, but it is she (with her daughters) who leads her forces into battle while her sons skulk at home.[13] She, and her other women companions excel at the martial arts – defeating the men by skill rather than by strength in a javelin-throwing contest – and women fight alongside men in the army. The narrator's brother, a renegade Roman military hero, is happy to enlist under her, and when they are defeated by a stratagem, it is Fausta, one of the women cavalry, who first sees the danger. Rome, under the Emperor Aurelian, is seen as masculine, brutal and short-sighted; Palmyra, under Zenobia, is feminine, civilised and almost Christian. Zenobia, it is whispered, may herself be Jewish – by inclination if not by race. Unlike Rome, Palmyra is a tolerant, intellectually open, and perhaps improbably democratic society.

At one level this does no more than follow Gibbon, who explicitly mentions Zenobia's beauty, leadership and martial skills – if not her democratic leanings;[14] but at another, this reflects Ware's own

---

[12] See, for instance, Richard Jenkyns, *Dignity and Decadence: Victorian Art and the Classical Inheritance*, Fontana, 1992.

[13] William Ware, *Zenobia, or the Fall of Palmyra*, 9th edn New York, 1866, vol. II, p. 74.

[14] *Decline and Fall*, vol. I, pp. 293–304.

background. William Ware (1797–1852) was not merely an American
(the son of a Harvard Professor of Divinity), and therefore not
predisposed to favour imperial ideals, but also a Unitarian – part of
what was probably the most liberal and intellectual section of that
society, which took for granted equal educational opportunities for
women. For fifteen years Ware was minister of the First Unitarian
Church of New York. It is hardly surprising therefore if Roman-
Palmyrene relations often resemble Anglo-American tensions in (say)
the War of 1812. Lucius Piso, the narrator, is permitted to stay with
friends in Palmyra during Aurelian's siege and observe without being
expected to take part. Fausta, the beautiful, and warlike daughter of
a Palmyrene senator, is also the American 'new woman' a generation
earlier than James' (amazonianly named) Isabel Archer.

But this female dominance in Ware's novel is not confined to the
battlefield or politics. Much of the book consists of long theologico-
philosophical discussions, where, unlike the women of Lockhart's novel,
who listen respectfully while the men converse and blush when spoken
to, the Palmyrene women play an equal part in the debates and are
often credited with the more penetrating insights. In one of the more
extraordinary passages Christianity is characterised as being 'feminine'
and therefore superior to the 'masculine' brutality of Roman paganism.
Though unlike *Hypatia*, there is no suggestion of an innate connection
between erotic and spiritual love, the pattern of female philosophic
leadership is clearly established. The educated women of the ancient
world, it is implied, are neither just athletic amazons nor sweet
Victorian helpmeets, but fully rounded figures (specifically in all senses
– some space is given to the flattering effects of Fausta's body-armour)
capable of giving intellectual, political and spiritual leadership. If
Kingsley draws his historical Hypatia from the pages of Gibbon, her
fictional origins are in Ware's Zenobia and her New World philosophic
court.[15]

Kingsley's own comments on the origins of *Hypatia* bear this out by
suggesting that, unusually for him, he was less interested in character or
plot than in working out a theme that is very close to that of Ware. In a
letter to F.D. Maurice of 19 January 1851, he wrote that

My idea in the romance is to set forth Christianity as the only really
democratic creed, and philosophy, above all, spiritualism, as the most
exclusively aristocratic creed ... Even Synesius, 'the philosophic' bishop, is an

---

[15] This is also true for lesser characters. Isaac, the omnipresent but benignly scheming Jew, is an
obvious origin for Kingsley's much more sinister Miriam.

aristocrat by the side of Cyril ... I have long wished to do something antique, and get out my thoughts about the connection of the old world and the new; Schiller's Gods of Greece expresses, I think, a tone of feeling very common, and which finds its vent in modern Neo-Platonism Anythingarianism.[16]

That last phrase is in fact an editorial emendation: instead of the rather vague 'modern Neo-Platonism' the original letter has 'Emersonian'.[17] In a letter to Parker, editor of *Frazer's Magazine*, where the novel first appeared in parts from January 1851, Kingsley makes it clear that, for him, Emersonian transcendentalism was the modern equivalent of antique paganism: the 'new foe with an old face'. Not least among its dangers is that it can sound beguilingly like the very Christianity to which, Kingsley believed, it was in fact fundamentally inimical. Thus Hypatia's own lectures sound, in places, astonishingly like Schleiermacher:

The elect soul, for instance ... A child as yet, it lies upon the fragrant bosom of its mother Nature, the nurse and yet the enemy of man ...
... the universal Soul thrills through the whole creation, doing the behests of that Reason from which it overflowed, unwillingly, into the storm and crowd of material appearances; warring with the brute forces of gross matter, crushing all which is foul and dissonant to itself, and clasping to its bosom the beautiful, and all wherein it discovers its own reflex ...[18]

What is similar, of course, is the imagery, not the actual argument. As phrases like 'the universal Soul' make clear, the difference is that this is pantheism – and, as Coleridge had discovered two generations earlier,[19] part of pantheism's attraction was that it eliminated the gap interposed between God and nature by Trinitarian Christianity, and in effect divinised nature by eliminating original sin. But as the plot amply illustrates, amid the convulsive and violent death-throes of the collapsing Empire a creed which had neither a satisfactory concept of evil, nor anything more than philosophic comfort for the afflicted, was as inadequate in practice as it was misguided in theory.

Nevertheless, the superficial similarity between Hypatia's Emersonian paganism and Schleiermacher's attempts to ground Christian religious experience in the very act of sense-perception itself is not accidental. Kingsley's point is that the attraction of Hypatia's (or, for

---

[16] *Charles Kingsley: Life and Letters*, ed. by his wife (Frances), Macmillan, 1895, p. 109.
[17] See Thorp, *Kingsley*, p. 111. His wife, always fearful of controversy, seems to have made a number of such unrecorded alterations when preparing his letters for publication.
[18] *Hypatia*, p. 125.
[19] See Thomas MacFarland, *Coleridge and the Pantheist Tradition*, Oxford: Clarendon Press, 1969.

that matter, Emerson's) philosophy was precisely in its resemblance to the real truth. Neither Raphael nor Philammon would have been drawn to Hypatia's Neo-platonism for a moment, whatever her personal charms, had not her philosophy seemed to offer the answer they were looking for. Paradoxically, the failure of her creed lay in the very quality also responsible for her most admired attribute: it was the same disdain for 'the brute force of gross matter' that made her beliefs so inadequate to real experience and kept her, virginal and 'pure', at arm's distance from her would-be lovers.

Kingsley insists, however, that in reality her philosophic paganism, with its superficial spiritualising accretions from Judaism, Christianity and the various gnostic cults then flourishing, was no more than a desperate attempt to 'sew new cloth into old garments':

[Hypatia] did not know yet that those who have no other means for regenerating a corrupted time than dogmatic pedantries concerning the dead and unreturning past, must end, in practice, by borrowing insincerely, and using clumsily, the very weapons of that novel age which they deprecate, and 'sewing new cloth into old garments' till the rent becomes patent and incurable.

At this point, one suspects, Hypatia's revived religion more resembles the Anglicanism of the Tractarians than Emersonian transcendentalism. That one was avowedly conservative, the other vaguely liberal, universalist and 'progressive' was beside the point. As far as Kingsley was concerned, what was fundamentally wrong with both was their contempt for the flesh: in the case of the transcendentalists this involved a scepticism towards the historical particularity of conventional Christianity – and especially the Incarnation; in the case of the Tractarians, their preference for monasticism and celibacy.

In this sense, *Hypatia* is a tract in favour of sexuality. Not a sublimated sexuality, but one whose very physicality is an essential part of what it means to be spiritual. As the title of Susan Chitty's 1976 biography of Kingsley, *The Beast and the Monk*, indicates, this was a theme that had become an obsession in his fiction, colouring almost everything he wrote. During his prolongued engagement to his wife, Fanny, he made and sent her a series of explicitly erotic drawings, culminating with a sketch of Fanny and himself copulating while lashed to a cross.[20] But though in *Hypatia* Kingsley is thus riding a very personal hobby-horse, it is a mistake to see this nexus of sexual and

---

[20] See plates between pp. 64 and 65.

religious feeling in isolation, and, as Chitty does, something peculiar only to Kingsley's personal pathology. As we have already seen, its roots can be traced back very clearly into mainstream Romanticism – and in particular to the no less obsessional desire for a totally integrated approach to human experience. The idea of a close relationship between carnal and spiritual love is less a private perversion of Kingsley's than a key quality in conversion or even behind 'perversion' – in the peculiar Victorian sense of changing one's religion, or apostasy[21] – and provided a theme common to many of the novelists of the period.

Though we first encounter the theme negatively, in the various levels of self-delusion among Hypatia's admirers, as the story unfolds it becomes clear that the very suspectness of this route from the human to the divine is part of its importance. In other words, a recognition of the route's deeply problematic ambiguity is for Kingsley, as, one suspects it was for Schleiermacher, an essential quality of the route itself. Certainly it lies at the very heart of Raphael the Jew's conversion to Christianity. As he is very well aware, he is finally drawn to Christianity by his love for Victoria, the daughter of a North African Prefect who had been defeated in Heraclian's abortive attempt to make himself emperor. It is Victoria's selfless devotion to her wounded father, and his concern for his own routed soldiery, that first gives Raphael an insight into what divine love might mean. In this he is following in a long literary tradition that includes both Lockhart's Valerius and Ware's Piso, but unlike either of these heroes, simply because he knows himself to be in love, he has severe scruples about converting to Christianity. Deeply sceptical of his own motivation, he is only too conscious that he is prepared to be impressed by Christianity for what he sees as totally unphilosophic reasons. In the end he goes to consult Synesius, Bishop of Cyrene, another of the real historical characters in the story, who almost alone among the Christians of the period, has been a friend of Hypatia, and who when he was made bishop, had made it a condition of his acceptance that he should be permitted to keep his wife.

To this Kingsley-like figure Raphael explains his problem:

'I have been tempted a dozen times already to turn Christian: but there has risen up in me the strangest fancy about conscience and honour ... I never

---

[21] See the account of William John Conybeare's novel, *Perversion; or, the Causes and Consequences of Infidelity* (1856) in Robert Lee Wolff, *Gains and Losses: Novels of Faith and Doubt in Victorian England*, New York: Garland, 1977, pp. 283–96.

was scrupulous before, Heaven knows – I am not over scrupulous now – except about her. I cannot dissemble before her. I dare not look in her face when I had a lie in my right hand ... She looks through one – into one – like a clear-eyed awful goddess ... I never was ashamed in my life till my eyes met hers.'

'But if you really became a Christian?'

'I cannot. I should suspect my own motives. Here is another of these soul-anatomizing scruples which have risen up in me. I should suspect that I had changed my creed because I wished to change it – that if I was not deceiving her I was deceiving myself. If I had not loved her it might have been different: but now – just because I do love her, I will not, I dare not listen to Augustine's arguments, or my own thoughts on the matter.'[22]

What seems in the end to resolve this crisis of conscience is an act of biblical re-interpretation.

As with Valerius and Piso, the way to conversion has been carefully prepared by a reading of the New Testament – in Raphael's case, appropriately enough, by his reading the Epistle to the Hebrews. But, as an educated Jew, he is an altogether more critical reader of the Bible than the upper-class Romans of the earlier novels. 'It is execrable Greek. But it is sound philosophy, I cannot deny. He knows Plato better than all the ladies and gentlemen in Alexandria.'[23] Fortified by the idea that it was not merely legitimate but necessary for the Christian to re-interpret the Hebrew scriptures, Raphael turns to that key work on erotic and heavenly love, the Song of Songs. Both Rabbinic Judaism and Catholic Christianity, he points out, however much they might disagree about the details, were united in insisting that it should be interpreted as a spiritual allegory. Raphael, however, has a 'dream' (whether literal or metaphorical is not made clear) that, on the contrary, the whole book must be read quite literally as a hymn in favour of sexual love, and how Solomon's

eyes are opened to see that God made the one man for the one woman, and the one woman to the one man, even as it was in the garden of Eden, so all his heart and thoughts become pure, and gentle, and simple; how the song of the birds, and the scent of the grapes, and the spicy southern gales, and all the simple country pleasures of the glens of Lebanon, which he shares with his own vine-dressers and slaves, become more precious in his eyes than all his palaces and artificial pomp; and the man feels that he is in harmony, for the first time in his life, with the universe of God, and with the mystery of the seasons; that within him, as well as without him, the winter is past, and the

---

[22] *Hypatia*, p. 293.   [23] *Ibid.*, p. 229.

rain is over and gone; the flowers appear on the earth, and the voice of the turtle is heard in the land.[24]

It is only through self-consciously sexual love that the Fall is to be reversed and humanity restored to its proper relationship with nature. This is certainly a Romantic vision both in the popular sense and in the very technical sense of its congruence with the religious intuitions of Schleiermacher. It is also Romantic in a third, and, perhaps, even more significant sense that Kingsley may have been less consciously aware of.

Behind Kant's revolutionary attempt to ground truth in the subjectivity of human consciousness lies the almost insoluble problem of the status of self-consciousness itself. It was his failure to offer an unambiguous solution in the Third Critique that opened the way for the Idealism of Fichte, Schelling and Hegel.[25] Indeed, if Derrida's work can be read as a commentary on how stories may be inseparable from ideas, so that the metaphors of philosophy cannot be abstracted,[26] one might interpret the work of Hare, Kingsley, and Newman in particular as just such an attempt to theorise the history of self-consciousness. One of the most interesting of the philological essays in *Guesses at Truth* concerns the way in which the use of the word 'I' in modern literature betokens a quite different quality of consciousness from that of the classical world. Hare cites the example of Seneca's play, *Medea*. At the point when she is deserted, she says bitterly *Medea superest*. 'An English poet', writes Hare, 'would hardly say "Medea remains".' Thus, he continues, 'a modern opera of little worth' solves the problem by Medea replying to Jason's question *Che mi resta?* with the simple pronoun *Io*. 'An ancient poet could not have used the pronoun; a modern poet could hardly use the proper name.'[27] This key point about the change in the consciousness of self is given further substance in another essay in the second volume which might have been written specifically with Kingsley's *Hypatia* in mind:

There was no vital indestructible essence in heathenism, to enable it, as Christianity has so often, to revive it in the very season of its greatest oppression, and to shoot out most healthily and vigorously, just after the world fancied it had cut it down. Thus the religious consciousness of the

---

[24] *Ibid.*, p. 289.

[25] Andrew Bowie, *Aesthetics and Subjectivity From Kant to Nietzsche*, Manchester University Press, 1990, pp. 41–3.

[26] *Ibid.*, p. 49.

[27] *Guesses at Truth* (1st edn), vol. I, pp. 116–17.

Romans was weak, when at variance with their political consciousness. Christianity has reversed this: it has set up the spiritual law of God in all its simplicity and purity high above the complicated machinery of human legislation: we are not merely to do what man commands; we are to look into our own hearts; we are to commune with them; we are to bring them into accordance with the Bible and into communion with God. In this way men have naturally been led to a stronger discernment of their own individuality.[28]

Hare's argument, which he illustrates at some length, goes right to the core of Raphael's religious experience in *Hypatia*. The young Jew's conversion is based first and foremost on an overwhelming sense of his own individual identity. It is not accidental that the word 'I' occurs no fewers than sixteen times in the speech to Synesius quoted above. Earlier, in an extended meditation at the beginning of chapter 13, Raphael, at the bottom of an abyss of scepticism, has already contemplated what it means to be himself. As Hare rightly notes, this sense of self as a philsophical and moral foundation is essentially a nineteenth-century romantic or post-romantic experience.[29] It is only the strangely modern consciousness of Augustine's *Confessions* (which, significantly, was translated into English by E.B. Pusey, the *de facto* leader of the Tractarians after Newman's 'perversion' to Rome) which prevents us from arguing the converse: that such a self-consciousness was impossible in the fifth century – but it was certainly exceptional.

Hare's argument, however, allows for that. It is not that such a sense of self is impossible for late antiquity, but that when it occurs it is a specifically, indeed, a *distinctively*, Christian quality. The Christian is not under the law but under the spirit. Under the new dispensation, legalism, whether Roman or Jewish, is replaced by a process of self-examination in the light of the scriptures which, argues Hare, is the origin of the modern (and therefore in our terms, romantic) sense of self. It is significant that Augustine was the first theologian to think historically. His *Confessions* are not merely the personal expression of this new sense of history, but also exemplify how the Christian study of the Bible promoted a new quality of self-awareness. 'I' is much more than simply a personal pronoun: it indicates a distinctive and individual centre of consciousness; a unique perspective on the world. As Walter Ong has argued, romantic self-consciousness represents the moment when literacy has been fully interiorised.[30]

---

[28] *Ibid.*, vol. II, p. 75.

[29] Though he does not make them, there are, of course, strong parallels here with Kierkegaard.

[30] *Orality and Literacy: the Technologising of the Word*, Routledge, 1982, p. 26.

This is a point Hare develops at greater length in subsequent editions of *Guesses at Truth*. We can judge the growth of self-consciousness by, among other things, the emancipation from mythology – not least, of course, biblical mythology. Once again we have the now-familiar metaphor of the child of nature.

When the mind of a people first awakes, it is full of its morning dreams, and holds these dreams to be, as the proverb accounts them, true. A long time passes, – it must encounter and struggle with opposition, – before it acquires anything like a clear, definite self-consciousness. For a long time it scarcely regards itself as separate from Nature. It lies in her arms, and feeds at her breast, and looks up into her face, and smiles at her smiles ...
This is the character of poetry in earliest times.[31]

It follows also from Hare's argument, of course, that the Bible has been crucial in shaping the modern consciousness – and it is at this point that we begin to realise the degree to which *Hypatia* is steeped in the hermeneutic debate of the time. Once again, we begin with a false trail: Hypatia's subtle and ultimately futile allegorisation of the Homeric myths. Only when her Emersonian uplift is set against what Kingsley sees as the reality of a biblical understanding of the world do we begin to realise how the counterfeit can only be known by the presence of the true.

Kingsley's use of the Bible runs at two levels throughout the novel. On the one hand underlying the whole action of the plot is an apocalyptic sense of a doomed and dying world. It is the theme of the opening paragraphs, as of the closing, and the action is punctuated by recurring references to the inevitable destruction of this whole society. The defeat of Heraclian's Roman expedition, for instance,

was but one, and that one of the least known and most trivial, of the tragedies of that age of woe; one petty death-spasm among the unnumbered throes which were shaking to dissolution the Babylon of the West. Her time had come. Even as St John beheld her in his vision, by agony after agony, she was rotting to her well-earned doom. Tyrannizing it luxuriously over all nations, she had sat upon the mystic beast.[32]

Nor do individuals escape this general doom. Raphael with his father and brother-in-law will die at the hands of invading Vandals at the siege of Hippo – and lie buried beneath its rubble. Only Victoria will survive for her allotted span, full of good works 'as an angel of mercy'

---

[31] *Guesses at Truth* (1871), pp. 38–9.   [32] *Hypatia*, p. 226.

– apparently 'content' that her menfolk had died 'the death of heroes'.

On the other hand, of course, within this rotting hulk the new life of Christianity offers a quite different prospect for those who can come to it. But it is emphatically not a case of salvation through the Church – but, rather, through an understanding of the written word. At this level, once again, the Bible emerges less as prophecy than as metatype. As Hypatia's death at the hands of rioting monks illustrates, the Catholic Church, under the politically motivated Cyril, is as corrupt as the rest of Alexandrian society. For such a vehement Protestant as Kingsley, it is the individualists, Synesius, Augustine and eventually Raphael, who reach a real religious understanding. These have fought their way through to a personal religion, and therefore to a 'modern' self-consciousness, by learning to read the Bible for themselves. Augustine is perhaps the strangest of these, for, as Raphael quickly recognises, much of his actual exegesis is unscholarly and even based on mistranslations; what is important about it, however, is that it is personal and therefore deeply felt.[33] First-hand experience, not taking on someone else's judgements, is the key. It is this stress on personal immediacy that explains also Philammon's movement from the desert monastery into the world of Alexandria, and finally back into the desert again. He does not return to the same state as before: he began with a second-hand faith; he returns with a personal one.

But as a monk, he too, is inevitably a part of the dying world. 'The Egyptian and Syrian Churches', explains Kingsley, 'were destined to labour not for themselves, but for us.'[34] It is the Goths, huge, blond, child-like men, capable both of extraordinary ferocity and great kindliness, who are the future. They represent one of the strangest and (in retrospect) least attractive parts of Kingsley's theory of history – spelled out most fully in his later Cambridge lectures, *The Roman and the Teuton* (1864). For Kingsley, they may be pagan barbarians, but they are the torch of the future, which will bring a new vigour and vision to the effete world of the Mediterranean. Above all (except when indulging in a little local rapine, or carrying with them their own floating brothel on a Nile cruise) they have a reverence for women and a belief in monogamy that will eventually find its true expression in North European Protestantism: especially Lutheranism and the Church of England.

---

[33] *Ibid.*, pp. 308–11.   [34] *Ibid.*, p. 9.

Those wild tribes were bringing with them into the magic circle of the Western Church's influence the very materials which she required for the building up of a future Christendom, and which she could find as little in the Western Empire as in the Eastern; comparative purity of morals; sacred respect for women, for family life, law, equal justice, individual freedom, and, above all, for honesty in word and deed; bodies untainted by hereditary effeminacy, hearts earnest though genial, and blest with a strange willingness to learn, even from those they despised.[35]

Only with this 'teutonic' understanding of the role of sexual experience as leading to religious experience will Raphael's prophetic vision of the Song of Songs be fulfilled. Left to itself, all the Roman tradition could come up with to counter the 'utterly indescribable' sins of the pagan world was the hideously unnatural practice of monasticism. For Kingsley, it is no exaggeration to say that without a proper understanding of sexuality, there could be no proper understanding of the Bible. The divine grows only through the human; the flesh, sanctified, leads ultimately to the spirit.

John Henry Newman had already begun work on his novel *Callista* as early as 1848, two years before the visit of Kingsley to the Roman amphitheatre at Trier which inspired *Hypatia*. The genre of the historical novel, so effectively relaunched by Scott, had by the middle of the nineteenth century become a strikingly popular form of fiction. As we have seen, works like the *Last Days of Pompeii*, *Zenobia* and *Valerius* had already made effective use of such colourful themes as Roman decadence, natural catastrophe and clandestine groups of early Christians. Kingsley's novel had, however, appeared at a particularly opportune moment. In 1850 the Catholic hierarchy, headed by Cardinal Wiseman as the new Archbishop of Westminster, had been re-established in England for the first time since the Reformation, and – opposed by a Protestant 'no popery' campaign of which Kingsley was a vocal member – Catholicism was suddenly in the news. Partly to counter the success of Kingsley's novel, one of Wiseman's first moves had been to establish his own series of historical novels with the title 'The Catholic Popular Library', designed to illustrate the 'condition of the Church in different periods of her past existence'.[36] He himself opened the series with *Fabiola; or The Church in the Catacombs* (1854). At Wiseman's request, Newman returned to his earlier novel, and in 1856 *Callista* appeared as number 12 in the Library.

---

[35] *Ibid.*, p. 7.   [36] Wolff, *Gains and Losses*, p. 61.

Given the fact that Newman was by this stage Kingsley's theological arch-opponent and that, at any rate in its final form, *Callista* was intended as a reply to *Hypatia*, to the modern reader the astonishing thing is not how much the two authors differ, but how close are their basic assumptions about conversion and the nature of religious experience – assumptions which in turn reflect common ways of reading the Bible and experiencing the world. Though, unlike Kingsley's, Newman's story is entirely fictitious, it parallels the psychological movement of *Hypatia* to an extraordinary degree. Even the plot itself can be read as almost an inversion of Kingsley's – summed up by Raphael's cynical prophecy to Orestes when the latter considers using force to make Hypatia agree to his plans for her:

'Most illustrious majesty – it will not succeed. You do not know that woman's determination. Scourges and red-hot pincers will not shake her, alive; and dead, she will be no use whatsoever to you, while she will be of great use to Cyril.'

'How?'

'He will be most happy to make the whole story a handle against you, give out that she died a virgin-martyr, in defence of the most holy catholic and apostolic faith, get miracles worked at her tomb, and pull your palace about your ears on the strength thereof.' [37]

The irony of this, of course, is that the unfortunate Hypatia, who does indeed show all the courage Raphael here attributes to her, is finally murdered not by the civil Roman power, but by a mob of bloodthirsty monks – and Kingsley is quite clear that there is something sexually perverted in the way that they strip her naked on the high altar before killing her. The incident was certainly vivid enough for Tennyson to write a note of protest to Kingsley about it.[38] Moreover, the episode certainly suggests that, though the Church could not recognise the true nature of its act, there was a Christ-like quality about her ritual sacrifice. Similarly in Newman's novel, Callista, a pagan, is caught by an anti-Christian mob while visiting the house of Agellius, her would-be lover and a baptised though somewhat lapsed Christian, and is thrown into jail on the entirely false charge of also being one. Her slow conversion to a religion she hardly understands only begins while in prison, and she is only received into the Catholic faith just before her

---

[37] *Ibid.*, p. 63.

[38] 'It is very powerful and tragic; but I objected to the word "naked". Pelagia's nakedness has nothing which revolts one ... but I was really hurt at having Hypatia stript' (Thorp, *Kingsley*, p. 114).

eventual execution. Nevertheless, she dies a martyr's death and is eventually canonised.

But the parallels with *Hypatia* are much more than simply appropriating and realising Raphael's cynical prediction. Callista, like Hypatia, is a beautiful Greek maiden living in North Africa. She is not merely a practising pagan, but like Hypatia, she is also a *professional* pagan, in that she and her brother earn their living by making religious images. Like Hypatia, too, she is a genuine seeker after spiritual insight. When she discovers that Agellius, her suitor, is more interested in her than his own religion, she explodes with pent-up anger:

'I had hoped that there was something somewhere more than I could see; but there is nothing. Here am I a living breathing woman, with an overflowing heart, with keen affections, with a yearning after some object which may possess me. I cannot exist without something to rest upon. I cannot fall back upon that drear, forlorn state, which philosophers call wisdom, and moralists call virtue. I cannot enrol myself a votary of that cold Moon, whose arrows do but freeze me. I cannot sympathize in that majestic band of sisters whom Rome has placed under the tutelage of Vesta. I must have something to love; love is my life.'

She was absorbed in her own misery, in an intense sense of degradation, in a keen consciousness of the bondage of nature, in a despair of ever finding what alone could give meaning to her existence, and an object to her intellect and affections.[39]

This is the voice of Kingsley's Hypatia as she begins to doubt her old certainties just before she is caught by the mob. It is also, of course, the authentic voice of romanticism, speaking of a kind of religious experience which, if it can be detected in Augustine's *Confessions*, is largely dormant again thereafter until the beginning of the nineteenth century.

But there is another quality to Callista's reply to Agellius that will also be familiar from Hare and Kingsley: her use of the word 'I'. Her whole speech rests upon a sense of self that is unique and different from any other – the kind of self-consciousness that Hare argues was scarcely possible in the world of antiquity until the advent of Christianity. As if to illustrate this thesis, Callista's real self-development begins with her reading of Luke's Gospel. 'It was the writing of a provincial Greek; elegant however, and marked with that simplicity which was to her taste the elementary idea of a classic author.'[40] What it does is to

[39] J.H. Newman, *Callista: a Sketch of the Third Century* (London, 1856), reprint New York: Garland, 1975, p. 103.
[40] *Callista*, p. 252.

accentuate her already-developed sense of personal identity: 'As the skies speak differently to the philsopher and the peasant, as a book of poems to the imaginative and the cold and narrow intellect, so now she saw her being, her history, her present condition, her future in a new light, which no one else could share with her.'[41] Newman is here making a very interesting hermeneutic point. As a succession of later writers have discovered,[42] it is peculiarly difficult to enter the state of mind of a martyr. It would be almost impossible to do so without attributing to the martyr a sense of personal identity and individuality so strong as to resist the ultimate sanction from his or her own society. The kind of 'romantic' self-consciousness attributed by Hare to Christianity and to the influence of the Bible is probably a necessary prerequisite for what we would understand as genuine martyrdom. Certainly it is noticeable in *Valerius*, for instance, that the only explicitly conscious self-examination in the novel comes from the Christian martyr, Thraso, at the point where he chooses death rather than sacrifice to the emperor.

Thus if *Hypatia* retains something of an adolescent adventure-story even in its philosophising, *Callista* is supremely a novel of interior consciousness. Its plot centres less upon the actions of its characters than upon slow changes in their mental state. For all its fictitious nature, the strength of *Callista* is that it is solidly based upon first-hand experience. Just as in his own life Newman had come to Catholicism because he had already been accused of being there, so Callista slowly becomes what she is already accused of being. As in Newman's own conversion, there is an inexorable inward logic to Callista's change of state that could neither be arrested nor hurried:

She might, indeed, have been able afterwards, on looking back, to say many things of herself; and she would have recognised that, while she was continually differing from herself, in that she was changing; yet it was not a change which involved contrariety, but one which expanded itself in (as it were) concentric circles, and only fulfilled, as time went on, the promise of its beginning. Every day, as it came, was, so to say, the child of the preceding, the parent of that which followed.[43]

Nor is that final image of sexual procreation an anodyne or clichéd expression. *Callista* is, in its own way, a novel as erotically charged as

[41] *Ibid.*, p. 254.
[42] See, for instance, Gerard Manly Hopkins' *Wreck of the Deutschland* or T.S. Eliot's *Murder in the Cathedral* and *The Cocktail Party*.
[43] *Callista*, p. 226.

Hypatia, and the implicit comparison here between her conversion and the slow but predictable course of a pregnancy is of a piece with the sexual metaphors that run throughout the whole book.

At first sight Newman appears very close to Schleiermacher on the fundamentally religious nature of all human perception:

There are certain most delicate instincts and perceptions in us, which act as first principles, and which once effaced, can never, except from some supernatural source, be restored to the mind. When men are in a state of nature, these are sinned against and vanish very soon; at so early a date in the history of the individual, that perhaps he does not recollect that he ever possessed them; and since, like other first principles, they are but very partially capable of proof, a general scepticism prevails, both as to their existence and their truth. The Greeks, partly from the vivacity of their intellect, partly from their passion for the beautiful, lost these celestial adumbrations sooner than other nations.[44]

Newman, of course, unlike Kingsley, had not read Schleiermacher: indeed, he is on record to the effect that contemporary Lutheranism was little better than a species of 'heresy or infidelity'.[45] If there is a common source, it lies not with German theology but with a common romantic heritage.[46] Even if Newman did not know Hare's *Guesses at Truth,* which he probably did, he certainly knew Wordsworth, and his theory of 'spots of time'. The differences between Newman and Schleiermacher are, however, as instructive as the similarities. Though both start with innate perceptions or intuitions that serve as 'celestial adumbrations', for Schleiermacher these are highly individual, while for Newman they are collective, even cultural phenomena that cannot merely be lost by particular people, but by whole societies or cultural groups. At the same time Newman is very clear that such instinctive products of an unfallen state of nature, once lost, can only be restored by a supernatural power. For him, therefore, Christianity was a restoration, through grace, to an original state of nature broken and disrupted by the Fall, where for the first time the kind of intuitive wholeness of perception described by Schleiermacher might become possible. But the most striking difference, of course, is that whereas for

---

[44] *Ibid.,* p. 76.
[45] *Essay on the Development of Doctrine* (1845), Sheed and Ward, 1960; see F.D. Maurice's comment on this passage in the Preface to his *Lectures on the Epistle to the Hebrews,* 1846, p. xii; and Stephen Prickett, *Romanticism and Religion: the Tradition of Coleridge and Wordsworth in the Victorian Church,* Cambridge University Press, 1976, p. 158.
[46] For Newman's Romantic inheritance see John Coulson, *Newman and the Common Tradition,* Oxford: Clarendon Press, 1970; and Prickett, *Romanticism and Religion.*

Schleiermacher such intuitions are part of a process of awakening consciousness, for Newman they are essentially a quality of the undifferentiated and unfallen intellect, and, as that last sentence makes very clear, the growth of individual self-consciousness is fundamentally inimical to their preservation.

This is at first sight an astonishing statement. That the very quality Newman valued so highly in himself, and in the novel, is made the *sine qua non* of Callista's conversion experience, should turn out to be, as it were, the first fruits of the tree of knowledge and a mark of the Fall, would seem quite extraordinary. Yet on consideration, such a move is typical of Newman's theology. For him Christianity (especially Catholicism) was not a way back to a lost, even infantile, condition, but a way forward. Humanity redeemed is not humanity returned to its unfallen state, but, as it were, an 'adult' consciousness which could comprehend the childish state without partaking of it. This is Augustine's *felix culpa*, the 'happy fault' by which the original innocence of mankind was exchanged for the far greater blessing of Christ's redemption. In Hare's terms, Callista's cry for help to Agellius is an instinctive reaching-out towards that state of more adult and heightened self-consciousness that is the distinctive hallmark of Christianity. In this sense, *Callista* can be seen as a fictional exploration of the distinction between 'notional' and 'real assent' that was to be the theme of Newman's last, and in many ways his greatest, philosophic work, the *Grammar of Assent*.

In stark contrast to this exploration of the meaning of post-lapsarian assent is Juba, Agellius' brother, who, while not being in himself an evil character, has no desire to be tied to the Christianity of his father, and prides himself on his independence of mind. Trying to hold a neutral position between the new religion and the old, he is bewitched by his mother, an evil sorceress, and like the man possessed of an evil spirit in the gospels, he roams through wild and rocky places living off fruit, berries and even roots.

had the daylight lasted, in him too, as well as Callista, Caecilius would have found changes, but of a very different nature; yet even in him he would have seen a change for the better, for that awful expression of pride and defiance was gone. What was the use of parading a self-will, which every moment of his life belied? His actions, his words, his hands, his lips, his feet, his place of abode, his daily course, were in the dominion of another, who inexorably ruled him. It was not the gentle influence which draws and persuades, it was not the power which can be propitiated by prayer; it was a tyranny which acted without reaction, energetic as mind, and impenetrable as matter.[47]

The message is clear. Consciousness of one's own individuality and moral integrity is not the same as moral self-possession or independence. Indeed, for Newman the idea of independence is an illusion – the more dangerous for its insidious attraction; true consciousness of self (as Schleiermacher elsewhere also argued) involves a recognition of humanity's absolute dependence upon God.

All this provides the philosophic backdrop for the ironies of the main theme – not least of which is that Newman, the Catholic celibate (and very possibly, as Kingsley hinted, the closet homosexual) has chosen to take on Kingsley on his own ground: sexual love. This is a tale of two loves: earthly and heavenly; *eros* and *agape*. Jucundus, Agellius' uncle and Callista's employer, runs a pagan image-shop. He is an easy-going man (even his name means 'pleasant') who thinks that if he encourages Agellius' obvious interest in Callista it will give him something to take his mind off all this Christian nonsense. For him it is perfectly obvious that sexual and spiritual love are mutually antagonistic and incompatible. The former will drive out the latter. To everyone's surprise, however, it turns out that they are not merely intimately connected, but that the former points to the latter. Callista's already-quoted outburst to Agellius is in many ways the key text:

Here am I a living breathing woman, with an overflowing heart, with keen affections, with a yearning after some object which may possess me. I cannot exist without someting to rest upon. I cannot fall back upon that drear, forlorn state, which philosophers call wisdom, and moralists call virtue. I cannot enrol myself a votary of that cold Moon, whose arrows do but freeze me. I cannot sympathize in that majestic band of sisters whom Rome has placed under the tutelage of Vesta. I must have something to love; love is my life.

Initially, we read this, as we are meant to do, in specifically sexual terms, but, as the novel progresses, it takes on retrospectively new shades of meaning, so that on the day of her trial she says to her jailor's wife 'I am ready; I am going home ... now I have espoused Him, and am going to be married today, and He will hear me.'[48] Again, at the trial, she announces 'I have found my true Love, whom before I knew not.'[49] For Callista earthly love leads straight to its divine prototype (her interest in Agellius was perfunctory and brief in the extreme). She

---

[47] *Callista*, p. 271.
[48] *Ibid.*, p. 227.
[49] *Ibid.*, p. 280.

is like George Eliot's Dinah Morris or Dorothea Brooke whose emotions are so powerful that they require an adequate object. It was a character-type that was to fascinate Newman, as it fascinated Eliot, and for the same reason: that it was in some sense a self-description.

if all your thoughts go one way; if you have needs, desires, aims, aspirations, all of which demand an Object, and imply, by their very existence, that such an Object does exist also; and if nothing here does satisfy them, and if there be a message which professes to come from that Object, of whom you already have a presentiment . . .[50]

Though this argument (or feeling) reaches back to Anselm's ontological proof of God, it was one that was to take on a peculiar force for many romantics and post-romantics – ranging from Newman himself, to such twentieth-century figures as C.S. Lewis.[51]

In many ways Schleiermacher, Kingsley and Newman are as diverse a trio of nineteenth-century theological writers as one could hope to find. That a Lutheran radical, a liberal Anglican, and a Catholic convert should all discover in erotic experience some intimation of divine *agape* is not perhaps in itself that improbable – conversion through the love of a good woman is almost a stock-in-trade of a certain kind of novel; but that they should all suggest that the former is in some sense the pattern or key to the latter is surely far more surprising. What is also clear is that the process of hermeneutic privatisation noted in the last chapter has become, if anything, more rather than less marked. This is especially evident in the case of Newman, and it is the more remarkable in that it runs directly counter to his declared antipathy to 'liberalism', or the exercise of private judgement in spiritual matters. Yet, as we have seen, Callista's conversion is essentially bound up with her strong and growing sense of individual identity, and her ability to make precisely such a 'private judgement' while isolated and in prison. Indeed, it is hard to see how 'conversion' in this sense of an individual's personal and considered choice could (or, for that matter, should) be other than a matter of private judgement. Callista's conversion is in some ways a more inward and personal affair even than that of the proto-Protestant Raphael Ben-Ezra.

What was conspicuously lacking in all these conversions, however, was any sense of a mythological dimension. Unlike Chateaubriand,

[50] *Ibid.*, p. 173.
[51] See *Pilgrim's Regress*, Dent, 1933, and *Surprised by Joy*, Bles, 1955.

who had been happy to see in Christianity a complete fulfilment of pagan mythology, none of the Victorian novelists we have examined was prepared to allow the immediacy of their 'historical' visions to be impaired by the suspicion that there might be some deeper general underlying sub-stratum to their narratives. Indeed, there is a very real sense in which the kind of self-consciousness arising from erotic experience so common in the romantic interpretation of religion is fundamentally inimical to the more collective consciousness implied by a mythological world-picture. For any kind of synthesis between these two apparent poles we must turn to the twentieth century, and a deliberate attempt to create a different kind of historical consciousness through the re-invention of myth.

THE FAMILY OF MANN: JACOB AND SON

No one remains quite where he was when he recognises himself.[52]

Thomas Mann's massive tetralogy, *Joseph and his Brothers*, was begun as early as 1926 and published between 1933 and 1943 – the first two volumes in Berlin (1933 and 1934), the third in Vienna (1936) and the final one (for obvious reasons) in Stockholm (1943). From the start the narratives are animated by a tension between the mythological, even timeless, nature of the biblical material itself and the turbulent twentieth-century context in which the novels were written. At one level nothing could be further removed from the crises of German identity that shook the world during that decade than a historical novel about one of the most ancient stories of the Old Testament; but at another level, of course, as we have seen with an earlier generation of historical novels, the story as it took shape had everything to do with Mann's contemporary situation – both personal and political.

Certainly the Nazi censor reponsible for reading the first volume in 1933, the writer Herbert Blank, saw its publication as a political act. 'It is simply not endurable', he wrote in his report on *The Tales of Jacob*, 'that, ten months after 30 January [the day Hitler became Chancellor], the emigrant Thomas Mann is able to retail in Germany a book full of Jewish tales.'[53] Mann had been marked down by the Nazis, immediately they came to power in 1933, as a 'liberal-reactionary'; he

---

[52] *Joseph and his Brothers*, trs. H.T. Lowe-Porter, Penguin, 1988, p. vii.

[53] Joseph Wulf, *Literatur und Dichtung im Dritten Reich: ein Dokumentation*, Rowahlt: Taschenbuch, 1966, p. 24. Cited by R.J. Hollingdale in *Thomas Mann: a Critical Study*, Hart-Davis, 1971, p. 23.

responded to their attacks by resigning from the Prussian Academy of
Arts as a public act of protest against the new regime in the same year,
and moved to Switzerland, where he lived until 1939. At the outbreak
of the Second World War he went to the United States, and in 1944, in
a no less political gesture, became an American citizen.

If a novel about the Book of Genesis, and what it meant to be a
displaced and enslaved Israelite within a powerful and imperial high
culture, had an immediate (indeed, prophetic) reference to the context
of Nazi Germany, it is also true that this, arguably Mann's greatest
work, arises uniquely from the German cultural tradition to which he
was heir – and which, during the 1940s, he explicitly appropriated to
himself. His famous claim in exile in California, *Wo ich bin ist die deutsche
Kultur* ('Where I am is German culture'), has, I think rightly, also been
seen in its context as not so much a piece of personal arrogance as itself
a 'necessary political act',[54] denying the competence of the crude and
chauvinistic Nazi 'cultural' propaganda, and stressing the surviving life
and continuity of an older German tradition of liberal culture. Yet the
papal resonances of that phrase[55] may also alert us to other levels, of a
personal, rather than a political, imperialism. It is not so far from his
1916 statement to Ernst Bertram that he had long believed the tragedy
of Germany to be 'symbolized and personified' by himself and his
brother,[56] which, in turn, foreshadows Mann's later affirmation of a
'mystical union' with Goethe in the novel *Lotte in Weimar* (1939) –
chronologically an interruption in the middle of the Joseph sequence.
In short, however we are meant to take his claim to embody the
cultural tradition of a whole nation,[57] it is hard to read it *simply* as a
statement about the necessary exile of the German literary tradition
during the Second World War. Mann stands unequivocally in the
tradition of German Romanticism, and it was not a tradition that ever
conspicuously down-played the artistic ego. His claim, moreover,
comes very close to Joseph's own to represent the Hebrew tradition,
made first in Potiphar's house, and then subsequently in the Egyptian
Court.

Though it is always dangerous to read too much of a writer's private
life into his novels, it is at least worth noting that Thomas Mann

---

[54] T.J. Reed, *Thomas Mann: the Uses of Tradition*, Oxford: Clarendon Press, 1974, p. 1.

[55] *Ubi papem, ibi ecclesia* ('Where the Pope is, there is the Church').

[56] Cited by Marcel Reich-Ranicki, *Thomas Mann and his Family*, trs. Ralph Manheim, Fontana,
1990, p. 4.

[57] Reed, *Thomas Mann*, p. 340.

himself, like Joseph, was a younger brother whose consciousness and identity were inevitably shaped by his sibling-relationships. Moreover, though Thomas Mann did not have ten elder brothers to contend with, he had the most formidable of all sibling-rivals for an aspiring writer – another, older, and successful novelist in the family: Heinrich Mann. Nor was that the end of the fraternal family conflicts: though Heinrich, like Thomas, chose to leave Germany because of the Nazis, Viktor, their younger brother (the 'Benjamin' of the family), not merely remained behind, but actively supported the new regime. It gives the dying Jacob's curious description of the youngest, Benjamin, as 'a ravening wolf'[58] – puzzling in the biblical text, and seen in the novel as referring to the future, perhaps in the rape and murder of the Levite's concubine – yet a new twist within the family of Mann.

Such a quest for evidence of the artist in the artifact is, perhaps, further justified by Thomas Mann's own unashamed Romanticism. Whereas, even before the rise of the Nazis, Heinrich had sought to distance himself from all aspects of German Romanticism, and looked instead to the more socially and politically engaged traditions of the French and even more the Russian novel,[59] part of Thomas' acute distaste for Hitler and his intellectual camp-followers stemmed from the fact that superficially they drew on very similar German aesthetic traditions to himself. His conscious identification with Schopenhauer, Nietzsche and Wagner[60] was uncomfortably close to the lineage many Nazis had attempted to claim as exclusively their own. Walter Benjamin has called attention to the fact that the most successful of the 'new mythologys' called for by the System-Programme and Friedrich Schlegel was that of the Nazis' 'aestheticising' of politics.[61] Even as early as 1926, when working on the sources for *Joseph*, Mann found himself using a new Nazi-orientated edition of Bachofen's classic study of mythology edited by Alfred Bäumler,[62] who, in 1931, was also to publish a similarly ideological selection from Nietzsche. Mann published an attack on Bäumler's introduction to Bachofen which was to involve him in immediate controversy with his Nazi opponents.[63]

---

[58] *Joseph*, p. 1190.
[59] Walter E. Berendsohn, *Thomas Mann: Artist and Partisan in Troubled Times*, trs. George C. Buck, Montgomery: University of Alabama Press, 1973, pp. 4–5.
[60] Hollingdale, *Thomas Mann*, pp. 11–13.
[61] Bowie, *Aesthetics and Subjectivity*, p. 57.
[62] *Der Mythus von Orient und Occident. Aus den Werken von J.J. Bachofen*, Munich: Beck, 1926.
[63] Reed, *Thomas Mann*, p. 307.

Other influences were less susceptible to exploitation by Mann's political enemies. Though, as we have seen, the word 'romantic' is never an unambiguous one, it has particular complexities in the German context where a sharp philosophic distinction is conventionally drawn between the so-called 'early Romanticism' of the Jena group and the 'later Romanticism' of Schopenhauer, Nietzsche and Wagner.[64] From the 1930s onwards, Goethe was as important to Mann as the later Romantics. Almost as important were the early Romantics, Friedrich Schlegel and Novalis, and in technical terms also Wackenroder, Tieck and Hoffman.[65] Certainly Mann, perhaps the most encyclopaedic and longwinded of major twentieth-century novelists, is not concerned with a theory of fragments. Still less is he trying to fill lacunae in Kantian philosophy. But the idea of the work of art as not so much a completed artifact as a process of self-creation has immediate relevance – as has the idea of a novel that would read the past by making its own selective 'anthology' from it, or that would also contain a theory of the novel. Indeed, it is hard to think that in writing *Jacob* Mann did not have in mind Friedrich Schlegel's famous programme for the 'Romantic' novel:

I would have ... a *theory of the novel* which would be a theory in the original sense of the word;[66] a spiritual viewing of the subject with calm and serene feelings; as it is proper to view in solemn joy the meaningful play of divine images. Such a theory of the novel would have to be itself a novel which would reflect imaginatively every eternal tone of the imagination and would again confound the chaos of the world of the knights.[67] The things of the past would live in it in new forms; Dante's sacred shadow would arise from the lower world, Laura would hover heavenly before us, Shakespeare would converse intimately with Cervantes, and there Sancho would jest with Don Quixote again.[68]

In his persona of Joseph, Mann, as it were, joins the great artists of the past: Dante, Petrarch, Shakespeare and Cervantes. Above all, however, what he was to find in Schlegel – as he had in Sterne and Nietzsche – was a sense of irony. Indeed, it will be part of our case that what many critics have noted as the unique authorial tone of

---

[64] See, for instance, Bowie, *Aesthetics and Subjectivity*, p. 41.

[65] Berendsohn, *Thomas Mann*, pp. 18–19.

[66] That is, 'contemplation'.

[67] 'This is where I look for and find the Romantic – in the older moderns, in Shakespeare, Cervantes, in Italian poetry, in that age of knights' (Friedrich Schlegel, *Dialogue on Poetry and Literary Aphorisms*, trs., introduced and annotated by Ernst Behler and Roman Struc, Philadelphia: Pennsylvania State University Press, 1968, p. 101.

[68] *Ibid.*, p. 102.

Joseph and his Brothers[69] arises in part from Mann's concern not merely to appropriate both the biblical narrative and the wealth of critical literature it has engendered, but also to show, and even discuss, this process in action, sometimes seriously, but as often as not ironically. It is in this, earlier, 'Jena' sense of Romanticism that we can also think of Joseph himself, emerging from myth to historical self-consciousness, as a Romantic.

This, surely, is also the meaning of the curious first chapter of the *Tales of Jacob*, entitled 'At the Well'. We first encounter the boy, Joseph, alone and half-naked, contemplating beside his father Jacob's well. As is repeatedly made clear, the well is itself a symbol of the unfathomable depths of the past – both for Joseph, as he looks back upon the history of his tribe, and the legends of surrounding societies which have inevitably formed part of Hebrew mythology, and, at the same time for ourselves, as we try to understand the outlook of Jacob and his favourite son over a gulf of more than three thousand years. But Joseph, at the moment we encounter him, is not so much gazing into the deep well of the past, but into himself – what Henry James called 'the deep well of the unconscious'. He is not in love – and is probably too egotistical ever to be so in the sense that his father was – but his state of contemplation has much in common with the condition of primary intuition which Schleiermacher describes as 'the highest flowering of religion'. For Jacob, like so many of the heroes of Romantic and post-Romantic novels, this state of self-conscious intuition was only to be reached through his sexual love for Rachel, his cousin, for whose sake he served his devious father-in-law for fourteen years. He had fled from his brother with only his life and the blessing. To become Israel, the father of the great people foretold in the dream at Bethel, he had first of all to learn to love something outside himself better than himself. His love for Rachel is at once his triumph and Joseph's immediate undoing, for from it stemmed Jacob's open favouritism towards Rachel's son and the consequent hatred of his half-brothers that was to send Joseph into the pit, and thence to the Midianite slavers and so to Egypt. All this is still in the future, however, and what we see in Joseph at this point is less a religious experience than, as it were, the readiness for it: the capacity for such intuitions as Schleiermacher describes, and the possession of what in Jacob's case is described as 'the copious flow of mythical association of ideas and their

---

[69] See, for instance, Hollingdale, *Thomas Mann*, p. 102.

capacity to permeate the moment'.[70] It is significant how often in the conversation with his father that follows he refers to himself in the third person. As the inheritor of the blessing, he must learn to say 'I'; and if we turn from these first pages to the final volume, *Joseph the Provider*, we find that this is precisely what his experiences have taught him.

Indeed, it is surely significant that Joseph himself, with his supreme and cheerful assumption of his own divinely protected destiny, offers us one of Mann's most fully developed portraits of the artist in society.[71] Perhaps not surprisingly Joseph is also more of a self-portrait than any of Mann's other protagonists. Just as, in *Joseph the Provider*, the last, and, in retrospect, most 'American' volume of the tetralogy, Joseph reshapes the Egyptian economy with what are, in effect, covert Hebrew values, so Mann saw himself not merely as the guardian of German traditional values, but also as their recreator in exile. 'I have no objection', he writes in his 1948 foreword to the English edition,

if ... critics say that the German of the 'Prelude in the Upper Circles' in *Joseph the Provider* 'is really not German any more'. Suffice it that it is speech, and suffice it that the entire opus is fundamentally a work of speech in whose polyphony sounds of the primitive Orient mingle with the most modern, with the accents of fictive scientific method, and that it takes pleasure in changing its linguistic masks as often as its hero changes his God-masks – the last of which looks remarkably American. For it is the mask of an American Hermes, a brilliant messenger of shrewdness, whose New Deal is unmistakably reflected in Joseph's magic administration of national economy.[72]

No culture, neither ancient Egypt nor, certainly, Germany in the 1940s, is static, or an island unto itself. Not least among the prophetic roles of the artist, as Julius Hare had observed, is the task of giving voice, and even structure, to those forces of change. Just as Luther, with his great sixteenth-century translation of the Bible, had virtually created the modern German language, so Mann, symbolically in exile in the new world, sees himself as inheriting and renewing that process – once again in relation to the Bible. Whether he would have wished that renewal of German culture to involve the degree of Americanising of the Federal Republic which actually followed the Second World War may be an open question, but, given what it replaced, we should not automatically assume a negative answer. Germany in 1945 was not merely a physical ruin, it was a cultural and spiritual void peculiarly

[70] *Joseph*, p. 57.
[71] Hollingdale, *Thomas Mann*, p. 114.
[72] *Ibid.*, p. xiii.

susceptible to the ideology of the conquerer – whether from east or west.

As the Nazi censor seems dimly to have perceived from *The Tales of Jacob* as early as 1933, to make the Jew, stateless, nomadic and infinitely adaptable, yet above all possessed of a unique vision, the type of the artist in society was a boldly polemical move. In that first volume Jacob/Israel has always a sense that his nomadic status is more than historical contingency, but a necessary attribute of his religion, for

one served a God whose nature was not repose and abiding comfort, but a God of designs for the future, in whose will inscrutable, great, far-reaching things were in process of becoming, who, with His brooding will and His world-planning, was Himself only in process of becoming, and thus was a God of unrest, a God of cares, who must be sought for, for whom one must at all times keep oneself free, mobile and in readiness.[73]

This is still the God of the great promises to Abraham and to Isaac, but whose nature is now apparently protean: one not merely of change, but of dynamic evolution. Nor is this idea of a divine *entelechy* simply a metaphor: in Mann's God there is a consistent tension between a sense of mysterious divine purpose and an ironic assumption that he is no more than a reflection of the qualities historically attributed to him. Thus at times the narrative has all the conscious anthropomorphism of a lecture on the higher criticism:

Israel, God fighteth, had always been the name of a warlike robber tribe of the desert ... Back in the wilderness their God had been a fire-breathing and storm-breeding warrior named Yahu, a troublesome sort of hobgoblin, with more demonic than godlike traits, spiteful, tyrannical and incalculable ... there was reserved for this sinister deity, entirely unknown to the civilized world, an extrardinary theological career, merely by dint of the fact that some of his followers had penetrated into the sphere of influence occupied by Abraham's thoughts about God.[74]

In a sense, as at least one critic has noted,[75] this God emerges as being essentially beyond good and evil. But this is very far from the Olympian detachment of a Goethe or even that assumed by Mann himself as narrator. Eliezer's instruction of Joseph in the mythology of his people portrays a deity who is more of a shifty politician than a First Cause: 'Had not God ... held His tongue and wisely kept silence upon the fact that not only righteous but also evil things would proceed from man,

---

[73] *Ibid.*, p. 31.
[74] *Ibid.*, pp. 83, 84.
[75] Hollingdale, *Thomas Mann*, p. 170.

the creation of man would certainly not have been permitted.'[76] Yet, at the same time, if only because Joseph himself never wavers in his own faith in God's providence, God retains an aura of being ultimately, if always inscrutably, in control. He is one of the great personages of the novel, but less as supreme governor and law-giver than as supreme artist: the great story-teller and ironist whose characters – Jacob, Joseph, even Mann himself – are but reflections of a creator who has ultimately shaped his world in story.[77]

And here, surely, is where we find the reflexive narrative centre of this extraordinary novel. With regard to Jacob's intuition of divine election behind his nomadic condition, Mann comments:

As for me ... I will not conceal my native and comprehensive understanding of the old man's restless unease and dislike of any fixed habitation. For do I not know the feeling? To me too has not unrest been ordained, have not I too been endowed with a heart that knoweth not repose? The story-teller's star – is it not the moon, lord of the road, the wanderer, who moves in his stations, one after another, freeing himself from each?[78]

Jacob's status as patriarch, prophet and seer is similarly grounded in his function of story-teller:

Such, then, are the tales of Jacob, written in the mien of the grey-haired man, as they passed before his swimming gaze, that got entangled in his eyebrows, when he fell into his solemn musing, either alone or with other people – and his look gave them a start, so that they nudged each other and whispered: 'Hush, Jacob is thinking of his stories!'[79]

In this respect, as in many others in this novel, Joseph, 'the Dreamer', is but the successor of his father. Indeed, no single dream of his ever has the importance accorded to it of the runaway Jacob's extraordinary vision at Bethel. Joseph's dreams are essentially utilitarian, concerning self-aggrandisement (the sheaves of corn), the fate of particular individuals (Pharaoh's butler and baker), or medium-term economic forecasting (the fat and lean kine); they do not, like Jacob's, reach up to heaven and out to all the families of the earth.

What in the last resort distinguishes Joseph from his resentful brothers, and binds him closer to his father, is that he, too, is both the holder of the blessing, and yet, at the same time, its usurper – who has

---

[76] *Joseph*, p. 28.
[77] I acknowledge taking the image from Brian Wicker's suggestive title, *The Story-Shaped World* (Athlone, 1975), although my conclusions are clearly very different from his.
[78] *Joseph*, p. 32.
[79] *Ibid.*, p. 207.

not come by his inheritance by openly legitimate means. At one level this is the final and most outrageous example of wilful favouritism:

it was since that time that Jacob, himself the first-born not in the way of nature, but only nominally and legally, conceived the plan of divesting Reuben of his right, depriving him of the blessing, to confer it not on Simeon, Leah's second, the next in order, but with the most arbitrary exercise of authority, on Joseph.[80]

At a more fundamental level, however, the bestowal of the blessing is simply a recognition of an existing state of affairs – as we see in Jacob's final summation of his sons on his deathbed.[81] Of all Jacob's offspring it is clear from very early on that Joseph is the only one who has what it takes. He has a charm, wit and intelligence conspicuously lacking in the sons of Leah and Bilhah. Even his faults are, in effect, the inverse of other assets essential to a holder of the blessing. His vanity and tale-bearing are also evidence of an emerging sense of personal identity. In his fascination with the history of his family and the myths of his own and other gods – which at one level are presented as no more than an extension to his personal vanity – can also be found a nascent sense of history and the foundations for an emergence from a mythological to a historical sense of the past. Finally, and apparently uniquely among the brothers, he is literate. Not merely can he read and write: increasingly he learns to read the course of his life as being itself a story in a book.

Though in the course of the novel the blessing is many things – fertility, land, perception, theological insight and divination – it circles constantly about this narrative centre. There is a sense in which the blessing actually becomes what its possessors say it is. It is as if it were, above all, a kind of creative articulacy: a means by which words shape their speaker into an ever-greater sense of his own uniqueness. Indeed, the whole book may be read in one sense as an extended discussion of the nature of the blessing, and it is clear even in the first few pages that what Jacob had stolen from his slower-witted brother is not a static possession, but a dynamic and constantly evolving destiny that owns its possessor rather than *vice versa*.

A blessing? It is unlikely that the word gives the true meaning of that which happened to him in his vision and which corresponded to his temperament and to his experience of himself. For the word 'blessing' carries with it an idea which but ill describes men of his sort: men, that is, of roving spirit and

---

[80] *Ibid.*, p. 52.
[81] 'The Last Assembly', *Joseph*, pp. 1184–96 (Genesis 49).

discomfortable mind, whose novel conception of the deity is destined to make its mark upon the future. The life of men with whom new histories begin can seldom or never be a sheer unclouded blessing; not this it is which their consciousness of self whispers in their ears. 'And thou shalt be a destiny': such is the purer and more precise meaning of the promise, in whatever language it may have been spoken.[82]

This is so close to Mann's later description of the role of the artist/ writer that we are hardly likely to miss the self-identification. One of the most striking features of the blessing, right from the start, is the way that the possession of it is publicly acknowledged. Laban, Jacob's devious father-in-law, however much he may mistrust his servant and son-in-law, has good reason to stand in awe of the blessing and, at least once, is apparently restrained from violence by fear of it.[83] Potiphar and eventually Pharaoh, who have much less reason to fear its power, are also secretly impressed by it, if only for the reason that it seems to be behind this slave's articulate self-confidence and belief in his own superiority.

Yet Joseph's route towards fulfilment of this dynamic and self-conscious destiny is a long and complex one, and forms one reason, at least, for the length of the novel. Eliezer, Jacob's steward, is a semi-mythological figure, both in his name, which is the same as that of the servant of Abraham who had found Rebecca at the well, and in his own consciousness, which does not fully distinguish between himself and his Eliezer-ancestors:

the old man's ego was not quite clearly demarcated, that it opened at the back, as it were, and overflowed into spheres external to his own individuality both in space and time; embodying in his own experience events which, remembered and related in the clear light of day, ought actually to have been put into the third person ... The conception of individuality belongs after all to the same category as that of unity and entirety, the whole and the all; and in the days of which I am writing the distinction between spirit in general and individual spirit possessed not nearly so much power of the mind as in our world of today ... It is highly significant that in those days there were no words for conceptions dealing with personality and individuality, other than such external ones as confession, religion.[84]

It is from Eliezer, as much as from his father, Jacob, that the young Joseph has learned his sense of the past. Not surprisingly, 'his ideas of time showed themselves to be hazy indeed; the past which he so

[82] *Ibid.*, pp. 6–7.
[83] *Ibid.*, pp. 242–3.
[84] *Ibid.*, p. 78.

lightly invoked being actually matter of remote and primeval dis-
tances'.[85] Even according to their own records, the gap between
Abraham's departure from Ur and Joseph's time was some six
hundred years – though, as Mann adds, 'six hundred years at that
time and under that sky did not mean what they mean in our western
history ... the frame of Joseph's life, his ways and habits of thought
were far more like his ancestors' than ours are like the crusaders' '.[86]
The point of this lengthy discussion of Joseph's mind-set right at the
start of the novel is to show both how (unlike his brothers) he is
fascinated by his family history and traditions, and, at the same time,
that his sense of that tradition, and his own place in it, is more
mythological than it is historical. The idea of the blessing is, as it
were, the dominant and organising historical myth by which the other
myths of origins are to be understood.

Indeed, without such a myth, he would lack a perspective to view
what Mann calls the 'time-coulisses' of history. The image is from the
theatre. A 'coulisse' is a piece of side-scenery in the wings of a stage –
one of the devices by which a conventional proscenium-arch stage gives
an illusion of depth. Joseph has also read verses and legends from
Assyrian clay tablets, and knows, for instance, the story of Tammuz –
the Hebrew name for the Babylonian deity Dumuzi, who was believed
to have journeyed to the underworld (and, in some versions, to have
returned). When Joseph is later cast into the pit for three days by his
angry brothers, Mann takes care that we shall feel the traditional New
Testament typological resonances with Christ before the Resurrection,
at the same time it is with Tammuz that Joseph compares, even
identifies, himself at this crucial point in his own career. Not for the
first time, Joseph is thus a link between pagan mythology and the
events of the New Testament.

But it is as well that Joseph does read himself into a part in that story
because it is itself one of the time-coulisses of the narrative, and is
already of unimaginable age. Though the story of Dumuzi comes from
a crumbling clay tablet, this, in turn is only a copy made in the time of
Asshurbanipal from a source perhaps a thousand years older and
'about as easy, or as hard, for Asshurbanipal's tablet-writers to read
and understand as for us today a manuscript of the time of Charle-
magne. Written in a quite obsolete and undeveloped hand ... it must
have been hard to decipher; whether its significance was wholly

---

[85] *Ibid.*, p. 13. [86] *Ibid.*, pp. 7–8.

honoured in the copy remains a matter for doubt.' But this is not the end of the process.

And then, this original: it was not actually an original; not *the* original, when you come to look at it. It was itself a copy of a document out of God knows what distant time; upon which, then, though without precisely knowing where, one might rest, as upon a true original, if it were not itself provided with glosses and additions by the hand of the scribe, who thought thus to make more comprehensible an original text lying again who knows how far back in time ... And thus I might go on – if I were not convinced that my readers already understand what I mean when I speak of coulisses and abysses.[87]

Mann's point, of course, concerns not merely the actual time-scales – what we saw in the first chapter were the unfathomable origins of the texts that have come down to us – it also concerns something even more difficult to determine: what may have been the actual protagonists' sense of time? Should we ask not merely what was the historical consciousness of the compliers of Genesis ('P', 'Q', 'J' and all their shadowy friends and relations) but also, more intriguingly, what was Jacob's, what was Joseph's sense of history?

The Tales of Jacob opens with a lengthy 'Prelude' discussing precisely these questions. As we see in the last quotation, Mann addresses his reader directly, commenting, explaining, questioning his sources. Elsewhere he obtrudes himself into the narrative even more insistently, telling us that he has visited the place where such-and-such event is supposed to have happened, and vouching at least for the truth of the setting: 'Here it was ... I myself went down into the depths and looked from the western shore of the evil-tasting sea of Lot, saw all with my own eyes, and that it is in order and agrees one part.'[88] It is difficult at first reading to be sure of the tone of such passages. Some critics have insisted on taking them at their face value,[89] others have pointed to the ironic possibilities of such interventions and seen, at any rate, a calculated gap between the writer and his fictive narrators.[90] So omnipresent is the narrator's voice in the *Joseph* tetralogy, however, that the question of tone is crucial to a reading of the whole novel, and it is here that an example may be useful. This is Mann, the narrator, on the Deluge:

87 *Ibid.*, p. 10.
88 *Ibid.*, pp. 241–2.
89 See, for instance, Hollingdale's comments, *Thomas Mann*, pp. 102–3.
90 See Reed's discussion of Mann's irony, *Thomas Mann*, pp. 8–14.

The Deluge, then, had its theatre on the Euphrates River, but also in China. Round the year 1300 before our era there was a frightful flood in the Huang-Ho after which the course of the river was regulated; it was a repetition of the great flood of some thousand and fifty years before, whose Noah had been the fifth Emperor, Yao, and which, chronologically speaking, was far from having been the true and original Deluge, since the tradition of the latter is common to both peoples. Just as the Babylonian account, known to Joseph, was only a reproduction of earlier and earlier accounts, so the flood itself is to be referred back to older and older prototypes; one is convinced of being on solid ground at last, when one fixes, as the original original, upon the sinking of the land Atlantis beneath the waves of the ocean – knowledge of which dread event penetrated into all the lands of the earth, previously populated from that same Atlantis, and fixed itself as a movable tradition forever in the minds of men. But it is only an apparent stop and a temporary goal. According to a Chaldean computation, a period of thirty-nine thousand, one hundred and eighty years lay between the Deluge and the first historical dynasty of the kingdom of the two rivers. It follows that the sinking of Atlantis, occurring only nine thousand years before Solon, a very recent catastrophe indeed, historically considered, certainly cannot have been *the* Deluge. It too was only a repetition, the becoming-present of something profoundly past, a frightful refresher to the memory, and the original story is to be referred back at least to that incalculable point of time when the island continent called 'Lemuria', in its turn only a remnant of the old Gondwana continent, sank beneath the waves of the Indian Ocean.[91]

The paragraph begins unexceptionably with a comparison between the Babylonian and the Chinese flood-myths, which, by deft sleight-of-hand it then reads as if they were datable historical events. We are thus prepared for the sinking of Atlantis, as if it, too, were an unquestionable piece of history, and so back to Lemuria, a hypothetical continent supposedly linking Madagascar and South East Asia in Jurassic times, and finally to the oldest of all, the ur-continent, Gondwanaland. In the process, of course, we have been swept from history to myth and away from the millennia of human existence into the aeons of geological time, so that the final conclusion, of the universality of the flood-myths pointing to the memory of original catastrophe somewhere between 70 million and 140 million years ago, when dinosaurs roamed the earth, seems for a moment not merely credible, but the only proper scholarly conclusion.

The pontificating delivery, the judicious weighing of evidence, the use of increasingly recondite sources, and the apparently logical progression all contribute to the parody of an academic style – and

---

[91] *Joseph*, p. 18.

should surely settle, once and for all, the question of whether Mann's weighty lucubrations in *Joseph* should be read entirely at their face value. But there is another aspect of this ironic style, familiar to readers of *Felix Krull* or *The Holy Sinner*, which leads us straight back to one of Mann's favourite authors: Sterne. We are hardly surprised to learn that during his work on *Joseph* Mann read and reread *Tristram Shandy*[92] – and, as we have seen, even as early as the sermons, the whole ironic style with its amassing of pseudo-evidence, the development of provisional hypotheses, and their judicious dismissal in the face of further evidence, is all part of Sterne's comic technique.

Yet there is one important difference. Sterne, we recall, was, if not a cause, at least symptomatic of the process whereby the Bible came to be read as a univocal and linear narrative. What Mann is doing is the opposite of that. He is taking an apparently linear source-narrative and so mythologising it, in the name of inclusiveness, that it becomes once again a polysemous and multivocal exposition. Lemuria is a case in point. It must rank as one of the briefest mythological continents of all time. It was first proposed by one P.L. Sclater, in 1864 to account for the prevalence of certain botanical and zoological forms across the Indian Ocean, but as early 1880 we find it being compared with Atlantis, and described as 'a good example of the survival of a provisional hypothesis which offers what seems to be an easy solution of a difficult problem ... long after it has been proved to be untenable'.[93] By this time it had been taken up by Madame Blavatsky and the Theosophical Society, who, unworried by the Jurassic dating of the original hypothesis, proceeded to people the continent with the Third Race, whose putative survivors included the Australian Aboriginal tribes.[94] The point is that nineteenth- (or, for that matter, twentieth-) century scientific mythology is as much mythology as any Babylonian stories of Gilgamesh and the flood. Mann is, in effect, remythologising the story of Joseph, linking it on the one hand with Babylonian and Egyptian stories, and on the other with its typological foreshadowings of the New Testament – with occasional forays into a scientific (or, at least, Theosophical) future, such as the Lemurian hypothesis.

The reason appears to be twofold. On the one hand, I suspect, is a

[92] Berendsohn, *Thomas Mann*, p. 90.

[93] A.R. Wallace, *Island Life*, 1880, vol. ii, pp. xix, 398.

[94] See Jenny McFarlane, 'The Theosophical Society and Christine Waller's *The Great Breath*', *Australian Journal of Art*, vol. 9 (1993), p. 122.

genuine interest in Joseph's own state of consciousness. He is in some ways seen as a genuinely 'modern' figure – as Mann himself says, stepping straight out of Rooseveldt's 'New Deal' – on the other hand he arises from a background of myth and legend and it would be incredible if he himself did not initially share much of that mythological framework of thought. Yet Mann is equally concerned to show how the Joseph stories resonate through later literature, themselves giving rise to new mythological patterns to be appropriated and celebrated by generations of artists and writers in societies not even dreamed of. It is as if he is stating, in contrast to the proud singularity of the nineteenth-century novel, that no narrative is an island unto itself: story links with story in an ever-widening ring of intertextuality. As the Jena Romantics knew well, meaning is never complete, never exhausted. There is always more to be said. Each generation will reread the past in its own new way.

Such, certainly, was the argument of a contemporary book on mythology which, not least because it actually names Mann (along with Byron and Nietzsche) as men conscious of an 'incurable tragic dualism at the very root of their being',[95] was to have a profound influence on Mann's thinking: Ernst Bertram's *Nietzsche, Versuch einer Mythologie* (1918). No doubt this naming of Mann in such company did much to recommend the rest of Bertram's argument to him, and in particular his idea of the construction of history. For Bertram, objectivity was essentially unattainable. What historians do, he argued, consciously or unconsciously, is to appropriate the past in order to impose upon it either their own values or those of some force they unconsciously serve. Thus a historic personality can only live as a myth or image capable of serving the present. History is not a report, reproduction or preservation of the past, but the active creation of such images. Knowledge is only raw material. Indeed, what we call the historical record is a palimpsest of the myths which changing perspectives have created.[96]

However accurate such a proto new-historicist argument may be as a description of historical practice, it is not difficult to see what use might be made of such a view by the new theoreticians of German nationalism. In a very different way, it is also the key to what Mann is doing in this novel. As has been suggested, Mann's Joseph emerges to individual consciousness from the mythological framework in which he has been brought up by Eliezer. Having descended into the pit and

[95] Reed, *Thomas Mann*, p. 327.　　[96] *Ibid.*, p. 328.

been, as it were, symbolically reborn, he has to learn in Egypt, separated from his family and tribal support-system, to be an individual. At the same time, Mann the author, by a whole armoury of techniques, some serious, many at various levels of irony, tries to make the reader see the events of the story within a much wider framework – in effect, to see in the saga of Joseph a myth for the twentieth century.

From our point of view *Joseph* offers a myth of a rather different, if related, kind. It will not have escaped anyone who has read thus far that almost every one of the multitudinous levels of appropriation so far touched on in relation to our history of the Bible and the development of literary consciousness is in some way represented by Mann in this novel. We have already seen how his metaphor of time-coulisses takes up our post-critical view of the Bible as layer upon layer of midrashic palimpsests where the original ur-text is probably both unreachable and, were it to be found, very likely unrecognisable as well. Mann is no less aware of how this distance is at once enhanced and concealed by the appropriative nature of successive translations. His handling of the tensions between linear novelistic narrative and the endless resonances of typological readings, has resulted in one of the most fascinatingly complex literary styles of the twentieth century. As perhaps no major European writer since Jane Austen, Mann has appropriated the traditional polysemous framework of biblical interpretation and has produced a work that in some ways more resembles the great mediaeval epics (Dante would be the supreme example) than any nineteenth-century novel. I doubt if we do adequate justice to Mann's ambition, or his carefully orchestrated self-construction, if we do not recognise that his great twentieth-century myth of origins seeks to place itself in the great tradition of Homer, Virgil and Dante – or that his proud claim, from exile in California, to represent the German tradition is not also a conscious echo of the earlier Florentine exile.

The difference, of course, lies in something he has appropriated from Sterne and his own fellow German Romantics:[97] irony. Though Dante is not without ironic passages, that sense of irony does not extend to, or in any way undermine, his entire metaphysical framework. He is still an orthodox Catholic. Mann, like Sterne before him, chooses to distance himself from his own creation. He has reason to mistrust the world-picture which he nevertheless faithfully portrays because he has no other. If he believes with Chateaubriand (and, in a

---

[97] For the German Romantic sense of irony, see Wheeler, 'Irony as Self-Criticism', in her *German Aesthetic and Literary Criticism*, pp. 17–20.

different sense, with Nietzsche) that the great tradition of his culture is essentially Christian, and without that religious construction of meaning at its centre there is a gulf of nihilism and emptiness, that does not mean that he can accept Christianity as anything more than a mythical system. Irony is almost inevitably the result of such a dilemma. It is perhaps inherent in the modern (or even post-modern) condition.

Yet it is not as if there were not always ironies enfolded in the original tradition of the blessing. A divine succession that is at once one of unyielding primogeniture, yet open to deception, theft or appropriation, is certainly not one devoid of irony. What, too, could be more ironic in its by-passing of the ethical than Jacob's dream at Bethel? As Kierkegaard saw, the blessing operates in the mysteries of the religious level not in the calculus of the ethical. But most writers, though they might not respond to the terminology, would probably acknowledge the experience.

Epilogue

If most studies of Romanticism have tended to underplay the degree to which it rested on a particular appropriation of the Bible,[1] almost none has noted that this is even more true of Romantic aesthetic theory than it is of particular works of literature. Yet, as I hope these chapters may suggest, we cannot begin to understand the way in which the Romantics actually use the Bible in poetry, drama and fiction (not to mention painting) without appreciating the degree to which particular applications rest (consciously or unconsciously) on more general theoretical assumptions. Moreover, few, if any, of these assumptions would have seemed obvious to writers of previous generations. As we have seen, the idea of the Bible as presenting a novel-like narrative, with character, motivation and plot, is, like the modern novel itself, no older than the eighteenth century. If those who created the Authorised Version in the early seventeenth century also read their world in terms of the Bible, their normative book reflected a very different world of typological correspondences and polysemous meanings. Similarly, the growing use of the Bible as a metatype was not unconnected with the new idea that expression was inseparable from theory, and which sought to create a universal whole out of many diverse fragments whose incompleteness was necessary and essential rather than accidental and contingent. Though such ideas would have been almost incomprehensible to the world of Locke and Newton, Dryden and Pope, in retrospect it is arguable that they are not so very far from that of Heisenberg and Dirac, Derrida and Barthes.

The greater the degree of individual self-consciousness, the greater the obsession with legitimation. At the heart of any legitimating process is a corresponding insecurity: a fear that the condition, event, or work

---

[1] Honourable exceptions would be Leslie Tannenbaum's, *Biblical Tradition in Blake's Early Prophecies*, Princeton University Press, 1982, or George P. Landow's *Victorian Types, Victorian Shadows*, Routledge, 1980.

in question may not carry the necessary authority to be accepted by others at the originator's own valuation. At one extreme such anxiety may be met by the assertion of individual autonomy, the total self-authentication of genius; at the other, by the idea of tradition. The undifferentiated consciousness of an Eliezer, still 'open at the back', is one with six hundred years of other Eliezers serving other nomadic patriarchs named Abraham or Isaac, and needing no further self-justification beyond that immemorial role. But self-consciousness is a second Fall. It is only when Jacob steals the blessing that he emerges as a fully autonomous individual, correspondingly prone to anxiety. Similarly, it is when Joseph discovers himself in a new situation, and new qualities in himself to meet it, that the endless re-enactments of an undifferentiated past can be consciously appropriated as myth. Such legitimating 'authority', whether seen as coming from the transcendent powers of the self, the possession (even by theft) of a divine blessing, or simply a literary tradition, is typically perceived in terms of a sequence or line of development, and the truth or power of any single link is dependent less upon the strength or even the endurance of the whole chain as simply upon its existence. Even legitimation by genius, an idea rapidly gaining currency at the end of the eighteenth century,[2] was ultimately as dependent upon the idea of *a sequence* of such transcendent figures, forming a secularised version of the biblical prophetic tradition, as the conventional classical idea of tradition where Dante invokes Virgil and the Bible, just as Virgil had invoked Homer and his shadowy construct of the Trojans. Under some circumstances the sequence could even be reversible. For Chateaubriand the Bible and the associated traditions of Christianity legitimated not only modern European civilisation, but also the pre-Christian pagan past. Volney's revolutionary synthesis, so far from attempting to draw a line under the *ancien régime* and start again, was elaborately legitimated by reference to the entire development of human religious consciousness over some seventeen thousand years. Similarly neither English nor German literature was immune to this need to construct a legitimating past.

Thus if the newest literary form, the aptly named 'novel', seemed to lack sufficient authority from approved past models, it could by-pass even well-known Roman antecedents[3] and appropriate for itself the

[2] See, for instance, Alexander Gerard, *Essay on Genius* (1774); Jean Paul Richter, *School for Aesthetics* (1804), trs. Margaret Hale, Detroit: Wayne State University Press, 1973, esp. pp. 28–32; S.T. Coleridge, 'On Poesy or Art' (*Biographia Literaria*, ed. J. Shawcross, Oxford, 1907, pp. 253–63).
[3] Apuleius' *The Golden Ass* had been in translation since the sixteenth century.

oldest of all literary traditions by reading back into the Bible itself the origins of narrative. It would be easy to dismiss the literally hundreds of biblical and early Christian romances of the Victorian period as being no more than a minor sub-genre of the great secular tradition of the novel, but, as we have suggested, that commonly assumed secularity of the mainstream rapidly begins to evaporate on closer inspection. *Mansfield Park* is not an exception. All but the most superficial reading of Leavis' 'great tradition', for instance, reveals the almost ineluctably religious tendencies of nineteenth-century literary consciousness. The covert religiosity of the atheist George Eliot has always drawn comment. Dickens is hardly less biblical in his imagery. Even Conrad is constantly groping after ineffable mysteries seemingly just beyond the reach of language. Indeed, there is a very real sense in chich the Roman and early Christian novels of Lockhart, Ware, Kingsley and Newman may better reflect the acknowledged biblical origins of the genre than the more realistic novels of contemporary life.

But compared with German, English literature could already draw on a long and rich prose fictional tradition of its own. Though the new national literature of the German Romantics – still more concept than reality – might seek to define itself polemically against the Gallic affectations of France or the crude bourgeois commercialism of Britain, it sought aesthetic legitimation with even greater urgency than either rival by constructing its own literary antecedents in classical and biblical writings. Like Virgil's Trojans, this was a past that could safely be appropriated without political side-effects. For the Schlegels the Bible offered not the thundering Lutheran revolution of faith over works but a literary metatype that by-passed contemporary British or French models by providing, in itself, a compendium and summation of all other aesthetic forms. For Thomas Mann, more beleaguered and isolated within his society than any Romantic predecessors could have imagined, the Bible provided much more: a source not only of myth and narrative but an ironic vision of a world where culture and consciousness themselves had to be redefined.

Yet though these Romantic appropriations of a biblical past have all the vitality predicated of *Aneignung*, they are not entirely free either from the darker ambiguities of the Anglo-French meaning of 'appropriation'. Nor is the primal tension between renewal and theft, so evident in the story of Jacob and Esau, much absent thereafter. Just as Capability Brown's 'expressive' open landscapes replaced the older 'emblematic' gardens of Kent and Bridgeman, so the romantically appropriated Bible was to prove a new source of narrative and poetic inspiration only at the cost of eliminating earlier traditional typological and spiritual meanings. As we have seen, the sense of loss and the corresponding need for new kinds of legitimation that we associate with Romantic self-consciousness are only one example of the much more widespread shift away from older, more collective ways of reading. What we have suggested may be seen as an innate religiosity in the nineteenth-century novel may equally well be interpreted as both a covert secularisation and a fictionalisation of what was once immutable Holy Writ. It is certainly significant that the very Evangelical groups most concerned with preserving a belief in the inerrancy of the scriptures should have been the most suspicious of the frivolity and sinfulness of novel-reading. Indeed, contemporary fundamentalism, with its attachment not to the traditional idea of divinely inspired meaning in the Bible, but to the literal 'historical' truth of the narrative stories themselves, is a modern development stemming from precisely this process of biblical novelisation.

The effect of the German historical criticism of the eighteenth century had been not merely to question the apparently unchangeable text of the Bible, but to call attention to successive previous polemical transformations. For the German Romantics, and, more slowly, also for the English, the Bible ceased to be the paradigm of textual stability, and was imperceptibly metamorphosed into its opposite: a model of textual fluidity, a moving target. Small wonder therefore if, for Friedrich Schlegel, the perfect 'Romantic novel' was 'a Bible', experienced less as a concrete artifact than as a process of *becoming*: a mode of self-consciousness. Certainly any age in which there is a perceived conflict between what are seen as eternal biblical verities and constantly shifting patterns of hermeneutic understanding has little cause to consider itself 'post-Romantic'. Such a tension was as real to Mann in the twentieth century as it was to Sterne in the eighteenth. I cited earlier Brevard Childs' observation that the canonisation of any text appropriates and implicitly assumes for it a meaning transcending that of its original context.[4] This is as true for the Bible as a whole as it is for any of its constituent parts. Indeed the canonical nature of the Bible is central to the phenomenon of its subsequent hermeneutic fluidity. Without having been initially prised loose, those historically heterogenous and diverse texts could never have been given the later

---

[4] Brevard Childs, *The New Testament as Canon: an Introduction*, London: SCM, 1984, p. 16.

typological, symbolic and narrative interpretations with which we have been concerned. It should come as no surprise to deconstructionists if the story of Jacob's blessing, initially one of legitimation within the specific context of a particular family and tribe, should, at the same time, question the very legitimacy it seeks to establish and itself become a key text in the process of appropriation, with the threefold blessing of the land, the descendants and all the families of the earth, justifying and giving meaning to endless applications over the last three thousand years.

Moreover, the subsequent history of that story, with its disturbing ambiguity between outright theft and the growth of a genuinely new kind of maturation and self-consciousness, may be seen as encapsulating a quality that is deeply endemic to Western Judeo-Christian society. Canonicity is only the final outcome of a long process of legitimation; the process by which a text moves, as it were, from context to myth so imperceptibly that we are only very occasionally made conscious of its passage. It is, perhaps, typical of the protean nature of Jacob's blessing that it is hard to say with hindsight whether the Romantics appropriated the Bible, or the Bible appropriated the Romantics. Such is the tectonic shift, or 'revolution' in thought, that occurred at the end of the eighteenth century that not merely have the landmarks changed, but even the theory of what constitutes a landmark has changed as well. In that sense, the idea of the blessing, the ambiguities of appropriation, the notion of the Bible itself as a moving target are all Romantic concepts. But so also is our idea of what constitutes a narrative. If that of Jacob's blessing provides a metaphor for the way in which the text of the Bible has presented itself to different periods, this is, not least, for its open-endedness, its mysterious suggestions of a narrative that is as yet incomplete, and whose meaning has always eluded closure.

Bibliography

Apart from publications of university presses, the place of publication, if not given in the entry, is London.

Aarsleff, Hans, *From Locke to Saussure: Essays on the Study of Language and Intellectual History*, Minneapolis: University of Minnesota Press, 1982.

Adams, Hazard, *Philosophy of the Literary Symbolic*, Tallahassee: Florida State University Press, 1983.

Albright, W.F., *Yahweh and the Gods of Canaan*, Athlone Press, 1968.

Allen, Ward, (ed.), *Translating for King James*, Allen Lane: Penguin, 1970.

Allison, Henry E., *Kant's Transcendental Idealism*, New Haven, Conn.: Yale University Press, 1983.

Armstrong, Karen, *A History of God: from Abraham to the Present: the 4000-year Quest for God.* Heinemann, 1993.

Arnold, Matthew, 'On the Study of Celtic Literature', in *Complete Prose Works of Matthew Arnold*, ed. R.H. Super, vol. III, Ann Arbor: University of Michigan Press, 1960–77.

Athenaeum 1798–1800, Stuttgart: J.G. Cotta'sche Buchhandlung.

Auerbach, Erich, 'Figura', trs. R. Mannheim, in Auerbach, *Scenes from the Drama of European Literature*, New York: Meridian, 1959.

Mimesis, Princeton University Press, 1953.

Austen, Jane, *Mansfield Park*, ed. R.W. Chapman, Oxford: 3rd edn., Clarendon Press, 1934.

Bahr, Ehrhard, and Saine, Thomas P. (eds.) *The Internalized Revolution: German Reactions to the French Revolution, 1789–1989*, New York: Garland, 1992.

Bakhtin, M.M., 'Discourse in the Novel', in *The Dialogic Imagination*, ed. Michael Holquist, trs. Caryl Emerson and Michael Holquist, Austin: University of Texas Press, 1981.

Barbéris, Pierre, *A la recherche d'une écriture: Chateaubriand*, Tours: Mame, 1974.

Barlow, William, *The Sum and Substance of the Conference ... at Hampton Court January 14 1603*, 1604. Gainesville: Scholars' Facsimiles and Reprints, 1965.

Barth, Karl, 'Schleiermacher', in *Protestant Theology in the Nineteenth Century*, Valley Forge: Judson Press, 1973.

Church Dogmatics, ed. G.W. Bromiley and T.F. Torrance, trs. G.W.

Bromiley, J.C. Campbell, Iain Wilson, J. Strathearn McNab, Harold Knight and R.A. Stewart, 2 vols. Edinburgh: T. and T. Clark, 1957.

Bate, Jonathan, *Shakespearean Constitutions: Politics, Theatre, Criticism 1730–1830*, Oxford: Clarendon Press, 1989.

Benjamin, Walter, 'The Work of Art in the Age of Mechanical Reproduction', in *Illuminations*, ed. Hannah Arendt, trs. Harry Zohn, Fontana/Collins, 1973.

Bentley, G.E., Jr, *Blake Records*, Oxford: Clarendon Press, 1969.
Blake Records Supplement, Oxford: Clarendon Press, 1988.

Berendsohn, Walter E., *Thomas Mann: Artist and Partisan in Troubled Times*, trs. George C. Buck, Montgomery: University of Alabama Press, 1973.

Best Geoffrey (ed.) *The Permanent Revolution*, Fontana, 1988.

Bicheno, James, *A Word in Season*, 1795.

Bickerman, E.J., *The Jews in the Greek Age*, Cambridge, Mass.: Harvard University Press, 1988.

Blome, Richard (ed.) *The History of the Old and New Testaments Extracted from the Sacred Scriptures, the Holy Fathers, and Other Ecclesiastical Writers ...*, 4th impression, 1712.

Blunt, Anthony, *The Art of William Blake*, New York: Columbia University Press, 1959.

Boccaccini, G., *Middle Judaism: Jewish Thought 300 B.C.E to 200 C.E.*, Minneapolis: Fortress Press, 1991.

Bowie, Andrew, *Aesthetics and Subjectivity: from Kant to Nietzsche*, Manchester University Press, 1990.

Bright, John, *The Authority of the Old Testament*, Grand Rapids, Mich.: Baker Book House, 1980.

Browne, Sir Thomas, *The Works of Sir Thomas Browne*, ed. Charles Saye, 3 vols., Edinburgh: Grant, 1927.

Bullinger, E.W., *Figures of Speech Used in the Bible*, Eyre and Spottiswoode, 1898. Reprinted Baker House, 1968; 15th printing March 1990.

Burnet, Gilbert, *History of his own Time*, 1725.

Burnouf, Emile, *The Science of Religions*, trs. Julie Liebe, 1888.

Burtt, E.A., *The Metaphysical Foundations of Modern Science*, Routledge, 1933.

Butler, Joseph, *Fifteen Sermons Preached at the Rolls Chapel to which are added Six Sermons Preached on Publick Occasions*, 4th edn, 1749.

Butler, Marilyn, *Jane Austen and the War of Ideas*, Oxford University Press, 1975.

Caird, G.B., *The Language and Imagery of the Bible*, Duckworth, 1980.

Carey, Edmond, *Les Grands Traducteurs français*, Geneva: Librarie de l'Université, 1963.

Carlyle, Thomas, *Life of John Sterling*, Chapman and Hall, 1893.

Carroll, Robert P., *Wolf in the Sheepfold: the Bible as a Problem for Christianity*, SPCK, 1991.

Casey, M., *From Jewish Prophet to Gentile God: the Origins and Development of New Testament Christology*, Cambridge: James Clarke, 1991.

Cash, Arthur H., *Laurence Sterne: the Early and Middle Years*, Methuen, 1975.

Chadwick, Henry, 'Philo', in A.H. Armstrong (ed.), *Cambridge History of Later Greek and Early Mediaeval Philosophy*, Cambridge University Press, 1967.

Chateaubriand, René François Auguste de, *The Genius of Christianity* (1802), trs. Charles White, Baltimore, 1856.

Mémoires d'outre-tombe, 1849–50.

Chaucer, Geoffrey, *Complete Works of Geoffrey Chaucer*, ed. F.N. Robinson, 2nd edn, Oxford University Press, 1957.

Childs, Brevard, *The New Testament as Canon: an Introduction*, London: SCM, 1984.

Chitty, Susan, *The Beast and the Monk*, Hodder, 1974.

Clark, Sir George, *The Idea of the Industrial Revolution* (Glasgow University Publications, no. 95), Glasgow: Jackson, 1953.

Clark, J.C.D., *English Society 1688–1832*, Cambridge University Press, 1985.

Clive, John, *Thomas Babington Macaulay*, Secker and Warburg, 1973.

Cochrane, Charles, *Christianity and Classical Culture*, Oxford University Press, 1944.

Coleridge, S.T., *Aids to Reflection* ed. T. Fenby, Edinburgh: Grant, 1905.

Biographia Literaria, 2nd edn. 1847.

Biographia Literaria, ed. J. Shawcross, Oxford University Press, 1907.

Biographia Literaria, ed. James Engell and W. Jackson Bate, Routledge, 1983.

Confessions of an Inquiring Spirit, 2nd edn, 1849.

Notebooks, ed. Kathleen Coburn, Routledge, 1957.

'The Statesman's Manual', in *Lay Sermons*, ed. R.J. White, Routledge, 1972.

Conybeare, William John, *Perversion; or, the Causes and Consequences of Infidelity*, 1856.

Coulson, John, *Newman and the Common Tradition*, Oxford: Clarendon Press, 1970.

Cross, F.M., *Canaanite Myth and Hebrew Epic*, Cambridge, Mass.: Harvard University Press, 1973.

Currie, Robert, Gilbert, Alan, and Horsely, Lee (eds.), *Churches and Churchgoers: Patterns of Growth in the British Isles Since 1700*, Oxford: Clarendon Press, 1977.

Curtius, Ernst, *European Literature and the Latin Middle Ages*, trs. Willard R. Trask, Routledge, 1953.

'Virgil', *Essays on European Literature*, trs. Michael Kowal, Princeton University Press, 1973.

Damrosch, David, *The Narrative Covenant: Transformations of Genre in the Growth of Biblical Literature*, San Francisco: Harper and Rowe, 1987.

Daniell, David, *Tyndale's New Testament*, New Haven, Conn.: Yale University Press, 1989.

Dante, *The Divine Comedy of Dante Alighieri*, trs. John D. Sinclair, New York: Oxford University Press, 1939.

Davson, Joanna, 'Critical and Conservative Treatments of Prophecy in Nineteenth Century Britain', unpublished D.Phil. thesis, Oxford, 1991.

Deconinck-Brossard, Françoise, *Vie politique, sociale et religieuse en Grande-Bretagne d'apres les sermons prêchés ou publiés dans le nord d'Angleterre 1738–1760*, Paris: Didier Erudition, 1984.

'England and France in the Eighteenth Century', in Stephen Prickett (ed.), *Reading the Text: Biblical criticism and Literary Theory*, Oxford: Basil Blackwell, 1991.

Desmond, Adrian, *The Hot-blooded Dinosaurs*, Blond, 1976.

Dilthey, Wilhelm, 'The Development of Hermeneutics' (1900), reprinted in David E. Klemm (ed.), *Hermeneutical Inquiry*, vol. 1: *The Interpretation of Texts*, Atlanta: Scolars Press, 1986.

Duckworth, Alistair, *The Improvement of the Estate: a Study of Jane Austen's Novels*, Baltimore, Md.: Johns Hopkins University Press, 1971.

Dunn, J.D.G., *The Partings of the Ways Between Christianity and Judaism and their Significance for the Character of Christianity*, SCM Press, 1992.

(ed.), *Jews and Chrsitians: the Parting of the Ways, A.D. 70 to 135*, Tübingen: Mohr (Siebeck), 1993.

Edmund Burke, *Letters ... on the Proposals for Peace with the Regicide Directory of France*, 1795.

Eichner, Hans, *Friedrich Schlegel*, New York: Twayne 1970.

Eitner, Lorenz, 'Cages, Prisons, and Captives in Eighteenth Century Art', in K. Kroeber and W. Walling (eds.), *Images of Romanticism*, New Haven, Conn.: Yale University Press, 1978.

Eliot, T.S., *Selected Essays*, 3rd edn, Faber, 1951.

Ernst, Cornelius, 'World Religions and Christian Theology', in *Multiple Echo: Explorations in Theology*, Darton, Longman and Todd, 1979.

Farrer, Austin, *A Rebirth of Images*, Dacre Press, 1944.

Faverty, Frederick E., *Matthew Arnold the Ethnologist*, Evanston, Ill.: Northwestern University Press, 1951.

Feuerbach, Ludwig, *The Essence of Christianity*, (1841) trs. George Eliot, 1854, New York: Harper, 1957.

Fielding, Henry, *Tom Jones*, ed. R.P.C. Mutter, Penguin, 1966.

Fisch, Harold, 'Bakhtin's Misreadings of the Bible', *Hebrew University Studies in Literature and the Arts*, vol. 16 (1988), pp. 130–49.

Forstman, Jack, *A Romantic Triangle: Schleiermacher and Early German Romanticism*, Misoula, Mont.: Scolars Press, 1977.

Frei, Hans, *The Eclipse of Biblical Narrative: a Study in Eighteenth and Nineteenth Century Hermeneutics*, New Haven, Conn.: Yale University Press, 1974.

Fruman, Norman, *Coleridge: the Damaged Archangel*, Allen and Unwin, 1972.

Fuller, R.C., *Alexander Geddes*, Sheffield: Almond Press, 1983.

Gadamer, Hans Georg, *Philosophical Hermeneutics*, trs. and ed. by David E. Linge, Berkeley: University of California Press, 1976
Truth and Method, Sheed and Ward, 1975.

Gibbon, Edward, *The Decline and Fall of the Roman Empire*, Everyman, 1910.

Gobineau, Joseph Arthur de, *The Inequality of Human Races*, trs. Adrian Collins, Heinemann, 1915.

Goethe, *Wilhelm Meister's Apprenticeship and Travels*, trs. Thomas Carlyle, 2 vols., Centenary edn. Carlyle: *Works*, Chapman and Hall, 1896–1903.

Gombrich, E.H. *Art and Illusion*, Phaidon, 1960.

Goodenough, E.R., *Introduction to Philo Judaeus*, 2nd edn, Oxford: Basil Blackwell, 1962 (1st edn, New Haven, Conn.: Yale University Press, 1940).

Grant, John E., 'Envisioning the First *Night Thoughts*', in David V. Erdman and John E. Grant (eds.), *Blake's Visionary Forms Dramatic*, Princeton University Press, 1970.

Grayston, Kenneth, 'Confessions of a Biblical Translator', *New Universities Quarterly*, vol. 33, no. 3 (Summer 1979), pp. 283–95.

Gruen, Erich S., 'Cultural Fictions and Cultural Identity', *University of California, Berkeley Transactions of the American Philological Association*, vol. 123 (1993), pp. 1–14.

Hammond, Lansing van der Heyden, *Laurence Sterne's 'Sermons of Mr Yorick'*, New Haven, Conn.: Yale University Press, 1948.

Hampshire, Stuart, *Spinoza: an Introduction to his Philosophical Thought*, Penguin, 1951.

Hare, Julius and Hare, Augustus, *Guesses at Truth*, 1st edn, 1827, 2nd edn, 1838, 3rd edn, 1871.

Harris, H.S., *Hegel's Development: Toward the Sunlight, 1770–1801*, Oxford: Clarendon Press, 1972.

Hatto, Arthur, 'Revolution: an Inquiry into the Usefulness of a Historical Term', *Mind*, 58 (1949), pp. 495–517.

Hennell, Charles, *Enquiry Concerning the Origins of Christianity*, 1838.

Hepworth, Brian, *Robert Lowth*, Boston, Mass.: Twayne, 1978.

Herder, Johann Gottfried, 'Essay on the Origin of Language' (1772), in *Herder on Social and Political Culture*, trs. and ed. F.M. Barnard, Cambridge University Press, 1969.

   The Spirit of Hebrew Poetry (Dessau, 1782–3), 3rd edn, Marburg, 1822. Trs. James Marsh: Burlington, Vt.: Edward Smith, 1833.

Holbach, Paul Henri, Baron d', *Système de la nature*, 1781.

Hollingdale, R.J., *Thomas Mann: a Critical Study*, Hart-Davis, 1971.

Holmes, Richard, *Shelley: The Pursuit*, Quartet, 1976.

Honan, Park, *Jane Austen*, Weidenfield and Nicolson, 1987.

Humboldt, Wilhelm von, *On Language* (1836) trs. Peter Heath, introduction by Hans Aarsleff, Cambridge University Press, 1988.

Hussey, Christopher, *English Gardens and Landscapes 1700–1750*, Country Life, 1967.

Ibn Hisham, 'Abd al-Malik, *The Life of Muhammad*, trans. Alfred Guillaume, Lahore, 1955.

Jacobs, Edward Craney, 'King James's Translators: the Bishops' Bible New Testament Revised', *The Library* (sixth series), vol. 14, no. 2 (June 1992), pp. 100–26.

Jeanrond, Werner G. 'The Impact of Schleiermacher's Hermeneutics on Contemporary Interpretation Theory', in David Jasper (ed.), *The Interpretation of Belief: Coleridge, Schleiermacher, and Romanticism*, Macmillan 1986.

   Theological Hermeneutics: Development and Significance, Macmillan, 1991.

Jenkyns, Richard, *Dignity and Decadence: Victorian Art and the Classical Inheritance*, Fontana, 1992.

The Victorians and Ancient Greece, Oxford: Basil Blackwell, 1980.

Jones, Sir William, 'Third Anniversary Discourse on the Hindus, Feb. 2, 1786', in *Works*, ed. Lord Teignmouth, vol. III, 1807.

Josipovici, Gabriel, *The Book of God*, New Haven, Conn.: Yale University Press, 1988.

Kant, Immanuel, *Critique of Judgement*, trs. J.H. Bernard, New York: Hafner, 1951.

Kearney, Hugh, *Scholars and Gentlemen*, Faber, 1970.

Kelly, L.G., *The True Interpreter: a History of Translation Theory and Practice in the West*, Oxford: Basil Blackwell, 1979.

Kelsall, Malcolm, 'The Iconography of Stourhead', *Journal of the Warburg and Courtauld Institutes*, vol. 46 (1983), pp. 133–43.

Kenny, J.F., *The Sources for the Early History of Ireland* (1929), reprinted Dublin: Irish University Press, 1968.

Kimmerle, H. (ed.), *Hermeneutics, the Handwritten Manuscripts*, trs. J. Duke and J. Forstmann, Missoula, Mont.: Scolars Press, 1977.

Kingsley, Charles, *Hypatia, or New Foes with an Old Face*, Everyman, 1907.

Kingsley, Frances, *Charles Kingsley: Life and Letters*, ed. by his wife (Frances), Macmillan, 1895.

Kipling, Rudyard, 'Proofs of Holy Writ', *Sussex Edition of Kipling's Works*, vol. XXX, Macmillan, 1937–9.

Kugel, James L., *The Idea of Biblical Poetry: Parallelism and its History*. New Haven, Conn.: Yale University Press, 1981.

Kuhn, Thomas, *The Structure of Scientific Revolutions*, University of Chicago Press, 1962.

Lacoue-Labarthe, Philippe, and Nancy, Jean-Luc, *The Literary Absolute: the Theory of Literature in German Romanticism*, trs. Philip Barnard and Cheryl Lester, Albany: State University of New York Press, 1988.

Lampe, G.W.H., and Woollcombe, K.G., 'The Reasonableness of Typology', in *Essays on Typology*, SCM Press, 1957.

Landow, George P., *Images of Crisis*, Routledge, 1982.

Victorian Types, Victorian Shadows, Routledge 1980.

Lasky, Melvin J., *Utopia and Revolution*, University of Chicago Press, 1976.

Lawton, David, *Blasphemy*, Hemel Hempstead: Harvester Wheatsheaf, 1993.

Lerner, Laurence, *The Truthtellers*, Chatto, 1967.

Levi, Peter, *The English Bible 1534–1859*, Constable, 1974.

Lewis, C.S., *Pilgrim's Regress,* Dent, 1933.

Surprised by Joy, Bles, 1955.

Lightfoot, J.B., *On a Fresh Revision of the English New Testament,* 2nd edn, revised, New York: Harper and Rowe, 1873.

Locke, John, *Essay Concerning Human Understanding*, 1690.

Lovejoy, A.O., 'On the Discrimination of Romanticisms', *Essays in the History of Ideas*, Baltimore, Md.: Johns Hopkins University Press, 1948.

The Reason, the Understanding, and Time, Baltimore, Md.: Johns Hopkins University Press, 1961.

Lowth, Robert, *Isaiah: a New Translation* (1778), 5th edn, 2 vols., Edinburgh, 1807.

Lectures on the Sacred Poetry of the Hebrews, trs. G. Gregory, 1787.

Lucretius, *De Rerrum natura*, ed. Cyril Bailey, 3 vols., Oxford: Clarendon Press, 1947.

MacDonagh, Oliver, *Jane Austen: Real and Imagined Worlds*, New Haven, Conn.: Yale University Press, 1991.

Malins, Edward, *English Landscape and Literature 1660–1840*, Oxford University Press, 1966.

Mann, Thomas, *Joseph and his Brothers*, trs. H.T. Lowe-Porter, Penguin, 1988.

Martin, H., *The Baptist Hymn Companion*, Psalm and Hymns Trust, 1953.

Mather, Increase, *Exhortations to Faith*, 1710.

Maurice, Frederick Dennison, *Lectures on the Epistle to the Hebrews*, 1846.

McCalman, Iain, 'Prophesying Revolution: Edmund Burke, Mad Lord George and Madame La Motte', in *Learning and Living: Essays in Honour of J.F.C. Harrison*, ed. Malcolm Chase and Ian Dyck, Scolars Press, 1995.

Radical Underworld: Prophets, Revolutionaries and Pornographers in London, 1745–1840, Cambridge University Press, 1988.

McFarland, Thomas, *Coleridge and the Pantheist Tradition*, Oxford: Clarendon Press, 1969.

Romanticism and the Forms of Ruin: Wordsworth, Coleridge, and the Modalities of Fragmentation, Princeton University Press, 1981.

McFarlane, Jenny, 'The Theosophical Society and Christine Waller's *The Great Breath*', *Australian Journal of Art*, vol. 9 (1993).

McNeice, Gerald, *Shelley and the Revolutionary Idea*, Cambridge, Mass.: Harvard University Press, 1969.

Mee, Jon, *Dangerous Enthusiasm: William Blake and the Culture of Radicalism in the 1790s*, Oxford: Clarendon Press, 1992.

Milton, John, *The Poems of John Milton*, ed. John Carey and Alastair Fowler, Longman, 1968.

Minnis, A.J., *Mediaeval Theory of Authorship*, Scolars Press, 1984.

Montluzin, E. L. de, *The Anti-Jacobins, 1798–1800*, New York: St Martin's Press, 1988.

Morrison, Karl F., 'Schleiermacher's Anthropology', in *'I Am You': the Hermeneutics of Empathy in Western Literature, Theology, and Art*, Princeton University Press, 1988.

Mosser, Monique, and Teyssot, Georges (eds.) *The History of Garden Design: the Western Tradition from the Renaissance to the Present Day*, Thames and Hudson, 1991.

Mozley, J.F., 'The English Bible before the Authorized Version', *The Bible Today*, Eyre and Spottiswode, 1955.

Mueller-Vollmer, Kurt (ed.), *The Hermeneutics Reader*, Oxford: Basil Blackwell, 1986.

Newman, John Henry, *Callista: a Sketch of the Third Century* (1856), reprint New York: Garland, 1975.

Essay on the Development of Doctrine (1845), Sheed and Ward, 1960.

A Grammar of Assent (1870), ed. C.F. Harrold, Longman, 1957.

Newsome, David, *The Parting of Friends*, Murray, 1966.

Newton, Isaac, *The Chronology of the Ancient Kingdoms Amended*, 1728.

Observations on the Prophecies of Daniel and St. John, 1733.

Newton, Thomas, *Dissertations on the prophecies, which have been remarkably fulfilled, and at this time are fulfilling in the world*, 3 vols., 1754–8.

Nida, Eugene A., 'Principles of Translation as Exemplified by Bible Translating', in Reuben A. Brower (ed.), *On Translation*, (Harvard Studies in Comparative Literature no. 23), Cambridge, Mass.: Harvard University Press, 1959.

Towards a Science of Translating, Leiden: E.J. Brill, 1964.

Nida, Eugene A. and Taber, C., *The Theory and Practice of Translation*, Leiden: E.J. Brill, 1969.

Norton, David, *History of the Bible as Literature*, 2 vols., Cambridge University Press, 1993.

Novalis, *Schriften*, ed. Paul Kluckhohn and Richard Samuel, Leipzig, 1929.

Nuttall, A.D., *A Common Sky: Philosophy and the Literary Imagination*, Chatto, 1974.

Openings, Oxford University Press, 1992.

O'Brien, Conor Cruise, *States of Ireland*, Hutchinson, 1972.

Ong, Walter J., *Orality and Literacy: the Technologising of the Word*, Routledge, 1982.

Orsini, G.N.G., *Coleridge and German Idealism*, Carbondale and Edwardsville: Southern Illinois University Press, 1969.

Paine, Thomas, *Complete Writings of Thomas Paine*, ed. P.S. Foner, 2 vols., New York: Citadel Press, 1945.

Palmer, Richard E., *Hermeneutics: Interpretation Theory in Schleiermacher, Dilthey, Heidegger and Gadamer*, Evanston, Ill.: Northwestern University Press, 1969.

Palmer, R.R., *The World of the French Revolution*, Allen and Unwin, 1971.

Parsons, James, *The Remains of Japhet* (1767), facsimile reprint, Menston: Scholar Press, 1968.

Paulson, Ronald, *Emblem and Expression: Meaning in English Art of the Eighteenth Century*, Thames and Hudson, 1975.

Representations of Revolution (1789–1820), New Haven, Conn.: Yale University Press, 1983.

Perkins, William, *The Art of Prophecying*, 1592.

Plumb, J.H., *The Death of the Past*, Macmillan, 1969.

Polanyi, Michael, *Personal Knowledge: Towards a Post-Critical Philosophy*, Routledge, 1958.

Pope-Hennessy, Una, *Canon Charles Kingsley*, Chatto, 1948.

Popper, Karl, *The Poverty of Historicism*, Routledge, 1957.

Porter, Dennis, *Rousseau's Legacy: Emergence and Eclipse of the Writer in France*, Oxford University Press, 1995.

Price, Richard, *Discourse on the Love of our Country*, 1799.

Prickett, Stephen, 'Church and University in the Life of John Keble,' in Geoffrey Rowell (ed.), *The English Religious Tradition and the Genius of Anglicanism*, Wantage: Ikon Press, 1992.

Coleridge and Wordsworth: the Poetry of Growth, Cambridge University Press, 1970.

England and the French Revolution, Macmillan, 1989.

'Fictions and Metafictions: *Phantastes, Wilhelm Meister* and the idea of the *Bildungsroman*', in William Reaper (ed.), *The Gold Thread: Essays on George MacDonald*, Edinburgh University Press, 1991.

'Hebrew Versus Hellene as a Principle of Literary Criticism', in G.W. Clarke (ed.), *Rediscovering Hellenism: the Hellenic Inheritance and the English Imagination*, Cambridge University Press, 1989.

Romanticism and Religion: the Tradition of Coleridge and Wordsworth in the Victorian Church, Cambridge University Press, 1976.

Words and the 'Word': Language, Poetics and Biblical Interpretation, Cambridge University Press, 1986.

'Wordsworth's Apocalypse: Robespierre and the Tribe of Moloch', *Graphé*, no. 3 (1994), pp. 87–99.

(ed.), *Reading the Text: Biblical Criticism and Literary Theory*, Blackwell, Oxford, 1991.

Qu'ran, trs. Mohammed Marmaduke Pickthall (1930), Star Books, 1989.

Rad, Gerhard, von 'The Beginnings of Historical Writing in Ancient Israel', in *The Problem of the Hexateuch and Other Essays*, trs. E.W. Dicken, Edinburgh and London: Oliver and Boyd, 1966.

Genesis: a Commentary, trs. John H. Marks, 3rd revised edition, SCM Press, 1972.

Old Testament Theology, trs. D.M.G. Stalker, 2 vols., Edinburgh: Oliver and Boyd, 1962.

Reed, T.J., *Thomas Mann: the Uses of Tradition*, Oxford: Clarendon Press, 1974.

Reeves, Marjorie, 'The Bible and Literary Authorship in the Middle Ages', in Stephen Prickett (ed.), *Reading the Text: Biblical Criticism and Literary Theory*, Oxford: Basil Blackwell, 1991.

Reeves, Marjorie and Gould, Warwick, *Joachim of Fiore and the Myth of the Eternal Evangel in the Nineteenth Century*, Oxford: Clarendon Press, 1987.

Reich-Ranicki, Marcel, *Thomas Mann and his Family*, trs. Ralph Manheim, Fontana, 1990.

Renan, Ernest, 'The History of the People of Israel', in *Studies in Religious History*, 1893.

The Life of Jesus, Watts, 1935.

Reventlow, Henning Graf, *The Authority of the Bible and the Rise of the Modern World*, trs. John Bowden, SCM Press, 1984.

Richardson, Alan (ed.), *A Theological Word Book of the Bible*, SCM Press, 1950.

Ricoeur, Paul, 'Appropriation', in *Hermeneutics and the Human Sciences*, ed., trs. and introduced by John B. Thompson, Cambridge University Press, 1981.

'Structure and Hermeneutics', in Don Ihde (ed.), *The Conflict of Interpretations*, Evanston, Ill.: Northwestern University Press, 1974.

Romer, John, *Testament: the Bible and History*, Michael O'Mara, 1988.

Said, Edward W., *Orientalism: Western Constructions of the Orient* new edn, Penguin, 1995.

Sanders, E.P., *Judaism: Practice and Belief 63 B.C.E. to 66 C.E.*, SCM Press, 1992.

Schiller, F.C., *On the Aesthetic Education of Man* (1795), trs. R. Snell, Routledge, 1954.

Schlegel, Friedrich, *Dialogue on Poetry and Literary Aphorisms*, trs., introduced, and annotated by Ernst Behler and Roman Struc, University Park: Pennsylvania State University Press, 1968.

Lucinde and the Fragments, trs. with an Introduction by Peter Firchow, Minneapolis: University of Minnesota Press, 1971.

Philosophical Fragments, trs. Peter Firchow, Minnespolis: University of Minnesota Press, 1991.

Schleiermacher, Friedrich, *Introductions to the Dialogues of Plato*, New York: Arno Press, 1973.

'Introduction to General Hermeneutics', in Kurt Mueller-Vollmer (ed.), *The Hermeneutics Reader*, Oxford: Basil Blackwell, 1986.

On Religion: Speeches to its Cultured Despisers, trs. Richard Crouter (1799), Cambridge University Press, 1988.

Schwartz, Regina, (ed.) *The Book and the Text: the Bible and Literary Theory*, Oxford: Basil Blackwell, 1990.

Shaffer, E.S., *'Kubla Khan' and 'The Fall of Jerusalem'*, Cambridge University Press, 1975.

Southam, B.C., *'Sanditon: the Seventh Novel'*, in Juliet McMaster (ed.), *Jane Austen's Achievement*, Macmillan, 1976.

Steiner, George, *After Babel: Aspects of Language and Translation*, Oxford University Press, 1976.

Stephens, Anthony, 'Socrates or Chorus Person? The Problem of Individuality in Nietzsche's Hellenism', in G.W. Clarke (ed.), *Rediscovering Hellenism: The Hellenic Inheritance and the English Imagination*, Cambridge University Press, 1989.

Stephenson, Roger, *Goethe's Conception of Knowledge and Science*, Edinburgh University Press, 1995.

Sterne, Laurence, *The Works of Laurence Sterne*, ed. James P. Browne, 2 vols., 1885.

Strauss, David Freidrich, *The Life of Jesus* (1835), trs. George Eliot, 1846.

Swedenborg, Emanuel, *Heaven and its Wonders and Hell: from Things Heard and Seen* (1758), New York: Swedenborg Foundation, 1978.

Sykes, Norman, 'The Authorized Version of 1611', in *The Bible Today*, Eyre and Spottiswode, 1955.

Tannenbaum, Leslie, *Biblical Tradition in Blake's Early Prophecies*, Princeton University Press, 1982.

Tanner, Tony, *Jane Austen*, Macmillan, 1986.

Taylor, Mark. C., *Disfiguring: Art, Architecture, Religion*, University of Chicago Press, 1992.

The Royal Bible or a Complete Body of Christian Divinity, with notes and observations by Leonard Howard, 2nd edn, 1761.

Thompson, E.P., *The Making of the English Working Class*, Gollancz, 1965.

Thorp, Margaret Farrand, *Charles Kingsley 1819–1875*, New York: Octagon Books, 1969.

Trilling, Lionel, '*Jane Austen* and *Mansfield Park*', in Boris Ford (ed.), *From Blake to Byron*, Harmondsworth: Pelican, 1957.

Trimmer, Mrs (Sarah), *Help to the Unlearned in the Study of the Holy Scriptures*, 2nd edn, 1806.

Van Seters, John, *In Search of History: Historiography in the Ancient World and the Origins of Biblical History*, New Haven, Conn.: Yale University Press, 1983.

Vico, Giambattista, *The New Science*, revised trs. of 3rd edn (1744), Thomas Goddard Bergin and Max Harrold Frisch, Ithaca N.Y.: Cornell University Press, 1968.

Voegelin, Eric, *Order and History*, 5 vols., Baton Rouge: Louisiana State University Press, 1956–87.

Volney, C.F.C. de, *The Ruins: or a Survey of the Revolutions of Empires*, T. Allman, 1851.

Voltaire, (François Marie Arouet) *L'Ingénu*, 1767.

Walker, Ralph C.S., *Kant*, Routledge, 1978.

Wallace, A.R., *Island Life*, 1880.

Ware, William, *Zenobia, or the Fall of Palmyra*, 9th edn, New York, 1866.

Weimann, Robert, *Structure and Society in Literary History*, Charlottesville: University Press of Virginia, 1976.

Wesley, Charles, *Hymns and Sacred Poems*, 1739.

Westermann, Claus, *Blessing in the Bible and in the Life of the Church*, trs. Keith Crim, Philadelphia: Fortress Press, 1978.

Genesis 12–36: a Commentary, trs. John J. Scullion SJ, SPCK, 1986.

Wheeler, Kathleen (ed.) *German Aesthetic and Literary Criticism: the Romantic Ironists and Goethe*, Cambridge University Press, 1984.

Wicker, Brian, *The Story-Shaped World*, Athlone Press, 1975.

Wilkinson, John, *Interpretation and Community*, Macmillan, 1963.

Willey, Basil, *Samuel Taylor Coleridge*, Chatto, 1972.

Wolff, Robert Lee, *Gains and Losses: Novels of Faith and Doubt in Victorian England*, New York: Garland, 1977.

Woodbridge, Kenneth, 'The Sacred Landscape: Painters and the Lake Garden at Stourhead', *Apollo*, 88, (1968).

The Stourhead Landscape, National Trust, 1991.

Wright, T.R., *The Religion of Humanity: the Impact of Comtean Positivism on Victorian Britain*, Cambridge University Press, 1986.

Zim, Rivkah, 'The Reformation: the Trial of God's Word', in Stephen Prickett (ed.), *Reading the Text: Biblical Criticism and Literary Theory*, Oxford: Basil Blackwell, 1991.

Index

Page numbers in bold print indicate extensive discussion of the headword.